Regional Studies in Political and Administrative History – No. 1

The Two Tipperarys

The Two Tipperarys

*The national and local politics – devolution
and self-determination – of the unique
1838 division into two ridings,
and the aftermath*

Donal A. Murphy

Published by

 Relay

Published in 1994 by
RELAY Publications
Tyone, Nenagh, Co. Tipperary

ISBN 0 946327 13 0 h.p.
ISBN 0 946327 14 9 p.b.

British Library Cataloguing-in-Publication Data
A catalogue record for this book
is available from the British Library.

Cover design: Deirdre O'Dowd – incorporating on the rear cover her drawings of Nenagh, Thurles and Clonmel courthouses, and on the front cover an aquatint by Michael Angelo Hayes, R.H.A., Clonmel, 'Arriving at the End of a Stage', from his set 'Car Travelling in the South of Ireland in the year 1856. Bianconi's Establishment'.

Typesetting: in house by RELAY

Typeface: Times, 11pt on 12 leading
Page size: 216 x 138 mm

Printed by Colour Books Ltd., Dublin

To
the legion of clerks and reporters,
printers and publishers,
archivists and librarians,
collectors and historians
who made this and many another work
possible

ADDITIONAL

re p. 207-10: Willie (Wm C.) Moloney, Clare County Manager designate, becomes the twenty-ninth chief executive to graduate from the two counties.

re p. 282: Ger Lewis resigned the chairmanship of TNR Co. Enterprise Board on 12 Dec 1994 and was succeeded by Jimmy Murphy.

A mix of national and local politics, analogous with the Tipperary and Waterford stories, occurred while the book was with the printers. The context was the greatest exhibition of political fireworks, tightrope dancing and somersaults in the history of the State. A delay in the Attorney-General's office re extradition of a paedophile priest; the appointment by the Fianna Fáil members of Government, despite a walk-out of Labour members, of A.G. Whelehan as President of the High Court; revelations as to who knew what and when; the resignations of Taoiseach Reynolds and Judge Whelehan; the collapse of both the Government and of negotiations for a renewed FF-Lab one – all culminated in a new Fine Gael-Lab-Democratic Left government. The two FG negotiators included the TNR TD Michael Lowry, Chairman of that parliamentary party, who became Minister for Transport, Energy and Communications on Thurs 15 Dec 1994. Meantime,

• Wed 14 Dec, the *Tipperary Star* issue of 17 Dec on sale; editorial spotlights both Lowry's prospects and the TRBDI campaign (see pp. 205-6): 'Deputy Lowry scarcely needs reminding, in view of his trenchant pursuit of Fianna Fáil's Michael Smith when a minister, that the onus to deliver on this project now lies with him.'

• Same day, the negotiated programme for the new 'Government of Renewal' promises: 'We will establish the TRBDI.'

• Same day, Smith as acting Minister for Education in the four-weeks-old caretaker Government announces on Tipp FM radio that it had 'accepted in principle the need' for the TRBDI.

• 24 Dec, *Tipperary Star*'s Anne O'Grady reports Lowry's 'no formal Government sanction' and outline of complex next steps; on the same page Eugene Hogan reports Smith's 'it is almost certain now to go ahead', and his outline of necessary next steps.

CORRECTIONS

p. xv, add *Oireachtas*: (in the context of pp. 83, 281) Dáil Éireann and Seanad Éireann – the lower and upper houses of parliament.

p. xxii, first par (also bibliography & notes): 'Seamus' should read 'Séamus'.

p. xxiii, final par: 'Geailge' should read 'Gaeilge'; 'ghuaiseacht' should read 'gluaiseacht'; 'i dTiobaid' should read 'i dTiobraid'.

p. xxiv, 4th line: delete 'i dtriochaidí'.

p. 10, Plate 2: 'Constantine Henry' should read 'Henry Constantine'.

p. 52, 9th line: 'the Prologue' should read 'pp. 45-6'.

p. 98, penultimate par: '1715' should read '1716'.

p. 104, first word: 'above' should read 'below'.

p. 108, 4th last line: 'p. 108' should read 'p. 110'.

p. 112, note 31, 3rd last line: delete 'details'.

p. 203, 7th last line: delete the first figure '32.'.

p. 205, 5th line, 3rd par: delete the figure '32.'.

p. 207, 11th line: 'geoprahical' should read 'geographical'.

p. 216, the final col. for Galway Co. Borough should include the figure '1' in respect of its Assistant Town Clerk.

p. 218, 6th last line: '1890s' should read '1990s'.

p. 267, 4th line, 2nd par: 'giver' should read 'given'.

p. 280, add: Noel Davern was an MEP (Member of the European Parliament) for Munster, 1979-84.

p. 281, 2nd line: delete 'Field'.

CONTENTS

Acknowledgments

Using a metaphor from the Preface, the foundations of this pillar and of another pillar were dug in an end-of-year paper for Professor Ronan Fanning's history class in the 1969-70 School of Public Administration. It was he who drew the neophyte's attention to the unique value of local sources held locally, supplemented by those generally available in the national repositories. The specific topic covered in that paper will arise in much expanded form as 'The Revolution of 1899', planned for publication in 1996. The experience gained in researching the original paper emboldened the taking on of this story of the 1838 ridings at the prompting of the late Des Roche, then Principal of the School. He kindly included a summary of its main elements as an Appendix in his monumental work mentioned above. The *Guardian* published work in progress in four parts, also in 1982, as part of its 'From Script and Stone' series encouraged by interim Manager Michael Moylan, and continued by its Managing Directors, Patrick A. Ryan and Mrs Brid Nolan, and Editor, Gerry Slevin. They afforded most generous research facilities in the goldmine which constitutes their archive of back numbers since 1838.

The fact that incremental work on this story has now taken place in three decades has more reasons than plausible excuses. I have to confess that its reaching the printing press owes a great deal to the patient prodding of John McGinley, County Manager of my vocational alma mater, Tipperary (North Riding) County Council, and of Nancy Murphy, my partner in all senses of the word. He has been largely instrumental in the Council's provision of much-appreciated financial assistance. She has been an incisive critic and map-maker as well as assistant researcher and typist of the first version – oft-times in parallel with and interrupting her own, greater, contributions to the county's, ridings and Nenagh's history and genealogy.

I am heavily indebted to those eight patrons and deeply appreciative of their several roles.

As indicated in the book's dedication, I am conscious of a special debt owed by historians, especially local and regional ones, and not always expressed by the beneficiaries. It is owed to the legion of persons whose skills have either preserved invaluable source material or analysed and packaged it in reference publications. Most of those who have had such an input into works on nineteenth century material are both dead and anonymous. Many are referenced in the notes. Those whose help has been more immediate and personally kind include successive Librarians, Assistant Librarians and Attendants of the

National Library of Ireland over twenty years whose individual names are too numerous to ascertain and list; the Librarians and staff of Trinity College Dublin and Limerick City Library; Mary Prendergast, Librarian of the Institute of Public Administration and staff – Renuka Page, Trudy Carroll, Marian Tannam, Eithne Cavanagh, Mary Guckian, Denise Moran, Paula Hilliard, Orla O'Neill; Brigid Dolan, Librarian, Royal Irish Academy, and staff; Martin Maher, County Librarian, Tipperary and especially its successive Assistant Librarians in charge of local studies: Mary (Moloughney) Murphy, Norma (Walsh) McDermott, the late Donal O'Gorman, Joe Gleeson, Tom Deegan and Mary Guinan-Darmody, also the Nenagh branch Librarian Eileen (Connolly) Bourke; John Power, Mary Immaculate College Librarian; Evelyn Coady, local studies, Waterford County Library; Dr Chris O'Mahony, Limerick Regional Archivist.

Elaine Burke Houlihan has been a tower of strength, having combined the functions of diligent researcher of multiple loose ends, percipient critic, typesetter and indexer. Cliona Lewis has researched and written the Cork appendix and part of the Waterford one, and at two stages given very helpful criticism on the main story. Margaret Gleeson and Fiona O'Brien also assisted the research, and the latter has also been a diligent proof reader and largely responsible for marketing. Daniel Grace at an early stage and Catriona O'Brien, a UCG undergraduate, at an advanced stage have read the typescript and made helpful observations. I am most grateful to them.

Spadework, sand-blasting and polishing in a variety of ways and stages have been furnished by the following also. It is a pleasure to place on record the thanks of all of the RELAY team and myself for their help and guidance.

T. J. Barrington; Noreen Bevans; the late Tom Brophy, County Manager, TNR; John Joe Buckley, D.C.C. and Mary Morris; Dr Donal de Buitléir; Michael Byrne; Siobhán Uí Chriagáin agus Siobhán Ní Mhurchú, Tiobraid Árann ag Labhairt; Jim Condon; Rodney Connor, Director of Environmental Services, Fermanagh District Council; William Corbett; Michele Crowe; the late Desmond, sixth Baron Dunalley; John Devane and Jane Toomey, Tipperary LEADER Group; Stephen Ellison, Deputy Clerk of the Record, Record Office, House of Lords; Dr Adrian Empey; Noel French, Meath Heritage Centre; Flan Galvin, owner of the *Clare Champion*; Tom Griffin, County Secretary, TNR; former Senator Des Hanafin; Richard B. (Dick) Haslam, UCC; Seamus Hayes and Ned O'Connor, Tipperary (S.R.) County Manager and Assistant County Manager, and Catriona Fitzgerald; Andrew

Hodgins; John Keanie, M.B.A., Town Clerk and Chief Executive, Derry City Council; Michael Killeen, Longford County Manager; Tom Kirwan; Frank Lewis; Patrick J. McCormack, County Registrar, Tipperary; Catherine McCullough, Curator, Armagh County Museum; Dr Thomas G. McGrath; Brian J. McNally, County Secretary, Waterford and Noreen Flynn; Carmel Maher; Dr Denis G. (Des) Marnane; William C. Moloney; Joan Neville; Dr William and Teresa Nolan; Tommy O'Doherty, FÁS; Jim O'Donnell, Head of Publications, IPA, and Eileen Kelly; Brendan O'Donoghue, Secretary, Department of the Environment; Liam Ó Duibhir; Nora O'Meara; Thomas P. Rice; Dr Joseph Robins; Niall Rooney, County Registrar, Waterford; John Ryan, TD; Pakie Ryan, V.S.;the late Senator Willie Ryan; Jacinta Shanny, County Secretary's Department, Limerick; Judge Noel Sheridan; Patrick F. Treacy; Sean Treacy, TD, Ceann Comhairle; Dr Brian Turner, Director, Down County Museum; Col. S. J. Watson; Dennis Warring & G. White, Belfast City Council; former Senator Liam Whyte.

Thanks also to the Tipperary People's Association in Galway, particularly Marie O'Connell and Paddy O'Meara; the Newport Historical Society, particularly Sean Guilfoyle; and a private party organised by Dr Tom McGrath – for the platforms they provided for talks on the subject which brought work in progress into sharper focus. Paul Dolan of Colour Books has been very generous with his time and advice in the design and printing stages. Deirdre O'Dowd has been a painstaking artist-designer.

Tipperary LEADER group has given much-appreciated financial assistance towards the publication.

Illustrations

Abbreviations
(not defined in the text or notes)

a.r.p.	acres, roods, perches – land measurement
c.	circa/approximate
c. = cap	as in cap. 67, meaning the 67th act of parliament passed in a year
C.A.	*Clonmel Advertiser*
C.H.	*Clonmel Herald*
C.J.	*Clare Journal*
D.E.M.	*Dublin Evening Mail*
D.E.P.	*Dublin Evening Post*
D.L.	Deputy Lieutenant
D.N.B.	*Dictionary of National Biography*
Encycl. Brit.	*Encyclopaedia Britannica*
IMPACT	Irish Municipal, Public and Civil Trade Union
Jn. Butler Soc.	*Journal of the Butler Society*
JP	Justice of the Peace
KC	King's Counsel
Lords' jn.	*Journals of the House of Lords* (U.K.)
Minutes, N.B.G.	Nenagh Board of Guardians Minutes
N.A.	National Archives
N.G.	*Nenagh Guardian*
N.L.I.	National Library of Ireland
Ormond Deeds	Calendar of Ormond Deeds, ed Edmund Curtis, 6 vols (Dublin, 1932-44)
PLG	Poor Law Guardian
PP	Parliamentary Papers
R.C.	Roman Catholic
R.S.A. Jn.	*Journal of the Royal Society of Antiquities of Ireland*
s.	section (of an act of parliament)
Sheehan, *N. & its N.*	E. H. Sheehan, *Nenagh and its Neighbourhood* (Bray, 1949)
Sp	Spring (Assizes)
SPO	State Paper Office, Dublin Castle, now incorporated in the National Archives
Su	Summer (Assizes)
T.C.	*Tipperary Constitution*
T.C.D.	Trinity College Dublin
T.F.P.	*Tipperary Free Press*
TC	Town Commissioner
TD	Teachta Dála = member of Dáil Éireann (parliament of the Republic of Ireland)

Thoms	Thom's Official Directories
TNR	Tipperary North Riding
TSR	Tipperary South Riding
W.C.	Waterford Chronicle
W.M.	Waterford Mail
£.s.d.	pounds, shillings, pence – the pre-decimalisation Irish currency (twelve pence = one shilling, and twenty shillings = one pound)

Glossary

(of terms not defined in the text or notes)

ach sin scéal eile (arís): that's another story (again).

affidavit: a written declaration on oath.

alderman: the borough councillor elected first in a ward.

ci-devant: previous/former.

civil parish: the smallest administrative unit.

Consolidation: merging all or parts of past acts of parliament by current legislation.

entente cordiale: cordial understanding/agreement.

eyre: a court of itinerant justices in the late twelfth and thirteenth centuries.

ex-officio: by virtue of office, as in a number of poor law guardian positions reserved to justices of the peace (magistrates).

fee simple: unconditional inheritance.

fiat: sanction.

fiscal business: the public expenditure end of the grand jury's functions.

flagitous: guilty of enormous crimes.

franchise: the right to vote; a grant, as with the liberties of a palatinate.

Gaol Delivery: 'by the law of the land, that men might not be detained in prison, but might receive full and speedy justice, commissions of gaol-delivery are issued out, direct to two of the judges and the clerk of assize associate, by virtue of which commission they have power to try every prisoner in the gaol, committed for any offence whatsoever' – John Burn, *A New Law Dictionary* (Dublin, 1792).

gaol: prison.

grádh: affection.

gríosach: hot embers, small live coals.

glebe: the land attached to a parish church.

in pectore: having an understanding, in mind.

in re: in the (law) case of.

irrefragable: irrefutable.

(Leas-)Cheann Comhairle: (deputy) speaker/chairman of Dáil Éireann.

memorial: petition.

Muintir na Tíre: 'people of the countryside', a community development organisation.

oyer and terminer: 'a court held by virtue of the King's commission, to hear and determine all treasons, felonies and misdemeanours ...; they must first enquire by means of the grand jury, or inquest, before they are empowered to hear and determine by the help of the petit [petty] jury' – Burn, cited above.

petit: of lesser importance.

plámás: flattery, palaver.

presentment: an estimate of expenditure presented to the grand jury.

Privy Council: an advisory council (to the Lord Lieutenant in Ireland pre-independence).

seanchaí: a story-teller.

sine die: 'without a day' (being fixed for resumption).

Tory: a member of the grouping which evolved to become the Conservative party (U.K.).

tuath: a Gaelic land division.

turnkey: gaol/prison warder.

uisce fé thalamh: undercurrents.

ulra vires: beyond one's power or authority.

urbs intacta: untouched town, applied to Waterford city for its loyalty to the Crown in resisting attack in the late fifteenth century.

vill: town.

Whig: a member of the grouping which evolved to become the Liberal party (U.K.).

Oireachtas : (in the context of pp. 83, 281) Dáil Éireann and Seanad Éireann – the lower and upper houses of parliament.

ℐOREWORD

This is a tale of two counties, not of two disparate counties but rather of Siamese twins formed from a single unit in the last century. It is a kind of administrative adventure story centred on Tipperary, as *Knocknagow* and *Sally Kavanagh* were in a different vein, and the Charles Kickham who supplies the local patriotism, the abounding detail and the administrative language is Donal Murphy of Nenagh. He has spent most of his working life in local government and health administration, and has added to these concerns a passionate interest in the local history of Nenagh town and of Tipperary at large, whether as a total county or as a brace of ridings.

Local government boundaries tend towards longevity, if not immortality – particularly those marking out rural areas. Urban populations are liable to increase, and their boundaries are accordingly constrained to adjustment. County boundaries are as nearly unchangeable as makes no difference, but they are inevitably subject to invasion by their urban equivalents – the county boroughs, boroughs, urban districts and town commissioners – most vividly reflecting the wave of urbanisation that has been flowing through the country. This contrasts with the solidity and relative antiquity of the county system, which emerged from the thirteenth to seventeenth centuries, and of the baronies which evolved from the cantreds that corresponded more or less with pre-Norman Irish kingdoms or 'countries'. One is compelled to admit an immutability in the county which cannot be matched by any other local unit.

What other local units? The Age of Reform had barely begun when, as the author makes clear, county authorities were empowered to divide their counties and constitute additional county towns for biennial assemblies of the grand juries. About the same time a general power was conferred on towns without municipal status to elect commissioners to levy rates for the purpose of lighting, paving, cleansing and generally improving their towns. But the major addition to local government was the creation of one hundred and thirty poor law unions with partly elected boards of guardians whose principal business was initially the management of their workhouses.

This work gives a detailed account of the evolution of a general power of dividing a county, to be wielded by the Lord Lieutenant. This power emerged in its earliest form in 1835, and was re-enacted in somewhat improved form a year later. The local demand was confined to Tipperary. There were counties like Cork and Galway so large and populous that the case for division seemed irresistible. The author mentions a degree of partial division in each case, but neither proceeded to achieve separation. Counties, especially large counties, are rarely if ever uniform in thought or sentiment. There are obvious differences between East Galway and Connemara; between West Cork and North or East Cork; between East and West Wicklow. But there would seem to be little reason why in the case of Tipperary there should be any marked difference between North and South Ridings. Yet I remember clearly that, when I had as a Department of Local Government Principal Officer to deal with water supplies during the 1950s and 1960s, there was a notable distinction between the two ridings. The southern one had an impressive programme of regional water supplies in prospect whereas the North Riding opted for a different course and has dotted the map with close on two hundred small group schemes with major community involvement. The curious feature was that Tipperary had a single county manager who ran both ridings with the help of an Assistant Manager. One would expect that the management system would produce the same effects in both ridings but in fact this was not so.

The Tipperary Manager was the well-remembered John P. Flynn, a leading figure in that group of first county managers who tended to dominate their councils by virtue of talent, long experience and the clear purposes of the 1940 Act. Add to these, in Flynn's case, the impression of Machiavellian guile which he conveyed to those with whom he worked.

On the subject of council-management, it is worthwhile calling to mind that following the City and County Management (Amendment) Act of 1955 the two councils, North and South, finally agreed that each riding should have a wholetime manager. De-grouping was effected in 1969 after much discussion, hesitation and prolonged disagreement. Details may be found in the Epilogue.

To return now to more substantial aspects of county structure, the reader will hardly need reminding that a major feature of local government reform in the 1920s was the concentration of local power and activity in the county councils and their subsidiary boards of health and public assistance, to the entire suppression of poor law unions and rural district councils that made up much the greatest part of the then sub-county tier of local government. Counties (and cities) have continued to hold a dominant position, either as agencies of action and planning or as units of composition.

However, the growth of the complexity and technological underpinning of government posed considerable problems of co-ordination and of possible economies of technological scale (e.g. major hospitals, roads, overall planning). In 1970, the health services were taken from the counties and concentrated in regions. But, as a result of a more or less spontaneous rise in regionalism, some years earlier counties had been grouped as Regional Development Organisations (RDOs) for planning and development purposes. These were moderately successful, but they were suddenly abolished in 1987, without warning or debate, or, be it said, significant public protest. Try doing that with the historic counties! This unexpected move was all the more surprising in view of the growth of European opinion in favour of a direct regional subvention. The Government had escaped from the dilemma of having to rely on the regional development organisations by its success in persuading the European Community to accept the whole State as a single region and by substituting a new set of bizarre sub-regions for the RDOs, differing from them in many respects, especially in origin and in breaching county boundaries. In this way the Minister for Finance held on firmly to his centralising authority in relation to the European Regional Fund.

It would be easy to see in this creation of a novel network of regions and the disappearance of an early county-based system, a shift of power from local to central government. There is nothing surprising about this. The process has been going on for decades. Occasional counter-moves promise reforms aimed at redistributing central power to the periphery. The author of this book and I were members of the Chubb ginger group which produced *More Local Government: A Programme for Development* in 1971 (reprinted in 1978); Dr Tom Barrington, Chubb and myself summoned up second wind in 1985 for the Muintir na Tíre Walsh group's *Toward a New Democracy? Implications of Local Government Reform* (reprinted in 1989). The latest statutory effort started in 1985 when a Local Government (Reorganisation) Act of that year added Galway to the county boroughs and, more relevant to our topic, divided Dublin County, like all Gaul, into three parts. Reform, while not at a pace many would have wished, continued with the Local Government Act, 1991.

That 1991 statute stemmed directly from the government's 1990 decision to establish a cabinet sub-committee, which was assisted by an advisory expert committee chaired by Dr Tom Barrington, as a further impetus to public service reform. It in turn received close to two hundred submissions from individuals and organisations. The government decided that the county and county borough are still to constitute the main tier of local government and they will continue to deliver the major services. However, the government has adopted the expert committee's proposal to set up eight regional authorities who will promote the co-ordination of both local and national services within their respective regions. Significantly, they will consist of groups of counties. That 1991 Act also re-christened the Dublin thridings, and more importantly, replaced the inhibitions attendant on the *ultra vires* doctrine by endowing local authorities with a general competence to promote development of its area, but without returning to local authorities the basic function of financing such discretion by raising significant funds through local taxation.

We have the promise of further decentralisation, properly so termed as distinct from the misuse of the word apropos the relocation of parts of central government departments from Dublin to other cities and towns. In October 1992 the government announced that county enterprise partnership boards were to be established in each county by incorporating the county development teams. The members of the boards will include the county manager and representatives of public agencies, trade unions, employers and local communities. The partnership boards are stated to have three key objectives: the development of small and start-up enterprises, employing up to ten people; training and education, especially as linked to enterprise development; and local community development. A forum of relevant local organisations is promised in each county quarterly, to ensure an exchange of ideas and feedback to local communities on the boards' activities. One awaits action on other aspects treated by the advisory expert committee and indeed explored exhaustively over recent decades: financing and sub-county/city structures – both having implications for the strength or weakness of democracy.

Donal Murphy's monograph on the Tipperary experience is an interesting account of an episode in re-structuring on a minor scale in the last century. That century was marked by much local experiments, climaxing in the great Local Government Act of 1898 which, incidentally, added Belfast and Londonderry to the four southern county boroughs but dropped Carrickfergus (Co. Antrim), Drogheda (Co. Louth), Galway and Kilkenny from their previous status as equivalent 'counties of towns', a status which had given them, for instance, their own sheriffs and assizes. Innovation continued through the first half of the present century, with city and county management and regionalism, as well as financial revision of dubious value. The recent resumption of the reform movement revives in Dublin the novel feature of county division tried only once before, in Tipperary.

Desmond Roche

Desmond Roche joined the staff of the Department of Local Government and Public Health (as it then was) in 1936. He was promoted Principal Officer in 1954 and took charge, inter alia, of a major campaign to develop rural water supplies to a tolerable level. In 1964 he was seconded from the civil service to become the first Principal of the School of Public Administration in the Institute of that name (IPA), followed by roles as Head of Administration in the Institute and editor of its quarterly ADMINISTRATION, posts he held with distinction until his retirement from the public service in 1973. He edited a second edition of John Collins's key work, 'Local Government', published in 1963. He followed this with his own monumental 'Local Government in Ireland', published in 1982. He died in March 1993.

Note: Since the Foreword was generously supplied by the late Des Roche, both the regional authorities and the county enterprise boards have come into existence.

$\mathcal{P}$REFACE

Why and how did Tipperary divide into two ridings, thus containing two administrative counties within its geographical bounds? Such has been a situation unique in Ireland, discounting the special cases of county boroughs in the major cities within some other geographical counties, from 1838 until 1994 when Dublin completed a division into three.

The answer to the question lies in a fascinating series of political, judicial and administrative events. The sources of the story are almost complete in the National Archives, in the microfilms of Clonmel newspapers in the National Library, in the files of the *Nenagh Guardian*, and in a small number of other repositories.

There is an impressive legacy in stone in Nenagh – the Courthouse and some components of the former County Gaol. It was the erection of these buildings and the population and business which they generated, together with the building of the military barracks in the previous decade and of the workhouse which opened just months before the gaol in 1842, that transformed Nenagh from a simple market town to an important centre.

The book is thus both local history and administrative history. On the one hand, it is the first of a modest number of monographs which can be deemed regional studies, worthwhile in themselves but also expanding the existing folders of national history. For the geographical area it focuses on, this present monograph might be grouped (by type, as distinct from any pretension to weight) with a small number of exceptionally valuable full-length works. Five are selected covering a span of time in the broad political arena: George Cunningham, *The Anglo-Norman Advance into the South-West Midlands of Ireland*; Dermot F. Gleeson, *The Last Lords of Ormond*; Denis G. Marnane, *Land and Violence: A History of West Tipperary from 1660*; Thomas P. Power, *Land, Politics and Society in Eighteenth-Century Tipperary*; James O'Shea, *Priest, Politics and Society in Post-famine Ireland*. It might be grouped also with the paramount selection of in-depth studies of particular personalities and topics in the nineteen chapters of William Nolan & Thomas McGrath, eds, *Tipperary History and Society*;

xxi

with a number of substantial and highly-focussed contributions to successive issues of the *Tipperary Historical Journal* (ed Marcus Bourke); with two pathfinder studies of emigrant groups: Bruce S. Elliott, *Irish Migrants in the Canadas,* and Max Barrett, *Because of These*; with the plentiful monographs on Gaelic Athletic Association clubs (and the twin volumes of *Tipperary's G.A.A. Story* by Canon Philip Fogarty and Seamus J. King plus the very recently-published biography of Maurice Davin, first President of the GAA, by a successor, Seamus Ó Riain), on religious communities and churches (two of which I dare select for their wealth of context material: Geraldine Carville, *The Heritage of Holy Cross,* and Sidney J. Watson, *A Dinner of Herbs: the history of Old St. Mary's church, Clonmel*), occasional ones on other sporting and cultural clubs and an outstanding one, in both senses of that word, Denis Foley, *Mullinahone Co-op: The first hundred years*; and with a number of archaeological studies in specialist journals.

Those above could be regarded as the vertical pillars in the construction of this region's history. The cross beams are largely the many parish histories covering a span of topics; strong elements of the successive histories of both dioceses of Killaloe by Canon Philip Dwyer, Dermot F. Gleeson and Aubrey Gwynn, and, outstandingly, Monsignor Ignatius Murphy plus the compendium of parish priests' biographies for the archdiocese of Cashel and Emly by Rev. Walter G. Skehan and Most Rev. Thomas Morris; just one outline sketch covering a wider area: Patrick C. Power's *History of South Tipperary;* and the social and political history arising in clan and family histories and in biographies or autobiographies of a diversity of figures ranging, alphabetically, from John Joe Barry, J. D. Bernal, Brendan Bracken, Dan Breen and Archbishop Thomas Croke to Terence Prittie, William P. Ryan, Bishop Joseph Shanahan and Sean Treacy. One substantial cross beam is loaded on this present vehicle: the general description of County Tipperary and the towns of Clonmel, Nenagh and Thurles in Samuel A. Lewis, *Topographical Dictionary of Ireland,* which received printer's ink, very happily for the purpose of its reprint here, in the year in which the conception of the twin ridings was confirmed.

Histories of the development of Irish local government are very scarce. Background sections within service-by-service chapters in Desmond Roche's *Local Government in Ireland*; Neil Collins, *Local Government Managers at Work*; Joseph Boland and others, *City and County Management 1929-1990/A Retrospective*; sidelights in Joseph Robins, *Custom House People;* incidental, highly specialised information in the successive reference volumes on local government law by George T. B. Vanston, Howard A. Street and Ronan Keane; and occasional contributions to the earlier issues of the quarterly *Administration,* together stand slim as local government pillars. The cross beams are notably the grand sweep of three chapters in Roche's major work, superseding a similar one by John Collins, a tiny number of Vocational Education Committee histories, and the sole county council history – Desmond Williams, *Donegal County Council 1899-1984.*

The former health wing of local government has fared a bit better, thanks to a number of distinguished administrators: Ruth Barrington, *Health, Medicine and Politics in Ireland, 1900-1970*; James Deeny, *To Cure and To Care*; Brendan Hensey, *The Health Services of Ireland,* and Joseph Robins, *Fools and Mad: A History of the Insane in Ireland,* plus a couple of mental hospital histories including Eamonn Lonergan, *St Luke's Hospital, Clonmel, 1834-1984.* That author has also provided *A Workhouse Story: St Patrick's Hospital, Cashel, 1842-1992.*

Eamonn Lonergan's double, of course, adds pillars to the history of the county, just as the chapter by Eamon McLoughlin in *Tipperary History and Society* does for local government generally (entitled 'Planning in Tipperary: A View of the South Riding 1964-1984'). Two studies in the 1992 *Tipperary Historical Journal* are further welcome accretions to both the local government and county pillars: Seán O'Donnell, 'The first election to the reformed Clonmel Corporation 150 years ago', and Thomas Deegan, 'Roscrea Poor Law Union: its administration 150 years ago'. Likewise, in the following issues of the *Tipperary Historical Journal* Dr Chris O'Mahony focuses on one aspect of the work of poor law guardians with 'Emigration from Thurles Workhouse, 1848-58' (1993) and a corresponding article in 1994 for Tipperary workhouse.

Focal scoir, mar gheall ar dhifríocht mhór idir muintir an tuaiscirt agus an deiscirt sa chontae. Rud ait é, ach bhí an Gaeilge níos láidre san deiscirt Normánach ná sa tuaisceart ina raibh smacht ag na clanna Gaelacha ar feadh na gcéadtha. Tá sin fíor, mar a chuir an Dr Gearóid Mac Gearailt in iúl sna páipéir aige, *Estimates for Baronies of Minimal Level of Irish Speaking Amongst Successive Decennial Cohorts: 1771-81 to 1861-71* (Royal Irish Academy Proceedings) mar gheall ar an naoú céad déag ina bhfuil an chuid is mó den leabhar suite. Ach san am i láthair is sa tuaisceart tá an ghuaiseacht TIOBRAID ÁRANN ag LABHAIRT ar siúl chun an dátheangachas a chur chun cinn i dTiobaid Árann Thuaidh. De thoradh a n-iarrachtaí tá forbairt mhór in úsáid na Gaeilge i bhfógraí, i gcomharthaí siopa agus leis na daltaí sna scoileanna.

Agus tá dhá ionad ina bhfuil gaelscoileanna sa tuaisceart – Aonach Urmhumhan agus Dúrlas Éile – agus áit amháin sa deisceart, Cluain Meala. Ar ndóigh, ní tré thimpiste a tharla gurb iad siúd an trí bhaile mór ba mhó fiontair i dtríochaidí sna deich mbliana dar thús 1830.

Tá súil agam go mbainfidh trí shórt duine beagán eolais – agus taithneamh freisin, b'fhéidir – as an scéal seo: muintir Thiobrad Árann sa bhaile nó i gcéin, lucht staire agus lucht polaitíochta pé áit iad, agus seirbhísig na phoiblí in Éirinn.

The extent of the Notes in this work, additional to quoting sources, arises from three considerations:

*   *firstly, to avoid as far as possible importing into the flow of the text information which is merely supplementary;*
*   *secondly, to cater for two categories of connoisseur – 'tracers and placers' who demand lavish information on local personalities, their descendants and relics, and those professionally interested in the fine points of local administration and impinging law, for whom precise information is needed ;*
*   *thirdly, to gather up in so far as has come within my ken what would sometimes be presented separately as 'suggestions for further reading'.*

𝔓ROLOGUE

'... shall henceforth be and remain one county for ever ...'

The geographical County Tipperary had two grand juries from 1838 to 1899 and two county councils thereafter. Coincidental with that phenomenon, because the grand juries had twin functions in the spheres of local government and justice, it was the only county having two towns holding the superior form of court – assizes (comparable to the modern High Court on Circuit) until a short time after twenty-six of Ireland's thirty-two counties became the Irish Free State in 1922. Comparable English cases, for instance the north, east and west ridings of Yorkshire ('riding' being a corruption of the Scandinavian *thriding* or *thrithing* or *thrithi*, meaning a third of a shire or county) disappeared in the reorganisation of their local government system in 1974.[1]

Galway had east and west ridings but only for the appointment of county surveyors and management of the police force; Cork had east and west ridings but only for the purpose of organising quarter sessions – a lesser breed of courts.[2] In each case there was only one grand jury and assize town for the county. The term 'riding' is not being used in the case of Dublin where it would have been literally correct upon that county's division into three administrative counties as of 1 January 1994.

NORMAN TIPPERARY

Tipperary county itself has its origins in the Norman organisation of Ireland in the thirteenth century. By 1211-12 Tipperary and Limerick together, called Munster, was a shire, the Saxon territorial division originally termed *scir* and adopted by the Normans in England. Tipperary and Limerick divided for courts about 1235 and for administration generally between 1251 and 1254.[3]

The King's chief representative in each shire was the *shire-reeve*, from which evolved the title sheriff. The sheriff was revenue collector, returning officer at a later stage for parliamentary elections, convenor of county meetings of magistrates or justices of the peace – occasionally sought to discuss matters of public importance as perceived by that

1

ascendancy class. He was also a civil officer of the courts of law, even presiding over minor cases in the county court. The nineteenth-century High Sheriff was appointed by the Lord Lieutenant of Ireland from a list of three names submitted by, in different eras, either the outgoing High Sheriff or the judge(s) at the assizes. At one period all the bench of judges vetted all county nominations. There was obviously scope for a High Sheriff, the Foreman of the grand jury or other dignitaries to have a word in the judge's ear at assizes.

The High Sheriff nominated twenty-three substantial landowners as a grand jury to act with the assize judges. The grand jury originated as Le Grande Inquest in 1166 and later added to its judicial functions by acquiring local government powers of taxation and repair of roads. Road works were the principal part of the local government end of the grand jury business, on the first day of Spring and Summer Assizes (they would have had little discretion on police and gaol expenses; a bit more, perhaps, on subsidies to hospitals). They decided the county cess (the equivalent of today's 'striking' the rate) upon selecting from presentments or budget demands which had been devised in sessions in the baronies by justices of the peace (magistrates), from 1833 in association with selected cess payers. A Local Government Inspector commented in 1878:

> The position of grand juror is usually regarded in Ireland as one conferring a certain stamp of social distinction. Selection for it, and especially for a high place on the list, is in consequence rather an object of local ambition.[4]

The assizes continued with up to a fortnight's hearing in the larger counties of civil and criminal cases by the presiding judges and petit or ordinary twelve-man juries. The grand jury's role in that field of justice was to decide whether there was sufficient evidence in the prosecution's indictments to send the accused forward for trial by a *petit* (petty) jury.[5]

The sheriff in Tipperary as of 1328 was appointed by the earl of Ormond as one of the earl's major privileges when Edward III granted Tipperary as a liberty (later termed a palatinate) to 'our dear cousin', James le Botiller (otherwise Butler), the first earl of Ormond, for the earl's lifetime. It was re-granted to the second earl, initially in 1347 for his lifetime and on 5 June 1372 to him and his male heirs.[6]

THE LIBERTIES

The palatinate privileges also included the appointment of sub-sheriff,

2

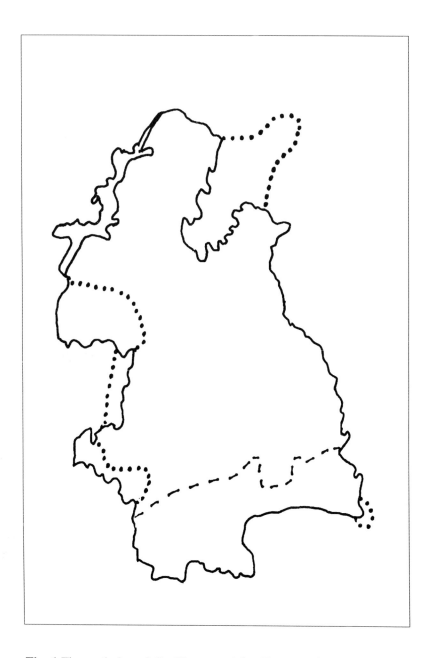

Fig. 1:The evolution of Co. Tipperary (after Empey). The dotted outlines denote territories transferred to King's Co., to and from Co.Limerick, and to Co. Kilkenny. The broken line denotes what may have been part of Co. Waterford.

the holding of courts, the appointment of justices and other court officers, coroners and other county officials, and the power of granting pardon for transgressions of the law. Those privileges were endowed by the Crown on loyal supporters who had the incentive of such devolved administrative power to keep their territory part of the English domain. The Butlers remained favourites longer than most feudal dynasties and Tipperary was the last palatinate to be extinguished in Ireland.[7]

For over three hundred years Tipperary county as a palatinate excluded Cross Tipperary or the County of the Cross which comprised the Church lands scattered throughout the geographical county. This County of the Cross had a separate sheriff and was under the judicial administration of the King's ordinary courts as distinct from the earl of Ormond's courts in the palatinate.[8]

It appears that the early palatinate included both Ely O'Carroll to the north-east and Duharra to the west. The exact status of both was uncertain, at least by the sixteenth century and became the focus of arbitration in 1605-6. The major portion by then of Ely O'Carroll (which originally incorporated also parts of Lower Ormond and Ikerrin baronies in County Tipperary and Clanadonagh barony in Queen's County which is modern County Laois), consisting of the baronies of Ballybrit and Clonlisk, were by Order of Council in 1605 annexed to King's County (now Offaly).[9]

A somewhat similar judgement in 1606 added 'Dugh Arra' to the County of the Cross. Duharra, also called Mac I Brien's country, was the old Gaelic *tuath* of Duitche Arad which became with slight modifications the modern half-barony of Arra.[10] It lies east of Lough Derg; and comprises the parishes of Portroe (whose civil parish name is Castletownarra), Youghalarra-Burgess (equal to the two civil parishes so called) and the west segment of Monsea civil parish (part of Puckane Catholic parish). The Arra parishes are in the Catholic Diocese of Killaloe – as distinct from its twin half-barony, Owney, which lies in the Diocese of Cashel.

Owney comprises the Catholic parishes of Ballina-Boher, Newport-Birdhill, Ballinahinch-Killoscully and part of Kilcommon-Hollyford, in total equating to the civil parishes of Templeachally, Kilmastulla, Kilcomenty, Killoscully, Kilvellane, Kilnarath and part Abington. Also in the early seventeenth century or slightly earlier, Owney seems to have joined the palatinate of Tipperary (leaving Owneybeg in County Limerick), as did another part of erstwhile County Limerick, around Emly, Lattin, Cullen, south of Tipperary town, and the Glen of Aherlow and northern slopes of the Galtee mountains, all in the modern

4

Clanwilliam barony. On the other hand Tipperary lost to Limerick that part of Okonagh cantred (a territorial predecessor of a barony) around Oola and Doon in the modern Coonagh barony.[11]

The tiny civil parish of Tiberaghny in Iverk barony, Co. Kilkenny, close to Carrick-on-Suir, Co. Tipperary, was part of medieval Tipperary until perhaps the late sixteenth century.[12]

It is impossible even yet to be definitive about the precise evolution of the county. For instance, the leading authority on the period, Dr. Adrian Empey, has recently suggested that those parts of the Diocese of Lismore north of the river Suir may have been part of the original Co. Waterford, e.g. those parts of the parishes of Inishlounaght, Clonmel, Killaloan, and Kilsheelan which lie astride the Suir. In the light of present knowledge it is not possible to date their transfer to Co. Tipperary, if they were in fact originally part of Co. Waterford.[13]

THE BUTLER MANTLE

One could not exaggerate the impact of the Butlers on the county and its fortunes from c.1200 to the early 1700s. L. M. Cullen puts it thus:

> The friendly mantle of the Butlers overlay the region. The Palatinate may well explain why more Catholic gentry or landowners survived in Tipperary: Kilkenny lacked the legal protection that the Palatinate's Butler-dominated jurisdiction had given Tipperary in the seventeenth century. Possibly more important than the legal framework was the centuries of relative peace, years of national warfare apart, which Butler political and military dominance had given to both counties.[14]

The dominance and the palatinate itself came under intense fire from the new wave of aggressive English administrators in the late sixteenth century.

> ... so long as any subiecte hath any jurisdiction pallatyne ... there will hardly be any sound and perfect reformacion in Munster.[15]

> The liberty of Tipperary, whereof the earls of Ormond have of long time been palatines, hath been and ever is, a great hindrance to the service, being too great a regality to be invested in a subject ... During this earl's time it may be permitted, but after him it were expedient it might be dissolved.[16]

The superb political ability of 'Black Tom', the 10th earl of Ormond, referred to in the latter quotation, added to the circumstances of his rearing at the English royal court, was the principal 'mantle'.[17] After his long reign as earl (1546-1614), there soon occurred one of the lengthiest of several breaks in the continuity of the palatinate.[18]

In 1662 a fresh grant of Tipperary as a palatinate by Charles II in favour of the first duke of Ormonde, James Butler, also twelfth earl and Lord Lieutenant, included both the County of the Cross and Duharra.[19] The county had finally attained its modern outline, but the status as a palatinate of that final shape was to last barely half a century. In 1715 the second duke of Ormonde espoused the Jacobite pretensions to regaining the English throne; Parliament under George I in 1716 passed 'An Act for extinguishing the royalties and liberties of the County of Tipperary commonly called the County Palatine of Tipperary', thus spelling the end of the palatinate. Its second section enacted:

> ... whatsoever hath been denominated or called Tipperary or Cross Tipperary, shall henceforth be and remain one county for ever, under the name of the County of Tipperary.[20]

CLONMEL AS CAPITAL

Clonmel was pre-eminent among the county's towns from their Norman initiation.[21] Positioned on the navigable Suir and in a fertile countryside, it had indirect access through Waterford to Welsh and English ports. Apart from commercial and later social stature, what made it the administrative capital? One necessarily defines such as the place where the principal court was held, both because rudimentary medieval public service was carried out largely in the courts and because the court sittings through the grand jury accrued prototype local government functions from the 1600s.

A south county choice was better than a northern one as the south of Tipperary was more heavily settled by Normans and therefore more stable politically than the north where the Gaelic lords were more assertive.

An inspection of a calendar of public documents reveals Cashel as the seat of royal courts, held by itinerant justices on tour (*eyre*) (which got underway 1212-21) in 1246, 1253, and 1267.[22] Mind you, there was a claim in 1297 that the county court was held in Tipperary town (*vill*) 'from time whereof there is no memory' until the archbishop of Cashel caused it to be removed to Cashel.[23] Presumably what was in question there was the sheriff's court (*tourn*) for lesser offences. Royal

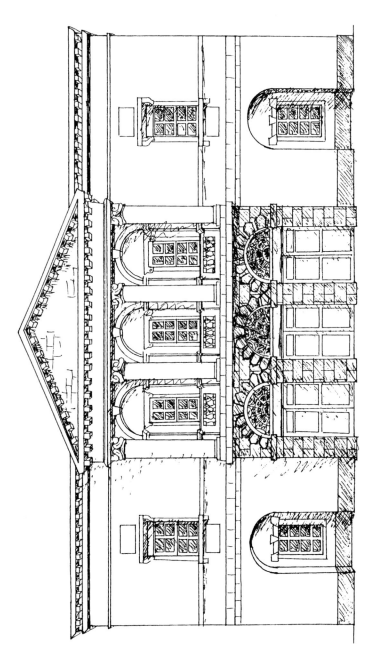

Plate 1: Clonmel Courthouse, built c.1800 to a design by Sir Richard Morrison.

Drawing – Deirdre O'Dowd, from a photograph.

7

writ prescribed 'the construction of a royal gaol at Cashel' shortly before 1275.[24]

The King's courts held by the King's justices gradually acquired the description assizes from that term being used for certain types of case involving land disputes.[25] The same calendar uses that term assizes for some of the cases held in Clonmel in 1278, 1288-9-90, 1293 and 1318.[26] Cashel had disappeared from that record of itineraries but another source has a wide range of cases held by those royal courts at Cashel between April 1317 and April 1318 – five sessions there as against one intervening at Clonmel.[27]

A decade later James Butler acquired the devolved rights of a palatinate. Whether he himself before his death in 1338 switched the county's own court to a venue independent of Cashel, which continued to host the King's courts for the County of the Cross, is unknown. By 1358, records become abundant again and show Clonmel firmly established from that date onwards as the site of the 'court of the liberty',[28] usually presided over by the seneschal/steward or earl's chief executive – corresponding at local level to the position at national level of justiciar, later Lord Lieutenant, as chief executive in Ireland for the King.[29] There were exceptions – courts were held at Crumpiscastell/Crumpstown/Crompstown, next door to Fethard and hardly eight miles north of Clonmel, on several occasions concentrated in 1410-11, once in 1421, on five occasions concentrated in 1457-8 and once more in 1551. They were also held at Lisronagh, four miles north of Clonmel on just three occasions, intermingled with Clonmel itself, 1434-7.[30]

Whether such out-of-town appearances coincided with flashpoints in the testy relations between the Butler earls of Ormond, lords of the palatinate, and the Fitzgerald earls of Desmond, owners of Clonmel town since 1338,[31] can be speculated on. Perhaps even the flaunting of the Butler arms in quasi-Fitzgerald territory might have been a factor in choosing Clonmel initially.

One can only presume that the King's judges on circuit resumed assizes in Tipperary between 1621 and 1662 when the palatinate was quashed. Again, that from 1662 to 1716, with the County of the Cross incorporated in the Palatinate, Cashel ceased to receive judges and juries.[32] When the palatinate finally disappeared from the political landscape in 1716, commonsense presumably dictated that the Clonmel site of its courthouse would continue to be the venue for assizes, now once more part of one of the five national circuits. It was replaced as courthouse by the present edifice c.1800 to Sir Richard Morrison's design.[33] There would have been little likelihood of any other assize town than Clonmel, still clearly through the 1600s the prime one in the county. In 1655 it had the 'County Gaole and Towne Hall'.[34]

Cashel got the county infirmary soon after an enabling statute of 1765. Clonmel got the county's first fever hospital following an Act of 1807.[35] Both institutions had a mix of grand jury and private funding; one must wonder at the unrecorded power politics involved in the choice of locations.

NEW ERA – NEW LAW

Two acts of parliament in the 1830s gave scope for a review of both assize venues and county divisions. The Assizes Act, 1835 gave the Lord Lieutenant the power, acting by and with the advice of the Privy Council, to name one or more assize towns in a county and, if more than one, to divide a county (as detailed in Appendix Two).

The Grand Jury (Consolidation) Act, 1836 repeated the endowment of that power to that personage and advisory body who were in effect the devolved government of Ireland. It was slightly more restrictive in one respect, by specifying just a second assize town, but it dropped a restriction embodied in the 1835 Act – that significant development is explored in Chapter One. The 1836 Act, which was the one utilised to divide Tipperary, was a wide-ranging update of centuries of grand jury law. The Bill was revised by the House of Lords in August 1836 and finally passed into law by the quill pen of William IV on the 20th of that month (the relevant sections are detailed in Appendix Three).

Like the county and its sheriff the Privy Council descended from a Norman institution. It was an advisory body to the Lord Lieutenant who was the viceroy or King's representative and Chief Governor of Ireland.[36] In its 1830s' Irish version it comprised senior judicial and administrative officials – organisational descendants of the medieval king's household – and peers and distinguished commoners – the contemporary equivalent of the feudal barons.

How could such a body and the personage whom it advised, the very essence of establishment, have open minds on upsetting the existing structure for the administration of the law and of local government and in addition deal adequately with the details of the Tipperary case as viewed from an apparently remote and lofty bench? One must advert to individual expertise, to the fresh political winds blowing throughout the whole United Kingdom, particularly throughout Ireland, and to the high profile of County Tipperary in the national consciousness.

Plate 2: ~~Constantine Henry~~ Henry Constantine Phipps (1797-1863), second earl of Mulgrave, created Marquis of Normanby in 1838, Lord Lieutenant of Ireland 1835-9 – photo, courtesy of the National Gallery of Ireland, of an oil on canvas sketch by Nicholas Crowley.

THE LORD LIEUTENANT

Come the crucial year of 1836, the Lord Lieutenant, at the apex of this array of power and privilege, was Henry Constantine Phipps, second earl of Mulgrave which title was also the name of the family seat near Whitby, Yorkshire. He was an English Whig or Liberal, governing Ireland since 23 April 1835, five days after Lord Melbourne began a second spell as Prime Minister of a Whig cabinet. Melbourne, as plain William Lamb, had been Chief Secretary in Ireland, 1827-8.

The change of government occurred following what was termed the 'Lichfield House compact', a tripartite one between the Whigs, a group of Radical MPs, and Daniel O'Connell and his thirty-three lrish MPs who were committed to a policy of repealing the Union of Great Britain and Ireland (1801). The O'Connellite influence on the new administration was comparable to that of any modern small party or group of Teachtaí Dála (TDs = members of parliament) holding the balance of power.[37] In his case it resulted in the appointments of Roman Catholics to local (unpaid) positions as magistrates and to high office, including that of Michael O'Loghlen to four successively higher honours (see Appendix Eleven). The alliance and the liberalisation evoked strong Protestant reaction, led in Tipperary by the earl of Glengall, and articulated most strongly within County Tipperary by the *Tipperary Constitution*. The headline 'O'Mulgrave the Buffoon and O'Connell the Clown', quoted by the *Clare Journal* from *Age* magazine, typifies the propagandist edge of the antipathy.[38] 'Ireland Mulgravised', a headline from the *Clonmel Advertiser*, was inspired by similar feelings on the occasion of Whig appointments to public offices in August 1836.

CREEPING CIVILISATION

The times that were in it can also be gauged by a select digest of recent reforms and progress which themselves gave the prospect of further progress:

• the abolition in British dominions in 1807 of trading in slaves (the culmination of a parliamentary campaign which commenced in 1776), following the example of Denmark as of 1792, and the abolition of slavery itself throughout British dominions in 1833, ten years after the formation of the first anti-slavery society;[39]

• the removal of barriers against admission to parliament and to civil offices, such as held by judges, mayors and sheriffs, for two million Protestant dissenters in 1828 and seven million Roman Catholics in 1829; mass 'Greenboy' civil rights marches throughout the Golden

Vale and particularly County Tipperary had some influence in converting the government of Wellington and Peel to the latter reform;[40]
• police reform succeeding military control, 1829, and elaborated on in Ireland, 1836. The Irish reform provided for a single force recruited on a non-sectarian basis under an Inspector-General with county inspectors. It replaced both the 1814 'peelers' or Peace Preservation Force, assigned as needed to districts, proclaimed as disturbed, and the 1822 constabulary, recruited through local magistrates, which had a chief constable in each barony under four provincial inspectors-general;[41]
• the removal in 1832 of house-breaking, sheep-stealing and forgery from the list of offences punishable by death;[42]
• the introduction in 1833 of a 48-hour weekly working limit in their first year of work for children under 11 years of age and a 69-hour limit for young people under 18;[43]
• the remission in 1836 of the 1834 sentence of transportation for seven years on the 'Tolpuddle Martyrs' – Dorchester agricultural labourers whose prototype trade union's rules forbade violence but whose initiation ceremony included Bible readings and solemn promises construed by their prosecutors as 'unlawful oaths';[44]
• the system of national education introduced in Ireland in 1831, controversial as regards its original non-denominational aims and also evoking muted objections to the absence of Irish history and language from the curriculum. Nevertheless the system attracted extensive support, influenced by its structure and funding. The school site was vested in local trustees. The diocesan bishop acted as patron and the parish priest or rector as manager. The construction of schools was paid for by the Commissioners of National Education. There were 941 applications in 1835 and a total of 4,704 schools in the system by 1851 with 520,000 children enrolled. The 1851 census recorded a drop in illiteracy among the population aged five and over from 53% in 1841 to 47% (it fell to 39% in 1861 and to 14% in 1901);[45]
• 205 miles of roadway through mountainous country in Cork, Kerry, Limerick and Tipperary built between 1822 and 1831 by Richard Griffith, initially to the orders of the Lord Lieutenant (1821-8 and 1833-4), Richard Colley Wellesley, first Marquess Wellesley, bringing remarkable improvements in agriculture (through access for lime as a fertiliser and access outwards to markets), in shops and in housing. The public works climaxed in 1828-31 with the Anglesey lines from Newport to Thurles and from Nenagh to Tipperary; they opened up 480 square miles of country 'throughout the whole of which there was no road passable for wheel-carriages'. They were authorised following

a personal examination on horseback by Henry William Paget, first Marquess of Anglesey, Lord Lieutenant (1828-9 and 1830-3). They were built by the Griffith innovations of direct labour – cutting out profit-taking contractors who were difficult to supervise – and of pay for measured piece-work, with its incentive to productivity rather than employment by the day;[46]

• the spread of railways, with statutory approval given in 1826 (one of fifty-four Railway Acts passed 1825-35) to the Limerick-Waterford line (it actually took until 1848 before its construction proceeded and reached Limerick Junction and Tipperary town). The first Irish line opened in 1834 from Dublin to Kingstown (now Dun Laoghaire) following the 1830 Liverpool-Manchester opening. The prospect of popular travel and commercial development was fulfilled, e.g. by 1888 when 55 companies managed 2,814 miles of rail which carried 23 million passengers and 4 million tons of goods;[47]

• an increase of almost 50% in the franchise in England and Wales by the Reform Act, 1832. It also brought a re-distribution of parliamentary seats from rural Britain, which was controlled by the landowners, to the towns and middle classes. The corresponding act for Ireland in the same year was far less generous, however;[48]

• poor relief by elected Board of Guardians under the surveillance of central Poor Law Commissioners – in Britain as of 1834 and now mooted for extension to Ireland. An 1833-6 royal commission, chaired by Dublin Church of Ireland Archbishop Whately, was followed in autumn 1836 by an Irish tour of survey by an English poor law commissioner, George Nicholls. His less radical proposals got statutory adoption in 1838, and 118 workhouses were occupied by 1845 with 4,000 paupers accommodated. The guardians for 130 poor law unions composed the first-ever countrywide structure of local democracy, albeit diluted by the ex-officio presence of non-elected justices of the peace up to one quarter (one half as of 1847) of the total membership, and also limited in its franchise to owners and occupiers of property, 'and a system of plural voting ensured that property had its rights as well as its duties';[49]

• the Municipal Reform Act, 1835, instituting elected town councils with paid officials and power over local finance and bye-laws, again due to be copied for Ireland;[50]

• the Assizes Act, 1833, which related to England and Wales, followed by the two Irish Acts of 1835 and 1836, already cited, which enabled the improvement of court and grand jury structures to accord with local needs, and a further 1836 Act which provided likewise for the lower tier of courts called quarter sessions.

IRISH REFORMS

The government's chief executive in Ireland, the Under-Secretary (as distinct from the political head, the Chief Secretary, Lord Morpeth, who spent long periods in London at parliament) was Thomas Drummond, a Scot. Drummond's reforming zeal ran to appointing stipendiary (paid) magistrates reporting to Dublin Castle and free of local landlord influence. He put the brakes on the Crown practice of challenging Roman Catholic jurors which had by-and-large excluded them from trials of their co-religionists. Catholics were encouraged to join the new police force. He stopped the employment of military in the enforcement of ejection orders and collection of tithes. He moved equally against the Orange Society – ultra-Protestant – and the peasant secret societies whose members were Catholic in religion. All this and the resulting ascendancy agitation enabled him to reply to a petition of Tipperary magistrates upon the murder of a landlord in April 1838 – Austin Cooper of Killenure, Dundrum – in the words now engraved on the base of Drummond's statue in City Hall, Dublin:

> Property has its duties as well as its rights; to the neglect of those duties in times past is mainly to be ascribed that diseased state of society in which such crimes can take their rise; ...[51]

This spirit of change throughout the United Kingdom must have developed a benign scenario which would influence the government attitude towards any semi-democratic stirrings for a change of administrative system, even at county level.

PUBLIC OPINION

There was the additional spur of a mobilised, informed and articulate public opinion. The mobilisation was becoming a habit from the initial public meetings seeking Catholic Emancipation, a strong habit from at least 1818, climaxing in Tipperary with the series of disciplined marches in September 1828 by thousands flourishing a variety of green emblems signifying liberty. The articulation as of 1834-6 was at a number of levels, and focused on Repeal of the Union and anti-tithes campaigns. In March 1834 R. L. Sheil, MP, presented petitions on those concerns to the House of Commons from Thurles, Nenagh and an unnamed parish in the county. In early April a meeting at the rear of the Ormond Hotel, Clonmel, mustered 98 signatures to another such petition.[52]

The most dramatic evidence of public awareness occurred on the nights of Saturday and Sunday, 11-12 March 1835. The newspapers reported 'a vast extent of country blazed with bonfires ... the modern species of telegraph ... causes very great alarm.'[53] Tipperary and its neighbours Clare, Kilkenny, Limerick and Queen's County were among those alight. Police reported fires on the hills about Thurles and Killenaule.[54] Police and papers were agreed that the resignation of Peel and his Tory Cabinet was the cause of this blazing from the hilltops.

MULGRAVE IN TIPPERARY

A further hidden factor was that Lord Lieutenant Mulgrave, under constant public pressure by the Tory opposition to introduce harsher methods to restore, as the catch-cry had it, 'Tipperary Tranquillity', had some familiarity with the county. And not just knowledge based on reports and memoranda read in London or Dublin, as is evident from the newspaper reports of his 1835 and 1836 tours of the south of Ireland.

Roscrea, for instance, in August 1835 was derided by the *Evening Packet* for an address made to His Excellency 'from a few priests, shopkeepers, brewers, the manager of Dan's bank [i.e. O'Connell's National Bank], an attorney, a retired shopkeeper ...'. The magistrates and 'other gentlemen of the neighbourhood' were in town for the fair day but 'left him alone in his glory'.[55] That was not quite true, for the newspaper's own account also described 'a son of the Hon. F. A. Prittie, who bestrided a horse belonging to Stephen Egan, a brewer'. Mulgrave had spent the previous night at 'the splendid mansion of Lord Dunally', young Prittie's uncle, en route from Limerick where he reviewed the army garrison, visited institutions and listened to several addresses including one from the Catholic clergy headed by the Bishop.[56]

An advertisement which conveyed to the public the terms of Borrisokane's address and Mulgrave's neutral expression of gratitude claimed that the address was made 'with the united consent' of seven parishes.[57] The Mayor of Clonmel refused to convene a meeting of the inhabitants for the purpose of addressing Mulgrave, on the grounds of non-precedence.[58] The requisitionists were clearly O'Connellite liberals, headed by Charles Bianconi, transport entrepreneur, O'Connell's close friend, and a future mayor. They included also John Hackett, proprietor-editor of the *Tipperary Free Press* and target of a libel action with political overtones, and John Luther, fellow Town Commissioner of the other two[59] and joint Treasurer with them of the National Bank branch foundation moves.[60]

In 1836, a February address to the Lord Lieutenant from Cashel 'purporting to be "the address of the nobility, clergy, gentry, freeholders and other inhabitants'" was countered by three columns of dissenting names in a March newspaper.[61]

Mulgrave was no simpering recipient of sycophancy. The hostile *Evening Packet* had reported from the Roscrea 1835 meeting that he 'read a lecture to the persons who had, during the last month, violated the law by assaulting the houses and persons of the Protestants of the town'.[62] A countywide address which itself vowed to bring Tipperary back 'from motives the most mistaken and selfish' – an acknowledgement of the catalogue of crime sampled in Chapter Two – was responded to even-handedly, as reported by the friendly *Pilot*:

> My first object was to establish a more efficient system for the prosecution of lawless outrage of every description ...
>
> I, within this hour, received an official report from the Cashel district, now the only disturbed part of the county, stating that 'a marked improvement' for the better had taken place in that part of the county since the steps recently taken of increasing the force at police stations and that the military patrolling is also considered to be attended with the very best consequences ...
>
> I can never forget that there is no thraldom so offensive as lawless intimidation ...[63]

AMNESTY

The familiarity with the county and its problems became very intimate indeed, as reported by the *Clare Journal* of 22 August 1836:

> Lord Mulgrave, on his visit to Clonmel on Saturday last, went to the House of Correction and desired that any persons who had suffered a long confinement and who during that period had behaved to the satisfaction of the gaol officers, should be pointed out to him. This was accordingly done and His Excellency used his prerogative by ordering the discharge of 47 men and 10 women. Nearly all the men were persons who had been sentenced to long periods of confinement and who had been from 9 months to 2 years in prison.

The House of Correction was attached to the County Gaol, but with a separate Governor. Mulgrave obtained the recommendations for release from the Governor of the House of Correction, its First Turnkey and its Overseer of the Works. The prisoners who were recommended included several convicted of affrays and assaults, which seem to have been part of faction fights, and who had served less than half of their eighteen-months sentences. Others released included brothers convicted of the manslaughter of their uncle; a man who had served almost a year and a half of his two years sentence for shooting at a person and attacking a dwelling house; and a man originally sentenced to transportation for life for forging a note or bond but which had been commuted to two and a half years alienation in Clonmel.

Under cross-examination by a Select Committee of Inquiry nearly three years later the Governor clarified that all fifty-seven had been released on a pledge to keep the peace, without formal entry into recognizances, and that all had kept the pledge. Although he made it clear that he would not have recommended some who were put forward by other officers and released, and though the Protestant Chaplain maintained that he would not have recommended one, the Governor confessed when questioned about the effect upon the ex-prisoners' relations and upon the population generally: 'I believe it had rather a good tendency on the feelings of the people in that part of the country'.

The controversy engendered for Mulgrave did not shake the confidence implied in his motto, *Virtute quies* (Content in virtue). Indeed he personified the change in the times in that his father, the first earl of Mulgrave, had been described as 'a high tory, and complete John Bull'.

Again, the contrasting opinions on Mulgrave's government of Ireland can be gauged from the following quotation from the speech of a Tipperary MP, Richard Lalor Sheil, in the House of Commons on 19 April 1839 to a motion by Lord Roden seeking an inquiry into the Lord Lieutenant's tenure. Mulgrave by that time was titled Marquess of Normanby.

> Charge Lord Normanby, if you please, with an abandonment of that policy by which Ireland was ruled so long, by the men who regarded that policy as the only means of preserving what is called British connexion and Protestant interests; charge him with having preferred the conciliation of an entire people to the mercenary sustainment of a decayed and impuissant faction; charge him with having grounded his administration upon a scheme of government subversive of that party which was held so long to be the garrison of the country. These are accusations worthy of him, and of you: but you should not stoop to a miserable criticism upon the appointment of subordinate officers in the police, and of stipendiary magistrates, whose only offence is to be found in their consanguinity with the member for Dublin [i.e. Daniel O'Connell]; upon the alleged liberation of men charged with

larcenies and assaults, without a strict compliance with technical formalities ... [64]

The *Dictionary of National Biography* concluded: 'In spite of a somewhat frivolous and theatrical manner, he was a man of considerable prescience and political ability'. As of 1835-6 his past included a parliamentary maiden speech in favour of Catholic Emancipation, a later one for parliamentary reform, two years as Governor of Jamaica which included suppressing a rebellion and overseeing the payment of compensation to the former owners of emancipated slaves, and appointment as Lord Privy Seal. His future would take in posts as Secretary of War and Colonies, Ambassador to France and to the Courts of Tuscany and Florence; in the interim the Queen offered him the Prime Minister's role in 1839, but he was unable to form a cabinet.

STATE OF MIND, 1830s
The man given charge of the government of Ireland as of 1835 can thus be seen as in spirit with the liberalising times – and well capable of withstanding reactionary elements. In a milieu of newly even-handed administration, he was likely to bring his independence of mind to any adjudication upon competing regional interests. He was the deciding authority on both local government and court structures in the regions, and he had made himself directly acquainted with the regions. In particular, he has been seen as very familiar with the condition of one large region, Tipperary. Its territory had evolved through an extraordinary history to a point about 120 years previously when it was designated as 'one county for ever'.

Notes
1. *Chambers English Dictionary*; *Encycl. Brit.* 19, 300b;. 23, 898d; 14, 147b. The system and term were thus brought to England by the Vikings, adopted by the Normans who set up riding courts, and applied to Ireland by the United Kingdom parliament and its Irish administration in Dublin Castle. Yorkshire, thus divided c.875, was the largest English county, over double the size of the next biggest, Lincolnshire, and almost four times that of Tipperary. Lincolnshire also had three 'Parts' or ridings: Lindsey, Holland and Kesteven. They preceded the formation of the county itself, stemming from the distinction of natural areas respectively of island, forest and fen. The total area of that county or shire was about sixty per cent greater than Tipperary's; the average area of its three ridings was slightly greater than the average of Tipperary's two.
2. John J. Clancy, MP, *A Handbook of Local Government in Ireland*, p. 50; Desmond Roche, *Local Government in Ireland* (Dublin, 1982), p. 31.

For Cork, see note 1, Appendix Twelve.

3. A. J. Otway-Ruthven, *A History of Medieval Ireland* (London, 1940), p. 174; C. A. Empey, 'The Settlement of Limerick' in James Lydon ed, *England and Ireland in the Later Middle Ages* (Dublin 1981), p. 16; C. A. Empey, 'The Norman Period 1185-1500' in Nolan and McGrath eds, *Tipperary: History and Society* (Dublin, 1985), pp. 71-91.

4. Roche, cited above, pp. 29-32; see also P. J. Meghen 'The Administrative Work of the Grand Jury', in *ADMINISTRATION*, Autumn 1958, for a more detailed account of the evolution of grand juries and their local government functions; Virginia Crossman, *Local Government in Nineteenth Century Ireland* (Belfast, 1994), pp. 25-41, draws extensively on private papers, parliamentary committee reports and even fiction to illustrate graphically the controversial exercise of their powers by these non-elected bodies. Her pp. 7-12 outline the fluctuating government edicts on the method of selection of High Sheriffs. The quotation is from p. 27 of W. P. O'Brien's report upon local government and taxation – PP (Commons) 1878, xxiii, 735. The 1833 reforms are outlined in note 39 to Chapter One. The limited extent of grand jury functions in the 1830s to mid-1840s can be gauged from the expenditure headings in Table 6 in Appendix Seven.

5. R. M. Jackson, *The Machinery of Justice in England* (1940), p. 82; V. T. H. Delany and Charles Lysaght, *The Administration of Justice in Ireland*, (Dublin, 1977), p. 44. The latter gives the Irish background, and moves on to the abolition of grand juries by the Courts of Justice Act, 1924 (assizes and grand juries had been effectively abandoned in the preceding few years because of the success of the Dáil Éireann courts system during the War of Independence). Delany-Lysaght, p. 45, outline the system of prosecution involving proceedings in the District Court, and subsequent involvement of the Attorney-General, 1924-74, and since then by the Director of Public Prosecutions. The grand jury procedure ceased in Britain in 1933 for most cases and in 1948 per the Criminal Justice Act of that year for remaining cases; it 'swept away all vestiges of the institution of grand jury' (*Encycl. Brit.*, 6, p. 712). Grand juries adjudicating on indictments as to whether to send the accused for trial are still in practice in the USA. Assizes were replaced by Crown Courts in Northern Ireland by the Judicature (N.I.) Act, 1978.

6. Carte, *An History of the Life of James, Duke of Ormond (1736)*, part i, lxvi; *Ormond Deeds* i, no. 693. Empey, in 'The Butler Lordship', *Jn. Butler Soc.*, vol. 1, no. 3, (1970-1), p. 177, speculates on the political motivations for the grant on 9 November 1328, apart from the fact that James was married to Eleanor de Bohun, Edward III's niece.

According to Blackstone, 'counties palatine ... are so called *a palatio*, because the owners of them had formerly in those counties *jura regalia* [royal rights/law/courts of justice] as fully as the King in his palace.' The Earl of a county was Lord of all the land in his shire that was not

Church land; and his jurisdiction was equivalent in all essential points to the jurisdiction of the King in an ordinary county. ... Included in the power to appoint officers of justice was the appointment of the sheriff; and with the functions of the sheriff in the palatinate no King's sheriff might interfere – C. Litton Falkiner, *Illustrations of Irish History* (Dublin, 1904), p. 109.

7. Appendix to Fifth Report of the Deputy Keeper of the Public Records (1873), pp. 33-6; V. T. H. Delany, 'The Palatinate Court of the Liberty of Tipperary' in *American Journal of Legal History*, 5, 1961; Empey in Nolan and McGrath, cited above, part v, 'The Liberty of Tipperary', pp. 89-91. All three outline the genesis, ebb and flow, and extinction of the palatinate. The Deputy Keeper quotes in full a 1621 legal document which spells out the extent of the 'liberties, privileges, franchises and jurisdictions', in so far as the various courts and their officers are involved. He appends schedules of 332 cases heard.

Delany outlines and puts in context the work of the county court of the liberty in two phases, 1328-1621 and 1662-1715, mentions inferior courts within the county, as did the Deputy Keeper, and goes on to potted biographies of the personnel in the latter period. Many judges progressed to the royal or national courts, facilitated by the lord of the palatinate, James Butler, Duke of Ormonde, being also Lord Lieutenant of Ireland during a key period. Both Delany and Empey sample cases recorded in the *Ormond Deeds*, ii, iii, iv, *Irish Manuscripts Commission*, Edmund Curtis ed (Dublin, 1934, 5, 7).

Empey summarises, with instances, the types of cases dealt with, and points to minor legislation actually enacted by the court of the liberty. One outstanding example is in *Ormond Deeds*, iii, no. 102, p. 97, c.1460, quoted in free translation in Patrick C. Power, *History of South Tipperary* (Cork, 1989), p. 34. It bans breaches of the peace, prohibits certain customs, proclaims annual sessions to be attended by spiritual and temporal dignitaries 'as well as ye Kyng may hole hys parlement', with the sessions to grant the lord [the earl] a specified 'subsidy'.

Although Sidney and Beatrice Webb in *English Local Government*, i, Book 2, pp. 310-17, outline aspects of palatinate privileges enjoyed by, e.g. Durham and Isle of Ely until 1836 and 1837, respectively, and Lancashire through the 1700s with its own court until 1873, Empey draws attention to Tipperary being the longest lasting in both islands to keep all privileges intact: 'unique in the world of common law in exercising its full medieval prerogatives undiminished by parliamentary legislation which had reduced the English and Welsh franchises to mere shadows of their former glory'. All 'thanks largely to the capacity of the Butlers to range themselves, if not exactly on the side of the angels, at least on the side of the winners'.

R. M. Jackson, cited above, p. 2, points out that the term county *franchises* 'always signifies the exclusive right of a private person to exercise functions which we now consider should be in public hands'.

The jurisdiction of the palatinate courts was 'nothing more than a replica in miniature of the Irish legal system at the time ... the same wide range of matters as that possessed by the King's Courts in Dublin' (Delany, p. 106). However, four pleas or types of case were reserved to the Crown in the original, renewal and fresh grants of the liberty: arson, rape, forestalling [assault on the highway] and treasure-trove (but not homicide). Delany, p. 112, instances inferior courts within the liberty or palatinate as the Town Court of Clonmel, the City Court of Cashel and the sheriff's county courts at Silvermines and Nenagh.

There seems to be no way of ascertaining whether roadmaking powers, as acquired per statute in 1634 by the grand juries of counties in general, applied to the palatinate on its renewal in 1662. Delany, p. 113, asserts that a process of malicious injury claims, originating in 1595 and 1696 statutes, applied with equal force in Tipperary. The records of any business of a local government nature were not calendared by the Deputy Keeper in 1872; any that did exist were consumed by flames in the Public Record Office in 1922 in a burst of fervour comparable to the destruction in Belfast's Linenhall Library in the past decade. But see note 13.

8. Empey, 'The formation of the county', pp. 75-6, and 'The liberty of Tipperary', pp. 89-91, in Nolan and McGrath, cited above, following his 'The Butler Lordship', in *Jn. Butler Soc.,* cited above, pp. 174-87; Otway-Ruthven, cited above, p. 174.

9. Dermot F. Gleeson, *The Last Lords of Ormond* (London, 1938), pp. 3-4; George Cunningham, *The Anglo-Norman Advance into the South-West Midlands of Ireland, 1185-1221* (Roscrea, 1987), Chapter Two, pp. 13-27; Seamus Ó Riain, *Dunkerrin: A Parish in Ely O'Carroll* (Dunkerrin, 1988), pp. 35-7. Gleeson touches on the subject. Cunningham teases out the extent of medieval Ely O'Carroll and Ormond and the bearing which that may have had on the 1605-6 arbitration. Ó Riain traces the gory saga of murder, invasion, treachery and politicking right up to Elizabeth's throne from 1589 onwards. It was so bitter an O'Carroll-Butler feud that Sir Charles O'Carroll actually petitioned government that 'his county may be reduced to shire ground, or else annexed to the King's or Queen's Counties' (*C.S.P.,* 16 July 1595, no. 34; 20 Aug 1595, no. 53.1). O'Carroll got Queen Elizabeth to defer his trial 'for the slaughter of some of the Cantwells' (Butler vassals) until the territorial claim was heard (*C.S.P.,* 73.1 & Carew MSS, 161, both 20 Aug 1595).

Her mention of O'Carroll's £100 a year tax paid to the Crown as an apparent factor is a wry reflection on her affection for O'Carroll's adversary, her 'beloved cousin', her 'black husband', Thomas Butler the 10th earl of Ormond. His delay, despite pressure from Carew, President of Munster, in taking military action against Ormond allies of the Tyrone rebellion (Gleeson, cited above, p. 28-9), his age and failing sight – he was 72 in 1605 – may have been factors in the hearing of the arbitration. He wrote to Elizabeth's successor, James I, one month after the hearing that he expected to die shortly (he survived another nine years), returning

21

'thanks for His Majesty's kindness and entreating the like for his successor' (*C.S.P.*, 1603-6, 472). But he lost his case.

10. Deputy Keeper, cited above pp. 33-4; the judgement was given on 6 Sept 1606 by a royal commission of four judges sitting at Cashel as capital of the County of the Cross.

11. Empey, in Nolan and McGrath, cited above, p. 73. The dates and rationale of these transfers do not appear to have been established. All of Owney seems to be in Co. Limerick in Francis Jobson's 1598 map. But, extraordinarily, if that is accurate, *Ormond Deeds*, iv, no. 78 has William and Daniel O'Mulriain of Annaghe and the abbey of Owney agreeing to give allegiance to the 10th earl of Ormond in 1557. That was to take the form of military service and money tribute, in return for which the earl promised fosterage of his first child with the O'Mulriains. Annagh and the abbey are in Owneybeg barony, Co. Limerick. Hence the question: was the territory's affiliation in doubt, or was it believed by the earl and those members of that sept to have been part of Tipperary? That it may have been in doubt, with Black Tom attempting a foothold via the O'Mulriain alliance, is suggested by his and the earl of Desmond both seeking a fee farm grant of Owney from the newly-crowned Elizabeth in 1558-9 (John Kirwan, lecture to Butler Rally, at Carrick-on-Suir, 11 Sept 1993). Another question for anyone to pursue might be: did the description Owney O Mulriain/Mulryan, so called, cover Owneybeg or Owney with Arra or both – writers differ.

Sir Charles O'Carroll, who features in note 9 above, as part of the feud with the 10th earl submitted 'a breve note of certain territories subtracted and concealed by the Right honourable the Erle of ORMOND, from her most excellent m^{ti}' to the Lord Lieutenant in 1595. He included 'Item, O'Mulrian is contré, called Wonymulrian' – quoted by John O'Donovan in JRSAI, vol. 1 New Series, 1856-7, p. 312.

12. C. A. Empey, 'County Kilkenny in the Norman Period' in Nolan and Whelan eds, *Kilkenny History and Society* (Dublin, 1990), p. 75, Figure 4.1. Tibberaghny/Tibberaghtne/Tiperaght appears in a roll of amercements [fines] on parishes in Co. Tipperary for 1370-90 – Newport B. White ed, *Irish Monastic and Episcopal Deeds* (Dublin, 1936), C4(7), p. 229. It figures in a number of Ormond Deeds up to 1560 as still in the same county, e.g. *Ormond Deeds*,. iii, no. 102 (1432) to v, no. 99 (1560). The first mention I can find of its Co. Kilkenny affiliation is as the address of a tithe payer in a report of a jury on tithes in that county for 1619-20 – White, XXXV, p. 279.

13. C. A. Empey, 'County Waterford: 1200-1300', p. 133, in Nolan & Power eds, *Waterford History and Society* (Dublin,1992). Empey has cautioned that his study is not based on a thorough examination of all available printed sources, and does not take into consideration some records which are in the National Archives and in the Public Record Office, London. Neither have I examined a vast set of uncalendared Ormond Deeds and other manuscripts in the National Library of Ireland, attention to which

was drawn by Empey and Kenneth Nicholls in two short summaries in *Jn. Butler Soc.*, vol. 1, no. 7, pp. 519-26.

14. L. M. Cullen, 'The Social and Economic Evolution of Kilkenny in the seventeenth and eighteenth centuries' in Nolan & Whelan eds, *Kilkenny*, cited above, p.274.

15. Lord Deputy Sidney to the Privy Council, 27 February 1576 (Collins, *Letters and Memorials of State*, 1, 89-97) quoted by Nicholas P. Canny, *The Elizabethan Conquest of Ireland: A Pattern Established 1565-76*, p. 106.

16. Sir George Carew to Sir Robert Cecil, 2 Nov 1600 (P.R.O., London, S.P. 63/207) quoted by Aileen McClintock, 'The Earls of Ormond and Tipperary's Role in the Governing of Ireland (1603-1641) in *Tipperary Historical Journal*, 1988, p. 160.

17. John Kirwan, 'Thomas Butler, 10th Earl of Ormond', Part 1, in *Jn. Butler Soc.*, vol. 3, no. 4, 1994.

18. The 'regality' or palatinate privileges first reverted to the crown during 1331-2 for reasons described by Empey in *Jn. Butler Soc.*, cited above, p. 178 (ref *C.P.R.* 1330-4, 336). They were renewed on 23 April 1337 (*Ormond Deeds*, i, no. 693) but again reverted to the crown upon the death of the first earl in 1338, when his son and heir, the second James, was only seven years of age. He was sixteen when re-granted it in 1347 (*C.P.R.* 1345-8, 429-30 and recited in *Ormond Deeds*, iii, no. 348). The 1372 grant was per *C.P.R.*, 41 Edw III and *Ormond Deeds*, iii, no. 348. The privileges 'were seized and resumed into the hands of Henry VII' by act of parliament in 1495-6 which act was made void in 1501-2, thus restoring the palatinate to the seventh earl James (*Ormond Deeds*, v, no. 68. which recites that story in the course of a fresh grant to the tenth earl, Thomas ('Black Tom') by (Queen) Mary on 11 March 1557). The longest break was from 1621 to 1662, beginning with Walter Butler, the eleventh earl, falling out of favour with James I and continuing through the Cromwellian control of England until the restoration of Charles II to the English throne.

19. Deputy Keeper, cited above, p. 34.

20. Deputy Keeper, cited above, p. 37; the title of the Act trumpeted on: 'and for vesting in His Majesty the estate of James Butler, commonly called James, Duke of Ormonde; and for giving a Reward of ten thousand pounds to any person who shall seize or secure him in case he shall attempt to land in this kingdom' (*Civil Survey*, ii, xxiii. no. 38).

21. Power, cited in note 7, pp. 19-21.

22. H. S. Sweetman ed, *Calendar of Documents relating to Ireland* (Dublin, 1875), i, no. 2820; ii, no. 187; G. J. Hand, *English Law in Ireland 1290-1324* (Cambridge, 1967), p. 8, n5.

23. Sweetman, iv, no. 419. This was kindly drawn to my attention by Dr Denis G. Marnane, Tipperary *vill.* The judgement was equivocal: to the effect that if the claim was true, the court be returned to Tipperary.

24. Edmund Curtis, 'Sheriff's Accounts for County Tipperary', 1275-6, in

Proceedings of the R.I.A., 42, C5.
25. See Richard H. Grimes and Patrick T. Horgan, *Introduction to Law in the Republic of Ireland*, pp. 22-32 for the development of feudal law and courts generally, leading on to their development in Ireland.
26. Sweetman, cited above, ii, no. 1520; iii, no. 263, no. 469, no. 622; iv, no. 107.
27. Hand, cited above, Appendix Four, pp. 230-2.
28. *Ormond Deeds*, ii, iii, iv, and v, ranging from 1358 to 1410, 1425-1457, 1508-25 and 1560-1582.
29. For a comprehensive account of 'The Government of the Norman-Irish State' as she titles Chapter Five, see Otway-Ruthven, cited above, particularly pp. 181-7 for the local government of the era.
30. *Ormond Deeds*, (Crimpiscastell) ii, no. 405; iii, nos 23, 44, 200; iv, no. 265; (Lisronagh) iii, nos 102, 129.
31. Elizabeth Shee and S. J. Watson, *Clonmel* (Clonmel 1992), p. 7.
32. I have not examined the assize rolls included in the Ormond MSS 'C' collection in the N.L.I., drawn attention to by C. A. Empey, referred to in note 13 above.
33. Shee and Watson, cited above, pp. 36, 38.
34. R. C. Simington ed, *The Civil Survey, i, Co. Tipperary* (Dublin, 1931), p. 387. This is illuminating for the disparity in extent and services between, for instance, Clonmel, Cashel, Thurles, and Nenagh (the latter – ii).
35. Power, cited above, p. 129.
36. Otway-Ruthven, cited above, pp. 145-150.
37. Charles Chenevix Trench, *The Great Dan* (London, 1986) p.b. edition, pp. 228-30. This is an especially readable work. The 1835-41 period is also dealt with succinctly and lucidly by Donal McCartney, *The Dawning of Democracy: Ireland 1800-1870* (Dublin, 1987), pp. 143-8, and by Gearóid Ó Tuathaigh, *Ireland Before the Famine, 1798-1848* (Dublin 1972), pp. 181-4. The British context is well set as 'The new structure', pp. 86-110 in Michael Bentley, *Politics Without Democracy, 1815-1914* (London, 1984). There is a marriage of the two perspectives by A. D. Macintyre in 'O'Connell and British Politics' in Kevin B. Nowlan and Maurice R. O'Connell eds, *Daniel O'Connell, Portrait of a Radical* (RTE Thomas Davis Lectures, Belfast 1984). See also D. George Boyce, *Nineteenth-Century Ireland: the Search for Stability* (Dublin, 1990), pp. 66-74.
38. *C.J.*, 30 Dec 1836.
39. *Encycl. Brit.*, 20, pp. 780-2.
40. Gearóid Ó Tuathaigh, *Ireland before the Famine 1798-1848* (Dublin, 1972), pp. 74-5; Fergus O'Ferrall, *Catholic Emancipation* (Dublin, 1985), pp. 4, 180, 337, 250; Donal A. Murphy, 'Emancipation and the Tipperary Marches, 1828', parts 6-9, *The Guardian*, 12 May, 2, 16, 23 June 1990.
41. The Constabulary (Ireland) Act, 1836, 6-7 William IV, c. 12; Ó Tuathaigh, cited above, pp. 92-3; Seamus Breathnach, *The Irish Police* (Dublin,

1974), pp. 24-6, 30-2, 36-7.

42. David Thomson, *England in the Nineteenth Century* (No. 8 of the Pelican History of England) (London, 1971), p. 17.

43. ditto, p. 47.

44. ditto, pp. 53-4.

45. D. J. Hickey and J. E. Doherty, *A Dictionary of Irish History since 1800* (Dublin, 1980), pp. 386-8; D. George Boyce, *Nineteenth-Century Ireland: The Search for Stability* (Dublin 1990), p. 81 which illustrates the strong feelings of Thomas Davis, the Young Ireland leader, who was however in a minority at the time; T Ó Raifeartaigh, 'The State's Administration of Education' in *ADMINISTRATION*, 2 no. 4, p. 74. He points to the Irish language being allowed as an extra subject only as of 1878.

46. PP (Reports on Commissions) Report of Mr Griffith, Engineer, On the Roads in the Southern District of Ireland, 1831 (119) xii; William Corbett, 'The Anglesey Road', *Tipperary Association Yearbook 1981-2* (Dublin) pp. 523; Gordon L. Herries Davies and R. Charles Mollan, *Richard Griffith, 1784-1878* (Dublin, 1980).

47. Hickey & Doherty, cited above, pp. 498-9; Donal A. Murphy, 'The Redwood Railway Reformer' ('From Script and Stone' series), *The Guardian,* 12, 19 April 1986.

48. Thomson, cited above, p. 74; Bentley, cited above, p. 88, assesses the possible increase in England and Wales as 80%. For Ireland see McCartney, cited above, pp. 122-4. He assesses the Irish franchise as 1 voter in 26 of the population in the boroughs and only 1 in 116 in the counties, as against Bentley's corresponding English figures of 1 in 17 and 1 in 24.

49. 1 & 2 Vic., c. 56 – An Act for the more effectual Relief of the Destitute Poor in Ireland, 1838, s. 24, amended by 10 Vic., c. 31, An Act to make further Provision for the Relief of the Destitute Poor in Ireland, 1847, s. 16; Roche, cited above, pp. 37-9.

50. Roche, cited above, pp. 33-4.

51. The letter from the meeting of (only) thirty-two magistrates, including only two from a northern barony, chaired by the earl of Glengall, at Cashel on 7 April 1838, and Drummond's reply of 22 May 1838 (incorporating umpteen references to 'His Excellency', demonstrating Normanby's backing) were printed as PP (Accounts and Papers), 1837-8 (735) xxxxvi. Nicholas Maher, a future MP, had meantime written to Drummond with a strong demur from the sentiments of the Cashel meeting (on 30 April, printed in *T.F.P.*, 4 May 1838). Drummond's reply evoked another Cashel meeting on 26 September, again with only a couple of northerners present and again chaired by Glengall. The latter's detailed analysis of Drummond's reply was contested by Hon. Cornelius O'Callaghan, a former MP, and John and James Scully, clearly liberals among tories (*T.C.* report, 28 Sept 1838).

52. *C.A.*, 1, 12 Mar 1834; *T.F.P.*, 5 Apr 1834.

53. *C.A.*, 18 Apr 1835, quoting also the *Kilkenny Moderator*.

54. W. Miller to Lieut.-Col. Sir William Gossett, 15 April 1835 (N.A.). Gossett was Under Secretary at Dublin Castle immediately prior to Thomas Drummond.
55. *Limerick Times*, 13 Aug 1835, copied from the *Evening Packet*.
56 *W.M.,* 10 Aug 1835.
57. *Limerick Times*, 24 Aug 1835.
58. *T.F.P.*, 29 Jul 1835.
59. ditto.
60. *C.A.*, 3 June 1835.
61. *The Pilot*, 19 Feb 1836; *T.C.*, 18 Mar 1836.
62. Quoted by the *Limerick Times*, 13 Aug 1835.
63. *The Pilot*, 19 Feb 1836.
64. Thomas Macnevin ed, *The Speeches of Richard Lalor Sheil* (Dublin, 1872), pp.180-1.

CHAPTER ONE

'... the ends of justice are defeated by the locality of our assize town'

The power given by the 1835 Assizes Act to the Lord Lieutenant, advised by the Privy Council of Ireland, to relocate assize towns and to divide a county prescribed an initiative by a majority of the county's grand jury. The 1836 Grand Jury Act required no such initiative, nor did it provide for any consultation with the grand jurors as a body. The repetition of the basic power within a year of the original statute, but now allowing a by-pass of a county's local government body, seemed curious.

The curiosity arose from the hostile attitude of the Grand Jury of Tipperary, as will be seen later, to the division which was now proposed. If the 1836 Act had not allowed their wishes to be ignored or at least over-ruled, Tipperary could not have been divided in 1838. The 1835 Act's limitation was expressed thus:

> ... it shall not be lawful for the Lord Lieutenant or other Chief Governor of Ireland and the Privy Council there to make any order changing the place for holding the Assizes in any County, or for dividing any County for the purposes of this Act, unless a Memorial shall have been presented to him or them by a Majority of the Grand Jury of the Assizes of such county, praying that such change or Division may be made.[1]

TIPPERARY INITIATIVE, 1828

The curiosity is satisfied almost completely by the evidence exhumed from contemporary newspapers, largely the four twice-weekly Clonmel ones, and from *Hansard*, the record of parliamentary debates, and the *House of Lords Journal*. The evidence reveals that Tipperarymen had considerable influence on successive developments. As early as 26 August 1828 the *Limerick Evening Post & Clare Sentinel* reported:

> It is said that the judges will recommend the removal of the Assizes

of the County of Tipperary from the Town of Clonmel to some more central quarter of the county.

At that point there did not exist any statutory power for government to act upon even if, as seems unlikely, it were judicious for judges to make such a recommendation. And in the absence of an enabling public general act of parliament at that stage, the alternative option of promoting a local or private bill in parliament, as occurred in the case of King's County (see note 22, Appendix Eleven), does not seem to have been pursued for Tipperary. Such may indeed have been in mind from the evidence of the following. For three months later, on 19 November 1828, the *Clonmel Herald* discarded much of the wool from the story and revealed:

> For some time back strenuous exertions, we understand, were made to procure signatures to a Memorial to His Excellency for returning Public Institutions from this town to Thurles and there, should these exertions succeed, it was intended to build a County Jail and Court-House to hold the Assizes, &c, &c, &c ... We now learn that a highly influential Nobleman, who is opposed to such an extraordinary project, has received an assurance from the *highest authority* that no alteration shall take place and we understand that the earls of Donoughmore, Kingston and Glengall are opposed to the plan; and that the earl of Llandaff and Lords Dunalley and Lismore are quite favourable to it. It is, we are informed, the intentions of the inhabitants of this town to oppose any candidate for the representation of this County who shall be supported by those who exert themselves in forming and maturing a plan so fraught with injury to this town and so calculated to increase the public burden. We believe the project, which would require the sum of £100,000 to complete it, will now be abandoned.

One could presume that the '*highest authority*', who could only be the Lord Lieutenant, had pointed out the lack of statutory power for such a 'project'. A further week on, the fellow townspaper and rival, the *Clonmel Advertiser*,[2] cut further into the meat of the story, in order 'to expose the fallacy and misrepresentations of that Statement, on which the Memorial is said to be grounded'. The paper set out to expose the 'Statement' as being based on 'an extract, purporting to be taken from the Inspectors' General Report on the Gaol of Clonmel'.

The Inspectors-General (there were two) had been accurately quoted by the offending Statement. Their report, dated 1 February 1828, had recommended 'the grand jury to present the necessary sum to provide for the accommodation of at least 100 additional prisoners.' In the 108 cells an average of 280 prisoners were accommodated and 'from the want of workrooms the male poor prisoners are wholly unemployed, contrary to Act of Parliament'. The report's preamble judged that the gaol 'now stands as low as it did stand high in the comparative scale of County Gaols.'[3]

THURLES CONSIDERED

The *Advertiser* revealed that the circulated Statement

> asks with great simplicity, if it would not be better to build an entirely-new Gaol at *Thurles*, which, with a Court-house, it alleges, would cost the County *only* £31,500 ... let the proposed plan be examined in detail:– It sets out by asserting that the ground will be given rent free. – By whom? who is this disinterested individual that is willing to make so great a sacrifice?[4]

The paper's examination in detail went on to probe alleged claims of savings to be made by a removal of assizes. It tackled the Statement's suggestion that 'perhaps the present Gaol could be converted into a district Lunatic Asylum, with the expense of the erection of which it threatens the County. The County is already aware that it possesses a Lunatic Asylum, attached to the House of Industry, which as yet has been found sufficient to meet the melancholy demands of that calamity'. Finally, it drew itself up to full height and pounded the rostrum:

> Clonmel in itself contains a multitude of respectable jurymen, to whose honest and unintimidated verdicts the County would look with confidence in times of public danger, such as arose during a late dreadful conspiracy. It is surrounded by a numerous and wealthy country population, by the towns of Carrick-on-Suir, Fethard, Killenaule, Cashel, Caher and Clogheen, from whence abundant jurymen may be obtained; – and it possesses a large Barrack, with a considerable Garrison, to give the necessary support to the King's commission – can all this be said of Thurles!
>
> It is urged that Clonmel, being situated on the borders of the County, makes it an ineligible place for the County Establishment. This objection did not prevail at the time Clonmel was chosen

for that purpose, or it is to be presumed it would not have been selected. But in point of fact most of the County Towns in Ireland, as well as in England, are, from their peculiar local eligibility, near the borders of their respective Counties, witness Cork, Limerick, Waterford, &c. &c.

The *Advertiser*, in its patriotic defence of its hometown, could not have foreseen what our hindsight reveals – that a genuine offer of Thurles land, rent free, would emerge; that a custom-built Lunatic Asylum would shortly be built in Clonmel; that Donoughmore's stance might not be readily presumed; and that King's County, Tyrone and Waterford would soon experience rumbles of disaffection on similar lines to Tipperary's.

The paper had indeed identified the two grounds on which pressure for change was based: the inadequacy of Clonmel's county gaol as perceived by the central government's inspector, and the peripheral location of that borough.

NENAGH UNDER SURVEILLANCE, 1833
Five years on, that pressure probably emanating from Thurles in 1828 was now centred on Nenagh. For a neutral outsider, the *Limerick Evening Herald*, in a second leader of 16 September 1833, revealed:

DIVISION OF THE COUNTY TIPPERARY AND QUEENS COUNTY

A correspondent of the *Tipperary Free Press*, whom we presume to be Mr Ronayne, the member for Clonmel, makes the following statement:

"I think, sir, that I ought here to apprise you of a fact that is perhaps known as yet but to a few, which is of great import to the inhabitants of Clonmel; it is that of measures being actually in progress to divide the county – making the baronies of Ikerrin, Owney and Arra and the two Ormonds, a separate jurisdiction; to which some Queen's Co. baronies will also be added – Nenagh becomes an Assize town. Of the merits of such a plan, I can at present form no judgement. It offers many views on both sides of the question; but the fact is as I state".

As far as the county of Tipperary is concerned, the arrangement appears to be judicious and advisable; but the effect, with respect to any portion of the Queen's County, would be to remove the inhabitants to a greater distance from the seat of justice than they are at present. There is no part of the Queen's

Co. so far from Maryborough – (with the exception perhaps of a small tract adjoining Carlow) – as every part of it is from Nenagh, the proposed Assize town. The communication with the latter place is inconvenient; and we are yet to learn the moral advantage to be expected, on either side, by bringing the Whitefeet of Upper Ossory and the Magpies of Lower Ormond into more immediate contact. They are too near neighbours already.

One notes the judicious expression of the warning bell rung for Clonmel by that borough's new MP, Dominick Ronayne[5] – presuming it was him; one questions the likelihood of anyone involving another county in the proposal – and if Queen's (Laois) why not King's (Offaly) also; one leaves aside the sideswipe at the faction fighters. Perhaps the greatest significance of the report is its timing. The Assizes Act, 1833, which applied to England and Wales, had been passed less than a month previously.[6] It gave power to re-allocate assizes to one or more places in a county and to divide a county. It may be that an impression was gleaned that the Act applied to Ireland.

ENTER BLOOMFIELD, 1834

Any such impression was not universal among political insiders or, if it was, had been well corrected by 22 April 1834, seven months later, when Lord Bloomfield wrote from Laughton, Moneygall, King's County, to John Hely-Hutchinson, Lord Donoughmore:

> It was with high hopes you were to have seen Lord W in the subject of the memorial. We depend upon your ascertaining how the English Bill was carried through Parliament and also upon your exertions to have the standing orders suspended if there is no other obstacle to our being brought forward this session. You have been very kind throughout this business and we are all greatly obliged to you. I have not been silent on the liberal offer you have made towards the furtherance of our interests in this question.
>
> The government has only to look over the map, to discover how completely the ends of justice are defeated by the locality of our assize town – some of my tenants are 60 miles from Clonmel. 'Tis a crying evil and one that calls for remedy without delay. In the King's County the Calendar of crime has already increased double since last assizes. ... I seem out of the Vale of Politicks save those affecting our hapless land.[7]

Some examination of those two correspondents' curricula vitae and analysis of their associates may give a degree of insight into the capacity of that particular Tipperaryman to influence affairs of State.

The supplicant was Benjamin Bloomfield (1768-1846), G.C.B., G.C.H., P.C., the first Baron Bloomfield of Redwood near Lorrha in the extreme north-west of the county. He resided at Laughton, Moneygall, a kilometre into King's County in Tipperary's former Ely O'Carroll territory. He owned 9,900 acres including lands in the Killoscully, Newport area on which he built Ciamalta House c.1836. As a young officer in the Royal Horse Artillery he had commanded the battery which had turned the tables in the battle of New Ross in 1798.[8] Following successively higher positions in the personal service of George IV through parts of that king's career as Prince of Wales, regent and monarch, during which Bloomfield was MP for Plymouth (1812-17), he rose to the rank of Lieut.-Gen. and served as Commandant at the Royal Military Academy for artillery cadets at Woolwich and Governor of Fort Charles, Jamaica. This career was interposed with nine years as Ambassador to Sweden, 1823-32, during which he negotiated with the Swedish cabinet some fine print of an anti-slavery treaty.[9]

The third earl of Donoughmore (as of 1832), John Hely-Hutchinson (1787-1851), had his seat at Knocklofty, four miles from Clonmel. He seems thus at first sight to have been unlikely to assist in any downgrading of his hometown. He was clearly a key figure – Lieutenant of the county and a member of the Privy Council.[10] Following a short army career which included the Peninsular War and Waterloo, he was an MP for Tipperary from 1826 to 1830 and from 1831 to 1832 when he succeeded his uncle to the title.[11] For the first of those periods his fellow MP was Francis Aldborough Prittie, brother of Lord Dunalley;[12] the Pritties will both emerge as confederates of Bloomfield in the northern campaign. This third earl's grandfather and uncle had been, like the Pritties, powerful advocates of Catholic Emancipation, among many such adherents of the Established Church of Ireland. In addition to army and parliamentary experience in common, there was another reason for vocational empathy: the second earl, who was the third earl's uncle, had also been an ambassador – to Russia, 1805-6.

The Donoughmore Papers show previous contacts between Bloomfield and two generations of Hely-Hutchinsons between 1804 and 1831, spanning three Donoughmore lordships. They range from Bloomfield's in 1804, while with the Prince of Wales's regiment at Brighton, asking a Hely-Hutchinson brother on behalf of the later second earl to urge the first earl to come to England because of

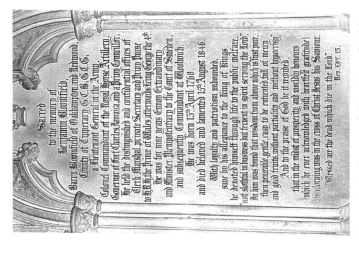

Plate 4: Wall memorial to Bloomfield in Borrisnafarney Church of Ireland church.

Plate 3: Benjamin Bloomfield (1768-1846), created Baron in 1825.

33

Plate 5: Ciamalta House c.1910, built c.1835-7 as a hunting lodge by the first Baron Bloomfield, in close proximity to the Mulcair river and Keeper Hill. Enlarged by the second baron, it became the family home of his sister Harriet Kingscote after his death. Her grandson inherited and it remained his family home until the mid-1920s when he disposed of it and emigrated to England. It is now owned by a German citizen – photo courtesy of Marie Scott, USA.

Plate 6: Bloomfield vault in the grounds of Borrisnafarney church.

impending developments centred on George III's 'precarious' health,[13] to Bloomfield as Ambassador to Sweden in early 1831 expressing to the second earl the 'pain ... caused me' because of the 1830 Tipperary election defeat of the later third earl.[14]

HIGH SOCIETY

The contacts also embrace Bloomfield's conveying the Prince Regent's 'most gracious sentiments' to the first earl;[15] the latter hosting Bloomfield at Knocklofty and sympathising with him on the loss of his position at Court in 1822 and the perceived inadequacy of his posting to Sweden;[16] and Bloomfield writing from the regency seat at Brighton to the second earl about promotion in the army for his nephew, 'young Hutchinson'[17] who was destined to be the third earl (then thirty years of age as against Bloomfield's forty-nine). The third earl and his countess, and Bloomfield and his lady were recorded as among a large party of guests at Castle Bernard in King's County in December 1833.[18]

These layers of mutual favours and close friendship (extending to concerned correspondence between the Hely-Hutchinsons themselves about Bloomfield's having suffered from Court intrigue in 1822)[19] explain Bloomfield's 1834 enlisting of the third earl's support in the division campaign.

The 'Lord W' referred to is probably Wellesley who was recorded by Francis Hely-Hutchinson in 1822 as having entertained himself and Bloomfield whom Wellesley 'has been covering with civilities'.[20] Wellesley, brother of the Duke of Wellington, was then Lord Lieutenant of Ireland as of four months previously.

Further spots of evidence of Bloomfield's pretty central position in the matrix of social and political relationships among the ascendancy, crop up in the 'Haut Ton' (literally, 'High Style') columns of the newspapers. For instance, he was among a party entertained in September 1833 by the new Lord Lieutenant, the Marquess of Anglesey.[21] Bloomfield was visited at Laughton the following January by Lieut.-Gen. Sir Richard Hussey Vivian, Commander of the Forces in Ireland and Groom of the Bedchamber to William IV, also an ex-MP, and, more importantly for the north Tipperary plotting and planning department, a member of the Privy Council.[22] There is a reference to Vivian as 'an old brother officer of the Duke of Wellington'.[23] Six months later the Bloomfields and Dunalleys 'and suite' were noted in the one breath as having arrived at Killarney for a visit to the lakes.[24]

Bloomfield had a constant homing instinct, despite his travels and as already indicated above in relation to his keeping in concerned touch with the 1830 parliamentary election for Tipperary. He is named in inter-Hely-Hutchinson correspondence in 1820 as 'the go between' in delicate fraternal Prittie contacts on a looming election.[25] In 1823 he is reported as leaving for Dublin from the Clonmel assizes with Captain John, the future third earl, obviously having stayed the duration at Knocklofty. Bloomfield had while there written 'a long letter yesterday' on the subject of a mail-coach contractor, pleading a case for the contractor vis-a-vis 'the Post'.[26] Close enough to home but fifteen years later he crops up as a patron of perhaps the first mid-west body, the Farming Society for the Counties of Limerick, Clare and Tipperary.[27]

Most significant, perhaps, is the fact that Francis Aldborough Prittie, brother of Lord Dunalley who was identified as pro-division in 1828, visited Bloomfield at Laughton as least three times in 1834. The first visit was less than three weeks before Bloomfield wrote to Donoughmore, as quoted above, and the second under three weeks after dispatch of that letter. The first visit seems to have lasted three days.[28]

Come a further six months again, as of January 1835, Bloomfield was even further 'well in' with the arrival in the vice-regal lodge of the earl of Mulgrave. Bloomfield had been in Fort Charles, Jamaica; Mulgrave had been Governor of that colony.[29] Their political alignment became public in late 1836 when each was named as a voter for the liberal Viscount Lismore in an election for representative peer.[30] Almost a decade into the future but indicative of the same or overlapping social circles is the marriage of Bloomfield's son and heir to the youngest sister of Mulgrave's wife.[31]

THE ASSIZES (REMOVAL) BILL, 1835

The Removal of Assizes (Ireland) Bill as introduced to the House of Commons on 26 March 1835 answered the Bloomfield prayer. But not directly: its inspiration was avowedly Waterford-based – a county meeting in Dungarvan which prayed for the extension of the English Assizes Act to Ireland. The Irish bill's sponsor was Michael O'Loghlen, MP for Dungarvan borough. He instanced counties Tipperary and Cork as needing the bill because of the distances witnesses had to travel to their assize towns.[32] The bill can be seen as a step in the devolution of power from the legislature to the executive – from parliament to the Lord Lieutenant and Privy Council. It was only three years previously that a noble agitator had to promote and guide through Parliament a change of location of the King's County assizes, already referred to. Some weeks previous to that again a similar transfer was proposed of the Norfolk assizes from Thetford to Norwich.[33]

Suffice it to say of the debate on the bill in general that it produced flashes of vintage politics of the grudging kind. Several of the honourable and learned members galloped up on hobby horses and charged the Solicitor-General. He was giving undue power to the Privy Council as advisers to the Lord Lieutenant – 'a tribunal, not only partial, but consisting wholly of one party when he [Charles A. Walker, MP, Wexford] knew that the Grand Juries in Ireland were nominated by the Orange Sheriffs, and the Orange Sheriffs of Ireland by the Orange Judges, and these Orange Judges forming a large and influential portion of the Privy Council of Ireland, he must say, that a more unjust proposal could not be imagined'.[34] Again, 'it would be necessary to erect new jails, and new court-houses. How could the country bear increased taxation?'[35]

One member used the occasion to ask the government to first 'commence assimilation of the laws of the two countries by a good Reform Bill, a good Registration Bill, and a good Municipal Reform Bill'.[36] The members for Waterford City attempted a classic six-months postponement and a Waterford County man claimed that the majority of Irish members were opposed to the bill. All four Waterford members and one other engaged in a 'desultory conversation' on the Committee stage but nobody pressed a vote of the House.[37] The impact of the bill on Waterford at home, including the questioning of O'Loghlen's position, is related in Appendix Eleven.

SETBACK

As an answer to Bloomfield's prayer it was negatived, however, by a simple amendment bursting like a shell in infantry ranks just as they seemed to have carried the day. The bill at first stage, as already stated, provided for the holding of assizes at one or more places in a county and, if more than one, for the division of that county. But the bill emerged from its final stage in the House of Lords on 13 August 1835 with an additional section providing that the powers to change an assize venue and divide a county could not be exercised unless a majority of that county's grand jury presented the Lord Lieutenant with a memorial praying for such change or division.[38] Appendix Two recites the detail.

Five days later, the House of Commons agreed the bill as amended; in a further three days it received royal assent and became law. Neither the *House of Lords Journal* nor the interested Tipperary or Waterford papers nor the leading Dublin dailies revealed who introduced the key amendment which scored a point for the decentralised local government which existed, albeit an oligarchy, but against the immediate aspirations of the north Tipperarymen.

Why so? Because northerners were invariably in a minority on successive Tipperary grand juries. The majority was inevitably from the south of the county because of the location of Clonmel and the unappealing prospect for northerners of travelling a distance and lodging there. So how could the majority be got to vote against its own constituency? The nett effect, in terms of persons with the power of initiative, was thus to prevent any cure of the cause of the problem. To put it another way and to adapt a more modern phrase, it was for Bloomfield a Catch 23 situation. Where exactly that number of grand jurors was drawn from will be seen in Table 1 and in Fig. 3.

THE GRAND JURY BILL, 1836

Things rested so for another eight months. On 28 April 1836 Viscount Morpeth, Chief Secretary for Ireland, moved for leave to bring in a bill 'to consolidate and amend the Laws relating to the Presentment of Public Money by Grand Juries in Ireland.'[39] Those laws reached back to 1634. It was a very wide-ranging measure which was to provide the basic structure of primitive local government in the counties for sixty-three years. There was no excitement raised by the practical clauses relating to arrangements for meetings, advertising for tenders for road works, fixing officials' salaries, supporting infirmaries, asylums, and the like. The only larger political perspective was that of a landlord who would later become a Young Irelander, William Smith O'Brien, who 'hoped, which he feared would not be the case, that the noble Viscount would introduce into the Grand Jury system of Ireland something of the principle of representation … of letting the people have a choice in the appointment of Irish Grand Juries'.[40] That hope was not fulfilled until 1899.

CATERING FOR TIPP

Then came the second north Tipperary assault, its first, albeit indirect, having been blunted in 1835. And with no Tipperary hand apparent, for the member up front was a Dr Thomas Lefroy.[41] The detail comes from newspapers of 8-19 July 1836, *Hansard* having failed to record the development.

> There are many important motions set down for this evening amongst which is one by Dr Lefroy in the shape of an amendment upon the Grand Jury Bill, brought in by Lord Morpeth 'to enable the Lord Lieutenant to divide the county of Tipperary into two ridings for the purpose of Holding Assizes in each'.[42]
> Commons: On the motion of Mr Lefroy a clause was added to

the bill giving the Lord Lieutenant the power of dividing the county of Tipperary into two ridings.[43]

Private Correspondence, July 16th. You will see by a reference to the proceedings last night that Dr Lefroy succeeded in his motion to have your county divided into two districts, for the purpose of holding Assizes in each, and to enable the Lord Lieutenant to make the necessary arrangements requisite for carrying that objective into immediate operation. I must repeat the remark I had before occasion to make on the absence of the Tipperary members. There was not one of them in the House, either to support the learned doctor's motion, or if they thought it injurious in its effects to oppose it.[44]

The Dublin media became confused as between the new concept in the Lefroy amendment and the provision in a virtually simultaneous bill for additional venues and division of districts for quarter sessions (see note 66 to Chapter Two):

The County of Tipperary, like Cork, is to have two ridings for sessions business and two Assistant Barristers.[45]

That quotation missed the point that the proposed division (it could not forecast that the term 'riding' would be used in implementing the 1836 Act which itself would not use the word) would be much more significant than the outlining of catchment areas for the function of justice only and that just at the lesser level of quarter sessions, as was the case in Cork since 1823.

County of Tipperary – There is no truth in the rumour that the county of Tipperary is to be divided into two Ridings, as Cork is at present – the division is only to facilitate the assize business of the county. The assizes are in future to be held both in Nenagh and Clonmel. There will not be two assistant-barristers.[46]

That second quotation seems not to have understood that the effects of the correct rumour, as implied by its reference to assizes business and two towns, were weightier than the quarter sessions rumour it was contradicting; its forecast of the two locations was quite premature.

Why Lefroy, 'a typical Irish Protestant Tory' who moreover represented Dublin University in parliament, 'steadily voted with Peel and opposed the Irish measures of the Melbourne administration',[47] should in effect deputise for the Tipperary Liberals is unclear. The only common denominator I can find was his and Lord Donoughmore's membership of the Privy Council.

MINDING THEIR SEATS?

The MPs for the county in 1836 were Richard Lalor Sheil, Longorchard, Templetuohy, near Templemore, and Robert Otway Cave, Castleotway, Templederry, both northerners but whose names do not surface in any aspect of the division saga. Sheil was a prominent orator on national questions whose residence was in the Thurles catchment; Otway Cave was within the Nenagh catchment. It may be that, drawing upon the votes of a mere two and one-half thousand electorate, they preferred not to choose in effect between Clonmel and the status quo, on the one hand, and Nenagh or Thurles and a partitioned county, on the other.

For the January 1835 general election, when they were returned unopposed by any Conservative/Tory nominees, Sheil was proposed by the parish priest of Fethard, Rev. Michael Laffan, and seconded by Edward Lalor, Cregg, Carrick-on-Suir, whose (presumed) brother or son Thomas will emerge as a strong anti-division juror. Otway Cave was proposed by James Roe, Roesborough, Tipperary, who was doubly influential as President of the Tipperary Liberal Club and an ex-MP for Cashel, and was seconded by Philip Fogarty, K.C., with roots in Cabra, Thurles. So three of their four leading patrons were southerners and one was from the mid-county.[48]

Or it may be that the lobbyists did not entrust them with enlistment in the cause. Or, in Otway Cave's case, that he was otherwise pre-occupied – according to the *Clonmel Advertiser* of 30 November 1836, the Court of Exchequer had appointed a receiver over his lands for unpaid tithes. Or a combination of circumstances, including or just simply that Lefroy was a recognised authority on grand jury law – he had been a contributor to the debate on the Grand Jury Bill of 1833.[49]

So far, so good for the north Tipps under the benign eyes of the Chief Secretary and House of Commons.

Similarly, some dexterous east Tyrone personages had accomplished the insertion of a provision, word for word a copy of the Tipperary one, except that 'the eastern part' was in place of the 'northern part' and 'Omagh' was in place of 'Clonmel'.[50] The House of Lords did, though, receive a petition from the Tyrone grand jury praying postponement of the bill.[51] Practically coincidental with these parliamentary manoeuvres, the west Waterford leaders were pushing ahead, through that county's grand jury, in their attempt to utilise the previous year's Assizes Act.

THE NATIONAL INTEREST

When the Grand Jury Bill reached the Lords, they had before them a number of petitions from interested parties in Ireland, including one

> ... from persons connected with the northern baronies of the county of Tipperary whose names are thereinover subscribed praying their lordships to grant an Assizes to be held at Nenagh, or some Town fixed on by the Lord Lieutenant, to which no reasonable objection can be made, as the Expense of a small Court House and Gaol, or enlarging the present one at Nenagh, would be most amply saved by the Arrangement and Diminution of the present Expenses.[52]

On 3 August 1836 the noblemen produced evidence in their Journal of a great deal of homework by way of almost eight columns of finely-crafted amendments.

One set of amendments focused on what became sections 176 and 177 of the Act as passed. As shown in Appendix Three the Lefroy addition to the bill was altered from the particular of County Tipperary and its northern parts to the general of counties in Ireland and their 'other parts'; the similar provision for County Tyrone and its eastern parts was likewise excised.[53] The *Clonmel Advertiser* had not caught up with that widening of the provision by its issue of 10 August, but in effect confirmed the gist of the Lefroy amendment to the bill, though Lefroy had not specified Nenagh as a location.

> We are credibly informed that the Bill for the division of this County which is, in fact, only a rider on the New Grand Jury Bill will pass the Lords this Session without opposition. Two additional assizes in each year will be added to the Judges circuit, to be holden at Nenagh, where a new Jail and Court House, must, of course, be built.

The final provision was for a second assize town and 'for that purpose' division of a county. Like the 1835 Act, the deciding authority was the Lord Lieutenant, advised by the Privy Council.

Unlike the 1835 Act there was no role, initiating or consultative, prescribed for a county's grand jury.

CONSPIRATORS, 1836

More leading personalities emerge from the shadows in the *Clare Journal* report of 12 September 1836, just a month after the passage

41

through parliament of that 1836 Grand Juries (Ireland) Act:

> Lord Dunalley, Maj.-Gen. Sir William Parker Carrol and several other magistrates have called a meeting for the 22nd inst. at Nenagh in consequence of the bad state of the public roads and with a view of applying to government for a second county surveyor in Tipperary.

Their aims were, or at least became, more basic and wider. On 29 November Cornwallis Maude, Viscount Hawarden wrote from Dundrum House in mid-county to George Ryan at Inch House near Thurles:

> I have seen a copy of a memorial which was sent to His Excellency, the Lord Lieutenant through Mr Drummond on the 21st inst. entitled 'Memorial of the undersigned the Committee' appointed by the Landed Proprietors and Inhabitants of the Northern Baronies of the county of Tipperary for the purpose of promoting the 'Division of said county into two Ridings according to 176 Section of 6 & 7 William 4th Cap 116'. It does not appear by this memorial that the Baronies of Kilnamanagh and Eliogarthy are to be included in the Northern Riding. The memorial was signed by Lord Dunalley as Chairman.[54]

Hawarden may have got a courtesy copy from Dunalley himself who was married to Emily Maude, Hawarden's sister, and whose niece moreover was married to Hawarden's brother.[55] Their views were not entirely on par, as already hinted at thus by Hawarden's apparent warning note regarding the proposed extent of the north riding. It would seem, from the date of the following, that Ryan and his neighbours were already alerted. On 30 November 1836, the *Clonmel Herald* speculated:

> The people of Nenagh are in high hopes that the county will be divided and that a new courthouse, etc., will be built in Nenagh; against this the people of Thurles will memorial in order to prevent the division.

The Thurles stance, by way of memorial or petition, was to become more subtle than that.

Early in that very month of November the campaigners for change in neighbouring County Waterford had a cooler reception before the

Privy Council than the strength of their own convictions might have anticipated. Appendix Eleven details the state of play there.

STATE OF THE COUNTY, LATE 1836

That Tipperary, would 'be and remain one county for ever', as proclaimed in 1716, was now in doubt. An official report had deemed its county gaol inadequate. That gave an opportunity to affected persons in the northern baronies to attack the location of the assize or principal court town, containing the gaol, at the southern extreme. Two acts of parliament now gave the opportunity to redress the grievance. The 1835 one stemmed from similar dissatisfaction in the neighbouring County Waterford. That act however, included a provision which amounted to a roadblock vis-a-vis the north Tipperary lobby. However, a key provision of the 1836 Act allowed them to circumvent that roadblock. That 1836 provision was directly inspired by a campaign of a few years standing, conducted through what could be termed quiet diplomacy.

Notes

1. An Act for the Appointment of convenient Places for the holding of Assizes in Ireland, 5 & 6 William IV, c. 26 (1835), s. III.
2. *C.A.*, 26 Nov 1828.
3. PP (Reports and Commissions)1829, xiii, Appendix to the Seventh Report of Inspectors-General on the Gaols etc. of Ireland.
4. *C.A.*, 26 Nov 1828.
5. Brian M. Walker, *Parliamentary Election Results in Ireland 1801-1922*, p. 261. Ronayne represented Clonmel as MP from 1832 until 1836, defeating John Bagwell in the general elections of 1832 and 1835, firstly by 262 votes to 212, and on the second occasion by 262 to 252. Ronayne was identified respectively as a Repealer and Liberal (Repealer) in those elections; Bagwell as a Conservative and of the family which 'held the patronage of the corporation for about the last thirty years' (evidence of William Chaytor, Mayor of Clonmel, to the Municipal Corporations Commissioners of Inquiry – *C.A.*, 12 Oct 1833). Ronayne had also contested the general election of 1830 for Dungarvan, unsuccessfully. He is described by Donal McCartney in *Decies*, no. 20, as 'a wealthy Catholic merchant with businesses in Youghal and Dungarvan, a distant cousin and friend of [Daniel] O'Connell'. In his own evidence to the 1833 Clonmel Inquiry, he identified his residence as in Youghal (*C.A.*, 23 Oct 1833). Although Walker gives the cause of a bye-election for Clonmel in 1836 as Ronayne's death, he was in fact active in July 1837. He was arrested during that year's general election, which was a repeat of his arrest during the 1832 general election; the causes of both

distinctions are described in L. F. Proudfoot, 'Landlords and Politics: Youghal and Dungarvan in the 1830s', *Decies*, no. 34, Spring 1987, pp. 41, 44-5.

6. Assizes Act, 1833, 3 & 4 William IV, c. 71.
7. Donoughmore Papers, MS, G 35/2, T.C.D.
8. Benjamin Bloomfield from New Ross to his brother-in-law, Tom Ryder Pepper at Laughton, 8 June 1798 – from a transcript made available by the owner of Laughton, Mr Guy Atkinson, through Mr Hardress Waller. Pepper bequeathed Laughton to Bloomfield; he died on 16 December 1828 at his residence 'from the effects of a fall from his horse in hunting' – *C.H.*, 17 Dec 1828.
9. Georgiana Baroness Bloomfield, *Memoir of Lord Bloomfield* (London, 1884) and *Reminiscences of Court and Diplomatic Life* (London, 1883); Mary T. Ryan, 'The First Lord Bloomfield' in *Newport News* 1990, pp. 99-102. Georgiana was the first Lord's daughter-in-law, married to John Arthur Douglas Bloomfield, the second Baron. Both barons Bloomfield are buried in a vault in the grounds of Borrisnafarney Church of Ireland church, Moneygall. Each has a marble wall tablet within the church, listing career accomplishments and paying tribute to personal character. Benjamin's religious fervour, as recorded by Georgiana, is emphasised on his tablet (see Plate 4). There are descendants of Benjamin through his daughter Harriet Kingscote. His great-great-great-granddaughter, Marie Scott, Florida, USA, visited Ciamalta and Laughton in 1990.
10. *Watson's Treble Almanack,*1832-4; *Pettigrew & Oulton*, 1835-8.
11. Donoughmore Papers, MS, T.C.D., general introduction by A. P. W. Malcolmson.
12. Walker, cited above, p. 239.
13. Donoughmore Papers, MS D/41/8, 16 Feb 1804, T.C.D.
14. Donoughmore Papers, MS E373, 11 Mar 1831, T.C.D.
15. Donoughmore Papers, MS D/38/2/3/4/, 5 Jan 1819, T.C.D.
16. Donoughmore MS D/38/20, n.d. between 21 Nov and 20 Dec 1822, T.C.D.
17. Donoughmore Papers, MS E313, 21 Dec 1817, T.C.D.
18. *C.A.*, 14 Dec 1833.
19. Donoughmore Papers, MS D/42/81, 4 Jan 1822, T.C.D.
20. Donoughmore Papers, MS D/49/1, 1 May 1822, T.C.D.
21. *C.A.*, 14 Sept 1833.
22. *C.A.*, 4 Jan 1834; *D.N.B.*
23. *C.A.*, 25 June 1834.
24. *C.A.*, 12 July 1834.
25. Donoughmore Papers, MS F/13/26, 1 February 1820, T.C.D., from the second earl to his brother Francis who was the third earl's father.
26. Donoughmore Papers, MS F/13/80, 28 March 1823, T.C.D., same to same.
27. *T.C.*, 2 Feb 1838. This was a 'remodelled' society who planned their first show for the second Saturday in May 1838 in the natural capital of

44

the region, Limerick city. Lord Dunraven, Adare, and Sir Lucius O'Brien, Clare, were among the other patrons.

28. Dunalley Papers, MS 29809 (16), NLI, transport bills from the representatives of J. Smallman, Roscrea: the dates were 3 April, returning 6 April, 10 May and 19 August.

29. *D.N.B.*

30. *C.A.*, 5 Nov 1836. It was an all-Tipperary contest: Viscount Lismore, himself Cornelius O'Callaghan, Shanbally Castle, Clogheen, and married to Lady Eleanor Butler, a daughter of the 17th earl of Ormond, a liberal, versus the winner, Viscount Hawarden, Dundrum, a conservative of whom more anon.

31. *Burke's Peerage.* Mulgrave's wife was Maria Liddell, the eldest daughter of the first Lord Ravenworth. Young Bloomfield's wife was his youngest daughter Georgiana. The marriages were as far apart as 1818 and 1845.

32. *W.M.*, 3 June 1835.

33. The House of Lords received five petitions against the bill, from inhabitants of the south-west, north-west and western parts of Norfolk. An amendment to read the bill in six months time was defeated – *Lords' jn.,* 64, pp. 285, 294.

34. *Hansard*, H.C., p. 27, col. 303, 26 Mar 1835.

35. *Hansard*, H.C., p. 28, col. 187, 27 May 1835.

36. *Hansard*, H.C., p. 28, col. 187, 27 May 1835.

37. *The Pilot*, 13 July 1835, reporting the proceedings of Wednesday 8 July.

38. *Lords' jn.,* 66, p. 554. The bill also emerged without the word 'removal' in its title, now formally: 5 & 6 Wm IV, c. 26, An Act for the Appointment of convenient Places for the holding of Assizes in Ireland; in common usage, simply the Assizes (Ireland) Act, 1835.

39. 6 & 7 William IV, c. 116. A major component of the 1836 Act was another piece of reforming legislation of a mere three years before, the Grand Juries (Ireland) Act, 1833. It was also the product of a Whig or Liberal government, with Lord Grey as Prime Minister, the Marquess of Anglesey in his second spell as Lord Lieutenant of Ireland, and the later Judge Crampton as Solicitor-General. That immediate parentage of much of the 1836 Act is seen in its s. 39 providing for the appointment of county surveyors, word for word taken from s. 37 of 1833; ss. 2-15 of 1833 prescribing special sessions in baronies to be fixed by the grand jury for consideration of public works applied for in a prescribed manner, by magistrates in association with cesspayers of the highest sums paid, with a form of rotation of cesspayers inbuilt (see Appendix Six) – all brought forward as ss. 4-17 of 1836, having dropped some stifling 1833 verbiage and altering the term to 'presentment sessions' – the grand jury's power of selecting public works was now limited to those approved at the baronial presentment sessions; s. 32 of 1833 introducing a compulsion on the High Sheriff to select at least one grand juror from each barony or half barony, repeated as s. 31 of 1836 with a double safeguard against any failure by him in this respect.

A couple of those features and other reforms were identified by Viscount Duncannon on their introduction to the House of Commons:

> He would detail a few of the alterations which the Bill would effect; it would associate those who paid the taxes [i.e. cesspayers] with the Judges of the Petty Sessions [i.e. magistrates], and thereby give them an interest in all works to be performed; it would, by the appointment of surveyors in each county in Ireland, give to those who paid the rates an assurance that the money raised was not more than requisite; by compelling all public works to be done by contract and open tender, it would assure the tax-payer that such works were performed at the lowest expense. One of the great complaints against the present system was, that all the business of the county was done by the Grand Jury, with closed doors; but the present Bill would compel the Grand Jury to act in open Court, and in the presence of the public.

Tight central government control over local government procedure has generally been regarded as stemming from the 1838 poor law. Here, however, in 1833 the Grand Juries Act had a number of schedules prescribing for the plethora of grand juries the actual standard forms to be used – bureaucracy at its most efficient and corruption-proof: separate forms of application for opening a new road, for repairs of roads, for widening roads, for lowering a hill and filling hollows, for erecting milestones and finger posts, and, significantly, for payment to contractors. If genius be attention to detail, there were some ingenious beavers at work in Dublin Castle.

And sufficient reform for the times, though such as the Tipperary MP, Richard Lalor Sheil, 'contended that those who taxed the people should be elected by the people, the Sheriffs ought to be so chosen, instead of being nominated by the Judges; and unless representation accompanied taxation in this Bill, it would be most injudicious now to proceed with it'.

40. *Hansard*, H.C., p. 33, col. 464, 28 Apr 1836. That February, in the course of a debate on a bill proposing county boards, to be elected by ratepayers, put forward by Joseph Hume, MP, Middlesex, Mr Trevor responded that there were enough elections of one kind or the other, without introducing any fresh ones; they did not tend to the good harmony of society, or the good order of the community, but that they were productive of much ill-will.

41. Thomas Langlois Lefroy (1776-1869), B.A., LLB, LLD, became a King's Counsel in 1806 and King's Sergeant from 1808 to 1830 when he resigned before entering parliament. He served in two successive judicial offices from 1841 to 1866 when he resigned as Lord Chief Justice of the Queen's Bench at ninety years of age – *D.N.B.* He presided at least once – as Baron Lefroy in Spring 1843 – over the assizes for the north riding whose creation he had facilitated – *N.G.*, 18 Mar 1843. His role in the formation

46

of the 1828 anti-Emancipation, anti-Liberal Brunswick Constitutional Club of Ireland, and other political moves, are described in O'Ferrall, *Catholic Emancipation*, pp. 208, 261, 274.

42. *T.C.*, 8 July 1836.
43. *D.E.M.*, 14 July 1836.
44. *T.C.*, 19 July 1836.
45. *Evening Packet*, 18 July 1836.
46. *D.E.P.*, 23 July 1836.
47. *D.N.B.*
48. *C.A.*, 17 Jan 1835.
49. *Hansard*, 19, col. 569, 11 July; 20, col. 283, 2 Aug, 1833.
50. See note 53 below. Dungannon would seem to have been pretender to a share of Omagh's power. Ms Kate McAllister, Senior Librarian (Irish and Local Studies), Western Education and Library Board, N.I., kindly supplied me with extracts from John J. Marshall, *History of Dungannon* (1929), and the *Dungannon Observer*, 27 Sept 1980, quoting a letter from a local historian, Mr W. R. Hutchinson. Dungannon was the assizes town until 1692 when post-Williamite war adjustments were made to the justices' itineraries. The extent of the Tyrone heave of 1836 has not been investigated through that county's newspapers; the Privy Council Minutes of 1834-40 do not contain any reference to petitions/memorials.
51. *Lords' jn.*, 21 July 1836, p. 736. There is another curiosity about the Tyrone situation. S. 182 of the Act (which is not printed in *Vanston* as it was repealed, presumably being redundant, by the Statutory Law Revision Act, 1874) commenced with a recital of diverse sums of money having being advanced from the Treasury for the execution of public works in that county. It followed with the story of proceedings taken against the late Treasurer for the recovery of a considerable balance on account of sums advanced. It then provided that 'by reason of the default and insolvency of the said Treasurer' it would be lawful for the Treasury to pay an amount of £8,000, already recovered, to the new Treasurer to be applied to the payment of contractors. S. 183 consequently enabled the grand jury to present the £8,000 to be levied by sixteen half-yearly instalments of £500 to be paid over to such bank or person as the Treasury would direct.
52. *Lords' jn.*, 25 July 1836, p. 741.
53. Prompted by the clear newspaper reports regarding Lefroy's amendment and armed with the set of House of Lords amendments, I first worked back from the act as passed to what the original Lefroy amendment must have been. It became clear that the House of Commons specifically provided for a division of Tipperary consequent on the location of assizes in a second, unspecified town in the northern part. Student thesis writers and case-hardened professors alike will recognise the warm feeling at that stage of journalist-detective-diviner of *uisce fé thalamh* which is the common historian. I then belatedly thought of the possibility of hunting down precise as distinct from deduced evidence, contacted the

House of Lords record office, and received confirmation of my deductions from its Mr Stephen Ellison. This took the form of two successive prints of relevant sections of the bill – the first as it left the Commons and reached the Lords; the second as it was presented to the Commons by Morpeth on 15 August as a new bill, laying aside the old bill because of the profusion of Lords' amendments (*Hansard*, 35, col. 1227). Appendix Three incorporates the wording of both first and second. The weight of Committee changes in the Lords was such that the section's side heading in the first print, 'County of Tipperary may be divided into Two Ridings or Districts', was erroneously brought forward into the second print by draughtsmen and printers who had obviously burned midnight oil. A second revelation was the presence of two further sections in the first print, summarised in their side heading, 'County of Tyrone may be so divided'.

54. Ryan Papers, courtesy of Mr Jim Condon.
55. *Burke's Peerage* (1878), p. 599.

Fig. 2: The counties of Ireland, 1830 – assize towns are in caps underlined thus: **<u>CLONMEL</u>;** 'pretenders'/aspirants to that status are thus: **Nenagh**. Note that Co. Kildare assizes alternated; King's Co., Tyrone, and Waterford, as well as Tipperary, had 'pretenders' to capital status.

49

CHAPTER TWO

'This county is to be turned topsy turvy'

The Grand Juries (Ireland) Act, 1836 had now established the rationale for 'a second Assize Town' and 'Two Districts or Ridings' thus:

> the great Extent of certain Counties in Ireland, and the inconvenient Situation of the Towns where the Assizes are now held in respect to other Parts of said Counties ... [1]

PRIME IN EXTENT CUM INCONVENIENCE

The unique applicability to Tipperary of that s. 176 of the Act, can be seen by reference to a contemporary directory and atlas.

In the five counties of greater extent, both in terms of acreage (Tipperary's was 1,061,731 acres or 1,659 square miles or 429,851 hectares) and length-breadth (approximately 70 x 40 miles or 113 km x 64 km), each had an assize town relatively convenient to all of its sizeable segments. These were Cork, 2,885 square miles (assize town Cork); Galway, 2,447 square miles (Galway); Mayo, 2,131 square miles (Castlebar); Donegal, 1,865 square miles (Lifford); and Kerry, 1,853 square miles (Tralee). Likewise the next to Tipperary in order of size – Clare, 1,294 square miles (Ennis), and Tyrone, 1,260 square miles (Omagh).

As to inconvenience, only Waterford and Wexford each had its namesake county town and Louth had Dundalk, all somewhat analogous to Clonmel's peripheral location within Tipperary. But Louth was the smallest county and the other two could hardly be judged to be of 'great Extent', their acreage being about half of Tipperary's, and their greatest lengths 52 and 55 miles as against Tipperary's 70. Yet Waterford had underway in that year, 1836, considerable agitation for and against relocation of its county assizes town, or 'removal' in the language of the 1835 Assizes Act which was the springboard in that county.

If one looks at five other counties of an elongated shape similar to Tipperary's, none of them were as 'long' and all had quite central assize towns: Roscommon (60 miles, Roscommon); Cavan (50 miles, Cavan); Leitrim (51 miles, Carrick-on-Shannon); Fermanagh (45 miles, Enniskillen); Antrim (56 miles, Carrickfergus).[2]

A factor aggravating any geographical inconvenience was that the population of Tipperary county then was third only to Cork and Galway, and it exceeded that of the other three counties of larger size. The 1831 Census figures were (excluding Cork city's 107,016 who were catered for by city assizes):[3]

Cork county and city	703,716
Galway county and city	414,684
Tipperary	402,563
Mayo	366,328
Donegal	289,149
Kerry	263,126

Tipperary and Clare had the fastest growing populations among all the counties in the four decades, 1800-1841, taken as a unit of time elapsed.[4]

THE COST OF INCONVENIENCE

There is some random evidence of the cost to northerners of the twice-yearly travel to Clonmel. Only four months after his wedding and six days after arrival with his bride at Tulla, Sir William Parker Carrol went to the Clonmel assizes on a Sunday. He returned on the Saturday, 'very late'.[5]

The expense of travelling solo may be gauged from Francis Aldborough Prittie's paying 19s. 6d. regularly for a pair of horses, presumably between shafts, from his home at Corville or Mount Butler outside Roscrea to Kilboy, Nenagh – his brother Lord Dunalley's abode. That equates to approximately £60, in early 1990s' values, for the approximate twenty-two miles.[6]

In the 1830s, an Ormond grand juror or litigant, witness or attorney, having got to Nenagh under his own horse-power, could set out from the town on a Bianconi car at 5 a.m. As the advertisement specified arrival in Waterford at 7 p.m. and the fare 11s. 6d., one can estimate arrival in Clonmel as at about 2 p.m. after nine hours on the road and the fare as 7s. 6d., say £23 in early 1990s' terms.[7]

The discomfort involved may be gauged by imagining the feeling in winter of those travelling in the style captured in the drawing reproduced on the front cover of this book. Or of those less protected than the Liberator himself in his description of an 1825 trip:

> The coach from Limerick carries six inside, and Dan O'Connell of Kilgorey and I were two so you may imagine how I was stuffed but I got an outside passenger to change with me in Nenagh – from that place up I travelled in a soft small rain but very comfortable for I had a large cloak and umbrella which kept off the wet effectively.[8]

The number of persons affected became greater as a result of a provision of the Grand Jury Act, 1833, summarised in ~~the Prologue~~ *pp. 45-6* and as indicated by the following reported scene at the 1834 Summer Assizes. One assumes that the newly-endowed right which is referred to was far more easily availed of by persons living near Clonmel and difficult to impossible for the lesser landowners who paid rates or cess and lived towards the northern parts of the county. The provision was thus in practice unintentionally discriminatory.

> COUNTY TIPPERARY ASSIZES. We have seldom witnessed so crowded a court, owing we suppose, to the number of ratepayers, &c., who from all parts of the county came to town, for the purpose of examining into the accounts, presentments, &c., which they now have the right of scrutinising.[9]

The nett effect of the cost of Clonmel's 'inconvenient situation' at the level of the corps of large landowners-cum-magistrates or justices of the peace from whom the grand jury was drawn can be shown by reference to the numbers of grand jurors sitting at the seven successive assizes prior to the Privy Council's deliberations in June 1837. They are categorised as coming from, respectively, the six northern baronies and the five southern ones. (The Summer Assizes 1834 did not have a full attendance).[10]

Assizes		Northern	Southern
Spring	1834	6	17
Summer	1834	4	17
Spring	1835	4	19
Summer	1835	7	16
Spring	1836	5	18
Summer	1836	6	16
Spring	1837	7	16

Hence the 'Catch 23' situation mentioned in Chapter One.

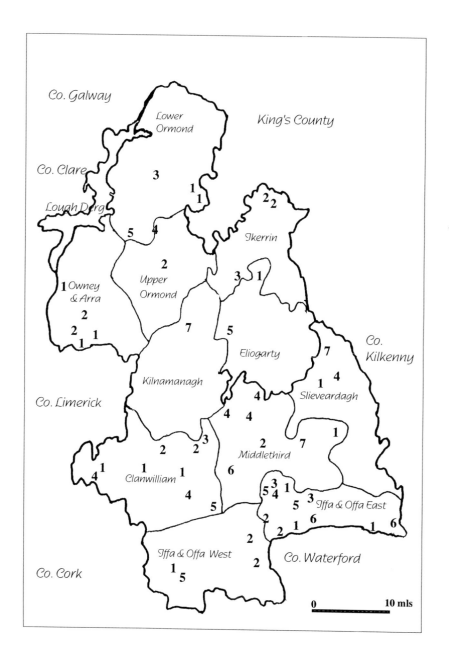

Fig. 3: The approximate residences of grand jurors for the assizes from Spring 1834 to Spring 1837 and the number of times each served in those seven assizes.

Table 1

The Members of the Grand Juries at the the final countywide Assizes, 1834-8 and at the January 1839 Special Commission

	Barony	Sp '34	Su '34	Sp '35	Su '35	Sp '36	Su '36	Sp '37	Su '37	Sp '38	Su '38	Jan '39
Atkins, Stephen Hastings, Birdhill	O & A			✓								✓
Bagwell, John, Marlfield, Clonmel	I & OE										✓	
Bagwell, John, D.L., Glenconnor, Clonmel	I & OE	✓		✓		✓			✓	✓	✓	✓
Bayly, John, D.L., Debsborough, Nenagh	UO		✓	✓					✓	✓	✓	✓
Baker, Hugh, Lismacue, Bansha	C		✓									
Barker, Wm Ponsonby, D.L., Kilcooly Abbey, Johnstown	S	✓		✓		✓	✓	✓	✓	✓		✓
Barton, Samuel Wm, Rochestown, Cahir	I & OW				✓	✓	✓	✓	✓	✓		✓
Bloomfield, Hon. John, Oakhampton, Newport	O & A							✓	✓			
Butler, James Archer, Garnavilla, Cahir	I & OW		✓			✓				✓	✓	
Carden, John, Barnane, Templemore	I											
Carden, Sir Henry, D.L., The Priory, Templemore	E				✓							
Carrol, Maj.-Gen. Sir Wm Parker, Tulla House, Nenagh	UO						✓	✓	✓			
Creagh, Laurence, Castle Park, Golden	C											
Creagh, Richard, D.L., Castle-Park, Golden	C			✓		✓		✓		✓	✓	
Dancer, Thomas Bernard, Modreeny, Cloughjordan	LO	✓								✓	✓	
Gason, Richard Wills, D.L., Richmond, Nenagh	LO	✓			✓	✓	✓			✓	✓	✓
Going, Ambrose, Ballyphilip, Killenaule	S									✓	✓	
Gough, Maj.-Gen. Sir Hugh, D.L., Rathronan House, Clonmel	I & OE	✓	✓	✓	✓	✓						
Head, William Henry, Modreeny, Cloughjordan	LO			✓	✓		✓			✓	✓	
Holmes, Peter, Nenagh	LO				✓		✓	✓	✓			
Hely-Hutchinson, Hon. Richard, D.L., Knocklofty, Clonmel	I & OW	✓		✓	✓		✓	✓	✓		✓	
Jacob, Mathew, D.L., Mobarnan, Fethard	M	✓		✓	✓	✓	✓			✓	✓	✓
Jacob, William	M											
King, Hon. James, Mitchelstown Castle, Co. Cork	I & OW			✓	✓	✓	✓	✓		✓	✓	
Lalor, Thomas E., Cregg, Carrick-on-Suir	I & OE		✓	✓	✓	✓	✓			✓	✓	✓
Langley, Henry, Coalbrook, Thurles	S	✓	✓		✓							✓

Name	Barony	Sp '34	Su '34	Sp '35	Su '35	Sp '36	Su '36	Sp '37	Su '37	Sp '38	Su '38	Jan '39
Lenigan, James, Castle Fogarty, Thurles	K									✓		
Lee, Henry, Barna, Newport	O & A	✓		✓							✓	
Lidwell, Richard, Clonmore, Templemore	I								✓	✓		✓
Long, Richard, D.L., Longfield, Cashel	M	✓				✓	✓	✓	✓	✓		
Lowe, Richard Butler Hamilton, D.L., Kenilworth, Clonmel	I & OE	✓	✓	✓	✓	✓	✓		✓	✓		✓
Maher, John, Tullamaine Castle, Fethard	M	✓	✓	✓	✓	✓	✓	✓	✓	✓		
Mansergh, Richard, Greenane, Tipperary	C	✓	✓		✓							
Millett, Matthew, Lismoynan, Fethard	M											
Moore, Edward Crosbie, Mooresfort, Lattin, Tipperary	C					✓						
Moore, Maurice Crosbie, D.L., Mooresfort, Lattin	C	✓		✓	✓			✓				✓
Moore, Stephen Charles, Glenconnor House, Clonmel	I & OE	✓		✓	✓	✓	✓	✓		✓		
Moore, Stephen, D.L., Barn House, Clonmel	I & OE	✓		✓	✓	✓	✓	✓	✓	✓		
O'Brien, John Bray, Turtulla, Thurles	E											
O'Callaghan, Hon Cornelius, D.L., Shanbally Castle, Clogheen	I & OW	✓		✓		✓	✓	✓	✓	✓		✓
O'Callaghan, Hon. George*	I & OW	✓	✓			✓	✓	✓	✓	✓	✓	✓
O'Meagher, Stephen, D.L., Kilmoyler, Cahir	C	✓										
Ossory, John (Butler), earl of, Kilkenny Castle*	?			✓	✓						✓	
Pennefather, Matthew, D.L., Newpark, Cashel	M	✓			✓	✓	✓		✓		✓	✓
Pennefather, Richard, Jun., D.L., Darling Hill, Clonmel	I & OE	✓		✓	✓	✓	✓	✓				✓
Pennefather, William, Lakefield, Fethard	M			✓								
Perry, Samuel, Woodroffe, Clonmel	I & OE		✓						✓			
Perry, William, D.L., Woodroffe, Clonmel	I & OE	✓		✓				✓		✓		✓
Phillips, Richard E., Mount Rivers, Newport	O & A						✓	✓		✓	✓	
Phillips, Samuel, Gaile, Cashel	M		✓	✓	✓		✓					
Prittie, Hon. F.A., D.L., Corville, Roscrea*	I	✓		✓				✓		✓		
Prittie, Henry, D.L., Corville, Roscrea,	I	✓		✓		✓	✓	✓	✓	✓	✓	✓
Purefoy, Lieut.-Col. W, Greenfield, Donohill	K	✓	✓	✓		✓		✓	✓	✓	✓	✓

55

	Barony	Sp '34	Su '34	Sp '35	Su '35	Sp '36	Su '36	Sp '37	Su '37	Sp '38	Su '38	Jan '39
Quin, William Jun., Loughlohery, Cahir	I & O W		✓				✓	✓	✓		✓	
Riall, William Henry, Westgrove, Clonmel	I & O E						✓	✓	✓	✓	✓	✓
Ryan, George, D.L., Inch House, Thurles	E	✓		✓	✓	✓		✓	✓			
Sankey, Martin Villiers, Coolemore, Fethard	M		✓									
Scully, James, Jun., Tipperary	C											
Scully, James, Kilfeacle, Tipperary	C					✓			✓		✓	
Scully, James, Jun., Shanballyard, Clerihan	I & O E	✓		✓								
Scully, John, Dualla, Cashel	M									✓		✓
Stoney, Thomas George, Arran-hill and/or Kyle Park Borrisokane	LO	✓	✓		✓					✓		
Trench, Frederick, Sopwell Hall, Cloughjordan	LO						✓		✓			
Trench, William Steuart, Sopwell Hall, Cloughjordan	LO									✓		
Wall, James William, Coolnamuck Court, Carrick-on-Suir	I & O E						✓					
Waller, Sir Edmund, Newport/Knockanacree, Cloughjordan	O & A/LO	✓										

*Foremen: 1834 Spring Assize: Hon George O'Callaghan; 1834 Summer Assizes: John, Earl of Ossory
1835 Summer Assizes: F.A. Prittie; 1836, 1837 and 1838 Spring and Summer Assizes and January 1839: Hon Cornelius O'Callaghan

Sources: 1834 Spring Assizes: C. A. 19 Mar 1834; Summer Assizes: C. A. 30 July 1834;
1835 Spring Assizes: C. A. 18 Mar 1835; Summer Assizes: C. A. 29 July 1835;
1836 Spring Assizes: C. A. 9 Mar 1836; Summer Assizes: C. A. 20 July 1836;
1837 Spring Assizes: C.A. 11 Mar 1837; Summer Assizes: C. A. 19 July 1837;
1838 Spring Assizes: C.A. 14 Mar 1838; Summer Assizes: T.F.P. 21 July 1838;
Jan 1839 Special Commission: T.F.P. 9 Jan 1839.

See Figure 3, p. 53

PRIME IN CRIME

Tipperary's density of population would in itself have imposed a strain on the legal apparatus and on local government, all things being equal. But the intensity of crime and the consequent pressure on the courts and their functionaries was not equal, Tipperary having an unrivalled reputation for lawlessness. The sheer statistics of Tipperary's being the premier county in this respect were examined by James W. Hurst.[11] He compared the ratios of committal for trial per 1,000 population for all Ireland and Tipperary.

	Ireland	Tipperary
1834	2.7	8.0
1835	2.7	9.7
1836	3.0	14.1
1837	1.4	10.2

A return of all crimes and outrages in the eighteen months from July 1836 to December 1837 yields ratios per 1,000 population of 1.52 for all Ireland and 2.85 for county Tipperary.[12] Those latter figures are in respect of all crimes reported – categorised as offences against the person, property and the public peace, and other. The Hurst figures are in respect of persons committed for trial; the disparity reflects the number of persons charged per crime. In other words, the turbulent Tipps were committing twice as many crimes as other Irishmen, but producing five times the number brought to trial. A crude comparison between the two sets of ratios seems to suggest that a higher number of persons per crime was also a Tipperary phenomenon – perhaps an early indication of a co-operative spirit in the county.

At the Spring Assizes of 1837, Judge Foster addressed the grand jury on the extent to which crime was unprosecuted and therefore unpunished.

> This difference between the amount of charge and prosecution is however in no degree attributable to official negligence and on the contrary no officers can be more efficient or more sincerely desirous to perform their duties than those to whom these prosecutions are entrusted but it is owing to the indisposition to give evidence, originating in a well-understood system of terror, which renders the administration of justice more or less difficult in various parts of Ireland and which in some counties goes the length of compelling the Crown to depend almost exclusively – either on the evidence of the police – or on that of approvers

about to be expatriated to the colonies at the public expense – or on that of the relatives of the deceased, in cases where their resentment got the better of their prudence.

I may be excused from the ungracious office of entering into comparison so far as other counties are concerned but I feel it my duty to assure you of the unwelcome truth that, in no other, is the difficulty felt to be so great as in your county.[13]

In June of that year 1837 the organ which kept an eagle eye on the neighbouring czars and proletariat, the *Clare Journal*, noted that 'Tipperary presents the heaviest weight of crime on any calendar in Ireland for Summer Assizes'.[14]

The types of crime, listed alphabetically, ranged from abandoning an infant and abduction to uttering counterfeit coins and vagrancy. Behind the statistical analysis lay, for instance, the cases of fifty-seven people charged with murder at the 1834 Spring Assizes, and forty-four that summer. The persons charged that year at those two Clonmel assizes totalled 410. It remained to be seen, if it were relevant, where the weight of the lawlessness lay – north or south.[15]

DISTURBED BARONIES
The following instances, drawn from a twenty-one-month period coincidental with early murmurings of the second assize town and division campaign, September 1833 to June 1835, all relate to crimes within the northern baronies. They are also selected as intimately affecting people involved in the campaign, whether as themselves or as fellow magistrates or landowners or relatives of the victims. The southern baronies, of course, endured a heavy crime rate also. A single issue of the *Clonmel Advertiser* reported a man driven from his own bog near Mullinahone by 'a large assemblage', a severe beating with bludgeons of a Marlfield man as punishment for a perceived unequal exchange of horses, and the houghing of a milch cow as a result of a legal action against tenants.[16]

Committed to our Co. Gaol since 16th inst. [incl.] by John B. O'Brien, _____ for the rape of _____ ; by F. A. Prittie, _____ for firing a shot and having arms and ammunition.[17]

Monday evening while Mr Pepper of Laughton House, was returning from Moneygall, within a quarter mile of his house, three men attacked him, two of them armed with pistols, and the third seized his horse by the bridle and they instantly demanded him to surrender the money which he had collected for rents which was £120. He flung them after some parley a pocketbook, but not finding money therein, they struck him with a heavy stone and cut him severely in the temple. He struggled and fortunately disengaged himself, galloping off to the Toomevara police station. The police turned out immediately, having left Mr Pepper behind, who was faint from loss of blood. They rapidly approached two suspicious looking men on the road, who took to the river on seeing the police, and they having called after them ineffectually, fired, and it is thought wounded one of the fugitives, as blood was traced in their route.[18]

SPRING ASSIZES Record Court eighth day, Mon., Judge Johnson: John Breslawn for sending a threatening message to O'Brien Dillon of Nenagh – Verdict guilty. The jury and Mr O'Brien Dillon recommended the prisoner to mercy which the court acceded to, and only sentenced him to imprisonment of three months.[19]

While Pennefather versus Bloomfield was under investigation at Newport last Tuesday,[20] and Lord Bloomfield's man who kept his Lordship's shooting lodge on the Keeper Mountain, was attending as witness, four fellows with their faces blackened and well armed, attacked the lodge, severely beat a man whom they found in care of it, and carried off a double and single-barrelled gun, and two cases of pistols.[21]

Dwelling house of Richard Minchin Carden of Fishmoyne maliciously set on fire and burnt to the ground.[22]

THE CAUSES OF DISTURBANCE
Hurst called this county 'Disturbed Tipperary'. That it was so recognised at the time is also testified to in a wealth of Parliamentary Reports and debates, newspaper editorials, and ballads.[23] It is not relevant to this work's main theme to explore the reasons for crime, just as Richard Dalton William's apocryphal fellow passenger failed:

Then he ventured on politics, spoke of the laws.
Of the crimes of Tipperary, *but not of their cause.*[24]

It is worthwhile mentioning in passing that, even at the time, the main cause was clearly perceived by some commentators, even in Great

Britain, to lie in the vast disparity in wealth and income which was itself basically attributable to the system of land ownership.[25]

The direct results of poverty included what had been variously described in 1834 as distress and famine. From June into August of that year there was in effect a preview of the Great Famine which was to occur just a decade later, with County Tipperary at the centre and Thurles in particular hard hit. The poor paraded there in June, a committee in July assessed 2,460 in a population of 7,000 'in absolute want', through July and August subscriptions funded the distribution of food and the employment of about one hundred men but leaving still 'one thousand able-bodied labourers, who have no wherewithal to purchase for themselves or families the smallest necessities of life'.[26]

Clonmel, Fethard, Carrick-on-Suir and Cahir had similar stories. The Cahir solution included at least three 'daring outrages' in the form of attacks on carts and robbery of their loads of flour en route from Grubb's mills.[27]

Richard Lalor Shiel, MP for the county, asked repeated questions in the House of Commons; the tone of the responses led the *Tipperary Free Press* to observe '… and yet the Government heard and knew so little? If it was necessary to make out a case for coercion, how readily these gentry would report every pig that tripped a peeler in the course of his duties'. Again: 'Let no politician after rail at the outrages committed by a starving peasantry'.[28] On the other hand, Lord Lieutenant Wellesley subscribed £50 directly to the Thurles fund[29] (the equivalent of about £3,000 in the early 1990s). Many landowners did help in alleviating the immediate distress; Rev. Mr Croake, the rector at Annacarty 'purchased flour and oatmeal to the value of £400 to £500 for poor parishioners'.[30]

Poverty and its causes, do not entirely explain 'Disturbed Tipperary', as evident in the flourishing state of faction fighting, violence for the sake of violence. Through 1834, while Bloomfield was conspiring through constitutional channels, personal and community vendettas were pursued between Shanavests and Caravats at the fair of Ballingarry near Thurles, between Rawlins and Cusheens at the Green of Cashel, Darrigs and Cummings at Roscrea and Pallates and Bawnies at Borrisoleigh fair, where both combined and attacked the interfering police. The Toomevara police, backed by the 36th regiment from Nenagh, prevented a riot between the Cummings and Whitefeet. Ballingarry Shanavests crossed the county border to tackle the Kilkenny Caravats at Callan.[31] Again, one must balance the story by adverting to similar ructions at the time, involving deaths, in north Cork and east Limerick.

NENAGH ORGANISES

Leaving aside now that stormy background through the couple of years of drawing-room diplomacy and legislative reform, the pace of constitutional change picks up in late 1836. The Nenagh lobby organised themselves into a committee and on 13 December they circularised potential subscribers of the sinews of law:

> It is ... expected that a considerable opposition to the Prayer of a Memorial will be given by Persons decidedly adverse to the Division of this county; and that in order to defray the expense of hiring Counsel, employing a Professional Agent to conduct the proceedings that may be advised, as also for the transmission of witnesses to give evidence before the Privy Council in support of the justice and expediency of the measure sought for, a sum of money must be forthcoming which though infinitely less than that which would be required for obtaining a specific Act of Parliament for the division of the County may be considerable ...[32]

The professional agent envisaged in the appeal for funds would turn out to be a Nenagh attorney, O'Brien Dillon (O'Brien being his Christian or first name). He was later a significant political figure in his own right and is the subject of Chapter Six.

Subscribers were to pay half immediately. A Treasurer in each of four baronies was to make a return of subscriptions by Monday 2 January 1837 and to lodge his collection by then in the National Bank, Nenagh. The leaders, obviously going to avail of Christmastide social contacts were:

as Chairman, the second Baron Dunalley of Kilboy, near Silvermines and Nenagh (1775-1854); born Henry Sadleir Prittie, Whig MP for Carlow 1797-1800 and for Okehampton, a borough in Devon, England, 1819-24, and whose support of the government in the passing of the Union of Great Britain and Ireland was reciprocated by his father's elevation to the peerage (hereditary of course – and his father died, aged 57, just over five months later); Dunalley was by now the second largest landowner in Tipperary with over 21,000 acres, headed in the rankings only by Viscount Lismore's close to 35,000 acres.[33]

Dunalley and his brother, Francis Aldborough Prittie, Corville, Roscrea (MP for Doneraile 1800, for Carlow 1801, and for County Tipperary 1806-12 and 1819-30) were 'for twenty years unchanged and un-changeable' ... 'in manifesting my anxious desire for the speedy emancipation of my Catholic fellow-countrymen'.[34] Henry was

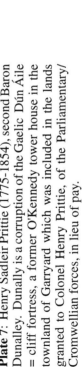

Plate 8: Francis Aldborough Prittie (1780-1853), younger brother of the second Baron Dunalley and father of the third; he lived in Corville House, Roscrea.

Plate 7: Henry Sadleir Prittie (1775-1854), second Baron Dunalley. Dunally is a corruption of the Gaelic Dún Áile = cliff fortress, a former O'Kennedy tower house in the townland of Garryard which was included in the lands granted to Colonel Henry Prittie, of the Parliamentary/ Cromwellian forces, in lieu of pay.

Plate 9: Kilboy House, built c.1771 by Henry Prittie who became Baron
Dunalley in 1800. William Leeson was the architect. It was burnt during the
civil war in 1922 and rebuilt by the fourth Baron minus its attic story. Death
duties and other financial constraints, exacerbated by prohibitive rates, caused
the sixth Baron to lower it to one-storey level in 1952 and cut it back by two
bays creating a bungalow-style appearance. Sold out of Dunalley ownership
a few years later, it was enlarged horizontally to what is now a very handome
private residence – drawing courtesy of Nenagh District Heritage Society.

identified as 'an Emancipator versus Castlemaine, a decided Orangeman'[35] during his successful campaign in 1828-9 for election by the Irish peerage as one of their twenty-eight representatives in the House of Lords, and backed by the government in the form of a circular issued by the Lord Lieutenant, Marquess of Anglesey, recommending him. Home Secretary Peel had cleared their support for Dunalley with Prime Minister Wellington who in turn thought it prudent to first obtain 'His Majesty's approval' – endorsement more royally comprehensive a baron could not dream of.[36] Shortly after Catholic Emancipation was approved of by His most reluctant Majesty, George IV, Lord Dunalley, together with The Liberator himself, Daniel O'Connell, were among the early contributors to a fund to erect a statue to the same Prime Minister, Duke of Wellington, 'in or near Dublin commemorative of this the most glorious of his public services'.[37] The Pritties' liberal views may have been influenced by a tutor who was engaged for Francis at home between 1796 and 1798. He was Rev. Henry Fulton, the Church of Ireland curate to their parish, who was transported as a convicted United Irishman;[38]

as Secretary, Major-General Sir William Parker Carrol, K.C.B., of Tulla, also near Silvermines, Nenagh (1776-1842); a hero of the Spanish Peninsular Wars, laden with honours which included a knighthood from King Charles III of Spain and twelve other foreign decorations, the freedom of the City of Dublin, a sword from the Irish bar, addresses from 'the noblemen and gentlemen of the Baronies of Upper and Lower Ormond and Owney and Arra' in 1811 and from the Grand Jury of Tipperary in 1816.[39] He was Governor of Malta from about 1822 to 1838, apparently being home for Christmas 1836, from there. Carrol was later brought out of retirement in 1839 to take command in Athlone of the army in the Western District;[40]

as Treasurer for Upper Ormond, Peter Holmes, Jun., of Johnstown, Puckane, the owner of most of the land on which Nenagh town was built;[41] as Treasurer for Lower Ormond, Richard Wills Gason of Richmond near Nenagh;[42] as Treasurer for Ikerrin, Henry Prittie, Corville, Roscrea, son of Francis Aldborough Prittie and who eventually succeeded his uncle, the Chairman, as the third Baron Dunalley;[43] as Treasurer for Owney and Arra, Richard Phillips of Mount Rivers near Newport.[44]

Among those leading campaigners only Carrol was not of colonist blood. Dunalley, Prittie, Gason and Phillips were sixth generation or so Cromwellian stock. So was Bloomfield's mother (a Waller); his father was an English soldier. The Holmes line in Ireland stemmed from an Irish colonial public servant. Carrol was of Gaelic lineage, his direct ancestry long converted to British service. All were Protestants, members of the (Established) Church of Ireland except that Bloomfield converted to Wesleyan Methodism while in Sweden and Dunalley became involved in an Independent chapel in Nenagh.

POLITICAL PLAY

As might be gauged from the range of their parliamentary seats and the second baron's successful bid for the upper house, the Pritties were adept and practiced politicians. F. A.'s first appearance in the Tipperary colours was in 1806, in tandem with Col. Hon. Montague J. Mathew, son of the first earl of Llandaff; they were unopposed for the two seats. It was probably the following year's contest, when they beat John Bagwell and Kingsmill Pennefather, south Tipperary conservatives, which evoked a note from Lord Donoughmore at Knocklofty. It indicated that he was 'withdrawing support' from Prittie because of his coalition with Mathew.

In 1812 the coalition again beat Bagwell; Pennefather did not run. In 1818 Richard Butler, Viscount Caher, topped the poll ahead of Mathew, with Prittie third and thus ousted. Early in the following year Caher became the second earl of Glengall (and as such appears later in this story). Accordingly, he resigned his Commons seat, but in liaison with Lords Lismore and Llandaff persuaded Prittie 'to resign pretensions to Bagwell on the present occasion and they would both join, and with Bagwell, in supporting him on the next vacancy'. Prittie agreed, and Col. Hon. William Bagwell got the uncontested seat. The caucus group redeemed their promise swiftly on Mathew's sudden death at a dinner party later that year; Prittie was unopposed for the bye-election.

F. A. headed the poll in 1826, ahead of John Hely-Hutchinson, the future third earl of Donoughmore. Two conservatives, Lionel Dawson and James Roe, were down the field. This election was probably the background to Glengall's note to Dunalley in 1828, promising support for the representative peer contest 'and believe me should be also equally glad never again to vote against your brother which would serve you <u>both</u>, contests and cash, as well as "trouble"'.[45]

OTHER ALLIANCES

Bloomfield's mother was a sister of the Tipperary MP Robert Otway Cave's grandmother; their grand-aunt was married to Gason's great-grandfather. Holmes was connected to the Pritties through a Bayly marriage.[46]

As illustrated already by the network of Bloomfield connections related in Chapter One, there is further evidence of lubricating sociability in a book by General Carrol's great-great-granddaughter, June O'Carroll Robertson, *A Long Way from Tipperary*, pp. 89, 108-9. She quotes an 1817 diary by Emma Sophia Sherwill, then Carrol's fiancé; he introduced her to Bloomfield and to Dundrum's Lord Hawarden (as well as to two royal dukes and four ambassadors) at a Grand Ball at Court in London. Later entries record her, by then married at Tulla, Nenagh, visiting the Dunalleys and two Holmes families.

Lord Dunalley and General Carrol, whose Big Houses were just 4.2 statute miles distant by road, had previously worked together in 1822 to devise an ingenious system of tithes-by-consensus in Kilmore parish. They had arranged the collection of his tithes for the Established Church Rector, Rev. Gilbert Holmes, who was also Dean of Ardfert diocese, in an atmosphere of peace and all-round goodwill, cut out the oppressive tithe proctor (collector) and relieved the tenant-farmers, almost all Roman Catholics, by voluntarily increasing their own share as large landowners. The formula for the latter feature was their agreement to pay tithes on pasture and parkland, in effect reversing a controversial exemption for those types of land which had been granted by statute, almost ninety years previously, in 1735. The popularity of this with the majority – tillage farmers who had hitherto borne the burden – and the prospect of making the hated proctor and his fees redundant, enabled the parishioners to elect their own assessors.

Carrol was the prime mover in this scheme; Dunalley was by far the largest landowner in the parish, followed by his own agent, William Trench, and Carrol.[47] Exactly one month after the arrival in Ireland of a new Lord Lieutenant, Richard Colley Wellesley, Marquis Wellesley – who was the Duke of Wellington's brother – Carrol forwarded him an account of the Kilmore treaty. Wellesley, bent on reform and already canvassing opinions from all sources, had his own proposals to some extent pushed into legislation by Chief Secretary Henry Goulburn as the Tithe Composition Act, 1823.[48]

Folklore has left a story of another cause for affinity between the Prittie-Dunalley and Carrol families. It tells of Carrol's father William, reputedly a noted swordsman and pugilist, deputising for a very young Henry Prittie, later our second baron Dunalley, in a duel with a British officer.[49]

THURLES ORGANISES

In the same week in December 1836 as the Nenagh-based committee circularised their landowner colleagues, an advertisement went from Thurles to the *Clonmel Advertiser* – Clonmel had four newspapers;

neither Nenagh nor Thurles had any. It convened a public meeting of the landed proprietors and inhabitants of the county – no baronialism evident there; at the Courthouse in the town of Thurles – where more central? It was 'to consider the best mode of remedying the great inconvenience and hindrance to due administration of justice caused by the remote situation (in reference to the greater part of the county) of the town of Clonmel'.[50]

The wording was a shrewd echo of the statutory enabling clause: 'the inconvenient Situation of the towns where the Assizes are now held in respect to other Parts of said Counties'.

The list of 136 signatures (see Appendix Four), all from the Thurles area, revealed a considerable degree of organisation beforehand. They were headed by three Deputy Lieutenants of the county – John Trant of Dovea,[51] William Fitzwilliam Mathew of Thurles, and George Ryan of Inch.[52] The meeting was held on Thursday 22 December 1836.[53] Ryan, a landowner of almost 1,700 acres, was moved to the chair; John Cahill, Main St, Thurles, Crown Solicitor, acted as Secretary.[54]

Mathew proposed the key resolution, seconded by Charles O'Keefe, brewer and malster, farmer and land agent, Thurles, who would himself within two years become a victim of the crime wave – murdered 'within a few yards of his residence':[55]

> That having learned that it is contemplated to divide this county for the purposes of assizes, it is the opinion of the meeting that no arrangement appropriating to the northern division of the county fewer baronies than six, viz. Eliogarty, Kilnamanagh, Ikerrin, Upper Ormond, Lower Ormond and Owney and Arra, can be satisfactory, and that no sufficient selection of jurors can be made in any small division of the northern district of the county for the administration of justice.[56]

The point of the resolution and the speaker's claim that the four baronies comprehended by the Nenagh memorial to the Lord Lieutenant amounted to only one-third of the county are borne out by reference to the 1831 census of population:

Lower Ormond	45,006
Upper Ormond	24,807
Owney & Arra	32,454
Ikerrin	27,077
Sub-total	**129,344**

Kilnamanagh	30,774
Eliogarty	<u>38,531</u>
Sub-total	**198,649**
Clanwilliam	48,152
Iffa & Offa East	38,702
Iffa & Offa West	40,192
Middlethird	44,103
Slieveardagh	<u>32,765</u>
Total	**402,563**

Speakers pointed out that Thurles had a population of 8,000 souls and was the 'the principal town in the northern division, with a river which, with very little expense, could be navigable, having the largest markets in the county, save Clonmel'.[57] The *Clare Journal* analysed the object of the meeting 'to have been to procure the appointment of Thurles to be the Assize town for the northern division of the county under the proposed division of the shire.'[58] Implied in that reporter's analysis was a presumption that the division proposal would succeed.

DUNDRUM DEMURS

It was now clear that Eliogarty, with Thurles as centre, wanted partition from the southern baronies and Clonmel.

But Kilnamanagh was different. The *Tipperary Constitution* reported that Viscount Hawarden, whose seat was at Dundrum in the southern segment of that barony and who had declined to act as chairman of the meeting,[59] retired from the meeting at that point, 'a circumstance which produced a great sensation amongst the friends of the intended change'.[60] Hawarden had in the previous year joined his brother-in-law Dunalley in the ranks of the Irish representative peers in the House of Lords.

John Bray O'Brien, JP, Turtulla, Thurles, seconded by Henry Langley, now proposed the appointment of Thurles for assizes as 'far superior to any other town'. Robert Lidwill, JP, Clonmore, Templemore; Rev. Albert Armstrong, Holycross; Capt. William Armstrong, JP, Farney Castle; Nicholas Maher, Turtulla; Charles Clarke, JP, Graiguenoe, Holycross; Patrick Kirwan, attorney, Thurles; and Dixon C. O'Keeffe, Killoran, Templemore were the proposers of a set of resolutions which formally endorsed a memorial, set up a committee, appointed a deputation to visit other towns to solicit support, and opened a subscription list. The Committee consisted of Ryan, Cahill, O'Brien, Lidwill, Maher, Kirwan, Francis O'Brien, Thurles, with Charles O'Keefe as Treasurer.[61]

DEFENCE OF CLONMEL

Clonmel had a prime interest against any downgrading and loss of business. Its *Tipperary Constitution*, as befitted the name, had entered the battle on behalf of the existing order on 30 December 1836 with an editorial of sardonic vision:

> This is the era for change. This county is to be turned topsy turvy in order to improve it; indeed for some time we have perceived it is upside down. Nenagh desires to have an Assizes held there, and Thurles wishes to have the Courthouse removed there. We understand that it is also contemplated to move the Gaol to Carrick-on-Suir, for the convenience of the inhabitants of that fine town, and to move the House of Correction to Newport, and the Lunatic Asylum to Mullinahone and the infirmary at Cashel to Borrisokane and the Clerk's of the Peace office to the Ragg, and the Crown Office to the Horse and Jockey. The river Suir, for the present, is to be allowed to run through Clonmel. We have no doubt that these various improvements can be effected at a very trifling expense, with great satisfaction and much convenience to the public.[62]

The degrees of Clonmel's indignation and sense of importance can be measured by comparison of its population (15,134) with those of Nenagh (8,466), Thurles (7,084) and Carrick-on-Suir (9,626), but more so with those of Mullinahone (1,175) and Borrisokane (1,185); the Ragg and Horse-and-Jockey were considerably less than 1,000. See also Appendix One. Extraordinarily, and as if the case so stated could safely rest, there were no indications in the following months of any Clonmel lobby being organised.[63]

It was to be almost six months before the memorials were heard, debated and judged by a Committee of the Privy Council. On the eve of those proceedings, in early June 1837, the *Clonmel Advertiser* commented: 'it appears admitted that the county is to be divided and the question will be whether the town of Nenagh or Thurles is to be the new assize town.'[64]

STRAWS IN THE WIND

A straw in the wind had blown by unnoticed in January of that same year. A rudimentary Tory party constituency body (160 of the 'rank, wealth and respectability of this great county'), chaired by the earl of Glengall, reorganised themselves into northern and southern divisions.[65] Glengall was the third Tipperaryman among the twenty-eight

69

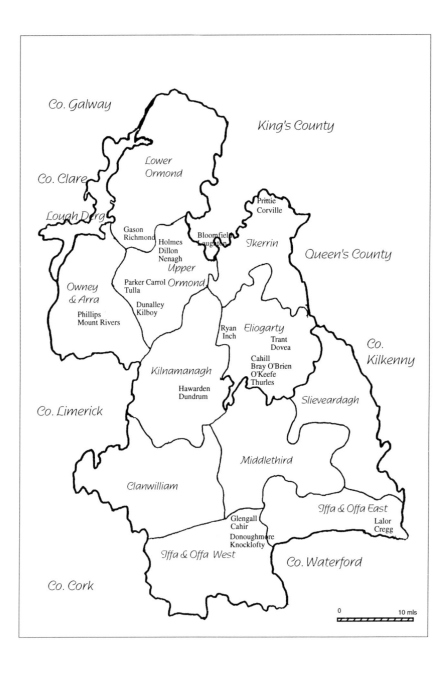

Fig. 4: The approximate residences of the key people involved in the initial moves for division, in the Nenagh and Thurles memorials, and in the opposition from the southern baronies.

representative peers in the House of Lords. Born Richard Butler of Cahir, he was the only titled holder of the surname which had shaped the county then resident in Tipperary. Whether he would have a stance on the question of dividing the former palatinate controlled by the Butlers, remained to be seen.

The Privy Council in a session of 24 December 1836 advised the Lord Lieutenant to divide the county into three parts for quarter sessions – the lower stratum of courts. Their considerations must have added to the high profile in general of County Tipperary in the official consciousness, as adverted to in the Prologue.

The baronies of Iffa and Offa West and Iffa and Offa East in what became advertised as the Upper Division were to be catered for by two sessions in Clonmel, one in Carrick-on-Suir and one in Clogheen.

The baronies of Clanwilliam, Middlethird, Slieveardagh and Compsey were proclaimed as a second, Middle Division. Three sessions in Cashel and one in Tipperary were now provided annually.

The Ormonds, Owney and Arra, Ikerrin, Eliogarty, Kilnamanagh and the three parishes of Kilcooley, Boulick and Fennor belonging to Slieveardagh barony were grouped as a Lower Division – remarkably like the north riding proposed by the Thurles lobby. That division was to be served at three locations: Nenagh and Thurles were to have two sessions each per annum and Roscrea one.[66]

None of this had any direct implications for assizes or for the working of the grand jury. It had, though, for the Lord Lieutenant's image in the eye of John Kempston's *Clonmel Advertiser*. Ten days before the Privy Council decision, on 14 December 1836, the editorial alleged Mulgrave's determination 'to open Sessions Courts in every little village that can number three or four hundred inhabitants ... the ostensible intention of its being, forsooth, to facilitate the ends of justice'. The *Clonmel Advertiser* recognised 'the real motive' as a Whig ploy to have the 'numerous host of the "Briefless"' – lawyer supporters of the O'Connell party which was the 'mainstay of the present Government' – 'reaping the reward ... in a translation from the empty honours of the spouting stool to the substantial enrolments of the judgement seat'.

STATE OF THE COUNTY, EARLY JUNE 1837

Tipperary county, singular both in the duration of its medieval constitution and in the degree of its people's contemporary lapse from law and order, in mid-1837 faced up to the prospect of another constitutional revision. By new statutory provisions, account was to be taken of the county's size and of the peripheral situation of its medieval and later capital, Clonmel, as assize town. The debate focused largely on the convenience of the county's ascendancy class in exercising separate functions in the spheres of justice and local government at bi-annual assizes. The first task dealt with public order and some private passions, through the courts; the second task largely consisted of maintaining an elementary roads system for the passage of the population, including the ascendancy and its tenantry in that very pursuit of justice.

There were two pro-division lobbies, themselves in opposition as to the location of the potential second assize town. The Ormonds and Owney and Arra baronies favoured their capital, Nenagh, and the Eliogarty lobby favoured theirs, Thurles. Ikerrin barony and its Roscrea capital (21 statute miles from Nenagh and 22 from Thurles) had not formulated a public position but presumably would be pro-division because of distance from Clonmel. There were muted anti-division sounds from Clonmel, naturally defending the status quo, and a hint of a burgeoning anti-division move from Dundrum, the focal point of mid-county Kilnamanagh barony. The potential protagonists in each lobby were led by men of skill and experience in public affairs, both national and local, with the Nenagh district's leaders pre-eminent in that regard.

The respective viewpoints would now have to be argued before a tribunal who would work within the remit of an 1836 statute, itself part of a corpus of modernising legislation. The statute and the legislation generally had encouraged elements of self-determination subject to central government decision.

Notes

1. 6 & 7 William IV, c. 116, s. 176, An Act to consolidate and amend the Laws relating to the Presentment Public Money by Grand Juries in Ireland.
2. *Philips' Handy Administrative Atlas*; *Thoms,* 1846.
3. PP (Census of Population 1831), 39 (1833) (23).
4. R. F. Foster, *Modern Ireland, 1600-1972* (London, 1989), p.b. ed., map 6 on p. 323 sourced to C. Ó Gráda, 'Demographic Adjustment and Seasonal Migration in Nineteenth-century Ireland', in L. M. Cullen and F. Furet eds, *Irlande et France XV IIc–XXc siècles: pour une histoire rurale comparèe.*
5. Emma Sophia Carrol's 1817 diary, in June O'Carroll Robertson, *A Long Way from Tipperary* (Upton-Upon-Severn, 1994), pp. 107-8.
6. Dunalley Papers, MS 29809 (16), NLI, bills from the representatives of J. Smallman, Roscrea.

7. *Limerick Evening Post & Clare Sentinel*, 29 July 1828.
8. Maurice R. O'Connell, *The Correspondence of Daniel O'Connell*, iii, letter 1254, O'Connell to his wife Mary, 27 Oct 1825.
9. *T.F.P.*, 30 July 1834.
10. Sources as for Table 1.
11. James W. Hurst, 'Disturbed Tipperary: 1831-1860' in *Éire-Ireland*, Autumn 1974, p. 58. The origins of the tag, 'The Premier County', perpetuated by sportswriters and in an occasional burst of political rhetoric, are unidentified by eleven other county-wide local historians whom I've consulted. This petit jury having failed to reach a verdict, the credit of the county shall go to whoever brings in a definitive judgement on the prime use of the term.
12. PP, xxxv (157), p. 427, 1846.
13. *C.A.*, Mar 1837.
14. *C.J.*, 29 June 1837. The sectarian element of much of the violence, including that of the 1832-3 Tithe War, is identified (as well as sectarianism in parliamentary election contests) in Dr Thomas G. McGrath, 'Interdenominational relations in pre-famine Tipperary', chapter 12, in Nolan and McGrath eds, *Tipperary History and Society* (Dublin, 1985).
15. *T.F.P.*, 12 Mar 1834; *C.A.*, 30 July 1834, 'Co. Tipperary Calendar for the Assizes'.
16. *C.A.*, 25 June 1834.
17. *C.A.*, 27 Nov 1833.
18. *C.A.*, 4 Jan 1834.
19. *T.F.P.*, 26 Mar 1834.
20. *C.A.*, 23 Apr 1834. The case was brought by Lysaght Pennefather, a barrister by qualification but with rare briefs except for fairly frequent self-endowed ones. This case, which was dismissed, was 'for keeping and using game dogs without a licence .... The case excited great interest and crowds assembled from all parts of the neighbourhood'.
21. *C.A.*, 23 Apr 1834.
22. *C.A.*, 10 June 1835.
23. The following specimen is by John O'Shea, then a journalist and contributor of verse on the *Clonmel Advertiser* and soon to accompany its proprietor family, the Kempstons, to Nenagh to found the *Nenagh Guardian*. The full ballad first appeared in *The Nenagh Minstrelsy*, a collection of verse (mostly his own) edited by O'Shea and published in 1838.

> Och, Barristhur Howley! Howley! Howley!
> Barristhur Howley, agragal, I vow
> You'll not lave among us a Darrig or Cummins,
> A Blackfoot or Whitefoot, to kick up a row.
> For shooting a Parson, or carding a Proctor,
> Or giving such fellows as Bailiffs their TAY,

'Tis a horrid hard case to be clapt in the dock, Sir,
Not at all to make mintion of 'Botany Bay'.
Och, Barristhur dear, if you would but be quiet,
Your praises we'd blaze in the rages of song;
Shure the Univarse knows, Sir, for ruxion and riot,
None equals 'Tipperary, the pride of the throng'.

The John Howley (1789/90-1866) thus addressed was a native of
Charlotte Quay, Limerick and resided later at Rich Hill, Castleconnell.
He was Assistant Barrister for Tipperary as of 1835 and thus chairman
of Quarter Sessions. He was a beneficiary of the Mulgrave
administration's positive discrimination in favour of Catholics to redress
the previous imbalance among office holders. Agragal = a grádh geal,
lit. oh, shining beloved. A proctor was a parson's tithe-collector; carding
meant tearing his skin with a rough instrument intended for cleansing
animal hides. TAY = tea. Darrig and Cummins were the names of two
factions from the Toomevara area in the heyday of faction fighting, the
1820s and 1830s. The Blackfeet and Whitefeet were secret societies using
violence to counter the tithe system and to remedy agrarian grievances.
Botany Bay was landfall for the first fleet transporting convicts to
Australia in 1791. Although their settlement was effected elsewhere, the
name 'Botany Bay' became shorthand for the convict colonies in New
South Wales.

References: Howley: *C.J.*, 11 July 1836; *N.G.*, 26 July 1851 and 17
Feb 1866; Con Costello, *Botany Bay: The Story of the Convicts
transported from Ireland to Australia, 1791-1853*.

24. 'The Cirilla Pulchella', pp. 155-161, *The Poems of Richard D'Alton
Williams* (Dublin, 1894). He is eminently quotable as the son of a landlord,
Count D'Alton who will be met in Chapter Five, and a woman of the
peasant class; he became a Young Ireland leader and poet in the later
1840s. His fellow passengers, under poetic licence, on 'the Toom
Caravan' (i.e. the Limerick-Dublin stage coach which he would board
in his shopping village, Toomevara) included also an admired young
lady who spiritedly answered the gentleman who had held forth on the
crimes of Tipperary.

When the beast of the forest is chased to his lair,
He turns and destroys in the rage of despair;
But men, fierce as they, must behold without ire
All they love, by your bloodhounds tormented, expire.
And, forsooth, all the crimes of the land they have done,
If, to thousands you murder, they immolate one;
If blood, fraud, and tears have built Widow-scourge Hall,
Shall we weep when the thing and its architect fall?

25. There is but one thing that surprises us in the state of Tipperary, and

that is the rarity, and not the frequency of the acts of desperation. House the peasantry of England like the peasantry of Tipperary; clothe them like the peasantry of Tipperary; feed them like the peasantry of Tipperary, which of all our shires would be half as orderly, half as patient, half as continent of the hand of rapacity or violence?

Ordinary diet of these stoics of the bog the vile potato ... execrable variety called the 'Lumper' ... 'dismal dens' in which they lodge, the tattered clothes they wear, nor the abject food they subsist on ... a depth of misery still to be sounded ... that cause is insecurity.

The landlords of Tipperary are indignant at being told that 'property has its duties as well as its rights' ... one of the 'duties of property' may be the clearing and improving of estates, but another certainly is to carry out the process with humane respect to the interests of the existing pauper population ... this pauper population is the creature of their own former acts and management when it was their sheer political interest to bid the people 'increase and multiply and replenish the earth'.
– *T.F.P.,* 1 Dec 1838, quoting *The Examiner*, London.

26. *T.F.P.*, 21 June, 9 July, 2 Aug 1834.
27. *C.A.*, 11, 14, 18 June 1834; *T.F.P.*, 23 July 1834.
28. *C.A.*, 2, 9, July; *T.F.P.*, 23 Jul 1834.
29. *T.F.P.*, 2 Aug 1834.
30. *T.F.P.*, 12 July 1834.
31. *C.A.*, 16 Nov 1833, 21 May, 9 Aug, 27 Aug, 20 Dec 1834.
32. Parker Papers, MS, 7331, N.L.I. A succession of Anthony Parkers lived at Castlelough on the lake drive from Nenagh to Ballina-Killaloe. See note 15 to Chapter Three.
33. Desmond, sixth Baron Dunalley, *History of the Prittie Family in Ireland, 1649-1981* (privately-held typescript); Local Government Board, *Land Owners in Ireland, 1876* (Dublin 1876 and Baltimore, USA, 1988). The name was spelt 'Dunally' more frequently in the nineteenth century. The remains of the second Baron and his two wives, Maria Trant (d. 1818) and Emily Maude (c.1800-c.1884) are interred in a vault in Kilmore graveyard. He died at Kilboy. Its grounds include the former Dolla parish church ruins, tastefully conserved by the present owner in the 1980s; most of the Pritties are buried in a family plot adjacent to the church. Kilboy House, renovated in a reduced form following arson in 1922, is now owned and its demesne farmed by Dr Tony Ryan, GPA.
34. The first quotation is Prittie's and the second Dunalley's, both from letters of apology for inability to attend a meeting in Clonmel, quoted in the *Tipperary Free Press* on 27 August and 3 September 1828 respectively.
35. *D.E.P.*, 25 Sept 1828.
36. Anglesey informed the Home Secretary, Sir Robert Peel, of the circular by letter of 17 September 1828 – *Memoirs by Sir Robert Peel, Part 1 The Roman Catholic Question, 1828-9* (London, 1856). Peel's and Wellington's clearances of Dunalley's 'best claim' were on 15-26 August 1828 – *Wellington: Despatches*.

37. Resolutions, committee, and subscribers 'passed at the London Tavern 6 May 1829' – printed list inserted at folio 132 of the Diary of Judge Day (Royal Irish Academy).

38. The Fulton story is the subject of the very readable blend of fact and fiction by Marjorie Quarton, *The Renegade* (London, 1991). His tuition of Francis, as distinct from the older Henry, was deduced by the author from the context. She kindly quoted me the reference for the tuition itself – in an unfavourable response by the local JP, Sir William Osborne, to an enquiry by Lord Claremont which in turn arose from a petition for clemency by three hundred of Fulton's parishioners – N.A. (Room 6 in the former S.P.O., 13.3.75).

39. Sheehan, *N. & its N.* pp. 45-6, 85

40. According to Sir Bernard Burke, *A Genealogical and Heraldic History of the Landed Gentry of Ireland,* second edition 1904, p. 84, General Sir William Parker (from his mother Susanna Parker) Carrol had three Williams in his immediate ancestry, the first of whom was a grandson of William of Balliecrenode in the civil parish of Kilkeary near Nenagh. That man, great-great-great-grandfather of General Sir William, had a daughter Elizabeth who married another Carrol, James of Tulla, son of Richard, Clerk of the Crown and Peace, King's County, and grandson of Thomas, Mayor and Alderman of Dublin, who was knighted in 1609. Burke states that Elizabeth brought Lissen (= Lisheen)/Kilkeary to James.

Strangely there are no Carrols/Carrolls in Ballycrenode/Ballycrynett or Kilkeary in the Civil Survey, 1640; Census, 1659-60; Hearth Money Rolls, 1665-7. But Donagh Carrol was in Ballykeveen (now Ballyquiveen) in 1640 and that townland is only separated by one townland and a mile across country from both Ballycrenode and Kilkeary. And a gravestone in Kilkeary cemetery records: 'Here lies the body of William Carroll of Ballygrenode Gentleman, who died the nineteenth day of February Anno. Dom. 1706'. He seems likely to have been the ancestor, five steps back, referred to above. The gravestone is a flat slab on the ground, close to the pyramid marking General Carrol's grave.

The Captain Carrol whose name is still associated in local lore with Lissenhall, another Big House in the family, was William Hutchinson Carrol, General Sir William's son. The Captain's daughters, Alice Isabel, Maude Rose and Florence Kate are the Misses Carrol of living memory in the Lissenhall district. They feature in June O'Carroll Robertson's warm-hearted family saga, cited above, using prime sources. The General-baronet is the central figure in its first section, 'The Age of Tulla'. Lissenhall house is now de-roofed.

41. According to Sheehan, *N. & its N.*, the first Holmes came to Ireland as Private Secretary to Wentworth, earl of Strafford, in 1630, and unlike his ill-fated master, kept his head and settled in Ireland.

The family's advent to North Tipperary dates from the purchase of Peterfield estate, Puckane, in 1728 by the first Peter Holmes from the family of Captain Benjamin Barry who was the grantee under the

Cromwellian Plantation of Grace, Hogan, Kennedy and Carroll lands. It comprised 'the lands of Killodiernan alias Johnstown, Ballyflin, part of Creagh (Creeagh/Criagh) and Clery (Claree), with the house and garden now or formerly enjoyed or in the occupation of Richard Haly, 540 acres, Irish Plantation Measure Total.' The modern townlands of Shanavally, Knockanacartan and Johnstown correspond; Johnstown probably acquired its name from John Barry, Benjamin's son. Sources: Registry of Deeds Lib 60 p. 81 No. 3995, Deed dated 19 February 1728, Matthew Bunbury and John Barry to Peter Holmes of Gallen in King's Co. for consideration of £4,437; 1768 map by John Moynahan of the estate of 625a 2r 45 p, statute measure, including Poulawee Lough's 65 acres; 1865 map by A. H. Crawford, County Surveyor, of the estate.

The Peter Holmes, Jun., of the 1830s was the fourth Peter, son of the third who had rotated his residence between Debsboro, Ballinaclough and the continent (he died at Lausanne in November 1843).

That third Peter's residence at Debsborough was due to the marriage of the daughter of his older second cousin, the second Peter, to John Bayly of Debsboro in a typically interwoven net of ascendancy families. That second Peter's wife had been Elizabeth Prittie of the later Dunalley dynasty (Peter and Elizabeth built Johnstown House, Puckane, in 1777). His father Robert Holmes had bought Nenagh in 1733 from Nehemiah Donnellan who had bought it thirty years previously from the second Duke of Ormonde, James Butler. The ownership of Nenagh manor and hence the ground rents of town property had passed down to our fourth Peter, Jun., from a brother, George, of Robert's father, the first Peter.

The fourth Peter predeceased his continental-hopping father by six months. The black-bordered *Nenagh Guardian* obituary eulogised:

Death of Peter Holmes, Jun., Esq., of Nenagh

With a sorrow as deep as it is unavailing, we announce the demise of the best of human beings; of one in whom were blended the rare qualifications of head and heart. One in whom the aristocracy of rank was only secondary to that of nature. It is with emotions of deep and poignant grief, that we announce the death of him whose name heads this obituary; who is now before the throne of his Heavenly Master, receiving the reward of just men made perfect. After an illness of some weeks which terminated in gout reaching the stomach, Mr Holmes, who was a Deputy Lieutenant, and Justice of Peace of this county, at his residence, Summerville, about the hour of Four o'Clock, on the 28th inst. ceased to be numbered amongst the living. He was the Lord of the Manor of Nenagh; and in the 45th year of his age. He has left an amiable Widow and three young children (a son and two daughters) to deplore, with deep and lasting sorrow, his decease. No obituary can do justice to his character. In him the Poor have lost a friend indeed; and well may they mourn his loss in the bitterness of grief; for his charity was extensive, and as liberal as it was secret. No calamity by death in this Riding could have created so deep and so general a sensation of sorrow and regret.

The Holmes connection with the Nenagh area continues in the presence of Mrs Rosalie Goodbody, née Holmes, best known as a former resident of 'St David's', Urra, on the shore of Lough Derg. She is in direct line from the George mentioned above and a grand-daughter of William Bassett Holmes who bought part of Nenagh town when it was sold under the Encumbered Estates Court in 1853. Johnstown House and Summerville no longer exist.

42. Richard Wills Gason (1774-1844) was a son of Richard Gason (1743-1829) and Alicia, daughter of Wills Crofts and Eleanor Freeman, Cork – the names Freeman and Wills Crofts were to figure as Christian names in later generations. Gasons lived on the Dromineer road on the outskirts of Nenagh in the townland of Richmond, formerly Killoshallo. He was great-grandson of Joseph Gason who was a descendant (possibly a grandson) of John Gason who bought Broder townland's approximate 640 acres in the early 1700s from the earl of Anglesey. Presumably John Gason was the one to re-christen it Richmond. Broder, partly in Monsea and partly in Nenagh parishes, had been Cleary and O'Brien lands until the Cromwellian confiscation and Charles II settlement saw them end up as shared by the then Arthur, earl of Anglesey (a royalist), Edward Worth who was Church of Ireland Bishop of Limerick, and William Rickerdicke or Bickerdicke, a Cromwellian soldier. A John Gayson, similarly identified by D. F. Gleeson in *The Last Lords of Ormond* as a Cromwellian soldier, had got 1,219 statute acres in Upper Ormond. Sources: the *Book of Survey and Distribution*; elaboration by Daniel Grace. R. W. Gason's great-grandfather, Joseph, married Dorothea, dau. of Richard Waller of Cully/Castlewaller, a Cromwellian grantee. R. W. was thus a third cousin of Lord Bloomfield whose mother, Charlotte Waller, was a daughter of Samuel Waller, Richard Waller's grandson.

The *Nenagh Guardian* (28 Sept 1844) obituary:

Died, at Kingstown, on Wednesday last, where, with his family, he resided for the last month for the benefit of his health, which, for some time past, had been declining, Richard Wills Gason, Esq. of Richmond, near Nenagh – a Magistrate and Deputy Lieutenant of the County – in the 70th year of his age. Mr Gason was a man greatly esteemed and highly regarded for his moral worth – his stern integrity – and his sound judgement. In the performance of his duties as a Magistrate, Grand Juror, and High Sheriff, he was zealous and impartial; – in his friendships, warm and sincere: – and his domestic ties and associations, most affectionate, beloved, and happy. As a Christian, he was like unto the 'just man for whom Death hath no terrors' – for his hopes were in Him 'who giveth and taketh away' – Mr Gason is succeeded in the family estates by his oldest son, Richard Gason, Esq.

There is a handsome wall memorial to R. W. in St Mary's Church of Ireland church, Nenagh. The Gason name ended in the Nenagh area in 1962 with the death of Richard's great-great grandson, Freeman. The Richmond house is de-roofed. Extra sources: *Burke's Landed Gentry* and Ormond Historical Society, *Kenyon St, Nenagh, Gravestone Inscriptions* (Nenagh, 1982).

43. Henry (1807-85), third Baron Dunalley as of 1854, got his turn as High Sheriff in 1840. The following year he married Anne Maria Louise O'Callaghan, the third daughter of Viscount Lismore.

44. Richard Edward Phillips (1804-63), Mount Rivers, is probably a descendant of the Parliamentary/Cromwellian officer, Thomas Phelps, who received grants of land in the Newport area in lieu of arrears of pay. A later generation married (c.1700) Joan, daughter of John Stumbles, a grantee of the townlands where Mount Rivers house was subsequently built. Richard Edward was magistrate for both counties Tipperary and Limerick for thirty years and a grand jury member for twenty-six years. His eldest son predeceased him and his second son died in 1867 leaving only daughters, the eldest of whom married Wyndham Gabbett and resided in Mount Rivers. The house, though no longer in Phillips ownership, is still occupied. Sources: *N.G.*, 31 Jan 1863; Mr Pakie Ryan, Newport; C. O. R. Phillips, letter to Nenagh District Heritage Centre, 4 Feb 1988. The Samuel Phillips of Gaile, Cashel, who served as a grand juror may be of the same family as the Newport Phillips but this has not been established. Phillips acquired Gaile by marriage with a daughter of the Max owner – Peter Meskell, *A History of Boherlahan-Dualla* (1987), p. 246.

45. Brian M. Walker, *Parliamentary Election Results in Ireland*, 1901-1922 (Dublin, 1978), pp. 238-9; Dunalley Papers, MS, PC 870, NLI, undated; Donoughmore Papers, D/28/4, Donoughmore to the earl of Kingston (whose Mitchelstown estate straddled the Cork-Tipperary border), 1 Mar 1819; Dunalley Papers, PC 873, Glengall to Dunalley, 20 Oct 1828. The political accommodation of 1819-26 between William Bagwell and F. A. Prittie, may have facilitated the marriage of William's nephew, John Bagwell, to F. A.'s daughter Fanny – Burke, *History of Clonmel*, p. 325. The Dunalley Papers, MS PC 870, NLI, included John's letter from Marlfield, Clonmel, on 2 May 1838 to Mrs Prittie 'begging permission to hand the enclosed to your daughter – an honest declaration of affection … patiently wait for your decision and your sanction'. Did F. A.'s arduous travels to the assizes occasion her company and hence fruitful social contact? R. V. Comerford, 'Tipperary representation at Westminster, 1801-1918' in Nolan and McGrath eds, *Tipperary History and Society* (Dublin, 1985), pp. 325-6 touches on this period.

46. *Burkes Landed Gentry*; Thomas P. Power in *Land, Politics and Society in Eighteenth-Century Tipperary* (Oxford, 1993) has a strong sub-chapter on marriage patterns among the 'landed society'.

47. Michael Delany, 'The Tithe Question in the Silvermines Area', *The Guardian* (Nenagh), 31 December 1938, quoting *Burke's Landed Gentry* and an unidentified newspaper of 24 August 1861.

48. Michael Delany, cited above, in this aspect drawing on the Wellesley MSS, MSS 37298, British Library Additional.

   The Irish Tithe Composition Acts comprised 4 Geo IV, cap 99 (1823), as amended by 5 Geo IV, cap 63 (1824) and 7 & 8 Geo IV, cap 60 (1827). To them we owe the Tithe Applotment Books, the prime family history and land use source for the 1820s, retained in the N.A., Bishop St. Dublin.

49. June O'Carroll Robertson, cited above, pp. 18-26 quotes one version of the duel, written in 1895 by John Ryan, the Dunalley gardener at Kilboy. The climax of the story is when a thrust of the Carrol sword sounds off armour worn by the officer. Carrol's second hints in Irish, a language that the Englishman would not know: 'Don't you know, sir, where Daly sticks the sheep in Tulla'. So Carrol takes the hint by plunging the sword in the officer's neck.

   I had heard the story previously, in a version which had the tip given by an old peasant woman who had somehow seen the officer don armour beneath his dress, and the killing of a pig alluded to rather than a sheep. A similar story is told by Desmond Fitzgerald, the Knight of Glin, apropos an ancestor whose family portrait hangs in Glin Castle.

50. *C.A.*, 17 & 21 Dec 1836.

51. John Frederick Trant (d. 1838), D.L., was married to a first cousin of Lord Dunalley, namely Caroline, daughter of Francis Brooke, Co. Fermanagh, and Hannah Prittie, Kilboy, sister of the first baron Dunalley. Trant's lands lay mainly in Dovea, in Loughmoe West civil parish near Thurles. His son, also John, became High Sheriff for the county in 1847 and was very much in the spotlight as a grand jury member in 1858 during the trial of Daniel and William Cormack who were charged with the murder of his land agent/steward John Ellis. They were found guilty and subsequently executed outside the County Gaol in Nenagh. His grandson Lawrence Dominick was the last Trant to farm the estate as it was sold in the mid-1940s. It is now the headquarters of the South-Eastern Cattle Breeding Association – *Burke's Irish Family Records* (1976).

52. George Ryan (1791-1884), lived at Inch on the Thurles-Nenagh road. He was third son of George and Mary (née Roche, Limerick) and great-great-grandson of Daniel Ryan (d. 1692) who had bought the former O'Fogarty lands in the parish of Inch from Edward Annesly the Cromwellian grantee. His paternal grandmother was McCarthy of Springfield and his great-grandmother a Mathew of Annfield. Inch was to remain in Ryan ownership until sold in the 1980s when the then owner, his great-great-grandson, Arthur George, emigrated to New Zealand. *Burke's Irish Family Records* (1976) and Mr Jim Condon, Thurles. The present owner is Mr John Egan, MCC, and a Chairman in recent years of Tipperary (N.R.) County Council.

53. *T.C.*, 22 Dec 1836.

54. John Cahill (1805-50) is doubly interesting. He was one of the second wave of young middle-class Catholics to benefit from the dismantling of the Penal Laws, thus allowing entry to the legal profession. He was the first son of Cornelius and Margaret (née Fogarty), Rathleasty, Thurles, and entered apprenticeship in Trinity term 1822. The necessary affidavit as to age and education was sworn by Philip Cahill, attorney, and probably John's uncle – he is described as the second son of John and Agnes (née Fogarty) whose affidavit was supplied by his brother Cornelius, on entering apprenticeship in 1808. That date suggests that Philip can be categorised with the Nenagh Dillons (see Chapter Six) as among the first wave of beneficiaries of relief from the Penal Laws. – King's Inns Admission Papers (Ir Manuscripts Commission, 1982).

John Cahill's second claim to elaboration is in the context of the Mulgrave reforms described in the Prologue. Cahill was one of the crown solicitors appointed by the Whig administration of 1835-41 who neatly combined positive discrimination for Catholic nationalists, to atone for the opposite practice of the past, with jobs for their own supporters under the pact with O'Connell. The following is from the same 1839 apologia by R. L. Sheil, MP, as is quoted in the Prologue.

> An itinerant crown solicitor goes down twice a year to the assizes of a county, in which he does not reside; the panel is called; and is he, from mere whim, or in a freak of authoritative caprice, to order respectable men, who have come, pursuant to a summons, a distance, perhaps, of forty miles, to be put aside? Why, Sir, the member for Tamworth [Peel, immediate past Prime Minister] ought to be the last man in this house to advocate such a practice; for his Juries Bill in this country was introduced, among other purposes, to prevent the packing of juries in criminal cases in this country. Sir Michael O'Loghlen did no more than act in conformity with its spirit in Ireland. With respect to the appointment of local crown solicitors at sessions, no measure has been more useful; and if Mr Howley, the assistant barrister of Tipperary, has won from men of all sides the most unqualified encomium – if his talents, his temper, his discrimination, his patience, and every other judicial quality, have been the theme of panegyric; and if he has put down, as he has done, the class of crime falling within his jurisdiction in Tipperary; it is right that I should add, that he told me, and authorised me to state, that he derived the most essential assistance from the local solicitor, Mr Cahill, a gentleman of great abilities and of the highest character, who was appointed under Lord Normanby's government.

55. *T.C.*, 26 Oct 1838.
56. *T.C.*, 27 Dec 1836.
57. *T.C.*, 27 Dec 1836.
58. *C.J.*, 29 Dec 1836.
59. *T.C.*, 27 Dec 1836.
60. *T.C.*, 27 Dec 1836. Cornwallis Maude (1780-1856), otherwise 3rd

Viscount Hawarden, was son of Cornwallis Maude, Baron de Montalt, who became Viscount Hawarden in 1793. The third Viscount had inherited the title on the death of his half-brother, the second Viscount, in 1807. The third Viscount was four generations on from Robert Maude of West Riddlesden, Yorkshire, who had bought lands in Kilkenny and Tipperary. Robert parented Anthony who became MP for Cashel in 1686 and High Sheriff for the county in 1695. Anthony's son Robert (d. 1750) was created a baronet of Ireland in 1705.

The Lord Hawarden of the 1830s was married to Jane Crawford, Buckinghamshire, and their only son, also Cornwallis, became the 4th Viscount. However, that man's only son and heir was killed in 1886 in the British-Zululand War, so the direct male line terminated on his own death in 1905. The 3rd Viscount's eldest brother was married to Martha Elizabeth, eldest daughter of Francis Aldborough Prittie and niece to Lord Dunalley – *Burke's Peerage & Baronetage*, 1878.

61. *T.C.*, 27 Dec 1836.
62. *T.C.*, 30 Dec 1836.
63. *C.A.*, 2, 9, July; *T.F.P.*, 23 Jul 1834.
64. *C.A.*, 3 June 1837.
65. *C.A.*, 11 Jan 1837. There is a profile of Glengall at the point of his late entry into the fray in Chapter Four.
66. Council Office Papers VI-VIC (N.A.). The corresponding Minutes of the Privy Council (also N.A.), folio 540, 17 December 1836, expressed its intention as to divide Cashel division into two districts. Apparently a 'Cashel division' had previously had quarter sessions alternating in Cashel and Clonmel, and another division had ones alternating in Thurles and Nenagh – the venues were specified, e.g. Cashel and Nenagh, Thurles and Clonmel, Clonmel and Nenagh, in newspaper advertisements.
    That meeting had before it reports from the Attorney-General on applications relating to various counties. The applications were for additional sessions and session towns and were enabled by section 53 of 6 & 7 William IV, c. 75, An Act to extend the jurisdiction and regulate the Proceedings of the Civil Bill Courts in *Ireland* (13 August 1836). County Mayo was also allocated three divisions on the same occasion; Antrim, Armagh, Donegal, Kerry, Kilkenny, King's County, Limerick and Louth also had some adjustments.

CHAPTER THREE

'The question excited the greatest interest
among the gentlemen connected with Tipperary'

BEFORE THE PRIVY COUNCIL

The Nenagh and Thurles memorials came before the Privy Council in February 1837 and were referred to a Committee of itself which sat on 16 June 1837.[1]

Two persons attended both the two Committee and two Council sessions which respectively recommended and took the crucial decisions in Tipperary's case. They were Anthony Richard Blake, Chief Remembrancer of the Treasury, prototype Department of Finance Secretary, once described as 'the backstairs Viceroy of Ireland', and Judge Louis Perrin, ex-MP for Cashel Borough (January-August 1835). The Lord Chancellor, Baron William Conyngham Plunket, and the Officer Commanding the Forces in Ireland, Lieut.-Gen. Sir Edward Blakeney, attended three of the sessions as did the only non-official regularly involved, Thomas Francis Kennedy, a Dublin lawyer. Two former Attorneys-General, now judges, John Richards, Fourth Baron of the Exchequer, and Michael O'Loghlen, Master of the Rolls, attended two sessions. The serving Attorney-General, Nicholas Ball, who attended the second Privy Council meeting which finalised the question, was the sitting MP for Clonmel Borough since the 1836 by-election.[2]

To put in perspective the high-level attention given to the case in an era of uncluttered administration one might contemplate the Council of State or a Joint Committee of Oireachtas front benchers and the judiciary conducting an inquiry, open to press and public, today on such a local issue.

The four peers who skipped the detailed committee investigations but signed the eventual proclamation, the Duke of Leinster, the Marquess of Headfort, the earl of Charlemont and Baron Cloncurry, had aggregate land holdings of 130,000 acres. They were in a position to appreciate the problems of expense and inconvenience reported from the Committee as pleaded by such as Lords Dunalley (21,000 acres) and Bloomfield (9,900 acres) for Nenagh, Nicholas Maher (4,500 acres)

83

for Thurles, and Lord Hawarden (15,300 acres) for Dundrum.[3]

THE CASE STATED

So, an atmosphere of political, social and administrative reform, as recounted in the Prologue, and a spirit of open enquiry, enlightened by judicial expertise and background knowledge, was present on 16 June 1837 for the Committee session appointed in February. I have failed to find either the Nenagh or Thurles written memorials but the presentation of the case and cross-examination of witnesses is recorded in the Council Office papers[4] and in the *Clonmel Advertiser* of 21 June 1837.

O'Brien Dillon, the Nenagh attorney, had drawn up the memorial for the Nenagh-oriented Dunalley/Carrol committee. Two King's Counsel, George Bennett and David R. Pigot (a future MP for Clonmel Borough, Solicitor-General as of February 1839 and promoted to Attorney-General in August 1840),[5] appeared for Nenagh, assisted by Charles Rolleston, a native of Glasshouse, Shinrone, just over the border in the old Ely O'Carroll territory long lost to King's County. O'Brien Dillon was named as their agent.

John Hatchell, KC, led for Thurles, backed by Philip Fogarty who had been among the 136 signatories to the requisition for the original Thurles rally and whose nephew, John Cahill, was the county's Crown Solicitor as of January 1836. Cahill and a 'Mr Hanley' (probably Joseph Hanly, Cahill's brother-in-law) were named as agents 'for the people of Thurles'.[6]

Pigot and Fogarty had served with Judge Perrin as Commissioners inquiring into the Municipal Corporations in 1835; they were two of the Catholics among the six who joined six Protestants in that example of the even-handed approach of the Whigs to government and administration. Again, Pigot and Fogarty had been involved as advocates in the most recent Special Commission to sit in the county; Hatchell had been sent down by the government to defend accused persons on that occasion, an early example of free legal aid and further evidence of liberal philosophy in high office.[7]

The question excited the greatest interest among the gentlemen connected with Tipperary, many of whom rallied behind their counsel upon the side to which they wished success. Among those who were favourably disposed to the northern division, or Nenagh, were observed Lord Dunalley and his nephew (Mr Prittie), Lord Bloomfield and the Hon. Mr Bloomfield, Captain Hayley, Messrs Poe, Falkiner, Bayly etc. Among the advocates of ... Thurles were Messrs Phillips (Gaile), Stephen Egan (Roscrea),[8] Mulcahy,

Hennessy, Meagher, O'Brien, etc., etc.[9]

General Carrol, secretary to the first lobbyists in the field, was a notable absentee; he was almost certainly out of the country at the time. The Nenagh camp had, however, a formidable acquisition in Bloomfield father and son. Lord Bloomfield, it will be recalled, was a prime mover in the campaign, at least as early as 1834. The son, John Arthur Douglas Bloomfield, second Baron (1802-1879), among the rallying gentlemen recorded, followed father's diplomatic career only, entering it at sixteen years of age. At the time of his appearance at the hearing of the Tipperary division case he was secretary to the United Kingdom legation in Sweden (father's former embassy) and later became ambassador in turn to Russia, to Prussia and to the Austrian Empire.[10]

RELATIONSHIPS

Further evidence of the matrix of political experience and of its practitioners' inter-relationships is given by that list of gentlemen in attendance. The Nenagh advocate, Dillon, and the Thurles supporters Egan and (the presumed) Thomas Hennessy were members of the Tipperary Society for the Suppression of Outrage and the Maintenance of Peace which had been formed in April 1836. The objectives incorporated in its name were seen, by its inaugural resolutions and by its list of duties for members of associations to be formed in each parish, to focus on 'every trace of agrarian outrages and factious riots in this county' and on 'bad characters', identifiable as Whiteboys and faction fighters.[11]

A large majority of the founders were Catholic and of that social class midway between the larger landowners and the peasantry – doctors, attorneys, businessmen, and farming middlemen who were sometimes also owners and land agents.[12] They had become highly politicised in the anti-tithes campaign and in the Catholic Association prior to Emancipation, 'an organisation that political scientists have argued was the first true mass political party in the world, ante-dating the Jacksonian Democrats in the United States by several years'.[13] Among the Committee members of the Tipperary Society with Dillon and Egan were Francis Aldborough Prittie, Attorney-General Ball, and Patrick Kirwan and George Ryan of the original Thurles pro-division lobby. Two others of the Thurles Committee, Robert Lidwill and Charles O'Keefe, were also founder-members of that Society.[14]

The Falkiners of Mount Falcon, Borrisokane, the Poes of Solsboro, Nenagh, and the Baylys of Debsborough, Ballinaclough, Nenagh, are names redolent of Ormond Protestant society. Frederick Falkiner was the County's Clerk of the Crown in 1837 and John Bayly became High Sheriff of the county in 1846. In another monograph in the series we will meet R. H. Falkiner and J. J. Poe as long-serving chairmen of the Borrisokane and Nenagh Boards of Guardians.[15]

It would become clear from the cases presented that the Nenagh lobby had obviously seen the wisdom of the Thurles stress on the need for six baronies in a northern division, rather than for the four only, which had been their original concern. No doubt, it would have been a consideration that such a common front on the primary question of division of the county would be more likely to impress the Privy Council. Divided opinions on the subsidiary question as to the most suitable new assize town had now emerged in Roscrea, more or less equidistant from Nenagh and Thurles, as seen in the lining up on opposite sides by Egan and by Henry Prittie.

THE CASE EXPLORED

Mr Bennett, KC on the Nenagh team, stressed that Tipperary was one of the most extensive counties in Ireland and proposed a division between six northern baronies and five southern ones thus:

	Acres	Population
N.	213,246	198,649
S.	212,932	203,914

Clonmel, he went on was on the verge of Waterford, 43 miles from Nenagh for jurors, witnesses and prosecutors. When litigious debtors chose to appeal, the creditor found it less expensive to give up his property, than go as far as Clonmel with witnesses .... In some instances, it was found that the respondent in an appeal had to remain six or seven days, with nearly as many witnesses in Clonmel, and when he finally succeeded in recovering the amount of his property, he was a considerable loser by his success.[16]

I have already noted that the Nenagh-Clonmel distance represented eight or nine hours travelling by horse-drawn coach. The mileages quoted throughout the hearing were in the Irish measurement which was longer than the British one later adopted in Ireland.

In the five years 1832-6, Bennett claimed, the respective case-loads for the six northern baronies and five southern were, respectively: civil bill cases – 9,235 and 5,997; crown cases – 8,616 and 5,875.

Mr Pigot took up the running with a breakdown of the 8,616 crown cases into 4,833 originating in the Nenagh area and 3,783 in Thurles.

His analysis of civil bills relating to Nenagh and Thurles respectively gave a ratio of 3 to 2.[17]

The Master of the Rolls, Michael O'Loghlen, now asked Mr Hatchell, KC, leading for Thurles, if he was prepared to show that the county should not be divided. Hatchell made a token mention of a majority of the Grand Jury being against it but negatived this by admitting that the majority of that body was from the southern division. Any division, he thought, should be as proclaimed recently for (quarter) sessions.[18]

NENAGH VERSUS THURLES

Hatchell swept on to claim the assizes for Thurles. Borrisoleigh (1,304 population) was only 6 miles distant as against 12 from Nenagh; Templemore (2,936) was 7 miles as against 16 or 17 from Nenagh. Memorials from those towns and Roscrea (5,512) protested against Nenagh (8,466) and preferred Thurles (7,084). Thurles was a superior market town.[19]

Baron Richards asked if it were a grievance to be made to go 18 miles to Nenagh instead of 22 to Clonmel. Hatchell responded that the badness of the Nenagh road made all the difference; it had a mountain barrier. Bennett interjected a denial – it was a level and excellent road.[20]

Hatchell continued that there was no plan or estimate for a Courthouse and Gaol at Nenagh. They would cost, say, £25,000, not including land purchase. At Thurles there was a Courthouse, Bridewell and any quantity of land which Lady Llandaff had promised to give free. With an addition of £7,000, all could be done.[21]

The Thurles counsel now called as a witness Patrick Leahy, County Surveyor for the east riding of Cork, who had been a land surveyor and shopkeeper in Thurles up to fifteen years previously. His evidence related to road mileages, and to a figure of £4,000 for extension of Thurles Gaol from its present bridewell accommodation of 70 to 130 or 140; his total for enlarging it and the Thurles Courthouse was £7,000. Judge Perrin intervened to tell Bennett that it was not necessary to cross-examine Leahy on the latter point as it was quite plain that he did not understand the building of gaols or courthouses.[22]

Nicholas Maher, Turtulla House, Thurles, later a Tipperary MP (1844-52), said they had very little intercourse with Nenagh; they did not want to pay for what would be a disadvantage.[23] Cross-examined by Rolleston, he said he did not know that 16,000 acres would be more convenient to Nenagh than Thurles.[24] Philip Fogarty, the Thurles junior counsel, countered Rolleston's argument on acreage by claiming that 19,132 people would be benefited more by a selection of Thurles.

He proposed Clonmel-Kilkenny-Thurles as a suitable circuit for Leinster judges.[25]

Stephen Egan, Roscrea, also gave evidence in favour of Thurles. He said that there was a regular car travelling between Roscrea and Thurles. There were two turnpikes on the Nenagh road. The Roscrea memorial was signed by the principal men of business; some signed who were from the Queen's County but he did not know how their names got onto it.[26] John O'Meara, Templemore, and Stephen Ryan, Borrisoleigh, weighed in for Thurles. Ryan claimed he travelled the Nenagh road the previous day and it was going to ruin.[27]

THE EXECUTIVE VIEW

A succession of public officials now took the stand. Richard Maybury Duckett, Sub-Sheriff and a Clonmel resident, led, and his evidence must have been a watershed. Neither town, he thought, had sufficient accommodation at present. There would be a sufficient supply of jurors from the six baronies. There was never a good attendance from Ormond at Clonmel: he was tired summoning them, although a considerable part of the business came from Ormond and Owney and Arra. Attendance, however, was good at both Nenagh and Thurles sessions, with a better record at Nenagh. There was a new military barracks at Nenagh, a small one at Thurles; military constantly escorted prisoners from Nenagh.[28]

Then came the unsurprising opinion, educed by Pigot, that Newport, Ballina, Toomevara and Cloughjordan (all small towns under 1,000 population in the Nenagh catchment area) would find Nenagh more convenient. Assuming that Thurles were the assize town, the three northern baronies would be more sufferers than the middle baronies would be benefited by Nenagh. Then the Lord Chancellor asked a key question: 'which would be the fittest town from his knowledge'.

Duckett: 'Nenagh would be the town.'

James Carmichael, Clerk of the Crown, gave a similar reply, but Thomas Sadleir, Clerk of the Peace and also a Clonmel resident, could not 'hazard an opinion'.[29] On one point he was clear, however – the Thurles-Nenagh road by Borrisoleigh which was complained of was one of the finest in Europe for he had made it himself. Although the Committee minutes did not record this professional opinion, the *Clonmel Advertiser* did and added: '(laughter)'.[30]

Major James Palmer, Inspector of Prisons (a central government official), put paid to any silent and absent Clonmel interest by echoing his own 1828 report: there was not sufficient gaol accommodation in Clonmel; it needed additions. He then turned to Thurles – it would be a mistake to enlarge its Bridewell. £14,000 would build a Gaol of 140 cells according to present fashion; a plainer building on the Barrack plan for £8,000 would not be so safe a one.

John B. Keane, architect, deposed that he had examined Nenagh and thought the locality favourable for the necessary buildings. He had estimated £15,000 for gaol and courthouse for 100 prisoners and four baronies.

Lord Dunalley, to nobody's surprise, believed Nenagh the most central and affirmed that there would be no difficulty in getting a sufficient attendance of grand and petty jurors.[31]

Lord Bloomfield tossed in Nenagh's proximity to slate quarries as an advantage. And countered the Thurles card of free land by expressing an understanding that Lord Norbury would give whatever ground was required, as he held property for ever under the Holmes family.[32] This assurance was the subject of an extraordinary story by 'a late professional gentleman' in a book published almost sixty years later. It is best told in Chapter Five in relation to the hearing of the Commissioners for valuing the land for courthouse and gaol at Nenagh.

It would be fanciful to suggest that Dunalley, the 62-year-old, and Bloomfield, the 69-year-old, had won the day by getting in last – bringing up the heavy artillery, so to speak, as their opponents' attack was spent. Sufficient whimsy to note that Dunalley's motto was *In omnia paratus* (prepared for everything); Bloomfield's was *Fortes fortuna juvat* (fortune favours the brave).[33]

THE COMMITTEE RECOMMENDS

The reality must have been that the factual evidence on distances and case loads was the principal influence on the recommendation of the Committee, recorded thus in the secretary's notes:

> County to be divided – Assizes to continue on Leinster Circuit and Report in favour of Nenagh as the assizes Town – New District to consist of the Six Baronies of Upper Ormond, Lower Ormond, Owney and Arra, Ikerrin, Eliogarty and Kilnamanagh.[34]

The *Clonmel Advertiser* of Saturday 17 June, the day following the hearing, could only report the call-up of witnesses to Dublin. But, true to form, it gave an editorial dig to the 'wanton and unnecessary expense' which another courthouse and gaol would involve. That, together with 'recently imposed imposts on this county must eventually impoverish all the farmers' – a heart-rending cry that has been echoed through the ages. Its issue of Wednesday, 21 June 1837 carried the report of the

Plate 10: Summerville, home of Peter Holmes, Jun., in the 1830s; also given as the address of O'Brien Dillon. It was a double house (rear portion partly visible) – photo courtesy of Hodgins family.

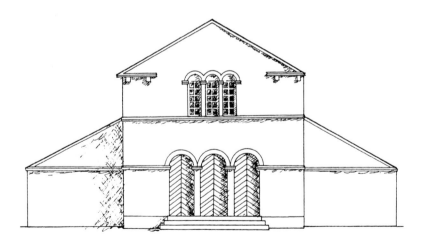

Plate 11: Thurles Courthouse
– drawing by Deirdre O'Dowd, based on the extant building and on Jim Condon's original drawing in the Co. Library, Thurles.

Committee hearing. It also reported that Lord Bloomfield had visited the Chancellor of the Exchequer on the previous day. It repeated the division story on Saturday 24 June and noted:

> On last Tuesday evening there was a bonfire made at the gate of Summerville, the residence of O'Brien Dillon, Esq., to honour him for the very active part he took in preparing evidence for the Privy Council relative to having Nenagh an Assizes Town.
> A large bonfire and general illumination is expected one of the coming evenings in commemoration of the decision of the Lord Lieutenant and Privy Council.

The paper added: 'We are of opinion that this is no time for rejoicement.' On the same evening as the bonfire, King William IV had died. Nenagh's enhanced status was to coincide with the opening of Queen Victoria's long reign.

STATE OF THE COUNTY, LATE JUNE 1837

The pertinent terms of the enabling statute, applied to Tipperary, were its great extent, the inconvenient situation of its assize town, Clonmel, and, if the county were to be divided, the designation of the baronies to form each riding and of a town 'most expedient' for assizes in addition to the traditional assize town. Each aspect had been debated before a tribunal of eminent national figures by experienced professional advocates who had as witnesses men of stature in the respective communities. Tribunal members, advocates and witnesses had a deep familiarity with the county and its constituent districts and had an accumulation of administrative skill and political acumen.

The 16 June hearing had produced a clear-cut set of recommendations. But they still had to be considered by the deciding authority – the Lord Lieutenant 'by and with the advice of the Privy Council'. Meantime, the first stage had seen an amazing absence of organised dissent by Clonmel from the proposed division, itself an indication of the weight of the case for division. It also appeared that the centre-county Dundrum-Kilnamanagh demur had lost by default at that crucial stage. But appearances could deceive.

Nenagh had secured endorsement of its case for the prize of assize town in the battle against Thurles by a combination of high-calibre advocacy, the disinterested opinions of county officials, and the evidence of case-loads as between the two towns' catchment areas.

Notes

1. Council Office Papers, VI-VIC (N.A., previously at the S.P.O.).
2. Brian M. Walker, *Parliamentary Election Results in Ireland 1801-1922*, p. 261.
3. Local Government Board, *Return of Owners of Land in Ireland, 1876* (Dublin, 1876 & Baltimore, 1988).
4. Council Office Papers, VI-VIC.
5. Walker, cited above, p. 262. Following the elevation of Nicholas Ball to the bench, Pigot was in effect imposed on Clonmel borough by the government. Dublin Castle persuaded Francis Aldborough Prittie to have his son withdraw his rumoured candidature. 'The rep of Clonmel is looked to with a view to place one of the law officers in the House of Commons and this arrangement will be entirely overturned if that point cannot be accomplished.' (Dunalley Papers, PC 869 & 870, N.L.I. MS).
6. *C.A.,* 21 June 1837. Agnes Margaret Cahill a sister of John Cahill (see note 54, Chapter Two) married Joseph Hanly, solicitor to the Ursuline Sisters, Thurles. The legal profession predominated Cahill vocations. John's brothers included Cornelius, solicitor, Llandaff Lodge, Thurles, and MacGrath, barrister, Dublin. Another sister, Charlotte Alicia, married George Bourke, solicitor, Liscahill House, Thurles. A Hanly daughter married Stephen W. Coppinger, solicitor, Thurles. The profession is still represented in Thurles town by Mary Barry, a great-grand niece of John Cahill. I am indebted to Dr Myles Shortall, a great-great-grandnephew of the Cahills for a detailed family tree, based on one drawn for him by his maternal grandmother. John Cahill and many members of that extended family are buried in Drom graveyard.
7. *T.F.P.,* 10 Jan 1839.
8. Egan was for a long time a leader of Catholic and Liberal circles in Roscrea. For the annual O'Connell 'Tribute' in 1833, 'as usual that steady patriot and friend Stephen Egan gave £5' (*Limerick Evening Herald*, 28 Nov 1833) – this headed the list of subscribers. In 1815 he and his brother Daniel had been the targets of a plot by the Church of Ireland curate, Rev. John Hamilton, which ended with their acquittal at the Clonmel assizes (Rev. John Gleeson, *History of Ely O'Carroll* (Dublin, 1915), pp. 392-3). Stephen was one of those consulted by Dr Kennedy, Bishop of Killaloe, in the successful plan to forestall the Greenboys' march on Shinrone in 1828 (Murphy, cited in Prologue notes, Part 7).
9. *C.A.,* 21 June 1837. Lord Dunalley's nephew Henry was a son of Francis Aldborough Prittie. He got his turn as High Sheriff in 1840 (*N.G.,* 29 Jan 1840) and succeeded to the title as third Baron in 1854.
10. Mary T. Ryan, 'John Arthur Douglas Bloomfield, 1802-1879' in *Newport News 1992*, pp. 27-30.
11. Evidence of John Cahill, Crown Prosecutor, to the Select Committee of the House of Lords appointed to inquire into the PP (State of Ireland in respect of Crime and Outrage), xi and xii, pp. 140-4, 1839.
12. Michael Beames, *Peasants and Power:the Whiteboy Movements and*

their control in Pre-Famine Ireland (Sussex, 1983), pp. 196-7.

13. Quotation: Tom Garvin, book review of Fergus O'Ferrall, *Catholic Emancipation* (Dublin, 1985), in *The Economic and Social Review*, p. 316.

14. State of Ireland inquiry, cited above.

15. John Bayly (1806-1865) was the eldest son of John and Mary Elizabeth Helena (née Uniacke) Bayly, Debsborough, some three miles south of Nenagh. He was the sixth John Bayly since his ancestor of the same name bought former Kennedy and Butler lands in Ballinaclough, near Nenagh in 1703. A second seat at nearby Debsborough was established by a later generation. He was a distant cousin of Lord Dunalley's and of Peter Holmes Jun., as Elizabeth Prittie of Kilboy and Bridget Holmes of Peterfield were his direct ancestors. Baylys continue to farm in Debsborough today. *Burke's Irish Family Records* (1976).

A Jack Poe features in evocative verse dated 1834 and relating to the Ormond Hunt. It was written by Nathaniel Falkiner of Mount Falcon. Also included are Parker (probably Anthony), Peter Holmes and Richard Wills Gason, of Richmond, all involved in the northern-Nenagh campaign. See biographical notes in Chapter Two.

> There's Solsboro' Jack, see how reckless he rides,
> There's Castle Lough Parker, who danger derides,
> For whom no gate is too high, no drain too wide,
> When he shouts Tallyho! in the morning.
> The Atkinsons too were never behind,
> Black Richard, from Richmond, the foremost you'll find,
> And dear Peter Holmes, so gentle and kind,
> Loved to cheer Tallyho! in the morning.

Source: Gems of Local Verse No. 31, *The Guardian*, compiled by Liam Doran, 3 Aug 1985.

16. *C.A.*, 21 June 1837.

17. There is some confusion, probably originating in Counsel's delivery, within and between the minutes of the Privy Council Committee meeting and the *Clonmel Advertiser* report; it is not clear whether the figures given are for one year or for a five-year period.

18. Council Office Papers, VI-VIC.

19. Privy Council minutes, 16 June 1837.

20. *C.A.*, 21 June 1837.

21. Council Office Papers, VI-VIC. Lady Elizabeth Mathew was the only daughter of Francis Mathew, 1st earl Llandaff, who had succeeded to all the Mathew seats in 1777 – Thurles, Thomastown, Annfield, and that in Wales. She was a sister of the late MP, Col. Hon. Montague Mathew. She was eight generations on and a direct descendant of George Mathew (d. 1636) Glamorgan, Wales, who had married Elizabeth (née Preston), widow of Thomas Butler, Viscount Thurles, and the mother of James

Butler who became the 1st Duke of Ormonde. What was left of his inheritance came to Elizabeth on the death of her brother Francis James, the 2nd earl, in 1833 – *Burke's Irish Family Records* (1976). The second earl had sold off some lands including Thurles Castle. After her death in 1841 the estates passed to her first cousin (her mother's nephew), Viscomte de Chabot, who sold Thurles and Thomastown in the Encumbered Estates Court in 1859 – Denis G. Marnane, *Land and Violence* (Tipperary, 1985), pp. 23, 94.

22. *C.A.*, 21 June 1837; Patrick Leahy was from Gortnahoe, Thurles. Mr Brendan O'Donoghue, a descendant, has kindly informed me that Patrick worked in the north of Ireland, 1810-13. He lived in Thurles in 1818 and in Clonmel from 1826.

On 14 Sept 1833 'Patrick Leahy & Sons, Civil Engineers Surveyor, valuer of lands etc.' advertised in the *Tipperary Free Press* their future commitment to this county 'having been engaged in England for the past two or three years … in the estimation of the most celebrated English Engineers "they may be equalled but certainly not excelled."' They had offices at 18 Ann St, Clonmel. The judge's dismissal of Leahy's competence in regard to gaols should be balanced by the commendation he received from Commissioner William Hanna at the Clonmel Corporation sworn inquiry: 'this gentleman's evidence was extremely interesting … there was a satisfaction and a pleasure in examining such witnesses'. – *C.A.*, 23 Oct 1833). In May 1834 Patrick was appointed as County Surveyor for Cork's east riding at a salary of £300 p.a. plus £50 for a clerk and £50 for an office. His son Edward got the appointment for Cork's west riding in the same competition for the whole country. It drew 239 candidates to a prototype local appointments commission which sat for fourteen days at the Custom House. The interviewers were Col. Burgoyne, Chairman of the Board of Works, I. Owen and John Radcliffe (*T.F.P.*, 26 Apr, 21, 28 May 1834). Samuel Jones was appointed for the undivided Tipperary; Samson Carter, son of Major Samson Carter, Resident Magistrate, Nenagh, became Kilkenny's first County Surveyor.

The Leahys combined public and private sector engagements; in 1840 a brother Denis became the contractor for Nenagh workhouse (*T.F.P.*, 1 Apr 1840, *N.G.*, 5 Mar 1842). Another son of Patrick's, also named Patrick, became Archbishop of Cashel and Emly, 1857-75.

23. Council Office Papers, VI-VIC.
24. ditto.
25. ditto, VI-VIC.
26. *C.A.*, 21 June 1887.
27. Council Office Papers, VI-VIC.
28. ditto.
29. ditto.
30. *C.A.*, 21 June 1837.
31. Council Office Papers, VI-VIC.
32. ditto.
33. *Thoms,* 1846.
34. Council Office Papers, VI-VIC.

CHAPTER FOUR

'Henceforth the County of Tipperary shall be divided'

COUNTER-ATTACK

It had seemed as if the division of the county was not being contested, whatever about the prize of designation as an assize town. But a counter-attack on the prestigious Privy Council Committee's recommendation came in the columns of the *Tipperary Constitution* three weeks afterwards, on 7 July 1837. The writer, from London three days previously, of an open letter to the grand jurors of the county thought it 'necessary to call attention to the proposed Plan'.

> The expense of building a courthouse and gaol at Nenagh is estimated at £15,000 and very probably that sum will not suffice, as estimates are not always to be trusted. A house of correction will soon be found to be indispensable and of course additional well-salaried officers must be appointed to it.

The correspondent, Richard Butler, Baron of Cahir and second earl of Glengall (1794-1858), had been MP for Tipperary in 1818-19 and was a representative peer for Ireland in the House of Lords since 1829.[1] He was a direct descendant of the third earl of Ormond[2] who had consolidated the move of the Butler lordship headquarters from Nenagh when he built Gowran Castle, County Kilkenny, and later purchased Kilkenny Castle.[3]

Glengall anticipated two chaplains, a surgeon, an inspector, a gaoler, turnkeys etc. He now set out to rebut points which had been made in favour of division and which had not been expressed in the minute of the 16 June evidence so clearly.

> The saving contemplated consists of a supposition that £3,000 per annum will be gained in the transmission of prisoners, and that the erection of a gaol at Nenagh will render the enlargement of the gaol at Clonmel unnecessary. Placing the contemplated saving ... against the annual deadweight, etc., I am of opinion that a most enormously increased burden of taxation will be

heaped upon our already heavily-rated county. I ... shall conclude by observing that when this proposal of dividing the county was first started, the four northern baronies agreed to pay the expenses of the necessary buildings and since which time it is now intended to place the expense on the whole county, and to add the baronies of Kilnamanagh and Eliogarty to the northern division which I conceive a most objectionable plan and one which is strongly resisted by the principal landowners of these baronies.

The nobleman signed off, in the style of the times, with the affirmation that he had 'the honour to be, gentlemen, your obedient servant'.[4]

THE GLENGALL STYLE

Lineage apart, what manner of nobleman was this servant of the public? He had survived an 1826 duel arising from his being allegedly libelled in *Age* magazine. His motto was 'God be my Guide'. In 1828 he could be perceived as among the great array of prominent Protestants who supported Catholic Emancipation. Like Dunalley, he sent a letter to a Munster meeting in August, explaining inability to attend and expressing support.[5] That October he helped the erection of a Roman Catholic chapel at Dunhill by providing a free site and 'considerable pecuniary assistance'.[6] And he was toasted in the same swig of liquor as the Liberal and Emancipationist earl of Llandaff at the inaugural county Liberal club that same month.[7]

We have already met him as the leading Tipperary Tory, hence predisposed to be at odds with the county's dominant Whigs or Liberals or Reformers. But surely not on a non-party political question. However, the true blue complexion deepens on reading the flavour of the *Dublin Evening Mail*'s report on an 1835 countywide body, a predecessor of the 1837 one mentioned at the end of Chapter Two and also chaired by him; in this instance he was named also as the founder. The portrait then becomes one of a full-blown reactionary on examining the reports of himself and the company he kept at a 'Great Protestant Dinner' in August 1834.

County Club of Tipperary now permanently established: Nobility and gentry may be said to have combined to stand together and assert their legitimate rights and their position in their native county; they have been driven to this measure from the overbearing insolence of the Priests and Demagogues. Chairman and founder earl of Glengall.[8]

96

The Dinner was in honour of the earl of Winchelsea at Morrison's Hotel. The guests included the earls of Longford, Bandon, Norbury and Glengall with the earl of Roden presiding. The toasts included one delivered by Roden to the Duke of Cumberland who had 'expressed strong sentiments of regard and interest for the Protestants of Ireland'; the Lord Lieutenant and prosperity of Ireland (cheers and laughter); the Rev. Charles Boyton and the Protestant Conservative Society (immense applause); the Resident Landlords of Ireland. The earl of Glengall confessed his error in voting for Emancipation.[9]

> I had been a supporter of the Roman Catholics of Ireland for many years, and I voted in favour of Catholic Emancipation. I was then, however, but a short time in Parliament, and I have lived, as I believe a great many others have lived, to repent that act (vehement cheering). Mine was an R.C. family, a family established for hundreds of years ... I believe I express the sentiments and feelings of a great many other peers, when I assert – for I have positively heard them declare – that they do regret the step they have taken with regard to Catholic Emancipation, because it did not answer to any single good, or produce one single beneficial, or advantageous result (hear). The government of the country have lost the confidence of the clergy, the landed proprietors, and the Protestants of Ireland generally; but how could it be otherwise? Every person of rank or property has been banished the precincts of the castle, which is now infested by a set of men who have lately been taken into conclave, who possess neither property in the country, nor the respect nor esteem of its inhabitants – men who are neither landholders nor fundholders, and who have existed more by their wits than by their talents (hear hear, cheers).[10]

In another aspect he fulfilled a role similar to that of his peers in leading local community development. A sample runs from his presenting 'the usual plate of £50 for Caher [thus spelt at the time] Races,[11] and being named with his Countess as the leading figures at the Caher Ball in the Assembly Rooms,[12] to chairing meetings in Cahir, Tipperary and Clonmel which promoted a Suir and Shannon Junction Company,[13] and becoming President of a County Tipperary Agriculture Society. His vice-Presidents in that Society were the neighbouring Lords Waterford, Clonmel, Lismore and Pennefather and, from the far north, Dunalley.[14] As a public man who had succeeded to the earldom at the age of twenty-five, the career of his love life in his fortieth year was most naturally under public scrutiny – worth recording in the notes simply to round out the portrait.[15] One will note there that the poor man was subjected to similar sycophancy from tenants and townspeople as was endured also by his peers.

GRAND JURY MOVE

So, here was a man of stature, a parliamentarian in the upper house, a community leader at home, taking a public stance not hitherto witnessed within the community. There were two drawbacks: he himself had become someone out of tune with the reforming times, and it was the thirteenth hour in the debate. Nevertheless, apparently triggered into action by the long-range missive of July 1837 from the earl, who was also Colonel of the Tipperary Militia, fifteen grand jurors signed a memorial to the Lord Lieutenant and Privy Council:

> praying that no decision on the subject should be made until an opportunity should be afforded to them to set forth such reasons and arguments as would show that any Division of the County is unnecessary.[16]

Although I have not found a record of the signatories, there were exactly fifteen of the summer 1837 Grand Jury drawn from the baronies in the proposed south riding. The northerners on that Grand Jury included Maj.-Gen. Sir William Parker Carrol; one wonders if he averted a formal vote of the Grand Jury (no formal records survive and the newspapers carried no inside stories).[17]

'A Subscriber' to the *Clonmel Herald* maintained in a letter published on 19 July 1837 that 'neither the Lord Lieutenant or the Grand Jury or any other single body have the power of severing this county … for the Act that unites them says: "Cross Tipperary and Tipperary shall from henceforth be one county for ever"'. He was adverting to the 1715 Act which formed the modern county and abolished the Butler palatinate or liberties, but he was ignoring the power to divide, clearly given by the Grand Jury (Consolidation) Act, 1836. And, to recapitulate, that power could be exercised by central government without the 1835 shackle of grand jury consent.

SEVERAL APPEALS

On 7 October 'a printed document purporting to be a petition to Lord Mulgrave, the Lord Lieutenant, and emanating from Borrisoleigh' was quoted by the *Clonmel Advertiser.* It was strongly pro-Thurles and anti-Nenagh. That document was not listed by the Privy Council's

Committee for a second meeting on 1 December 1837, five and one-half months after the first meeting which had recommended division on the basis of six baronies in the north. Its lists did include two memorials from the inhabitants of Kilnamanagh barony, which included Borrisoleigh town, against the division and against their inclusion in any northern division. That such inhabitants were from the southern/Dundrum end, rather than from the northern/Borrisoleigh end of that sprawling barony, may be inferred from the submission of two similar memorials by Lord Hawarden. His seat was Dundrum and it will be recalled that he walked out of the December 1836 Thurles meeting, presumably because the trend of the discussion indicated a presumption that the division of the county was assured and because the attendance favoured the inclusion of Kilnamanagh in the north.

There was a memorial from Glengall against the division. He hedged his bets by also opposing Kilnamanagh's and Eliogarty's being 'attached to the Nenagh Division, supposing that such Division should take effect'. The Committee's plateful was completed by the fifteen Grand Jurors' memorial and a similar anti-division letter from the High Sheriff of the county for the previous year, Maurice Crosbie Moore. Lord Bloomfield was present as sentry on his project and remonstrated against 'Grand Jurors who had never come forward with evidence in support of allegations made by them'. That concise statement drew attention to the weight of evidence examined earlier in the year, and on such an anti-climactic note the debate on the basic issue of division died.[18]

COMPROMISE

There was a definite whiff of a gentlemanly chat beforehand about the resolution of the Kilnamanagh problem. Charles Rolleston, junior counsel for the north, proposed that four parishes of the barony be attached to a northern division. This was assented to by counsel for Hawarden and Kilnamanagh,[19] thus relieved of sharing the expense of building a courthouse and a gaol by way of cess on the valuation of the Viscount's 15,000 acres. The settlement may have been facilitated by Hawarden and Dunalley being brothers-in-law. And/or by the neighbourliness of the brethren at law involved, three of whom had their offices at numbers 8, 12 and 18 Merrion Square.[20] The fact that Charles Rolleston was married to a daughter of John Richards, Baron of the Exchequer, absent from the June Committee meeting but present on 1 December, may well have assisted any preliminary diplomacy.[21]

All that lubricating influence aside, a sense of justice must have predominated, together with simple commonsense from a look at the

Plate 12: Dundrum House, the seat of the Maude family/Lord Hawarden. The house underwent a dramatic change (spiritually, not architecturally) c.1908 when it was bought by the Presentation Sisters. Its vast accommodation was used as convent, orphanage and boarding school (domestic economy). purposes. After a few years as a private residence in the 1970s it was bought by Austin and Mary Crowe and is now a hotel of international repute – photo courtesy of the Crowe family.

Plate 13:   A fireplace in the dining room.

shape of the map and at the roads carrying coach-driven passengers at a speed of eight miles per hour.

The Committee secretary's notes include two alternative draft responses to the Thurles counsel Philip Fogarty's belated proposition 'that certain portions of Eliogarty were similarly circumstanced as the four parishes in Kilnamanagh'. The first draft provided for an adjournment as Fogarty was unprepared with evidence. But the second draft, which was adopted, ignored the rumblings and amended their June decision by accepting only the Rolleston proposal, as agreed by counsel. This was to include only four civil parishes of Kilnamanagh in the northern division, described as Castletown, Mealiff, Glenkeen and Templebeg (see note 1, Appendix Five).[22]

The Privy Council itself met on 22 December in the presence of the Lord Lieutenant and made an order 'confirming said Reports and referring same to Her Majesty's Attorney and Solicitor-General to prepare the proper forms of Order to carry the said Reports into effect.'[23] So Borrisoleigh was in the north, Dundrum in the south and the case closed as far as the legal luminaries and bureaucrats were concerned. But not so for the landowners in south Tipperary.

GRAND JURY REACTION

The Spring Assizes in March 1838, however, went by with County Surveyor Samuel Jones presenting his estimates for alterations and improvements to the Thurles-Nenagh road 'as in all probability it will soon become of greater importance'.[24] The Grand Jury passed petitions against the Poor Law Bill and Medical Charities Bill. The former was 'unjust to the landed and agricultural interest of the kingdom'. As regards the second, 'the petitioners have seen, with surprise and alarm … [the intention] to rest exclusively in a Board of Medical Men, the power to erect hospitals and establish dispensaries'. Not a murmur of disagreement with the Privy Council's decision, though southerners had a majority of 14 to northerners' 9.[25] But, four months later, the *Clonmel Herald,* reporting the Summer Assizes, revealed a certain lack of recognition of reality or a sourness generated by the failure of some to fight their corner in due time:

> A smart discussion took place yesterday among the Grand Jury, respecting the division of the county. All the Ormond gentlemen on the Jury, and there were many, were in favour of it, but Thomas E. Lalor, Esq., opposed it with all his influence, which was great. He at length moved that such a division was unnecessary and inexpedient, which being put to a vote Mr Lalor's motion was

101

carried, 13 having voted with Mr Lalor and 8 against it. One of the Grand Jury, the Hon. Mr King, did not vote on the question. For the present this question is lost but if the division should ever take place which is now very problematical, a strong effort will be made by those gentlemen of the grand jury who voted with Mr Lalor to have the Assizes of the county held only in one place and that place is to be Thurles.

Great praise is due to John Bagwell, Matthew Pennefather, Matthew Jacob, Ambrose Going and Col. Purefoy who took an active part in supporting Mr Lalor's motion.

Since writing the foregoing, we find that the Hon. Judge Moore is charged by the Government with documents decisive of the division of the county.[26]

Two days later *The Tipperary Free Press* reported in similar vein but gave the outcome of 'a very animated discussion' as a vote of 13-9. Significantly, it added that 'the foreman intimated that before he would affix his name to the resolution he would consult the court upon the matter'.[27]

One week later the infant *Nenagh Guardian*,[28] in its Vol. 1, No. IV, copied the *Herald* story word for word with two amendments. In line politically with its secondary title, *Tipperary (North Riding) and Ormond Advertiser,* it omitted the words, 'Great praise is due to' and 'who'.

Two weeks further on the *Nenagh Guardian* amplified the story and proclaimed:

It has been stated by some of the Clonmel papers that on the question of division of the county being brought before the Grand Jury the votes were 13 against the division and 8 in favour of it. We are asked to mention that the numbers were 12 against and 9 for dividing this vast county and also that neither the foreman nor the Hon. Mr King voted. The judge remarked that the Grand Jury might vote as they pleased but the question had passed the Privy Council for sanction by the Lord Lieutenant ...[29]

THURLES RE-CONSIDERED

The thirteenth-hour resurrection of the idea of Thurles as assize town for a unitary county came just a decade after the original idea – on both occasions surfacing only in newspaper reports but no doubt based on well-informed sources. At first thought it seems odd that the Thurles lobby did not take steps in late 1835 or early 1836 to activate the 1835

Assizes (Removal) Act. Their difficulty would have been to mobilise a majority of grand jurors. That would have required convincing Bloomfield and company in the Ormonds and Owney and Arra that such a move would have a better chance of success than a proposal for division. And of enlisting another cadre from Kilnamanagh Lower, Clanwilliam, and the more northern parts of Middlethird and Slieveardagh baronies outside the immediate pull of Clonmel to add up to a majority, i.e. twelve grand jurors.

It is here that the person constituting the one-man tribunal selecting the twenty-three good men and true becomes important. A glance at the succession, scheduled below, of those High Sheriffs in the crucial years firstly illustrates the preponderance in general of southerners, as already seen, from Table 1 and Fig. 3, among the grand jurors they selected. It suggests, again at first thought, that under Moore's stewardship in spring 1836 was the only chance to have a more neutral grand jury – because of his equally remote situation from Clonmel and Thurles, and always presuming that he did not have compliments to repay to the Clonmel-oriented interests. But at that assizes there were 4 northerners and 19 southerners[30] – and then one realises that Moore felt strongly enough as an anti-partitionist, as already noted, to forward his own 1837 memorial to the Lord Lieutenant.

1834 John Bagwell, Marlfield, on the fringe of Clonmel in Iffa and Offa East barony.

1835 John Butler, earl of Ossory, with an address at Kilkenny castle in neighbouring County Kilkenny, related to Richard Butler, earl of Glengall, and to Cornelius O'Callaghan of Clogheen in the deep south of Iffa and Offa West, son of Lady Eleanor Butler.

1836 Maurice Crosbie Moore, Mooresfort, near Lattin and Tipperary town, in the western spur of Clanwilliam barony.

1837 Stephen O'Meagher, Kilmoyler, close to Cahir, at the eastern edge of Clanwilliam barony.

1838 F. A. Prittie, Corville/Mount Butler, Roscrea, at the northern tip of Ikerrin barony, and who managed to empanel nine northerners in both 1838 assizes, as against the usual four to seven.

By late 1836, the Grand Jury Act of that year having superseded the need for a majority, any removal ploy was too late; the Ormonds had their eyes focused on a realistic ambition of division.

It is possible to argue that if the Butlers had selected Thurles as palatinate headquarters and assizes location in medieval times, whatever complaints might have surfaced, such as the 'Ormond Freeholder's'

below,
~~above~~, would have bowed before the relatively central position of
Thurles. But, who knows? Would Bloomfield have been unhappy even
then, and/or would Donoughmore and Glengall have activated a move
to adopt Clonmel as assizes town for a south riding?

PROCLAMATION

The *Nenagh Guardian* had the right air of it; work was well advanced
on the preamble, 81 clauses and appendix which were issued as a
Proclamation of the Lord Lieutenant and Privy Council from its meeting
of Thursday, 8 November 1838 (see Appendix Five).[32] The same Lord
Lieutenant was still in office; the title earl of Mulgrave now, however,
gave precedence to his freshly-acquired one: Marquess of Normanby.
The Privy Councillor signatories were Lords Plunket, Charlemont and
Cloncurry, the Duke of Leinster, the Marquess of Headfort, L. Perrin,
A. R. Blake, T. F. Kennedy and N. Ball, all identified at the start of
Chapter Three.

The Proclamation provided for two ridings and directed that for
grand jury purposes each should 'be considered, deemed and taken to
be a separate county'. It directed the building of a gaol at Nenagh to
provide for not less than 140 male and 25 female prisoners, enabled
the enlargement or building of a courthouse there and directed a levy
for both on the north riding only (contrary to Glengall's foreboding).
Consequently the south riding grand jury could no longer levy the
north for Clonmel gaol expenses except in respect of any guests from
the north during the transitional period.

The north was to pay two-fifths and the south three-fifths of old
loan repayments, of the salaries of geographical county-wide officials
such as the Co. Surveyor, his clerk and assistants, the Secretary to the
Grand Juries, the Clerks of the Crown and of the Peace, sheriffs, and
the judges' crier, and of other common expenses. Expenses of the
county infirmary and the house of correction were to be paid in
proportion to the number of patrons from each riding.

Statutes relating to valuation, bridges and public works were applied
to each riding. Transitional arrangements were set out, including a
direction to the final county-wide grand jury to divide Kilnamanagh
into two half-baronies.

In the sphere of justice the Proclamation provided that offences
committed within five hundred yards of the border on either side could
be tried in either riding. Grand jurors for either assize could come
from either riding. There was to be 'but one jurors' book for the whole
of Tipperary', but 'in summoning such jurors ... the sheriff ... shall
have regard to the convenience of the said jurors as to their place of

residence'. Jurors on a special jury in one riding could not be drawn from the other riding.

And it is further ordered that this proclamation shall commence and take effect from and after the tenth day of December next.

THE TIMES AND THE ECHOES

The *Nenagh Guardian* carried the Proclamation tightly set into a page and a half, in each of three issues – Saturday 8, Wednesday 12 and Saturday 15 December 1838. Much of the usual proportion of foreign news and of the Haut Ton and State of the Country columns was therefore squeezed out of its normal four pages. In the first category they did report a Radical Meeting in Birmingham with two to three thousand cheering Fergus O'Connor, a rebellion in Canada, and items from Persia, Russia and the USA. In the second category, the earl and Countess of Norbury had arrived at the Shelbourne Hotel.

And in the third, the ongoing chronicle of violence, Tipperary men had crossed the Shannon into Clare and carried away a sixteen-year-old girl to be married. There had been an assault near Moneygall. A letter from Valentine Maher, MP, copied from the *Morning Chronicle*, defended the memory of the murdered Charles O'Keefe against 'wicked calumny'. Francis Wayland, Ballywalter, had died 'after lingering for 8 months from the effects of the shot he received' – on the occasion of Austin Cooper's murder which had led to the Glengall-Drummond exchange. And Sergeant Kelly, Golden, had arrested Cornelius Hickey, charged with Cooper's murder.

There was a rumour reported that the Duke of Sussex was being appointed to succeed Lord Normanby (he wasn't and didn't). There were facts reported relating to the imminent appointments of a nephew-in-law of Daniel O'Connell, Captain Richard Leyne, late of the 58th Regiment, as stipendiary magistrate to be stationed in Roscrea, and of Count Peter D'Alton of Grenanstown, Toomevara, as High Sheriff of the full geographical county for 1839, with Malachi Ryan, Tyone, Nenagh, as his sub-Sheriff.

Supplemented by stories of the new Poor Law Commissioners promising to commence erection of a workhouse in Nenagh in the spring, and of the opening shot in a fresh rationalisation campaign, avowedly inspired by 'the principle of two ridings', according to the letter-writer, 'An Ormond Freeholder'. This man was concerned with the allocation to Thurles, Roscrea and Nenagh of all the northern division's quarter sessions. He wanted a Roscrea-Borrisokane division and a Nenagh-Thurles division with Borrisokane getting its share of sessions. 'The chief evil' was the position which 'Thurles bears to the northern limits of Lower Ormond barony' – 30 miles; the 5*d*. Borrisokane-Nenagh post was also a factor (the whopping equivalent of approximately £1.25 in the early 1990s). And, needless to say, only a small outlay would be needed on the present petty sessions house and bridewell. Nenagh got its workhouse but Borrisokane did not get quarter sessions. Nor did Nenagh and Dromineer, on the Shannon's Lough Derg, get the canal to join them which was mooted over those three issues of the *Nenagh Guardian*. The paper's management was forcing the pace with an estimate commissioned by them from W. J. Hughes, Civil Engineer, 6 Westland Row, Dublin, of £58,927 (say £3.5 million in the early 1990s). Echoes of the other campaign sounded here by way of the names of the leaders – Peter Holmes in the chair and O'Brien Dillon as secretary of the promotional meeting held in the old Courthouse in Pound Street. Other community leaders bearing names familiar to followers of the division saga appeared in the role of patrons at the head of a report of the Nenagh Savings Bank's annual accounts – Dunalley and Bloomfield.

Thurles could be said to have evened the score against Nenagh, almost a century later, albeit unconscious of the 1837 debate. Nenagh was designated *in pectore* as the location of the third of the country's four sugar beet processing factories, with concomitant employment, business and stature. At the last moment, alert Thurles politicians who had superior clout with the Government of the day stole the prize.[31]

BACK TO BASICS
And in those successive issues of the *Nenagh Guardian* – sufficient proclamation that the race in microcosm in North Tipperary had not neglected matters more fundamental than all of the most inspired public service – there appeared
• a half-column filler, probably syndicated, of advice on Managing a Husband,
• notice of the marriage of Lt. F. S. Prittie, 70th Regt, to a daughter of the Hon. Peter Rose,
• notice of the birth on 11 December, one day after that of the two Tipperarys, of a son 'to the lady of O'Brien Dillon, Esq., Solr., Nenagh'.

POLITICAL FERMENT
Tipperary's consciousness of and involvement in national politics, as noted in the Prologue, was still notable in those last months of 1838. There was a 'Great Anti-Tithe Meeting' at the Green, Carrick-on-Suir,

on 1 November. That was followed by that town's meeting on 5 November to demand speedy completion of the railways – 'to leave the South-East of Ireland without direct communication with the metropolis was manifestly impolitic and unjust'.[33]

A swift response to another lead by The Liberator came through October into December. Daniel O'Connell had formed the Precursor Society in August 1838. Its ambitious aims included full justice for Ireland from parliament, equality with Great Britain in respect to franchise, privileges and rights, and also the total abolition of tithes. When forming that Society O'Connell already had intentions of forming a repeal association. He was giving the Precursor Society one year to gather interest, which it failed to do sufficiently, its members being easily counted.[34]

A branch of the Precursor Society was formed in Carrick-on-Suir on 14 October,[35] and in the united parishes of Ballyneale and Grangemockler on 4 November.[36] At Donaskeagh on the same date, after concluding its business of forming a branch and passing six other resolutions, 'the great meeting separated, first giving three cheers for The Queen, three cheers for Marquess Normanby, and three cheers for O'Connell'.[37] Meantime Moycarkey and Borris parishes combined had an acknowledgement from the national body of £21.60 subscriptions.[38] Archdeacon Laffan capped this with £56.30 from the union of Fethard and Killusty and recruited 1,063 members.[39]

The Precursors clearly prefigured the Repealers in the heady design of their public occasions. When O'Connell's progress through Tipperary in early November 1838 reached Thurles his reception included 1,400 men on horseback. He paid his respects to the Archbishop in his palace, to the populace in the open air at the Market House, and to his leading supporters in response to their tributes at a dinner in Mrs Boyton's hotel. The beneficiaries of Donaskeagh's three times three cheers were among seventeen toasts reported. The one to the monarch was followed by one with a republican ring: 'The People, the genuine source of legitimate power, and the best support of good government'. And the toast to that dominant and ubiquitous presence, though an absentee on this occasion, the Marquess of Normanby, and its reception by the audience spoke political volumes: 'He has given wholesome, but to some people rather unpleasant advice (cheers and laughter) and has provoked a little anger because he told them the truth (loud cheers and continued laughter).[40]

During all this period not one of Clonmel's three surviving newspapers uttered a line of comment on their own county's constitutional revision. Nor throughout the several years of discussion

107

of discussion had the name of the absentee earl of Clonmel been reported.

One might note at this point who were the holders throughout most of the 1830s of the two principal offices held with some continuity, as distinct from that of High Sheriff which changed annually. They had been fellow-MPs, as seen in this chapter; they had both been social and political colleagues of Bloomfield, as seen in the previous chapter. They were the earl of Donoughmore and F. A. Prittie. They held, respectively, the offices of Lord Lieutenant of the county and Custos Rotulorum, neither of which office has in itself any bearing on this story.

But perhaps it can be reasonably assumed that a Clonmel man and a Roscrea man in vocational harmony would have put the public interest before any pull towards a No Surrender stance by the Clonmel man's neighbours. And that as holders of high office, they would have had the ears of even higher.[41]

STATE OF THE COUNTY, 1839
10 December 1838 had become the birthday of the two Tipperarys. The following table shows the effects of the division in terms of population, of area, and of valuation of property for the purpose of county cess.

The compromise halving of Kilnamanagh barony resulted from successful, self-centred politicking by Viscount Hawarden. The population figures, compared with the schedule in Chapter Two, show that it produced a less even divide than that proposed by the Nenagh and Thurles lobbies.

Riding	Population	Acreage	Valuation		
			£	s.	d.
North	201,161	524,920	286,560	16	8
South	234,392	536,811	448,800	2	1
Total	**435,553**	**1,061,731**	**735,369**	**18**	**9**

The basic objective of the pro-division movers had been to lessen the inconvenience to themselves and to their tenants of the time-consuming administration of justice in a solitary and peripheral assize town and in the face of increasing crime. The effectiveness of the outcome in that regard can be judged by the figures on p. <del>108</del> 110.

One might endow the leading campaigners, with their hereditary addiction to mottoes, with the collective and complimentary *Quod est demonstrandum.*

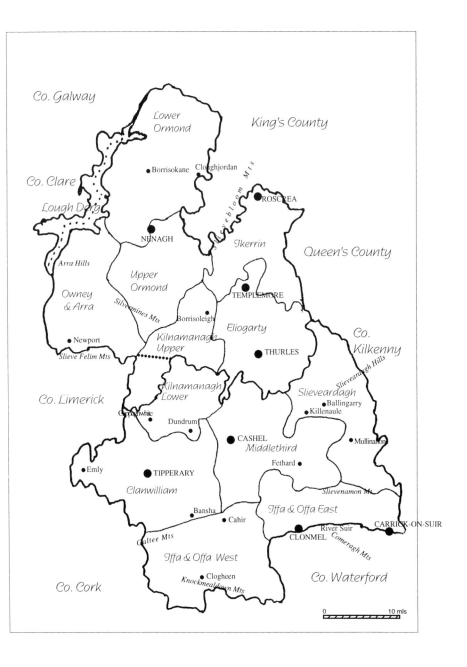

Fig. 5: Co. Tipperary after division showing the principal towns and villages. The area below the line of dots in Kilnamanagh Upper was transferred to the South Riding after the Local Government (Ireland) Act, 1898.

109

Assizes	Location	Duration (days)
Spring 1838	Clonmel	12
Summer 1838	do.	9
Spring 1839	do.	6
do.	Nenagh	7
Summer 1839	Clonmel	7
do.	Nenagh	6

The boundary between the two ridings was to remain intact for just over sixty years. In 1899, at the introduction of county councils, the south-west portion of Kilnamanagh Upper was switched to the South Riding (see Note 1, Appendix Five, and the final paragraphs of 'Partitioning Cork' in Appendix Twelve). Even then, 'the entire county of Tipperary' continued to be one county for the registration of voters and the functions of sheriff, lieutenant and other officers. In those sixty years no other county was divided. The enabling sections of the 1836 Grand Juries Act were repealed in 1898, as were those in the 1835 Assizes Act which had provided for more than one assize town and division.[42]

Notes

1. *Burke's Complete Peerage.*
2. Lord Dunboyne, *Butler Family History*, 3rd edition, p. 26.
3. Dermot F. Gleeson and Harold G. Leask, *The Castle and Manor of Nenagh* (Nenagh, 1971), p. 253 reprinted from the *R.S.A. Jn.*, lxvi, December 1936.
4. *T.C.*, 7 July 1837.
5. Rev. William P. Burke, *A History of Clonmel*, p. 154 (the duel); *Limerick Evening Post and Clare Sentinel*, 29 Aug 1828.
6. ditto, 17 Oct 1828.
7. *T.F.P.*, 11 Oct 1828.
8. *C.A.*, 18 Apr 1835.
9. *C.A.*, 20 Aug 1834.
10. *C.A.*, 23 Aug 1834.
11. *C.A.*, 14 Sept 1833.
12. *The Pilot*, 25 Feb 1835.
13. *T.F.P.*, 14 Sept 1836; *C.A.* 28 Sept 1836; *T.C.*, 14 Oct 1836.
14. *C.A.*, 30 May 1835.
15. *C.A.*, Wed 30 Oct 1833: Lord Glengall is to be united in a few days to Miss Mellish, daughter of a wealthy contractor.
    C.A., Sat 3 Nov 1833: We are authorised to contradict the report that Lord Glengall is about to enter a matrimonial alliance.
    T.F.P., 26 Feb 1834: Married on Thursday last by special licence, at St.

George's, Hanover-square, London, by the Very Rev. Dean of Carlisle, the Right Hon. the earl of Glengall, to Margaret Laurette, youngest daughter of the late W. Mellish Esq. of Woodford, Essex and Dover Street, Picadilly.

C.A., Wed 2 Apr 1834: earl and Countess Glengall, newly-married, arrive in Paris.

C.A., Wed 20 Aug 1834: Arrival of the earl of Glengall in Caher. The earl and Countess, the Countess Dowager, the Ladies Butler and Mrs Mellish and suite arrived in Caher amid the cheers and heartfelt rejoicing of the earl's numerous tenantry and the inhabitants of Caher generally. At dusk the town was splendidly illuminated which, together with repeated discharges of two pieces of ordnance, completed as animated and cheering a scene, such as we have seldom witnessed.

C.A., Wed 3 Dec 1834: On Saturday the 29th ult in Sackville St, Dublin. The Countess of Glengall of a daughter which, together with the Countess, is in the enjoyment of perfect health.

The Pilot, Fri 24 July 1835: The earl of Glengall has had a new yacht of 500 tonnes launched at Cowes. She is called *The Margaret* in compliment to his Countess.

C.A., 4 Sept 1835: The Earl and Countess of Glengall, it is expected, will arrive in this country in a week after, and remain during the winter.

The earl (d. 22 June 1858) and his countess (18 Feb 1811-2 Apr 1864), are handsomely entombed in the grounds of St Paul's Church of Ireland church, Cahir, together with a daughter and his mother. The combination of foreign holidays, a marine residence in the Isle of Wight, a town house (now Cahir House hotel) and a London house at 34 Grosvenor Square, (presumably) reduced rents during the Great Famine, and philanthropy which included the building of an Erasmus Smith school for which the leading architect John Nash was engaged, and St Paul's, contributed to his bankruptcy in 1855. His eldest daughter Margaret and husband Col. Richard Charteris later re-purchased the estates. Nash's Swiss Cottage, built for the first earl, was opened to the public in 1989 following local initiative and pressure which led to restoration by the Office of Public Works and FÁS, funded to a large extent by American and Irish foundations and South Tipperary County Council. Itself and the Earl of Glengall restaurant in the town are worth visiting for reasons additional to nostalgia – *Limerick Reporter and Tipperary Vindicator*, 6 July 1858; *Cahir Tourist Guide* (Junior Chamber, Cahir).

16. Council Office Papers, VI-VIC, (N.A., formerly at the S.P.O.).
17. *C.A.*, 19 July 1837.
18. Council Office Papers, VI-VIC.
19. ditto.
20. *Thoms*, 1846.
21. C. H. Rolleston, *Portrait of an Irishman* (London 1939) – plate facing p. 3, p. 4. Charles Rolleston of Glasshouse, Shinrone, five miles from the

patrimonial seat at ffranckfort castle, Dunkerrin, married Elizabeth
Richards c.1832. He became Rolleston-Spunner on inheriting an estate
in 1867 from Thomas Spunner, JP.

22. Council Office Papers, VI-VIC.
23. ditto.
24. *T.C.*, 3 Mar 1838.
25. *C.A.*, 14 Mar 1838.
26. *C.H.*, 23 July 1838.
27. *T.F.P.*, 25 July 1838.
28. The *Nenagh Guardian* (1838-) was the first of six weekly local
    newspapers to use that declaratory title, arriving into a world of flag-
    waving Standards and Constitutions and more prosaic Advertisers,
    Heralds, Chronicles, Journals, Times, Gazettes. The others were *The
    Armagh Guardian* 1844-1892, (Wexford) *Guardian* 1847-56, *Sligo
    Guardian* 1849-50, *Ulster Guardian* c.1907-c.1920, *Ballymena Guardian
    and Antrim Standard* 1970- – Hugh Oram, *The Newspaper Book* (Dublin,
    1983).
29. *N.G.*, 29 Aug 1838.
30. *C.A.*, 9 Mar 1836.
31. Though I do not have documentary evidence, the sources of the lore are
    first-class. John Scroope, Nenagh UDC 1942-50, and later chairman-
    managing director of Castle Brand, tells of that firm's predecessor, the
    Irish Aluminium Company, being founded in a bounce-back by the
    disappointed Nenagh Industrialists. He was told of Dr James Ryan, TD,
    Minister for Agriculture, actually having a Nenagh appointment to
    announce the allocation of the factory. The then Senator Des Hanafin, in
    the course details of a television election vox pop on the streets of Thurles
    in recent years, told with some glee of his father Johnny Hanafin, UDC,
    and others of the ruling party, Fianna Fáil, pulling off the coup.
32. Council Letter Book 8A6 8 (N.A.).
33. *T.F.P.*, 7 Nov 1838.
34. Charles Chenevix Trench, *The Great Dan* (London, 1986), pp. 244-5.
35. *T.F.P.*, 17 Oct 1838.
36. ditto, 7 Nov 1838.
37. ditto, 10 Nov 1838.
38. ditto, 7 Nov 1838.
39. ditto, 15 Dec 1838.
40. ditto, 10 Nov 1838.
41. The Lord Lieutenancy of a county was the more senior honour, identified
    by the Webbs for across Channel and O'Brien for Ireland as being in
    command of military forces in the county. Crossman, however, identifies
    a certain reliance on some of them as the local eyes and ears of central
    government, and having a role in recommending appointees to the
    magistracy and to an extent seeing to their adequacy in office. The Custos

Rotulorum, literally keeper of the county's records, was a civil office dating in England from 1546. He administered the oath of office to the sub-sheriff and, until 1877, appointed the clerk of the peace – Sidney and Beatrice Webb, *English Local Government*, Vol, I, Book 2, p. 285; W. P. O'Brien, *Report on local government and taxation of Ireland* [C 1965], H.C. 1878, xxiii, 735; Virginia Crossman, *Local Government in Nineteenth Century Ireland* (Belfast, 1994).
42. 61 & 62 Vic, c. 37, Local Government (Ireland) Act, 1898 Sixth Schedule, Part I (re 1836) and Part VI (re 1835).

CHAPTER FIVE

'Thousands upon thousands have been ... spent upon the ... dirty old tumble-down town of Nenagh'

THE IMMEDIATE AFTERMATH

Even prior to the formal proclamation of the division of the county, in fact within four months of the crucial Privy Council's Committee recommendation, one percipient Clonmel entrepreneur saw an opportunity for business northwards. John Kempston, Jun., printed a notice in his father's *Clonmel Advertiser* of 17 March 1838, of a proposal to publish from the following 2 June a newspaper to be called the *Nenagh Guardian and Tipperary North Riding Advertiser.*[1] The move was explicitly stated to be because of Nenagh's selection as assize town. Anyone 'who wished to forward the undertaking' could communicate with the *Advertiser* office or with John Kempston, Sen. (c/o Mr John O'Shea, Nenagh).

The paper appeared on Saturday 21 July 1838 with an enhanced title fine-tuned to the market in its catchment area, *Nenagh Guardian, or Tipperary (North Riding) and Ormond Advertiser.* On the following Wednesday, its advent was greeted in sour fashion by the *Tipperary Free Press*:[2]

> The journal, the *ci-devant* 'Clonmel Advertiser', having changed its local habitation and its name, started into life on Saturday last, as the organ of the left wing of Conservatism in Tipperary. ... The great inaugurating article is composed of as wanton, as malignant, and as cowardly an attack on an unoffending individual in Clonmel as has disgraced a newspaper.

On 8 December the *Guardian* editorialised, without a trace of modesty:

> When we proposed establishing a Journal in this locality we were influenced by the consideration that the great resources of Nenagh and its neighbourhood were not duly appreciated, or, if known,

that they were allowed to lie dormant, because of the apathy which hung over the people of Lower Ormond, and which can always be best dispelled by the exertions of an independent Paper. Already we are enabled to congratulate our neighbours and friends that our efforts have not been unavailing. We hope to see Nenagh a well-lit, well-paved, well-cleansed town.

The practicalities of implementing the latter hopes are recounted later. On the following 9 March the *Guardian* was able to quote evidence of success in its first five months to the end of 1838. The official Return of Stamps (duty) showed it to have sold 400 per issue; it appeared twice-weekly, on each Wednesday and Saturday. Its four pages cost $4^1/2d.$ or almost 2p in modern currency but equivalent to £1.15p approximately in 1994 on allowing for inflation.[3] The weekly total of 800 compared with the *Clonmel Herald's* 130, the *Tipperary Constitution's* 666 and the *Tipperary Free Press's* 718. Clonmel's fourth paper, their own *Advertiser*, had meantime ceased publication.[4]

The *Guardian* carried an advertisement one week later which gave evidence of the new internal tourism attendant upon selection as an assize town:

THURLES & NENAGH
A DAY CAR

The public are respectfully informed a well-appointed car leaves Mr Boynton's hotel, Thurles, every morning at 6 o'clock during the Assizes, for Nenagh and will start its departure from Nenagh every day at 3 o'clock for Thurles. To commence on Monday 18th inst.

On and after the 27th inst a car will leave Thurles at 1 o'clock after the arrival of the Kilkenny car for Nenagh, for Mondays, Wednesdays and Fridays, and will leave Nenagh at 8 o'clock in the morning on Tuesdays, Thursdays and Saturdays for Thurles.[5]

THE FIRST ASSIZES

One further week on, 23 March 1839, it reported the milestone of the North Riding's first assizes and shook hands with itself and all concerned in an editorial ecstasy:

We may now congratulate the patriotic and spirited Noblemen and Gentlemen of North Tipperary, upon the commencement of this practical result of their efforts to elevate the district which they serve and adorn by their residence, in the scale of social importance, and to confer upon it those advantages which must lead to the diffusion of wealth, to the spread of employment and to the increase of comfort and happiness among its inhabitants.

Hitherto the inhabitants of Nenagh, and of the surrounding district, have been revelling in something like a dream of the imagination. Everyone knew that Nenagh had been made an Assizes town, in other words, that it had become the capital of North Tipperary – but the pleasing truth, the glad result is now brought home to every breast. We see our town filled with strangers who never visited it before – we see the gentlemen comprising the Grand and Record Juries, the Judges, the Lawyers and Attorneys, and the witnesses – we perceive attention called to our local interests – we find that buildings are about to be erected, and valuable establishments created – and all this is a matter of rejoicing and of congratulation. We need hardly inform our patrons that the 'Nenagh Guardian' should devote its best energies upon the present occasion – and that the proceedings of our first Assizes will be fully and accurately reported.[6]

It did indeed report fully over five issues in three weeks all aspects of both the fiscal business of that very first North Riding Grand Jury and the hearing in two courts of cases involving fifty-one people.

The Grand Jurors comprised the aristocracy of our County, and reflected the highest credit, for their selection, on our High Sheriff, Count D'Alton.[7] Petit Jurors were chiefly composed of highly respectable country gentlemen, and the principal merchants and traders and shop-keepers of Nenagh; and, with a solitary exception, men of sound judgement and understanding.[8]

It must remain forever and a day a mystery as to who was the exception whom the editor, and he not too many wet days in the place, could soundly judge and understand not to be so sound.

Not alone did the resident *Guardian* mark the milestone occasion with a flourish; the leading Clonmel paper, the *Tipperary Free Press,* sent its own man.

This town today presented a busy and exhilarating scene – the novelty of the first assizes has attracted numbers. The Press (the fourth estate) is amply represented, as, beside the reporters for the County papers, there are several from the London, Dublin and Limerick Journals. I was deeply impressed with the justice

Table 2   GRAND JURIES, 1839:
North Riding of the County of Tipperary

	SPRING	SUMMER
Bayly, Richard Uniacke, Ballinaclough, Nenagh	√	√
Bloomfield, Hon. John D., Loughton Hse, Moneygall	√	√
Butler, James, Park, Templemore	√	
Carden, John, Barnane, Templemore		√
Carden, Richard Minchin, Fishmoyne, Borrisoleigh	√	
Carroll, William Hutchinson, Tulla House, Nenagh		√
Dancer, Sir Amyrald, Modreeny, Cloughjordan	√	
Dancer, Thomas B., Modreeny, Cloughjordan		√
Dwyer, Lieut. Col. Henry, Ballyquirke Castle, Lorrha	√	√
Finch, William, Tullamore Park, Nenagh		√
Gason, Richard Wills, Richmond, Nenagh	√	√
Hackett, Thomas, Riverstown, Parsonstown/Birr		√
Head, William Henry, Modreeny, Cloughjordan		√
Henchy, O'Connor, Lissenhall, Nenagh	√	
Holmes, Peter, Johnstown, Nenagh	√	√
Hunt, Vere D, Woodbine Lodge, Rathnaleen, Nenagh		√
Hutchinson, James D, Timoney, Roscrea		√
Jackson, George, Mount Pleasant, Ballymackey, Nenagh	√	
Lee, Henry, Barna, Newport	√	√
Lenigan, James, Castle Fogarty, Thurles	√	√
Lidwell, Robert, Richmond, Templemore		√
Lloyd, John, Esq., Lloydsborough, Templemore	√	
Minchin, George, Busherstown, Roscrea	√	
Phillips, Richard E., Mount Rivers, Newport	√	
Prittie, Henry, Corville, Roscrea	√	√
Prittie, Hon. F.A., Corville, Roscrea*	√	√
Ryan, George, Inch House, Thurles	√	
Sadleir, Thomas Jun, Ballinderry Hse, Borrisokane	√	√
Stoney, Thomas George, Kylepark, Borrisokane	√	√
Trench, William Steuart, Sopwell Hall, Cloughjordan	√	
Waller, Sir Edmund, Knockanacree Hse, Cloughjordan	√	√
Webb, Daniel James, Woodville, Templemore		√
Willington, James, Castle Willington, Nenagh	√	√

*Foreman – Spring and Summer Assizes

Sources: Spring Assizes – *N.G.* 9 Mar 1839
          Summer Assizes – *T.F.P.* 24 July 1839

See Figure 6, p. 136

and good policy of dividing this County as well as by my long journey hither as by what I have seen of the people and the country – Tipperary, for population and extent being one of the largest shires in Ireland .... I have employed this day in viewing Nenagh, which is very superior in size and appearance to the notion I had previously formed of it ... three banks ... the Joint Stock bank is about mid-way between the Agricultural and the National, in Castle St adjoining Mr Loman's extensive wine and grocery establishment and is a very handsome building.[9]

THE FIRST TNR GRAND JURY

The grand jurors for the first two assizes in both the North and South Ridings are listed as Tables 2 and 3.

Among the pioneers constituting that first North Riding Grand Jury for the Spring Assizes of 1839, the names of Prittie, Bloomfield, Holmes, Ryan, Gason and Phillips will be recognised as participants to varying extents in the division campaign.[10] Among the thirty-three men who were on either the Spring or Summer Assizes of that year, there were no less than seventeen who had not been on any of the previous eleven grand juries stretching from the spring of 1834 to the Special Commission of January 1839. The phenomenon arises from the paucity of men from the north in those countywide grand juries, as adverted to in Chapter Two. The involvement of this large number of new participants in public administration must be regarded as a benefit arising directly from the division.

There was fulfilment of a forecast of 'additional well-salaried officers' when the Grand Jury carried a motion, proposed by Richard Wills Gason and John Bayly, for the appointment of a second surveyor for the geographical county, to be stationed in the town of Nenagh. Horace Uniacke Townsend became first County Surveyor for the North Riding; Samuel Jones continued in that role for the South Riding. The Ormond agitators' particular target of 'a second county surveyor in Tipperary', as identified by the *Clare Journal* in 1836, was thus met. Townsend was in office by the Summer Assizes when he was granted two assistants after a grand jury vote on the two versus only one assistant.[11]

Ambrose Lane, the Treasurer of the Grand Jury, continued to fill that office for both the grand juries. Likewise Edwin Sadleir as the Secretary of both, but during 1838 he moved residence from Clonmel to Nenagh. During 1844 the offices of Clerk of the Crown and his Deputy became two Clerks of the Crown, one based at Clonmel and the other at Nenagh.[12]

118

FISCAL POLITICS

Applications seeking 'the honour of the Treasurer's account' were received by the inaugural Grand Jury from the Tipperary Joint Stock Bank at Nenagh, and from the newly-founded Provincial Bank who had to admit that it was not their intention to open a branch in Nenagh (one did come in 1856). 'The contest appeared to have excited much interest'; it was won by the local bank by 17 votes to 6 and its Manager, Thaddeus O'Shea, 'was warmly congratulated'. And why wouldn't he, with two of the congratulating Grand Jury voters, Holmes and Bayly,[13] listed in an advertisement in the same issue of the *Nenagh Guardian* as local directors of the National Loan Fund Life Assurance Society for which O'Shea as Bank Manager was Agent.[14]

Two other aspects of this vote are, however, puzzling. Firstly, why there was no application from either the Agricultural and Commercial Bank or the National Bank, each having branches in Nenagh, Thurles and Roscrea? Particularly the National as it had been chosen for lodgement of the Ormond, Owney and Arra and Ikerrin fighting fund in 1836. Perhaps a transition in management might explain its absence; it had a new manager as of January, succeeding none other than Thaddeus O'Shea.

The Tipperary J. S. B. had poached O'Shea on opening its Nenagh branch on 15 January 1839. The occasion was noted by the *Nenagh Guardian,* along with 'the kind and gentlemanly deportment of Mr O'Shea and the banking knowledge and judgement evinced by him during the period of his management of the National Bank here.' The terms of the newspaper's welcome for the Bank seem to shed light on the Grand Jury vote, six months later: 'Its principles have been carefully enquired into by the leading gentry of our neighbourhood, whose promised support is the best proof of their confidence, and the most gratifying testimonial that could be given to Mr O'Shea's character and capability.'[15]

Secondly, why the voters for the Provincial Bank – Bloomfield, Henry Prittie, Lloyd, Trench, Minchin and Dwyer – were all from what could be described as an expanded Roscrea district – was that simply coincidence? Roscrea, or indeed Thurles, did not have a Provincial Bank branch either.

The answers to both questions may lie in bank structurings. G. L. Barrow has discovered that the Agricultural and Commercial's 'special appeal was to the small tenant farmers, "the frieze-coated men", as both shareholders and customers'. And far from frieze were the grand jurors reared. The National Bank had two alienating elements. It had a majority of English capital as against Irish and had its headquarters in

119

London. Its active Chairman, Daniel O'Connell, was to most grand jurors an offensive Repeal-of-the-Union demagogue, however much he was an asset to the bank in attracting nationalist Irish support. So neither bank might have felt itself welcome in the inaugural jury room. More importantly, each was at that point having its own problems of transition. As of early 1839, the Agricultural and Commercial, whose very first branch had been opened as recently as 1 November 1834 – in Nenagh – was operating under the uneasy gaze of a public who were fascinated by its liquidity crisis of 1836-7, induced by over-rapid expansion of branches. The National, also founded in 1834, was engaged in a re-structuring as between its English and Irish members and as between its headquarters and branch company shareholdings.

In contrast the Grand Jury's choice, the Tipperary Joint Stock Bank, had a unique relationship with the Bank of Ireland, involving the issue of notes, discount facilities and letters of credit and rights, which 'made the Tipperary a virtual extension of the Bank of Ireland in its operations, though not in its management'.[16] The Bank of Ireland was the elder statesman of Irish commerce, having enjoyed a monopoly from 1782 to 1824, was unanimously seen as the financial agent of the ascendancy and was apparently immune to the birth-pangs of its youthful rivals.

Standing in attractiveness between that mature establishment of College Green and its infant Tipperary satellite under Thaddeus O'Shea on the one hand, and the thrusting and perhaps preoccupied novices on the other, was the Provincial which attracted the minority vote. It had opened in 1825 and pioneered banking-by-branches; branches were opened in Clonmel and Limerick in that first year. There is one final clue to the politics of the Grand Jury vote. Holmes, Ryan, Gason and Phillips, all voters for the Tipperary Joint Stock Bank, were members of the final county-wide Grand Jury for the Summer Assizes, 1838, along with James Scully, Kilfeacle, founding director of that bank.[17]

JUSTICE

Many degrees lower than the warmth of high position, patronage and commercial success were the fifty-one defendants at that first assizes. There were sentences ranging from hanging, for James Blake for the murder of his wife,[18] and transportation for life of William Murphy and James Hayes for arson, through imprisonment for twelve months with hard labour of Thomas Carroll for cow stealing and of Mary Fitzpatrick for issuing base coin, to 50s. (£2.50p) fines and security to keep the peace on John Kennedy, Denis Kennedy and Thomas Connors for riot.

120

Thirty convicted men and two women, who had initially been conveyed to Clonmel from the scenes of their arrests throughout the North Riding, were escorted out of town and bound for Clonmel gaol by a strong guard of the 34th Regiment and some horse police.

The convicts were followed out of town by a large mob of persons and when the party arrived at Toomevara, they were met by a concourse of people amounting to several thousands and, but for a strong military force that accompanied the criminals, the wretched creatures might have perhaps attempted a rescue.[19]

BUILDING FOR THE FUTURE

All of which underlined the wisdom of the Grand Jury's immediate appointment of commissioners to erect a County Gaol. This fulfilled both the Privy Council's instruction in its proclamation of the division and Judge Philip Cecil Crampton's[20] exhortation at this first assizes, accompanied by a warning:

the transmission of prisoners from the North Riding to the Gaol at Clonmel … might be attended with consequences that every man would deprecate.[21]

The quarter sessions in Nenagh in that January of 1839 had resulted in sixty-nine sentences of between one month and two years imprisonment, largely for assault, affray and larceny. The 'sixty-nine convicts' and eleven other prisoners required an escort to the county gaol in Clonmel of a captain, a lieutenant, three sergeants and seventy rank and file of the 34th Regiment.[22] The journey in reverse also caused logistics problems during this transition period while the north riding had assizes but not yet a gaol. One year on, forty-nine prisoners had to be conveyed under escort from Clonmel to Nenagh for the second Spring Assizes.[23]

The hazards of the highway were not confined to unsolicited salutation of prisoners, as is clear from a vivid description by the Clonmel reporter of the first north assizes.[24] His account serves to underline the difficulties encountered by northern litigants and jurors in pre-division times on the trips to Clonmel and on the return journey

The greatest difficulty we had to surmount in forwarding the proceedings of the Assizes for publication in the Free Press was the want of a direct communication with Clonmel, all letters and parcels being obliged to be sent via Limerick or Roscrea, in either case a round of 20 miles ... there never was a more disgraceful thoroughfare than that portion of the turnpike road leading from Cashel to Thurles ... the public conveyance on which we travelled from Nenagh was obliged to be driven over the pathway, the high road being there perfectly impassable.

Judge Crampton, who was actually locum Lord Chancellor on the first day of those 1839 assizes, was joined on the bench for his opening address in the Crown Court in the old courthouse in Pound Street[25] by Lord Dunalley, no doubt an acknowledgement of his lead role in the successful campaign by Nenagh and the north.

The Pound Street 'Sessions House' was quite inadequate, according to the County Surveyor, Samuel Jones. He urged the building of a new courthouse conjointly with the gaol.

John B. Keane, Dublin,[26] was appointed as architect for the gaol and later for the new courthouse. He also designed Tullamore[27] and Waterford[28] courthouses, the House of Correction attached to Clonmel's County Gaol,[29] Queen's College, Galway (now U.C.G.)[30] and St Francis Xavier church, Upper Gardiner St, Dublin.[31] In the locality he was awarded commissions for Borrisokane courthouse and bridewell[32] and the altar in Nenagh's R.C. chapel in Chapel Lane.[33]

John Hanly, 27 Summerhill, Nenagh became the contractor for both Nenagh's gaol and courthouse. He had built Grawn R.C. church in Cloughjordan parish (1830), the Military Barracks in Nenagh (1832) and Carrig R.C. church in Monsea parish (1833).[34]

The contract amounts were £18,000 for the gaol and £7,000 for the courthouse.[35] One must recall Keane's estimate of a total £15,000 at the June 1837 Committee hearing and the earl of Glengall's foreboding: 'very probably that sum will not suffice, as estimates are not always to be trusted'. But Keane's 1837 estimate was for 100 prisoners drawing on four baronies. Meantime the catchment had been finalised at five and a half baronies and the gaol plans provided cells for 192 prisoners.

NORBURY MUNIFICENCE
'We understand that the ground selected for the site of the new gaol is that which was offered as a grant by the late and much lamented Lord Norbury'. Behind that information lay a footnote to the story of Nenagh's selection as assize town, revealed in an 1865 book.[36] The author, Robert Maunsell, tells of passing by Dublin Castle on his way to court and being told that the Privy Council was considering the partition of Tipperary into Ridings, and the selection of an assize town for the northern division.

So I went up, out of curiosity, to see what decision would he come to, little doubting that Nenagh – which partly belonged to an esteemed friend of mine – would be chosen in preference to any other. On entering the council chamber, however, I was mistaken; my then friend Charley R–, who was professionally concerned as counsel for the inhabitants of Nenagh, came running up to me and said, 'we are fairly undone, unless you afford us relief, for', says he, 'there's that horrible Jesuit man, Anthony Richard Blake who offers ground free of rent in Lady Elizabeth Mathew's ancient town of Thurles, whereupon to erect the Court House and Jail and all other requisite buildings; if you, on behalf of your client the earl of Norbury, will alike undertake on behalf of the town of Nenagh, we will carry the day'. So I said, 'get me pen, ink, and paper … .

Blake, being a long-sighted man, looked forward to the time when – and that in a great measure through his own instrumentality – the judge of assize, the counsel, and petit jury would all be Romanists, and he was desirous to provide good spiritual comfort for them, which he well knew from experience was to be had in great abundance in the convents, nunneries, and monasteries of Thurles where mother abbesses, nuns and priests abound without number, because Anthony, no doubt, often himself did penance in one or other of these convents, and he therefore considered it essential that these officials should have an opportunity twice a year, at least, to cleanse themselves from the impurities contracted in passing sentences of death and incarceration upon the many culprits arraigned before them ….

Maunsell's piece of paper was thrown on the scales, so to speak, by Lord Bloomfield late in the evidence on 16 June 1837 with a timing born of his two brilliant careers in the army and Court-diplomatic service. Charley R– was clearly Charles Rolleston, the junior counsel for the Nenagh lobby. Maunsell's memory as regards the Thurles advocacy was, however, dimmed by the thirty-year lapse between the event and the recounting of it, and by sectarian prejudice which is clear in his Blake-Thurles fantasy. Blake was in a judicial role on the Committee; it was John Hatchell, KC, who made the offer for Thurles on behalf of Elizabeth or Elisha Mathew, Lady Llandaff.[37]

NORBURY MURDER
Two years on, Lord Norbury, born Hector John Graham Toler, second earl and second son of the first earl, John Toler (the 'Hanging Judge'),[38]

was dead. He had been a Deputy Lieutenant of King's County, living in Durrow Abbey near Tullamore.

> Walking in his plantation accompanied by his steward and probably devising some plan for which to give employment to hundreds of men, he was brutally shot in the heart by one of that race who know no code of morality.[39]

The murdered second earl, of Beechwood, Nenagh ancestry, had 3,598 acres with 156 tenants in King's County. He also employed large numbers directly. Landlord-tenant relations in general were good, but a small number of evictions had occurred. There is some evidence that these were attributed to harsh attitudes by his agent, George Garvey, but still Norbury was widely given tributes such as 'kind', 'benevolent', 'good', and including such words as 'respect', 'affection'.[40]

Six months later a valuation inquest was held to determine what compensation should be paid to occupiers of the land and buildings on the intended site of the gaol and courthouse. John O'Brien, Peter Holmes's legal agent, informed the jury that Mr Garvey, the third earl of Norbury's agent, had told him he would acquaint him before that day if Lord Norbury were making a claim. Mr Gason as Commissioner reported a conversation with Garvey and confirmed to a juryman, Mr Burr, that Garvey's declaration was binding on Lord Norbury. Mr Maunsell requested that Lord Norbury's waiving of a claim be noted down together with Garvey's declaration to Gason. O'Brien went on to say that Peter Holmes was waiving the head rent of £14 16s. 2d.[41]

In fact it would appear that George Garvey had no legal grounds for inferring that his employer might make a claim. The second earl had on 17 December 1838, only two weeks before his murder, renewed a lease from Peter Holmes for three fields in the vicinity of the castle. Extraordinarily, in the following two weeks prior to his murder he had surrendered, to the lessor Peter Holmes, five acres and ten perches of the three fields.[42]

One presumes that the son and his agent Garvey were not fully aware of that legality and were consciously honouring the offer made on his father's behalf by Maunsell in 1837; the earl's motto required him only to be 'Faithful to my king and country'.[43]

Or it may be that other matters weighed on his mind. Under the headline 'Alleged Seduction by Lord Norbury of his housemaid', the *Nenagh Guardian* reported a claim by Martha Woodland for expenses incurred upon the accouchement of her sister Elizabeth. Elizabeth had been housemaid to the Lord at Brighton and 'in consequence of something that occurred there he had brought her to London'. Letters from Norbury to both Elizabeth and her sister clearly made him liable for recoupment of the expense involved. The newspaper passed no comment this time on lack of adherence to a code of morality.[44]

The total compensation awards, despite the free land from Norbury, amounted to £1,524.[45]

DEVELOPMENT

The chronology of the two buildings which were jointly to become the catalyst of much town development was as follows. The grand jury at that spring assizes in late March 1839 presented the sum of £18,000 for the new county gaol which obtained the judge's fiat or go-ahead. It was to be advanced from the (National) Consolidated Fund and repaid to the Collector of Excise over twenty years in forty half-yearly instalments of £450. Several names now familiar headed the list of Commissioners to carry the project into effect; they included six of the appointing Grand Jury.

Lord Dunalley, The Hon. F. A. Prittie, Peter Holmes, R. W. Gason, R. U. Bayly, George Jackson, James Willington, Caleb Going, Traverston, Dolla; John Bennett, Riverston, Nenagh; Stephen Hastings Atkins, Birdhill; James Dempster, 19 Castle St., Nenagh; Malachi Ryan, Tyone, Nenagh.[46]

In mid-June the Commissioners examined three tenders obtained for the gaol and appointed John Hanly as contractor.[47] In mid-July they held the inquest, already mentioned, for the valuation of lands to recompense the displaced occupiers already mentioned.[48] In the last week of August architect Keane supervised the laying out of the boundaries, with seventy labourers levelling and excavating.[49] A few days later the foundation stone was laid.[50] Two years and ten months on, in July 1842, Hanly handed over the County Gaol to the Grand Jury, having at one stage conceded an increase in wages upon a strike by the tradesmen and labourers.[51] Francis White, Inspector-General of Prisons, had inspected the gaol on 25 July 1842 and reported thus to its Commissioners:

I feel called upon to express my perfect approbation of this extensive establishment and also express my decided approval and admiration for the arrangement, classification, accommodation and construction of the several sections of the prison so perfectly calculated to carry out all the modern improvements of prison discipline. Indeed Gentlemen, I have no hesitation in stating that your new gaol at Nenagh is one of the most perfect prisons in Ireland, and may be forthwith occupied by prisoners.[52]

His full report for the year 1842 elaborated.[53] Apart from smoking chimneys and a leaking roof, a need for some alterations in ventilation and heating, the Inspector found 'strict cleanliness and a proper systematic discipline' and 'very efficient' officers.

The complex consisted of an octagonal Governor's House and seven male cell blocks radiating from it, a female prison to the rear, between them providing 192 sleeping cells, male and female infirmaries, nine day rooms, seven workshops, nine turnkeys' apartments, twenty-eight airing yards, two chapels, a laundry, a forge, stores, a treadwheel, drains, a thirty-foot wall surrounding all and culminating in an imposing entrance fronting the gatehouse which itself incorporated four condemned cells.

The twelve wholetime and six part-time jobs created by the advent of the gaol were scheduled in the report: Governor, Deputy Governor, Head Turnkey, gate turnkey and six turnkeys, Matron and assistant, a local Inspector, medical attendant, Secretary, apothecary and RC and Church of Ireland chaplains.[54] The Inspector commented that the Deputy Governor 'conducts the Office Department with much ability, and the different Returns forwarded to me, showed accuracy, clearness, and business-like habits.'

The gaol was a hive of industry with male prisoners engaged in tailoring, shoemaking, stone-breaking, teasing hair, tread wheel and prison duties, while the female residents were occupied with needlework, washing and mangling, spinning and carding, nursing and prison duties.

The Inspector noted that the Board of Superintendence for the running of the gaol 'included one above the number directed by Law'. They included six who had been among the commissioners for the erection of the gaol.

The Hon. Mr Prittie	James Butler
Peter Holmes	James Willington
R. Wm Gason	Jonathan Walsh
Richard Bayly	R. E. Phillips
Joshua R. Minnitt	George Jackson
Caleb Minnitt	Thomas G. Stoney
John Bennett	

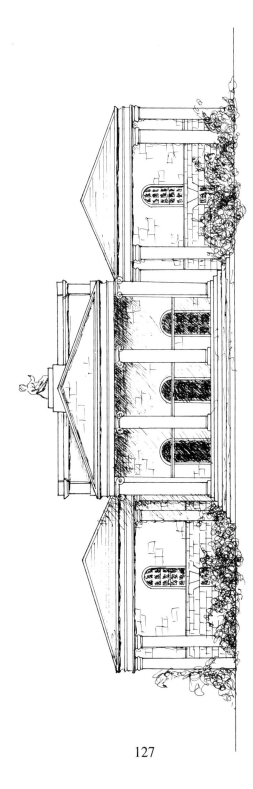

Plate 14: Nenagh Courthouse, with the figure of Justice over the pediment. Fashioned in cement, the statue's weight caused the pediment to crack; on the advice of a consultant architect the grand jury agreed to its removal in 1896.

Drawing – Deirdre O'Dowd, from a Lawrence photograph.

The first execution in Nenagh took place on 17 August 1842 when a man convicted of murder was hanged in public from a scaffold erected at the entrance. The scene attracted 'a multitude' who knelt and prayed following his speech which protested innocence. The *Nenagh Guardian*'s graphic account of 'the awful spectacle' was supported by an editorial and followed a week later by another editorial, both making an eloquent case for the abolition of capital punishment.[55] The patrons averaged 90 in the first six months.[56] In modern terms, the 33,000 bed-nights per annum obviously helped to bring trade to the 'new shop fronts appearing in our street'.[57]

COURTHOUSE & STREETS

In April 1840 tenders were sought and opened for the new courthouse adjoining the gaol.[58] In February 1841, midway through the gaol contract, Keane was laying out the courthouse site and just three years later John Hanly handed over his second major job for the Grand Jury.[59] Meantime gaol labour had constructed an underground passage from inside the gaol wall to the dock in one of the semi-circular courts in the courthouse.[60] The Spring Assizes were held there in 1844.[61] Its former venue, the redundant Courthouse or Sessions House in Pound Street, went into service at intervals as an auxiliary barracks, ballroom and theatre, and coach factory.[62]

The street which was cut from the main street, Castle Street, to the new gaol was given the Christian name of Nenagh's proprietor, Peter Holmes.[63] This gave rise to an early example of urban renewal. Advertisements appeared as early as March 1840: 'a plot of ground in Peter Street in the most central part of town';[64] again, in May 1840,

> over 3,000 feet OF FINEST BUILDING GROUND admitting the deepest gardens at the rear, in the large spacious street recently opened, offering incalculable advantages to those desirous of laying out their money IN A TOWN where not a foot of eligible building ground is to be had, not a private house to be let.[65]

Another road, New Cudville Road, was built by John Hanly from the Courthouse Square to Richmond Row.[66] Not without problems; the *Nenagh Guardian* reported in May 1846 that the townspeople were surprised that the new line was not opened. Work had been recommended by the Town Commissioners, and a special presentment at the Lower Ormond sessions had put forward a figure of £250.[67] Houses were built for the gaol turnkeys in Grace's Street, itself cut through the fields in mid-1839.[68]

COMMERCIAL SUCCESS

> … thousands upon thousands have been, in consequence, spent in the – till then – dirty old tumble-down town of Nenagh, and property quadrupled in value in consequence, and every spring and every summer the judges and barristers exhibit their persons and wigs, and make speeches, and with the grand and petit juries spend large sums of money amongst the inhabitants.[69]

TOWN GOVERNMENT

Just three months after the birth of the *Nenagh Guardian* and some weeks before the formal proclamation of Nenagh as an assize town, its leading citizens and neighbours took further action to enhance the town's status and development. Fifty-four persons started the procedure whereby twenty-one or more householders could seek an order from the Lord Lieutenant to convene a meeting which would consider adoption of an 1828 Act that provided for the lighting, watching, cleansing and paving of a town.[70] The signatories to the application included some omnipresent names: Lord Dunalley, Sir William Parker Carrol, Peter Holmes, John Kempston, Jun., Rev. Ambrose O'Connor, Parish Priest, Rev. James Hill Poe, Rector, John Dobbs, Barrack-Master, seven doctors and four solicitors/attorneys – the latter including, of course, O'Brien Dillon.[71]

The subsequent meeting, in November 1838, decided after 'a most turbulent scene' and by a majority of eighteen to adopt the Act.[72] They went through the process of election of twenty-one men to be Commissioners – women were a long way from eligibiity for the vote or for public representation. Then somebody – surely one of the solicitors – discovered 'an informality on the part of the government'. The Lord Lieutenant's clerk in Dublin Castle had addressed the convening order to 'the Mayor or Chief Magistrate of Nenagh'.[73] There was of course no Mayor and there was no provision in the Lighting of Towns Act, 1828, as it became known, for involvement of a chief magistrate. Samson Carter, the stipendiary or paid Resident Magistrate, had been *ultra vires* in acting on the order.[74]

A second memorial elicited a proper convening order addressed to two Justices of the Peace 'resident within ten miles of the town', namely Peter Holmes, Nenagh, and John Bayly, Debsboro, Ballinaclough.[75] They convened a meeting which was held on 10 January 1839.[76] Influenced no doubt by the previous turbulence, the *Nenagh Guardian* worried about the outcome and went on record in clear pro-development terms.

129

IMPROVEMENT OF NENAGH

We do most earnestly hope that the respectable Householders of Nenagh will be early in attendance on Thursday (10 Jan) next at the Court-house, and by their presence and support, endeavour to carry into effect the Provisions of the Act of 9th Geo. IV in the County town of North Riding of Tipperary. We have learned that a fractious few – who perhaps do not appreciate the benefits their town will receive in this measure, or who may be prejudiced or influenced against the contemplative improvement intend to give opposition on the occasion. We therefore again repeat our hope that those who desire to see their town improve in its appearance, as much as in progressing in importance, will be at the Court-house EARLY.[77]

A stirring debate centred on fears of the high cost of improvements and therefore of rates to be levied on the householders. It ended in a 90-76 vote for 'cleansing and paving'.

The other functions enabled by the 1828 Act, 'lighting and watching', i.e. the employment of a night watchman, were not adopted and had to await further developments in 1847.[78] This despite the *Nenagh Guardian*'s succinct yet graphic outline the previous November of the benefits of lighting and watching:

Those unfortunate females by whom our streets are disgraced and disturbed each succeeding night could no longer, under the shelter of darkness, be the temptation and ruin of the rising generation.[79]

The statistics show that about 40% of eligible householders took part in that vital first step in democracy – that decision to adopt this new form of public authority which would provide and maintain those basic amenities.

Only ten of the twenty-one invalidly selected on the previous abortive occasion were among the twenty now designated Nenagh's first Town Commissioners,[80] due to remain in office for three years (the Act allowed any number from nine to twenty-one). This is a puzzling feature in that the eleven not elected on the second, valid occasion were, by and large, very significant figures. They included Peter Holmes, the proprietor of the town, the Parish Priest, the leading industrialists, two doctors, at least one landowner of substance, and a man who would prove a vote-getter later that year in the Board of Guardians' elections.[81] Did some mature reflection by them upon the

130

previous turbulent proceedings cause them to regard the Commissioners as beneath their dignity; did some absent themselves on the second occasion; did some lose out in an unreported vote? There are no clues in the Press. Another indication of the healthy volatility in early town politics is that only five of the pioneering twenty were among the second crop elected in 1841, and only six of the first twenty were elected in 1843.[82]

There were only three of the inaugural commissioners who were not among the requisitionists who initiated the two householders' meetings and who are listed in Appendix Eight. O'Brien Dillon was elected Chairman at the first meeting on 25 January 1839 when the thirteen who attended were 'sworn into office' by Messrs Holmes and Bayly; the remainder, who 'were unavoidably absent', were due to be sworn in at the next meeting. George O'Leary became the first Clerk.[83]

BRIDGING FINANCE

Those first Commissioners did not let grass grow under their paving, so to speak. Because it was 'quite impossible to raise any money under the assessment in time for cleansing the town previous to the Assizes,' in a March 1839 advertisement they 'respectfully intimate to the nobility and gentry in the vicinity of Nenagh, who are outside the rated boundary, that the Commissioners will attend at the Record Court, from the hour of 1 to 2 o'clock in the afternoon of Monday, 18th inst for the purpose of receiving voluntary contributions'.[84]

By April they had contracted with William Sullivan, 4 Ellen St, Limerick for the laying of flagged footways, and he advertised for six operative masons. 'Nenagh men would be preferred if found competent'.[85] In late June the *Nenagh Guardian's* editor (who had not become a Town Commissioner) praised the Agricultural Bank for advancing a loan of £250 for two years in order to do the job at once rather than piecemeal.[86] He praised the Commissioners, 'and we further hope that as soon as their own immediate neighbourhood is finished they will direct the contractor's attention to the upper end of Castle Street' (where the *Guardian* works were situated, opposite its present location at No. 13 Summerhill; that part of Castle Street was so re-named in September 1839).[87]

At the 1840 Summer Assizes the Grand Jury had before them an application from the fledgling town authority for help. John Bayly supported a presentment for flagging the footways of the town. 'The sum of £300 had already been raised by subscriptions and expended on flagging the town by which it was considerably improved and he was sure they had done more for their town than had been done for any other town in the county'. But Lieut.-Col. Dwyer, Lorrha, opposed it: 'the taxes already on the county were now, in consequence of the gaol, courthouse and other local improvements, double what they were before, and on the principle that it would increase the burden which the ratepayers were already scarcely able to bear he should oppose it'. The presentment was lost by 11 votes to 10. The former High Sheriff for the full County Tipperary, Count Peter D'Alton, Grenanstown, Toomevara, and Thomas George Stoney, Borrisokane, were absent; D'Alton, at least, might have been expected to vote for his shopping town's interests.[88]

However, persistence paid off. At the 1842 Spring Assizes the grand jury passed and the court gave its fiat to another presentment for 'flagging and improving the town of Nenagh', although opposed by a Mr George. Two years later another £100 was provided for flagging.

Meantime and without the town commissioners' involvement, the ultimate in demonstrating the times that were in it for Nenagh's new status, appropriately placed on the building which was the springboard for all these developments:

> A splendid clock, with two dials and which chimes the quarter hours, has been just erected in the turret of the Governor's House in our new Gaol. This is a most valuable acquisition to our town not having any public clock heretofore in Nenagh. It has been manufactured by MacMaster of Dublin and its cost is £140.[89]

PROPERTY TAX

In that first year the inaugural Commissioners raised £159 16s. 10^1/2d. by way of rates and spent it on paving, flagging and cleansing. Over two hundred houses whose annual value ranged from £5 to £10 were rated at 4^1/2d. in the £; almost one hundred valued at £10 to £20 at 6d. in the £; and just over another hundred valued at £20 and upwards at 9d. in the £. Those differential rates would read 1.875p, 2.5p and 3.75p in today's decimal currency; to make a comparison in early 1990s terms, one should multiply by approximately sixty-one to take fallen money values into account.[90]

The differential rates draw attention to two features of the 1828 Act: householders whose houses had an annual value of £5 or more were eligible to take part in a meeting to adopt the Act and vote in the election for commissioners and be levied for rates; only those valued at £20 or more were eligible for election.[91] The first commissioners are therefore seen to have imposed a rate on themselves of double that which they imposed on the majority of householders.

132

WHAT HAPPENED CLONMEL

Sixty-four other towns throughout Ireland opted for local democracy by adopting the Lighting of Towns Act, 1828. This movement was aided by the scrapping of fifty-eight municipal corporations of medieval origin – ineffective and often corrupt oligarchies. The statute responsible, the Municipal Corporations (Ireland) Act, 1840, also reformed the franchise by extending it to householders of £10 valuation and upwards (double the minimum required for towns with commissioners).

Although six decades away from an extensive liberalisation of the local government franchise, the not-so-plain people of Ireland were developing political muscle. Among the ten reformed borough corporations two at least signalled this dawn to the watching nation. In late 1841 Daniel O'Connell became Lord Mayor of Dublin. In 1843 John Hackett, editor of the *Tipperary Free Press,* who had printed Drummond's 1838 address to the Tipperary magistrates for widespread distribution as a broadsheet, became 'the first Catholic Lord Mayor of Clonmel since the reign of James II'.[92] He was followed by O'Connell's friend and patron, Charles Bianconi, who had come to Ireland as a young Italian pedlar, put a horse and outside car for passengers on a daily Clonmel-Cahir run in 1815 and had now 1,300 horses and 100 vehicles travelling 3,800 miles per day to service most corners of Ireland at reasonable fares – a naturalised British subject since 1831.[93] The capital of the South Riding may have lost its pull on half a county but it had gained meaningful borough status and the reflected fame of a national figure of immense popularity whom it had nurtured.

Side by side with borough status it had gained town commissioners; it was one of the first towns in the country to exercise self-determination by adopting the Lighting of Towns Act, 1828. On 17 September 1828 the *Clonmel Advertiser* carried a notice by the Mayor, W. Chaytor, of the requisite householders' meeting. It was held on 25 September 1828 and elected the first commissioners for watching and lighting, supplying with water and abating nuisances. The provisions of the Act for cleansing, repairing and paving the streets were not adopted because the corporation already exercised those functions.[94]

The inaugural twenty-one did not include three prominent names already encountered – Bianconi, John Hackett and John Luther. However, they were all among the third set of commissioners elected unanimously 'after much discussion' in July 1834 [95] and, on a sampling of reports, Bianconi and Hackett were among the fifth set elected in 1840.[96] Hackett can be termed the O'Brien Dillon of Clonmel in that he was both Chairman of the Town Commissioners and Lord Mayor in 1843. Six others doubled as borough councillors and town commissioners in that year. Hackett did not compete in the inaugural elections in 1839 for Poor Law Guardians to govern the novel poor law unions. Bianconi did and headed the poll in the Clonmel electoral district.[97] Nine others of those first guardians (see note 97 to Chapter Six) appear as borough councillors and/or town commissioners in the limited sample in notes 94-6 to this chapter.

THE FIRST TSR GRAND JURY

As stated above, the pioneering 1839 grand jurors for the first two assizes in both the North and South Ridings are listed as Tables 2 and 3.

Among the thirty-three men who were on the South Riding Grand Juries for either the Spring or Summer Assizes of that year, there were only six who had not been on any of the previous eleven grand juries stretching from the Spring of 1834 to the Special Commission of January 1839. The phenomenon arises from the preponderance of men from the south in those countywide grand juries, as adverted to in Chapter Two.[98]

The High Sheriff for the year, Count D'Alton from the north, had little or no problem in selecting his men. It will be noted also that there was a bias towards gentlemen from Iffa and Offa, both West and East, as heretofore.

At the Spring Assizes the first South Riding Grand Jury took cognizance of a problem arising from the transition from one county to two. It was dealt with in a practical and honourable manner arising from the following recommendation of the County Surveyor.

> The Proclamation of the division of the county has placed the North Riding in a very novel position, in as much as the Grand Jury of that portion have no funds at their disposal, nor is there even so much as may be necessary to honour the Court Orders or other demands necessarily growing out of the division, for while there are some balances to the credit of the northern baronies, still I believe the grand jury of the South Riding have alone the power of allocation of same; under those circumstances, and taking into consideration the peculiar position of that riding, it would be justice to re-present such balances in aid of the baronies off which they were originally levied, and placed at all events at the disposal of the North Riding grand jury, by which means an available fund amounting to £1,961 18*s*. 6*d*. will be at once created.[99]

Table 3	GRAND JURIES, 1839: South Riding of the County of Tipperary	
	SPRING	SUMMER
Bagwell, John, Marlfield, Clonmel*	√	√
Barton, Samuel W., Rochestown, Cahir	√	√
Barton, Thomas Barker, Grove, Fethard	√	√
Butler, James Archer, Garnavilla, Cahir	√	√
Creagh, Lawrence, Castlepark, Golden	√	
Creagh, Richard, Castlepark, Golden		√
Going, Ambrose, Ballyphillip, Killenaule	√	
Jacob, Matthew, Mobarnan, Fethard		√
Jephson, Lorenzo H, Carrick House		√
King, Hon J., Mitchelstown Castle, Co. Cork	√	
Long, Richard, Longfield, Cashel	√	√
Lowe, Richard Butler H, Kenilworth, Clonmel	√	√
Maher, John, Tullamaine Castle, Fethard	√	√
Mansergh, R.S., Greenane, Tipperary	√	
Millet, Matthew, Kyle, Fethard	√	
Moore, Edward Crosbie, Mooresfort, Lattin, Tipperary		√
Moore, Maurice Crosbie, Mooresfort, Lattin	√	
Moore, Stephen, Barn, Clonmel	√	√
O'Callaghan, Hon C., Shanbally Castle, Clogheen**		√
O'Donnell, William, Cottage, Ardnageha, Clonmel		√
O'Meagher, Stephen, Kilmoyler, Cahir	√	
Pennefather, Richard, Knockeven, Clonmel	√	
Pennefather, William, Lakefield, Fethard		√
Perry, Samuel, Barona, Clonmel		√
Perry, William, Woodrooffe, Clonmel	√	
Power, James, Ballydine, Carrick-on-Suir	√	√
Purefoy, Col. William, Greenfields, Tipperary	√	
Quin(n),William, Loughlohery Castle, Cahir	√	√
Riall, William H, Clonmel	√	√
Roe, James, Roesboro, Tipperary	√	√
Sadleir, Richard, Scallaheen, Tipperary		√
Scully, James, Kilfeacle, Tipperary		√
Scully, John, Dualla, Cashel	√	√

*Foreman, Spring Assizes
**Foreman, Summer Assizes

Sources: Spring Assizes – *T.F.P.* 6 Mar 1839
        Summer Assizes – *T.F.P.* 13 July 1839

See Figure 6, p. 136

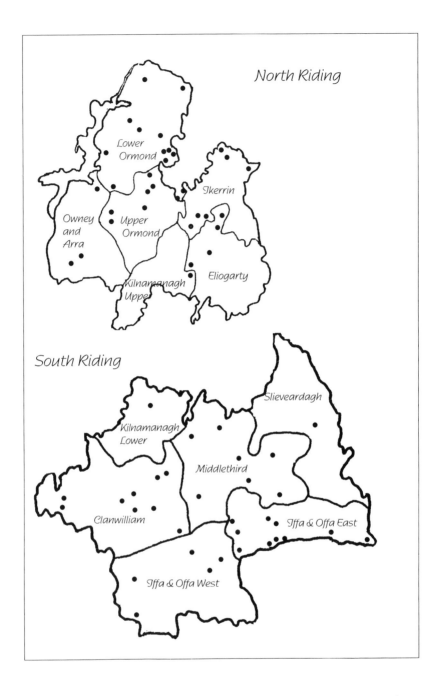

Fig. 6: The approximate residences of the 1839 Spring and Summer Assizes grand jurors.

Some evidence of how firmly the county's division was already established is furnished by a *Tipperary Free Press* report of 3 April 1839 of a meeting to protest against any change in the Corn Laws. The meeting was expressly for people from the 'southern division'; the list of participants was headed by no less a person than the thirteenth-hour objector to the division, the earl of Glengall.

THE SOUTH RIDING'S GAOL

It will be recalled that an initial reason or excuse for seeking a second assize town and division of the county was the inadequacy of the County Gaol at Clonmel as reported upon in 1828 by the Inspectors-General of Prisons.

Clonmel at the time of the report had a house of correction, a county gaol, a sheriff's gaol and a marshalsea for debtors. There was also a House of Industry, sometimes called a workhouse, dating from 1811. Originally it housed vagrants, lunatics, prostitutes, petty criminals, the old and infirm and, as of 1822, orphans. Changes in the gaol structure and the advent of the district asylum in 1834 saw the removal of criminals and lunatics from the confines of the gaol, leaving only the poor, the infirm and orphans.[100]

In 1830 the grand jury took the first steps to rectify the gaol's problems by initiating the erection of a new, additional house of correction which was completed in 1834. The following year the Inspector expressed himself highly satisfied with the system in operation in the new building which held 100 male prisoners serving sentences.

> ... There are five classes ... with a turnkey to each, every prisoner is employed by day and has a single cell by night, various trades are taught and a considerable degree of silence is preserved ... [101]

The report indicates that the improvements in the system were achieved by one Thomas Ryan whom the Board of Superintendence had appointed Master of Works. Indeed Clonmel was the first gaol to implement the section of an 1826 Act[102] which allowed for such an appointment.[103] This practice was continued after Ryan was appointed Governor of Waterford County Gaol – his extraordinary achievement there is recounted in Appendix Eleven.

Notwithstanding that the old house of correction, still in use, and county gaol buildings were still grossly overcrowded, the 1841 report was in the same laudatory vein. 'It is', he wrote, 'gratifying to report the state of efficiency in the Gaol and House of Correction ... the whole prison is heated by Arnott's Stoves, with tin pipes, at a very trifling expense and great saving of fuel, should this plan stand the test of experience it may be adopted in every Gaol in Ireland ... Trades are taught, chiefly Carpenters, Sawyers, Tailors, Shoemakers, Tinware, Blanket making and Smith's work.' He also praised the innovation in the female prison of taking in washing for the townspeople as being 'profitable and useful', with the observation that this was an unusual experiment for a country gaol. On a negative note he expressed regret that the female prisoners were not yet 'clothed in Prison Dress'.

He forecast that the daily average of 340 prisoners 'would be greatly reduced when Nenagh Gaol is occupied ...'.[104] The report for 1843 indeed showed that outcome. Clonmel gaol had 156 prisoners on 31 December while Nenagh had 172.[105] The 'removal of prisoners to Nenagh gaol' had also brought about the enlargement of the debtors section of the gaol.[106]

STATE OF THE TOWNS, 1839

To adopt the phraseology of the *Nenagh Guardian*'s assessment, the patriotic efforts of the noblemen and gentlemen to elevate the district in the scale of social importance had among its practical results that Nenagh had become the capital of North Tipperary. The impetus created had brought to the new capital an increase in business and employment, a major complex of public buildings, a newspaper, and its first taste of immediate, local self-government. Significantly, two other North Tipperary towns, without this massive accrual of self-confidence, did not adopt Town Commissioners until much later – Templemore in 1860, Thurles in 1861. Roscrea never did, even during the 1980s which saw that development in three growing towns, Shannon, Co. Clare, 1982, Greystones, Co. Wicklow, 1984, and Leixlip, Co. Kildare, 1988. Roscrea did toy with the idea as early as December 1828 by requisitioning a public meeting but I failed to find any follow-up.[107]

The south Tipperary towns appear to have had considerably more self-assurance than their northern counterparts. Tipperary was the first to follow Clonmel's lead by electing commissioners in January 1834. Carrick-on-Suir followed in October 1836, Cashel in 1840, and Fethard at some unidentified stage before that again.[108]

Whatever loss occurred to individual businesses in Clonmel by way of the reduction of supplies to its gaol, both prisoners and their keepers had benefited enormously within four years of the county's division.

The noblemen and gentlemen continued the oligarchy in the county. Land ownership being the basic qualification, almost all the grand jurors were Protestant. Patrick C. Power has identified only four Catholics,

O'Donnell, Power and the two Scullys, on the first South Riding grand jury. With Ryan alone on the first North Riding Grand Jury, they underline the scarcity of Catholics in the upper echelons of landholders.[109] The towns, however, were now giving a political outlet to both the Catholic majority of the population and the trader, businessman and professional. Nenagh's first crop of twenty commissioners included at least eleven Catholics, eleven businessmen, four attorneys and two doctors (it is not possible to identify the religion or occupations of all).

It may be appropriate in the next, concluding chapter to seek hints, by examining the personality and activities of one of those new power brokers, as to what manner of men were these rising people.

Notes

1. John Kempston, Jun. (1789-1851), was a son of John Kempston, the owner of the *Clonmel Advertiser*. John Jun. was an active promoter of Nenagh's interests from arrival until his death in 1851 aged 62. He is buried in Kenyon St graveyard in Nenagh.
2. *T.F.P.*, 25 July 1838.
3. Consumer Price Index, mid-May 1994 to base July 1914=100; figures for the further period are extrapolated by 'empirical estimates for 1846-1922', kindly supplied by Mr John O'Hagan, Central Statistics Office, with the caution that they are in no sense official estimates.
4. The *Clonmel Advertiser* ceased publication late in its twenty-seventh year with the issue of 7 April 1838. Its editorial that day both explained Clonmel's loss and Nenagh's gain, and pompously affirmed its conservative or unionist stance:

> The announcement of a new undertaking, conveyed to our friends in the prospectus which appeared in several successive numbers of our Journal, had already prepared them for the line we are about to write that from this day the *Advertiser* ceases to be published in Clonmel.
>
> We did intend continuing the publication of the advertisement until the *Nenagh Guardian* had assumed its paternal care over the principles of the Constitution in the North Riding of Tipperary, but we found, upon mature consideration, that it would be better to devote the short interval of time left to us between this and the 2nd June to a full and adequate preparation for the duties which lie before us.

None of the other three Clonmel papers referred to the *Advertiser's* passing, except by way of the *Tipperary Free Press* implying that it had merely changed name and address. The same *Press* played tough by incorporating the name *Clonmel Advertiser* as a sub-title to its own as of later 1837. The name was repeated twice more for short-lived publications. The first in 1843 had the tag, ' ... *and Literary Journal*',

139

and was more magazine than newspaper. The second, in 1884, was a brave try by a two-page halfpenny sheet, printed from the type and press of the *Tipperary Free Press* which had expired in 1881. Its owner was Edward McDonald, Abbey St, the former foreman printer with the *Press*. There is some piquancy in noting that, 110 years later, the (Nenagh) *Guardian* which has outlived threefold the longest survivor of its early Clonmel contemporaries, published an obituary of Edward McDonald's daughter Ciss who died eight days short of a 105th birthday. And just as John Kempston, Jun., and John O'Shea brought Clonmel expertise to Nenagh, Edward McDonald's son Tom, with his brother-in-law Pádraig Ó Meadhra, compiled *The Spirit of Tipperary* (Nenagh, 1939) – Very Rev. William P. Canon Burke, *History of Clonmel* (Clonmel, 1907), pp. 351-7; 'Passing of Toomevara's Oldest Resident', *The Guardian*, 12 March 1994.

5. *N.G.,* 16 Mar 1839.

6. ditto, 23 Mar 1839.

7. Peter D'Alton, (1775-1851), Grenanstown, Nenagh, was a son of Edward D'Alton, Lieut.-Gen. of the Austrian Army who was killed at the siege of Dunkirk in 1793, and who had been named as a Count of the German and Holy Roman Empire by Maria Theresa. Peter was the natural father of Richard Dalton Williams (1822-62), medical doctor, poet and Young Irelander.

   The first Peter D'Alton, from Dundonnell, Westmeath, had obtained 1,528 acres by the Act of Settlement of 1666 in Traverstown, Ballinenagh, etc., and probably purchased Grenanstown from Captain Salt, a Cromwellian grantee of what was John Grace's land in 1640. In the year of Count Peter D'Alton's birth, 1775, the Kilboy MSS recorded that the estate was valued at an income of £1,000 yearly – Donal A. Murphy & Nancy Murphy, 'The Toomevara Shamrock in Louisiana,' Part One, *The Guardian*, 3 April 1993.

8. *N.G.,* 23 Mar 1839.

9. *T.F.P.*, 23 Mar 1839.

10. *N.G.*, 9 Mar 1839.

11. *T.F.P.*, 24 July 1839. Townsend remained only until 1845 when Andrew H. Crawford commenced a forty-six year tenure until the year of his death, 1891, aged 80 – Ormond Historical Society, *Ballinaclough Gravestone Inscriptions* (Nenagh, 1982).

12. *Pettigrew & Oulton*, 1835 to 1839;*Thoms*, 1842, p. 241, 1844, p. 265, 1845, p. 273, and 1846, p. 574.

13. Richard Uniacke Bayly (1807-81), Ballinaclough House was a younger brother of John Bayly, Debsboro. An elected member of Nenagh Poor Law Guardians, he was chairman when he survived an assassination attempt in 1847 for which three men were later hanged, though Bayly had petitioned the Lord Lieutenant for a reprieve for one. ('The Gaol Story' display in the Gatehouse of Nenagh District Heritage Centre).

14. *N.G.*, 6 July 1839.

15. ditto, 16 Jan, 20 Mar 1839. O'Shea had come from Limerick city as Nenagh's National bank manager in 1836 (*C.J.*, 15 Dec 1836). He departed Nenagh for the Carlow branch of the Tipperary Joint Stock Bank in 1845 and was replaced by W. C. Moroney from the Roscrea branch (*N.G.*, 15 Oct 1845). In 1854 a William Healy was at the Nenagh branch, named as the agent for the National Loan Fund Life Assurance (*N.G.*, 18 Feb 1854). The National's new manager, succeeding O'Shea in January, 1839 was a Mr Gough, late accountant at Ballina, Co. Mayo.

16. The Tipperary Joint Stock Bank collapsed in February 1856. There is a full account of the tragedy in Marnane, *Land and Violence*, cited already, pp. 74-6.

17. *T.F.P.*, 21 July 1838; G. L. Barrow, *The Emergence of the Irish Banking System, 1820-45* (Dublin, 1975): Bank of Ireland, pp. 1-3; Provincial Bank, pp. 75-8; Agricultural and Commercial Bank, pp. 116-20 (quotation pp. 117-18); National Bank, pp. 120-5; Tipperary Joint Stock Bank, p. 161, including quotation; bank branch opening dates, Appendix Three, pp. 215-9. Nenagh's Provincial Bank branch opened in Burr's, Barrack St, early in 1856 (*N.G.*, 27 Feb 1856), almost coincidental with the Tipperary Joint Stock Bank's collapse. The Provincial moved to new premises at the corner of Peter St and Dwyer's Lane (renamed Bank Place) in 1864 (*N.G.*, 9 Mar 1864). The premises became the Garda Síochána station in 1986 following the Provincial's amalgamation with Munster & Leinster as AIB (Murphy, *Walkabout Nenagh*, pp. 85-6).

18. 'On Wednesday last, 17 April, James Blake was executed in front of the County Gaol [Clonmel] for the murder of his wife near Urlingford. This unfortunate man, we understand, felt quite reluctant to submit to his awful doom and he approached the fatal drop with much fear and trembling. He did not address the multitude assembled to witness his ignominious exit from this world, and when he launched into eternity died, apparently, without a struggle. The Rev. Mr Power, R.C.C. attended him in his last moments. – *Free Press* '(*N.G.*, 24 Apr 1839).

19. *N.G.,* 3 Apr 1839.

20. Crampton had been Solicitor-General from 1830 to 1834, immediately preceding Michael O'Loghlen. In 1834 he had the distinction of polling six votes to the other two candidates' 307 and 260 in an 1834 by-election for Dungarvan borough – L. J. Proudfoot, 'Landlords and Politics: Youghal and Dungarvan in the 1830s' in *Decies,* no. xxxiv, Spring 1987, p. 40.

21. *N.G.*, 23 Mar 1839.

22. ditto, 30 Jan 1839.

23. ditto, 14 Mar 1840.

24. *T.F.P.*, 30 Mar 1839.

25. The 'Sessions House, Pound St' was built circa 1760 in Jacobean style; it remained the venue of both assizes and Quarter Sessions until the new courthouse was handed over in 1844.

26. Keane's address is given in *Watson's Almanack*, 1825-30 and in *Thoms*,

1847, as 19 Mabbot St. *Watson* 1840 had Keane at 44 Mabbot St. Keane died in 1859.

27. Michael Byrne, *A Walk Through Tullamore* (Tullamore, 1980), p. 27.
28. Information courtesy of Mr David Slattery, Senior Architect, O.P.W.
29. *C.A.*, 8 Feb 1832. The contractors for the House of Correction were Messrs Murray, Dublin.
30. *D.N.B.*, 10, p. 1156. Here he is erroneously named as Joseph.
31. Maurice Craig, *Dublin 1660-1860* (Dublin, 1969) p. 292 and Corrigenda; its index is incorrect in giving the name as Joseph B. Keane.
32. *N.G.*, 27 July 1843.
33. ditto, 15 July 1843. The altar was executed by William Harding, Nenagh.
34. Nancy Murphy, *Walkabout Nenagh* (Nenagh, 1994), p. 103.
35. *N.G.*, 17 Mar 1841.
36. *N.G.*., 23 Mar 1839; Robert Maunsell, *Recollections of Ireland*, by 'A Late Professional Gentleman' (Dublin, 1865), pp. 156-7. The identity of the anonymous author as published is revealed in the National Library of Ireland index as R. Maunsell, further identified from *Thoms*, 1846, as Robert, a King's Counsel.
37. Council Office Papers, V–VIIC N.A.
38. John Toler (the 'Hanging Judge') (1745-1831) was born at Beechwood (formerly Graigue), Nenagh, son of Nicholas Toler (d. 1732) and brother of Daniel who was High Sheriff of Tipperary in 1766, the year Rev.. Nicholas Sheehy was tried and executed in Clonmel.
39. *N.G.*, 6 Jan 1839.
40. M. Byrne, 'Who Killed Lord Norbury?', *Ireland's Own,* Summer Annual 1988, p. 54; Howard Bury Papers, Longford–Westmeath Co. Library, D/10-13, 16, 34; PP, State of Ireland in Relation to Crime, xi, xii, 1839, evidence pp. 1927, 6545, 10151.
41. *N.G.*, 17 July 1839.
42. Holmes Deed 2814, Limerick Regional Archives. These were storied acres in the vicinity of Nenagh Castle, sold by James Butler, the second Duke of Ormonde in 1703 to Nehemiah Donnellan, Chief Baron of the Exchequer. They passed from him to Robert Holmes in 1733 – Sheehan, *N. & its N.*, p. 74.
43. *Thoms,* 1846, p. 95.
44. *N.G.*, 24 July 1839.
45. ditto, 17 July 1839.
46. Sheehan, cited above, p. 25.
47. *N.G.*, 19 June 1839.
48. ditto, 17 July 1839.
49. ditto, 31 Aug 1839.
50. ditto, 4 Sept 1839.
51. ditto, 18 Mar 1840.
52. ditto, 27 July 1842. In 1984-5 the Governor's House and Gatehouse of the County Gaol were renovated as a Heritage Centre by a voluntary

committee, with funding from Bord Fáilte/Shannonside Tourism, the local authorities, and the long-term lessees of the building, the Sisters of Mercy. The Governor's House features exhibitions of social history, including a recreated schoolroom – the building was for decades part of the Sisters' secondary school. The Gatehouse features the condemned cells, execution room, and site of the scaffold.

53. Appendix to Twenty Second Report of the Inspectors-General of Prisons Ireland (1843), pp. 77-8.
54. The Inspectors-General's 1842 report, p. 77, scheduled 'the Names and [annual] Salaries of the various Officers of this Prison. The Salaries are upon an exceedingly moderate scale. The Salaries to be given to the Chaplains (the Rev. Mr. Poe, and the Rev. Mr. O'Connor, R.C.) have not yet been specified.' Jonathan Smith, Governor, £150; Thomas Rock, Deputy Governor and Clerk, £80; Robert Purtill, Head Turnkey, £30; William Grady, Gate Turnkey, £30; Turnkeys: H. Cole, J. Mills, T. Ellis, T. Greene, W. Greene, A. Chalmers, £25 each; E. Kelly, Matron, £30; M. Switzer, Assistant; Mr. Abbott , Local Inspector, £50; Dr. Quin, Medical Attendant, £30; Mr. E. Sadleir, Secretary, £25; Michael Harty, Apothecary, £5.
55. *N.G.*, 17, 24 Aug 1842: 'For it were better that ninety and nine guilty men should escape than one innocent man should suffer'; '… if the convict was innocent the sacrifice of his life was awful – but not a feather in the balance compared to the awfulness of his precipitation into eternity if he was guilty, guilty not only of murder, but of the abomination of premeditated falsehood'.
56. Appendix to Twenty-first Report of the Inspectors-General of Prisons etc. in Ireland (1842), pp. 77-8 N.A.
57. *N.G.*, 20 Feb 1841.
58. ditto, 3 Apr 1840.
59. ditto, 24 Feb 1844.
60. ditto, 30 Sept 1843. This exit from this passageway was boarded up in the late 1960s when a new liturgy of justice ordained the removal of the dock.
61. ditto, 23 Mar 1844.
62. Murphy, *Walkabout Nenagh*, pp. 25-6.
63. *N.G.*, 14 Sept 1839.
64. ditto, 18 Mar 1840.
65. ditto, 6 May 1840. This advertisement was addressed 'TO CAPITALISTS' and promised: 'The return for money so expended in building must be unusually great: and as an encouragement, no rent whatever will be charged till the Houses are in actual state of profit, and make a return to the builder. Application to Doctor Finucane, Castle Street, Nenagh.'
66. Actually, New Cudville Road (now Ashe Road) stopped short of Richmond Row (later Richmond Road, now St Conlon's Road), its actual terminus being that part of Pound Road which incorporates a row of

houses long known as Cudville.

The 1852 Primary/Griffith's Valuation lists only a Cuddyville Lane with three houses on the new stretch, whereas New Cudville Road does appear in the map drawn up in 1858 for the Holmes's Sale of Nenagh.

67. *N.G.*, 30 May 1846.
68. ditto, 28 Aug 1839 recorded that John Egan Grace, a solicitor, and 210 men 'cut a new street from that part of Castle St., between this office and Ivy House to Batchelors Walk', i.e. including what is now known as Church Road.
69. Maunsell, cited above, p. 157.
70. Lighting of Towns Act, 1828, 9 Geo IV, c. 82.
71. *N.G., 30 Oct, 7 & 14 Nov 1838.
72. ditto, 28 Nov 1838.
73. ditto, 24 Nov 1838.
74. ditto, 17 Nov 1838.
75. ditto, 29 Dec 1838.
76. ditto, 12 Jan 1839.
77. ditto, 9 Jan 1839.
78. Similar reticence occurred in Cavan where cleansing was put into effect and lighting rejected by the votes of public meetings, both in 1837 and 1840 (after a gap in the Commissioners' existence). Cavan adopted lighting in 1851 – T. S. Smyth, *The Civic History of the Town of Cavan*, pp. 70-1.
79. *N.G.*, 24 Nov 1838.
80. The inaugural 1839 Town Commissioners, as of that birthday of municipal government in the new county capital, 10 January 1839, were (the addresses, where given, have been assembled from *Pigot's Directory*, 1824, and *Slater's Directory*, 1846: Michael Harty, Apothecary [6 Castle Street]; B. Crane [Pound Street]; James O'Brien, Merchant [1 Castle Street]; Patrick Cane, Post Master [51 Castle Street]; Anthony Nolan, Shopkeeper [79 Castle Street]; Francis Byron, Linen & Woollen Draper [13 Castle Street]; John O'Brien, Sen., Attorney [8 Barrack Street]; Edward Lee, Attorney [23 Summerhill]; John Woulfe, Attorney [24 Summerhill]; Rody Spain, Merchant [2 Castle Street]; James Dempster, M.D. [19 Castle Street]; O'Brien Dillon, Attorney [Summerville]; Patrick (O')Meara, Chandler & Grocer [22-23 Castle Street]; J. Kennedy; Daniel Tracy, Apothecary [59 Castle Street]; David Brundley, [The King's Arms, 12 Castle Street]; William Bourke; Thaddeus O'Shea, Agent [Tipperary Joint Stock Bank, 30 Castle Street]; O'Neill Quin, M.D., [94 Silver Street]; Rice Lewis, Wool Factor [36 Queen Street]. – *N.G.*, 1 Aug 1840.

Crane, James O'Brien and Woulfe were the three not among the requisitionists listed in Appendix Eight. In fact Crane had spoken strongly against adoption of the Act.
81. Rev. A. O'Connor, P.P.; John Finucane, M.D.; John Darcy; Peter Holmes, prop of Nenagh; Geo Frith, Druggist; Wm Burr; Geo Burr; T. T. Abbott; W. Cantrell; John Bennet, Riverston; W. T. Carey.

82. James O'Brien, Rody Spain, O'Brien Dillon, Anthony Nolan and Rice Lewis were re-elected in 1841 – *N.G.*, 24 July 1841. Dillon resigned in April 1843. The other four were re-elected in 1843, joined by Patrick Meara and Patrick Cane of the 1839 pioneers. – PP (Accounts & Papers), 1843 (632) l.373.

83. George O'Leary was probably a son of Dr George O'Leary, Castle Street – *N.G.*, 6 Jan 1839.

84. *N.G.*, 16 Mar 1839.

85. ditto, 10 Apr 1839.

86. ditto, 26 June 1839.

87. ditto,14 Sept 1839.

88. ditto, 27 Sept 1839.

89. ditto, Wed 30 June 1841.

90. As for note 3.

91. Roche, *Local Government in Ireland*, p. 33.

92. Very Rev. William P. Canon Burke, *History of Clonmel* (Waterford 1907, Kilkenny 1983), p. 181.

93. M. O'C. Bianconi & S. J. Watson, *Bianconi King of the Irish Roads* (Dublin, 1962).

94. *T.F.P.*, 27 Sept 1828; PP (Accounts & Papers), 1843 (350) l. 57. The first commissioners were (the occupations and addresses, where given, have been assembled from *Pigot's Directory*, 1824, and *Shearman's Directory*, 1839):

The Rev. D. H. Wall, Rector of St Mary's [Mary St]; Dr. Fitzgerald; James Morton [Quay]; Michael Williams [Ironmonger, Main St]; Robert Grubb [merchant miller, Richmond St]; Ambrose Lane [Upper Johnson St]; Sam Morton [brewer, Morton St]; William Lonergan [New Quay]; Edward Sargint [corn merchant, Irishtown]; Sean Gordon [possibly Samuel, Spring-Garden]; Rev. William Stephenson, curate of St Mary's [Mary St]; Jeremiah Kelly; Henry Pedder [Oakville]; Thomas Stanton [23 Upper Johnson St]; William Whitten [Boat owner, Old-quay]; Patrick Grady [butter merchant, Quay]; Thomas Greer [Raheen]; Wm. Markham [possibly Anne St]; Anthony Guy Luther [2 Anne Street]; Wm Edmundson [Mary St]; Thomas Hughes [probably merchant miller, Old Bridge (1824) but possibly corn merchant, Quay (1839)].

95. *T.F.P.,* Wed 9 July 1834: 'THE NEW COMMISSIONERS (unanimously elected after much discussion):

John Hackett [bookseller & printer, 101 Main St]; John Luther [commission agent, stamp distributor & wine merchant, 24 Main St]; Richard Shanahan [pawnbroker, 41 Johnson St]; Patrick O'Neill [spirit dealer, 5 Dublin St]; John Butler; Patrick Corcoran [corn & spirit, Quay St]; Patrick Grady [butter merchant, Quay]; Patrick Quin[n] [tobacco manufacturer, 45 Main St]; Edward Phelan [M.D., Bagwell St]; William Sheedy [saddler, 34 Johnson St]; Thomas Scully [M.D., 2 Gordon St]; John Lacy [woollen draper, 8 Main St]; Eccles Green

145

[baker, 23 Irishtown]; Thomas O'Brien [woollen draper, 14 Main St]; Charles Bianconi [Silver Springs]; William Lonergan [New Quay]; Joseph Kenny; Lawrence Davis; James Forrestal [6 Dublin St]; William Crean [leather seller and tanner, Irishtown]; John Dunphy [grocer, wine & spirit merchant, 27 Main St].' – The occupations and addresses have been assembled from *Pigot's*, 1824, and *Shearman's*, 1839.

96. *PP* (Accounts & Papers), 1843 (632) l. 373: William Cahill, Clerk to the Commissioners, signed the report which stated that 'the present Commissioners are in office since the last triennial election which took place in July 1840'.

John Hackett, alderman and merchant (Chairman); Philip Daniel, merchant; John M. Murphy, merchant; Thomas Stokes, Bank director; Joshua Malcomson, merchant; Henry Pedder, gentleman, attorney; James Burke, woollen draper; Bernard P. Phelan, wine merchant; Henry Tydd, J.P., gentleman; Patrick Quinn, alderman and tobacconist; Edmund Phelan, medical doctor etc.; Patrick Fennelly, bacon merchant; Charles Bianconi, coach and car proprietor; James O'Farrell, merchant; William Smith, merchant; Thomas Prendergast, tanner; John Lacy, woollen draper; Richard Guiton, merchant; Patrick O'Neill, grocer etc.; Denis F. O'Leary, wine and spirit merchant.

To enable any local historian to examine the coincidence of names in those early public bodies in Clonmel, the names of the first reformed Corporation or Borough Councillors of 1843 are given here from Burke's *Clonmel*, pp. 228-9. See also the first Poor Law Guardians of Clonmel Poor Law Union in Chapter Six.

Aldermen: East Ward – William Byrne, John Luther, Patrick Hearn; West Ward –John Hackett (Mayor), Thomas Cantwell, Patrick Quinn; *Councillors:* East Ward –William Forristal, Thomas O'Brien, Edward Phelan, Charles Bianconi, Patrick Fennelly, John Cary, Thomas Holmes, Edward O'Neill, William Singleton. West Ward – William Keily, Thomas Stokes, Eccles Greene, Patrick Rivers, Daniel O'Brien, Patrick Corcoran, Thomas Prendergast, David Clancy, Patrick Egan.

Seán O'Donnell, 'The first election to the reformed Clonmel Corporation 150 years ago' in *Tipp. Hist. Soc. jn.* 1992 has a graphic account of the election itself and of the Liberals' 'primary' election, together with the votes cast for each candidate in both polls.

97. *T.F.P.*, 3 May 1839.

98. *N.G.*, 9 Mar 1839.

99. *T.F.P.*, 3 Apr 1839.

100. Burke, cited above, pp. 198-9.

101. *PP*, 1836 (523) xxxv. 485, Appendix to the Fourteenth Report of the Inspectors-General of Prisons Ireland,

102. 7 Geo. IV, c. 74, An Act for Consolidating and Amending the Laws relating to Prisons in Ireland, 1826.

103 *PP*, 1839 (91) xx. 403, Appendix to the Seventeenth Report of the Inspectors-General of Prisons Ireland.

104. *PP*, 1842 (377) xxii. 117, Appendix to Twentieth Report of the Inspectors-General of Prisons Ireland.
105. Schedule B, Appendix to Twenty-Second Report of the Inspectors-General of Prisons Ireland (1844). (NA).
106 Appendix to Twenty-Second Report of the Inspectors-General of Prisons Ireland 1844 (N.A).
107. *C.H.*, 3 Dec 1828.
108. *PP* (Accounts & Papers), 1843 (632) l. 373.
109. Patrick C. Power, *History of South Tipperary*, p.125.

CHAPTER SIX

'The People: the source of all legitimate power'

A MAN OF THE PEOPLE

O'Brien Dillon had been staff officer to the generals in the strategy of the 1836-7 northern campaign for the division of the county and was now as of 1839 commanding officer of a new force in the battle for the fruits of general political reform. He deserves as good a portrait as the available snapshots allow one to draw. Over his shoulder one can discern the misty outlines of an emerging nation, and get a telescopic view of some political concerns, movements and structures. His involvement in one new, semi-democratic body gives some insight into the development of expertise in the exercise of power by people who had long been frustrated in the seeking of it.

He was born in March 1799, a son of one of the expanding Catholic middle class, Garret Dillon, who was in business in Nenagh as an apothecary at least as early as 1788,[1] and of his wife, Mary née Smith.[2] An older son, also Garret, was born in 1794[3] – two years after the fourth stage of relief from the Penal Laws had allowed Catholics to practice as solicitors and barristers.[4] Garret Jun. became a barrister and the younger O'Brien a solicitor.[5]

EMANCIPATIONIST

Garret senior and junior were two of the eleven convenors of a typical civil rights meeting of Catholics in Nenagh in 1818; the eleven also included Dr George O'Leary and Thomas Nugent of Nenagh Mills.[6]

Ten years on, the younger O'Brien was a leading political figure in his native parish. He was a proposer of one resolution at a parish meeting to petition against an act of parliament which prevented (largely Catholic) tenants sub-letting property without the consent of their (largely Protestant) landlords. He was the principal speaker at a parish meeting on 1 January 1828, twelve days ahead of the other 'simultaneous meetings' held in two-thirds of the island's parishes.[7] Dillon's speech, presided over by the parish priest, Rev. Ambrose O'Connor, to 'the aisle of the chapel ... crowded to excess and the

148

gallaries presented a galaxy of female fashion and beauty for which the town of Nenagh is pre-eminently distinguished' (this, mind you, from a Limerick paper)[8] was a model of demagoguery, using sardonic humour and dramatic effect and spoken vis-a-vis the ruling class with loyal plámás in one cheek and unveiled threat in the other.

> I confess when our claims were last rejected I felt myself desperately mortified. I make use of the word 'desperately' because I felt, in common with the great body of Irishmen, that as every constitutional measure had been tried, none but a desperate remedy could have accompanied our rights.[9]

Dillon believed that 'this darling project' of simultaneous meetings 'which was first thought of by my distinguished friend Mr Sheil'

> ought to have the most irresistible effect on … friendly advocates in parliament … Protestant friends … It should go to assure, if not to convince, our Protestant thinking enemies in England and the gang of Orange reptiles here, that were we to use these powers in a hostile concentration of physical might on a given day, which we now make use of in a peaceful and constitutional manner seeking for our rights, what terrible consequences might ensue to the enemies of a people maddened by insult and trodden down by degradation and oppression. (cheers) …

The phrases 'desperate remedy' and 'hostile concentration of physical might' and the consequent cheers must have caused shivers down the spines of 'thinking' Catholics and of Protestants of all mentalities. Everyone then over, say, forty years of age would have had vivid memories of the nightmare of 1798 and the preceding years of terror in Tipperary. Dillon continued, however, with a more politic line.

> Will our abstaining from embarrassing the Ministry give us our rights as British subjects … We Catholics want but the opportunity of strengthening the power of the Crown, the power of the Government, and the resources of the Empire …

One year later, he acted as secretary to a similar meeting and gave the keynote address. This was a well-structured one summarising progress on emancipation. One suspects the secretary-attorney's hand was the one which drew up a series of resolutions which were adopted and entrusted to Lord Dunalley and the new Clare MP, Daniel O'Connell, for presentation in the houses of parliament.[10]

Meantime, it was he who forwarded to the Catholic Association the Nenagh subscriptions of £1 each from twenty-one 'gentlemen' plus £3 each from himself and Thomas Nugent.[11] Dillon was reported in the Press as one of those town householders who illuminated their houses upon news of the election of Dunalley the 'Emancipator' as Representative Peer.[12]

WIDENED HORIZONS
His talents found a larger stage. In 1826 Dillon the political attorney had a less than conciliating and constitutional role at the seminal Waterford election. That saw a breakthrough in switching the voting allegiance of Catholic tenant-farmers from their Protestant landlord masters to the Catholic Association; parish contingents marched to record their votes in public for the youthful emancipationist, Henry Villiers-Stuart, himself a Protestant landlord, and against their landlords' orders to vote for the outgoing MP, Lord George Beresford, son of the Marquis of Waterford. Dillon was, apparently, a provocative advocate in the emotional atmosphere, for on 30 June 1826 he engaged in the socially acceptable level of violence of the times.

> DUEL. Wednesday a.m. at 4 o'clock a meeting took place at Rockshire in the County of Kilkenny, between O'Brien Dillon of Nenagh in the County of Tipperary, Esq., and Charles Maunsell of Tallow in the County of Waterford, Esq ... The dispute, we understand, originated in some altercation upon administering the bribery oaths to a voter of Mr Stuart's. After the first fire, Mr Maunsell (for whom the message was sent) requested that some concession should be made, which being distinctly refused by Mr Dillon, a second fire took place, happily without effect, when by the interference of the friends, an accommodation was effected and the parties advanced to meet each other and shake hands.[13]

Some months later he was still engaged as an agent of a body set up to deal with the drastic consequences for Beresford tenants of their courageous votes.[14]

Sectarian politics and his profession meshed on 16 August 1828 at the Summer Assizes in Clonmel; he extracted a pledge to be of good conduct from policemen 'arraigned for a riot at Toomevara' fair.[15] The police had ordered away a ballad singer who had 'sung all day about O'Connell'. When the singer's appreciative audience remonstrated, the police charged the crowd with fixed bayonets. Stones thrown were met by police fire and a young man was killed and several wounded.[16]

Meantime, that July he was identified by no less than the potential Liberator himself, O'Connell, as apparently the leading local emancipationist.

> Mr O'Gorman and myself as soon as the court rises on Saturday proceed for Clare. We will hear Mass at Nenagh on Sunday. We will then proceed from Nenagh and my friend, O'Brien Dillon has promised me reinforcement of 3,000 cavalry from that to Limerick.[17]

Whether Dillon travelled to the making of another increment of history at that Clare election is not on record. But he was among those requisitioning and organising a 'great Munster meeting' in Clonmel on 25-6 August 1828, organised as a heave towards emancipation.[18] That was just before the escalation of Greenboy marches throughout Tipperary and parts of neighbouring counties which impressed the government sufficiently at least to advance their moves towards an Emancipation Bill. That October he was on the inaugural Committee of Management of the County Tipperary Liberal Club, one of eight northerners in a committee of thirty-one.[19] The exertions of the inaugural meeting at Mrs Riall's Hotel in Cashel were followed by a dinner at which Dillon was one of a host of public figures, mostly national ones, who were toasted. He was acclaimed as 'the fearless asserter of the people's rights'.[20] Early in the following year the *Tipperary Free Press,* in the course of signposting yet another meeting called for Nenagh, complemented him thus:

> the name of that sterling patriot O'Brien Dillon is sufficient guarantee that it will be conducted in that conciliating and constitutional spirit which is one to reflect credit on the clergy and the people of Nenagh.[21]

Late in the following decade, he still seems to have been the only one from the Ormonds, outside the grand jury cadre, to be well known in the south – in this instance as a member of a committee to raise the estimated £800 damages and costs incurred by the owner-editor of the *Tipperary Free Press,* John Hackett, in a legal action. That nationalist-liberal organ was not to 'be left walk alone against the combined efforts of our opponents'.[22]

Leaping ahead to May 1843, he was still a public leader. He chaired a banquet for that grand marshal of the national majority, Daniel O'Connell, on the occasion of one of O'Connell's monster Repeal of the Union meetings at Grange, Nenagh.[23] Dillon proposed the toast: 'The People: the source of all legitimate power'.

THE BOARD OF GUARDIANS

Apart from town commissioners self-selected like Nenagh and spotted around the Irish map, the first countrywide semi-democratic institutions _ the poor law unions, signposted in the Prologue as part of creeping civilisation – came into being in 1839. The first elections, with a wider franchise and more local impact than parliamentary ones, had enhanced excitement. For the first time Catholic and Protestant tenant-farmers were to join their landlords in boardrooms, as Poor Law Guardians (PLGs). The landlords were, by and large, present as a result of an internal election among magistrates; in the Nenagh Poor Law Union, for instance, there were eleven seats out of forty-four reserved to them 'ex-officio'. Before the boards of guardians reached the novel and heady exercise of patronage in the appointments of clerk and treasurer, valuators and rate collectors, wardens and vaccinators and workhouse contractors, there were the first fruits of a democratic spring – the elections of officers of the boards.

Two men prominent in the campaign for Nenagh's enhancement competed for the chairmanship of the inaugural Nenagh Union Board of Guardians on 30 May 1839. The common cause of Nenagh and district's welfare was a battle won and past. Now it was 'party discord' with reverberations in the local press and *Dublin Evening Post*. [24]

The Liberal attorney, O'Brien Dillon, he for whom the bonfire blazed in June 1837, defeated the Conservative landlord Richard Wills Gason, the division campaign's Treasurer for Lower Ormond, by 17 votes to 12. Captain Gason's vote was identified by the *Nenagh Guardian* as including all the Conservatives and four Roman Catholics – the report thus giving a reflection of the sectarian politics of the 1830s.

The spring double by O'Brien Dillon as Chairman of town and poor law union was followed by a similar achievement on the part of the Tipperary Joint Stock Bank, already Treasurer to the Grand Jury and now to the Guardians.[25] Its Manager/Agent, Thaddeus O'Shea, was one of the Town Commissioners serving under Dillon. The first Clerk appointed by the Guardians was John O'Brien, Jun., whose father, John O'Brien, Sen., was also a Town Commissioner, legal advisor to the influential Peter Holmes and soon to be the Guardians' legal agent.[26]

To Dillon's apparent attributes of energy and oratory must be added organising ability as evidenced by his mobilising the power of the people through their newly-acquired votes for the election of Poor Law Guardians. In the inaugural 1839 elections he attempted double indemnity by running in the Lisboney and Nenagh divisions. He was elected in Lisboney and defeated in Nenagh. The *gríosach* was still alive from the bonfire almost three years before. In 1840 he did make doubly certain by being elected both in Nenagh and Castletown. Entering a second decade, in 1849, he was the runner-up in the Nenagh three-seater, with 204 votes behind 240 for the Board's vice-Chairman, J. J. Poe. The following year he reversed the top placings, 279 to 225.[27]

LEADER
The impressive gathering of votes out in the field continued into the boardroom. For his successful 1839 bid for the Guardians' chair, he was proposed by Edward Kennedy, Bantis, representing Cloughjordan division, and seconded by John Darcy, one of the three ahead of him in the Nenagh poll. The vice-Chairman was elected unanimously – Caleb Going, Traverstown, Dolla, a magistrate and one of the minority ascendancy. The Deputy vice-Chairman was John Darcy, elected by an 18-10 vote on similar lines to that for the chair. Darcy was proposed by Cornelius Hogan, who represented Newport division, and seconded by Edward Kennedy. He defeated John Falkiner, Prospect, Puckane, who was probably a member of the prominent Mount Falcon, Ardcroney, landed family which included national figures in law and the Church of Ireland.

The following three years seem to show a degree of statesmanship, with party discord diminished to the point of unanimous elections of all three officers. An expertise in inter-personal relationships had obviously developed across racial and social barriers, good turns accepted and repaid; one can visualise the delicate manoeuvrings before the annual meetings. Dillon, Darcy and Hogan were obviously the leaders of the majority. In 1840 Dillon was unanimously re-elected Chairman on the proposition of Darcy and Hogan. Darcy moved up to the vice-chair on the proposition of Michael Darcy, Youghal division, seconded by George Thorn, Kilcomenty division. Denis Kennedy, also Youghal, became Deputy vice-Chairman, put forward by the two Darcys.

Neither Dillon nor John Darcy contested the 1841 officerships. *Entente cordiale* continued; power-sharing was its practical product. William Finch, Tullamore Park, Nenagh, a Protestant landowner and magistrate, and a descendant of a Cromwellian grantee, Col. Symon Finch, proposed as Chairman the grand juror R. U. Bayly,

Ballinaclough, Nenagh, a descendant of a purchaser from Cromwellian hands of former Kennedy and Butler lands. He was seconded by Cornelius Hogan, bearer of a surname than which there were none with deeper Gaelic roots in the area. A third Protestant-magistrate-grand juror, Thomas George Stoney, Kylepark, Borrisokane, and Dillon proposed Caleb Going as the vice-Chairman to replace Darcy and thus regain his 1839 office. Finch of the ascendancy and Darcy of the risen people proposed the re-election of Deputy vice-Chairman Denis Kennedy.[28]

In 1842 Bayly retained the chair and Kennedy the deputy vice-chair. James Willington, another of the minority, was elected vice-Chairman, after Dillon had declined the offer.[29] Dillon proposed Joshua R. Minnitt, Annaghbeg, a magistrate, as Chairman in 1852[30] and Poe as vice-Chairman in 1854.[31]

He was himself at least once more in the chair, in 1855,[32] and chaired a meeting in 1858 in the absence of the officers.[33] He served until the board year 1861-2 inclusive, with gaps totalling three years in the later 1840s – a total of twenty years as PLG. From the spotty Press reports of the era, one gleans his annual election placings as varying from heading the poll at least once more, ahead of J. J. Poe, 261-240 in 1853,[34] down to third place in the three-seater in 1855.[35]

The capacity of Dillon to work with all shades of opinion was underlined in the resolution proposed by R. W. Gason, his 1839 antagonist for the chair who had been his 1836-8 co-operator in several local development projects. It was seconded by Finch and carried unanimously; Dillon, in attendance, did not dissent:

> That O'Brien Dillon merits the thanks of the Board of Guardians of the Poor Law Union of Nenagh for his upright conduct and gentlemanly demeanour as Chairman of the Board for the last two years, and that the resolution be recorded in the minutes of the Union in testimony of the good feeling of the Guardians of the Union.[36]

EXECUTIVE COMMITTEEMAN

Dillon's lead role is also reflected in the frequent appearance of his name in a sample of Board minutes. The record of his actions coincidentally gives a taste of some pre-occupations of a new body in difficult times. He seconded a proposal to adjourn a reactionary resolution which sought to impose a twelve-month in-Union-area residence qualification for admission of paupers to the workhouse (the adjournment had the effect of the resolution being withdrawn at the next meeting).[37] He was the proposer of a candidate, who was defeated, for a Nursetender post.[38] It was he who proposed the £8 p.a. salary to be paid to the Nursetender, a salary increase for the workhouse physician from £40 to £50 p.a.[39] (this won on a vote of 23-10), and a salary of £60 p.a. for the Clerk (this was defeated 24-12).[40]

In 1846 he questioned the expense of newspaper advertising by the board. He suggested that handbills distributed throughout the town would meet their needs 'except in certain cases when the heart of the subject matter of the advertisement exceeded £50'.[41] In 1849 he was one of three guardians appointed as a Committee to report to the Board on the expediency of lighting the workhouse with gas.[42] In 1858-9 he was one of five appointed on occasions to undertake tasks such as an examination of rates arrears sheets and a stock-taking of clothing in the workhouse.[43]

As early as 1843 he was one of five who examined a bill of costs submitted by the Board's legal advisor, John O'Brien. They recommended a certain amount, O'Brien sued for the full amount, and none other than Dillon himself was engaged 'to enter an appearance to the writ'.[44] In 1846 he was similarly engaged to counter the suit of a Mr Scroope for £300 for services as valuer, alleged 'irregularities' in his valuation books being under scrutiny.[45] One week later, Dillon recommended that the £300 be paid pending the attendance of Mr Scroope and the ascertainment of any 'discrepancies'.[46] He also acted as attorney for occasional Board legal actions from 1850 to 1862 in the recovery of outstanding poor law rates and other debts.[47] Thus providing a service as attorney, whatever conflict of interest it might seem to involve, was not apparently regarded as a contract which would have disqualified him as a guardian.[48]

POLICY MAKER
In January 1843 O'Brien Dillon gave notice of an intended motion:

> That a new valuation of the entire Union to meet the exigency of the times be made. When Mr. Dillon had fully explained his reasons and sentiments thereon he withdrew his notice of motion. Mr. Dillon then handed in the following notice: for appointment of a Committee to prepare a petition from the board to parliament praying that the present poor laws may be abolished and a more suitable and less expensive remedy be substituted by the legislature for giving relief to the destitute poor of Ireland.[49]

The proposer himself – writer also, one recalls again, of the

155

successful county division memorial – was, naturally, deputed to draft the 'Humble Petition' which was unanimously signed in February.[50] The Board requested that it be presented by Lords Dunalley and Donoughmore in the House of Lords, and by the county's two MPs, Robert Otway Cave and Valentine Maher, in the House of Commons.

It pointed out that the laws for the relief of the poor had not been preceded by public meetings nor had landlords or the public generally been consulted. It went on to claim historical differences between the English and Irish patterns of leasing land and between the comparative levels of rent when the respective poor laws were introduced. Because Ireland was heavily agricultural, a direct tax 'bears heavily on the farming population ... poor rates ... the most grievous and likely to become the most intolerable burthen.' Redolent of anti-taxation pleas in all eras, it concluded:

> Your Petitioners therefore humbly pray that Your Honourable House will Repeal the Irish Poor Laws and not consent to the enacting of any other Statute in place thereof or of similar import without fully & publicly consulting the Landed Interest and public of Ireland generally.

Dillon's absence from the Nenagh Board coincided with three years of the Great Famine: 1845-6, 1847-8 and 1848-9. His absence was interrupted by a very active presence throughout 1846-7. In that September 1846 he proposed and got unanimous agreement to advertise in the *General Advertiser,* Dublin, for a contract for the supply of Indian Meal for 12 months to be 'delivered free of expense at whatever times and in any quantities as the Board may require'.[51] This followed attempts by a Limerick supplier to increase his tendered price of £11 per ton to £12 in two steps while a contract was being finalised.

The horrific problems presented to an organisation only seven years in existence are also reflected in two successive Board minutes of early December 1846. At the first meeting Dillon proposed a committee and was appointed on it, to calculate the number of wives and children who were in the workhouse but whose husbands were employed in public works, 'with a view to their expulsion to make room for the really destitute'.[52] At the next meeting an outbreak of fever was reported at the workhouse which was 'full to suffocation'. Dillon was against a motion to admit new inmates but the motion was carried by a majority of one.[53]

Outside that local authority structure Relief Committees were set up in most areas. Dillon was among sixteen guardians appointed to

156

one for Lower Ormond barony, with sub-committees for four parishes, along with numbers of people in separate categories of magistrates, clergyman and landed proprietors. His subscription to the Nenagh town relief fund for April 1846 was £3, one of only ten in that amount, in the company of the rector and parish priest, R. U. Bayly, one doctor, three large landowners, and the Burr brothers, who were brewers and 'as philanthropic, a family as ever proved a blessing to any community.' Only three banks and two businessmen had subscribed higher.[54] Most of the doctors, attorneys and businessmen of substance were in the £2 and £1 listings.

TOWN COMMISSIONER

The reasons remain clouded behind our man's reported resignation as a Nenagh Town Commissioner in April 1843, towards the end of a second two-year term of office.[55] O'Brien Dillon resumed as Town Commissioner at some stage between 1843 and his re-election as Chairman in 1850,[56] proposed by David Brundley at the T.C.s' meeting held in the ballroom of Brundley's very own Hotel which premises happened to be held under a lease, which was renewed the following year, from – O'Brien Dillon. A sampling of Press reports finds Dillon a T.C. in 1851, 1859 (when the Commissioners discussed the poor state of the streets), in 1860 and 1862 (when the candidate he proposed for the vacant office of Rate Collector and Town Sergeant – a son of the deceased office-holder – got only his own and the seconder's votes against six for the opposition).[57]

That the gap in his T.C. service was short is suggested by a *Nenagh Guardian* report in October 1862 on the election of seven to replace the one-third of the total who were obliged by law to retire but who were eligible for re-election.[58] On that occasion two outgoing T.C.s did not go forward and were replaced. 'The other five' (including Dillon) 'have been commissioners since the introduction of the act into Nenagh'. The report on that 1862 election yields a sidelight both on the diminution of democracy since its heady birth in 1839 and on the media or at least one reporter's perception of the lack of importance of the town governors' role. Dillon and commissioner Pine, also re-elected, were not present. Five T.C.s, without the aid of the few other householders present, rotated the proposing and seconding which ceased when the required number was reached. One can sense an atmosphere all too familiar to the faithful core in a voluntary body on a downward slide or at a ticking-over stage.

... so little interest did the affair create that there were scarcely

157

half a dozen present at the hour fixed for nomination, nine o'clock. The chair was occupied by Mr Rody Spain, JP, and the only other Commissioners present were: – Messrs. Ryan, Nolan, Kilkelly, Roche, Tucker, and Gill … There being no other candidates to be proposed, the Chairman declared the seven candidates duly elected, and the town is thus spared the turmoil and excitement of an election.

There was, however, some minor excitement a year later. Four new candidates were proposed in addition to the seven outgoing commissioners, who so little anticipated such turmoil that they 'had not canvassed a single voter, nor had they thought it necessary to do so'. It was only after the new nominations and while polling was in progress that they attempted to canvass.

DEVELOPER

For a number of years Dillon was also an indispensable participant, often in a key role, in development projects. R. W. Gason and himself – the 1839 opponents for the inaugural poor law union chair – were respectively chairman and secretary in November 1836 of what was described as a 'baronial meeting of gentry, merchants, traders and farmers' of the two Ormonds and Owney and Arra. The meeting's objective was to give public backing to a new bank.[59] In October 1838 he acted as secretary to a meeting chaired by Sir Amyrald Dancer of Modreeny House, Cloughjordan, and which passed various resolutions related to railways in Ireland (the meeting was wholeheartedly in favour of construction by private enterprise – but with government assistance).[60]

That December and into January 1839 he was again in the secretary's seat, beside Peter Holmes in the chair, when meetings deliberated on a possible Nenagh-Shannon canal starting at either Dromineer or Youghal Bay.[61]

In 1840 he was secretary of another Gason-chaired committee, set up to suitably commemorate the brewer William Burr who had recently died. Gason, Dillon and three others were deputed to 'determine the best means of effecting subscriber intentions'. One plan under consideration was for a fountain in Peter Street, to be designed by John B. Keane, and incorporating a statue of Niobe, the grieving mother in Greek mythology whom the gods transformed into a weeping rock. Those waters, no more than a canal's, never flowed.[62]

And in 1846 he was a Director, with R. U. Bayly as Chairman and J. J. Poe, John Kempston of the *Nenagh Guardian* and some T.C.s among the other Directors, of a project which did come to fruition – the Nenagh Gas Company with whom the Town Commissioners entered into a contract for the lighting of the streets.[63]

Through the eyes of the *Nenagh Guardian,* and not forgetting the orange-tinted glasses which that beholder wore in that era, one gets further glimpses of the two Dillon personalities – the universally-respected one and the duellist. Firstly, the *Guardian* saluted the better profile after his 1839 Board of Guardians defeat in Nenagh electoral division (when Lisboney saved him), albeit in the course of a condemnation of 'the future of "Universal Suffrage" which has shown itself in this case and which, if carried to elections generally, would be a curse to the country'. The editor bracketed Dillon with his Canal task force chairman, Peter Holmes, and the town businessman William Burr in its regret:

> It will be an everlasting blot on the town of Nenagh ... three gentlemen which every person must acknowledge as among the most prominent of all that is most likely to be good to the Country ... Their persons and their services are ever at the command of the public ... [64]

POLEMICIST

The *Nenagh Guardian* unveiled Dillon's other profile as a partisan and demagogue in April 1840 when he presided at a local meeting held to petition parliament against Lord Stanley's Irish Registration Bill which was being put forward from the Tory opposition benches. It would have restricted further the Irish franchise; O'Connell declared that it would nullify both the Emancipation Act and the 1832 Reform Act which had expanded the franchise, and he whipped up a widespread furore in Ireland. Part of Dillon's speech led to the *Nenagh Guardian* editor's understandable reproof which itself drew a Dillon riposte and in turn a scathing report in the paper of Dillon's laying the foundation stone for the Guardians' workhouse. Unlike the Waterford election duel of fourteen years previously, both parties could now be said to have drawn blood.

Thus Dillon in full flow of speech, generously endowed with capitals and exclamation marks by the editor:

> He would not speak sedition, but he was ready to be in arms against this Bill. He was one who had some property to lose, and knew the 'Vile Orangemen' would be glad to give information about him.

159

If this bill was passed, HE WOULD BE READY TO TAKE UP ARMS IN DEFENCE OF HIS COUNTRY AND HIS RELIGION. HE COULD YET GRASP A MUSKET AND BRANDISH A BAYONET!!! If this bill should pass I, FOR ONE, WOULD THINK THAT I NO LONGER OWE ALLEGIANCE TO HER MAJESTY! ! ![65]

This man of some property and conditional allegiance, only a month previously had been a signatory among fifty-seven freeholders who had requisitioned a public meeting 'for the purpose of adopting an Address to Her Majesty, congratulating her on her marriage; and also an Address to His Royal Highness Prince Albert, on the same auspicious event'.[66] He was one of six probable Catholics among the lot. His name was third from the end of the list, almost all large landowners, headed by Dunalley, Bloomfield, D'Alton and Prittie. The apothecary's son from Pound Street had joined the gentry.

But not in the perception of his *Nenagh Guardian* adversary of the moment. Thus its report of yet another milestone event in the development of the town of its birth under the loaded heading, 'PAYING FOR POPULARITY':

> On last Thursday, Mr O'Brien Dillon, adorned with a masonic apron, was supported by Mr Leahy, the architect, the Clerk to the Poor Law Guardians and some six or seven undistinguishables, bearing wands, proceeded from the Court-house to Tyone, for the purpose, which had been placarded, of laying the *foundation-stone* of the Poor-House of the Nenagh Union. ... How unlike the laying of the foundation-stone of the New Gaol by Lord Dunalley was the present exhibition. It was the scene burlesqued. One was attended by the respectability of the County and an accompaniment of music while the ceremony was being performed by a Nobleman whose high station entitled him to the laying of the stone as a prerogative of his order: the other had neither attendance nor respectability beyond what we have already stated; and to add to its indignity the chief actor of the drama was one eschewed by the aristocracy because of his assumption of privileges which belong alone to them... .[67]

That, to put it in context, was a year before the peaceful boardroom co-existence between the aristocracy, whose chief privilege was to have inherited the earth, and the representatives of the rising people, 'the source of all legitimate power'.

EXPERT

O'Brien Dillon's evidence to the 1844 Devon Commission ('to inquire into the occupation of land in Ireland')[68] illustrates the style of the man and of the lawyer: forthright, clear and concise, masterful of detail, meticulous in answers to specific questions on the local scene, and imaginative in suggestions on remedies for the crucial, national land problem. The printed version of the 166 questions put to him and of his answers identifies eighteen amendments to the record made by Dillon subsequent to the hearing. Although he was legal agent as well as tenant of Stafford O'Brien, he instanced that landlord as one who made no allowance in the rent for improvements effected by the tenant. He drew a contrast between this failing and the practice by Lord Norbury of allowing one-half for building walls and houses; he gave credit to Lord Dunalley also for good practice.

Dillon's radical suggestions, six years before the Tenant League formulated objectives of Fair Rent and Fixity of Tenure, were for a statutory allowance for improvements; for extension of tenure; for election by £20 freeholders of two or three commissioners in each townland who would value land every three years, proprietors thereafter to be obliged to charge the rent thus fixed; for a farm of 100 acres to be attached to each workhouse on which the paupers, presumably meaning resident ones, would be obliged to work.[69]

MAN OF PROPERTY

O'Brien Dillon described himself to that 1844 Devon Commission as a 'small landed proprietor, and a solicitor and attorney at law, holding land in Westmeath in fee and by lease in this county'.[70] He gave his residence as Laurel Lodge, Nenagh. That house was of a class which could be called comfortable, the holding also taking in the adjoining twelve acre Lough Field. His previous residence as of 1836, Summerville (rented from Peter Holmes), was more sizeable and was classed as a gentleman's residence.

Before that again he resided in and had his office in the 1820s in a good street dwelling which he had inherited that from his father.[71] In 1846 his office address was Chapel Lane.

In the 1850 Primary Valuation he was the occupier of three premises – a medium-size house with offices and yard in the new Peter Street, probably his office; a small office and yard at Bourne's Lane – beside Laurel Lodge or possibly a part of which he had retained; and a medium-size house at Nenagh North which may have been his residence.

In those successive residences he was a tenant, but he was also the 'immediate lessor' of two substantial properties in the town. One in

161

Barrack Street was originally held jointly with his father; it was the Burr brewery and maltings with dwelling house. His equally valuable interest was Brundley's Hotel.[72] Of lesser value was a house among the sixty-one which were closely packed into unsalubrious Ball Alley Lane, although its valuation was quite a cut above that of the neighbours generally.

He was the occupier of land on the fringe of the town totalling over 97 acres and with five houses thereon, four of them rented to tenants. Recourse to Poor Law Rate Books[73] for the period reveals him as the occupier of over eleven acres. He was the occupier of over 13 further acres in Nenagh North in 1853.

His landed interest in County Westmeath at 1863 was in the barony of Kilkenny West – just over 39 acres held in fee simple and three and one-half acres leased by him.[74]

FAMILY MAN
At the height of the final drive for Catholic Emancipation, in late August or early September 1828, Dillon married Anastasia Keogh of Crumlin, Dublin, daughter of a deceased barrister.[75] They had eight known children whose names by and large seem to indicate both respect for the tradition of repeating first names in successive generations and, in two cases, political sentiment. The eldest got his own name, O'Brien.[76] Garret (1831)[77] was obviously named for the child's paternal grandfather. Theobald (December 1838),[78] not apparently an immediate family name, was probably in tribute to Fr Theobald Mathew, the Capuchin priest born in County Tipperary who had launched his temperance crusade that year.[79] Their eldest daughter bore her paternal grandmother's name, Mary.[80] Their second daughter was named Margaret,[81] perhaps indicating the name of her maternal grandmother or aunt (a Margaret Keogh was one of young Garret's sponsors).

In December 1840 twin girls were named Anna (origin not identified), and Anastasia Victoria.[82] The latter's first name was, of course, her mother's; the second coincided with that of the young monarch of the United Kingdom to whom the allegiance of O'Brien Dillon had been put in question by his rash speech of eight months previously. The eighth child, Dominick (1845),[83] was given the same name as one of his sponsors, Dominick Keogh, presumably Anastasia's brother and the child's uncle.

ADVERSITY
O'Brien Dillon's eventual obituary in the *Nenagh Guardian* issue of 14 November 1874 revealed:

About sixteen years ago adverse circumstances set in, and, after a struggle of four years [i.e. circa 1858], he had to succumb and sell out his property. He then emigrated to New York, where he soon became himself again, and formed some influential connections.

Whatever the circumstances, and with due caution as to the retrospective dating by the paper, Dillon acted for his tenant Richard Burr against the Tipperary Joint Stock Bank in March 1859.[84] He was one of three solicitors involved in the September 1860 deed of conveyance of the 'Castle plot' (which included the Nenagh Castle keep) from Margaret and Daniel O'Meara, merchant, to the Bishop of Killaloe and other 'trustees for the use of the Roman Catholic parishioners of Nenagh'.[85]

In November 1861 he reported to the Board of Guardians as their solicitor on a matter of arrears of rates; he was still a member of the Board and present as such.[86] And as late as March 1862 he was similarly engaged by the Board to appear in an appeals case against the Board by two ratepayers.[87] On 4 September 1862 the Board passed for payment his bill of costs for 'election law'.[88]

Dillon was active as a guardian up to the penultimate weekly meeting of the 1861-2 Board on 15 March 1862. That represents his curtain call; he was not present at the new Board's first meeting on 29 March nor at any subsequent meeting. The *Nenagh Guardian* reports do not say if he was among the contestants in the Nenagh district election that March. However, his fellow guardians of many years at that first meeting named him with five citizens of substance as the Nenagh Dispensary District Committee of Management.[89] A year later, still unreported as an election contestant, his name again appears in the Minute Book among six placed on the new Dispensary Committee but, tantalisingly, is then crossed out in the same ink.[90]

One can only speculate in the light of the following that he was known to be planning his departure from Nenagh by that March 1863 and that he may have been in arrears with his own rates perhaps as early as March 1862 and, if so, disqualified from voting in an election and hence from a guardianship. That would not have been a factor with the separate Town Commissioners whose meetings he attended up to and including January 1863.[91] That body moved to fill his vacancy, 'caused by the removal from town of Mr O'Brien Dillon', in October 1863, coincidentally with filling vacancies upon the deaths of commissioners R. Spain and John Carroll that September.[92] The timing suggests that Dillon left Nenagh for a New World during the summer.

Despite and ironically in the light of the adverse circumstances, he was among twenty-nine clergy, landowners, businessmen and professional men, several of them Town Commissioners, named on a committee, reported upon in February 1863, to collect subscriptions for the relief of distress in Nenagh.[93] Significantly, his name was not among those of sixty-four leading citizens who requisitioned the public meeting which set up that committee.[94] That very same issue of the *Nenagh Guardian* recorded the sale of his Westmeath lands for £500 and four lots of Nenagh property interests for a total of £1,315.

The sale of his long lease of the Barrack Street premises which were sub-leased to the Burrs, who filled double roles as petitioners to the court and purchasers of most of the interests, was adjourned. Going on the advertised profit rents,[95] it probably realised about £450 after negotiations, bringing the total yield close to £2,300, equal to about £140,000 in early 1990s money. This betokened distress at a rather higher level than most and must have both assisted his fresh start in the USA and cleared the presumed debts built up in the 'struggle of four years'.

A spot-check of Brooklyn City Directories for Dillon's years in the U.S.A. disclosed that he was listed as a lawyer at 110 Ryerson Street in 1864. By 1866, when he was aged sixty-seven, however he had no occupational tag and was resident at Douglass, Hoyt. By 1870 he had moved to 50 Carroll Street.

O'Brien Dillon died at 246 Harte Street in the 10th Ward, Brooklyn, on 22 October 1874, aged 75 years and 7 months. He was buried at Holy Cross cemetery on the following day. His death certificate was signed by Dr G. A. Plunkett who attributed the causes of death to, 'FIRST, general debility', and 'SECOND (remote and complicating) uraemia', three months being specified as the 'period from attack till death'.[96] Dillon's wife survived him. I do not know if any of his family and their spouses or children were among four families resident at that address. Back home, the *Nenagh Guardian,* which had reported his doings at times favourably and at times critically, mourned the exile:

> To know Mr Dillon was to respect him, for he was one of the most perfect gentlemen ever known in his profession (solicitor)… He was a ready and polished writer, to dash off a poetic squib or a scathing satire was to him but the matter of a moment. In society he was a most agreeable companion; most cheerful and inoffensive, courteous in all his bearings. ... On the whole, O'Brien Dillon was a man of whom Nenagh might be well proud, and many of his old friends and admirers will, in spirit, visit his grave

at Brooklyn, and think of the many noble qualities that once animated the generous and impulsive heart now stilled for ever by the cold hand of death.

STATE OF THE RACE, 1839

The portrait of this key figure is thus one of alternative demagogue and diplomat, a leader among his peers and acknowledged in a larger circle as capable, inheriting talent and a degree of affluence, suffering setbacks – some self-inflicted – recovering but leaving business incomplete. It could be a portrait of native Irish political leadership over a century and a half. He was, in varying degrees, a district's O'Connell, Parnell or De Valera. He was the precursor of hundreds of district liberators, uncrowned kings and chiefs who demonstrated a native genius for exploiting the gradually expanding 'curse' of 'universal suffrage'.

These new power brokers were challenging the old – mostly sixth and seventh generation descendants of the grantees and purchasers from grantees in the Cromwellian plantation of the 1650s. Clonmel Poor Law Union commenced its government remarkably like Nenagh did – discord followed by rapport.[97] Thurles and Roscrea unions in 1839-41 were having their power struggles, somewhat akin to Nenagh's. Ach sin scéal eile, as is the one of how the practice of power in those new institutions sharpened the native genius and culminated in the 'revolution' of 1899 when a greater degree of democracy swept the grand jurors from power with the introduction of another form of county government – the county councils. Both stories will be told in a companion volume.

For the six intervening decades the far-from-meek inheritors of the earth, or at least of Irish soil, formed the virtually self-perpetuating grand juries. The earl of Glengall wrote to the earl of Donoughmore concerning a rumour of moves 'to put Bianconi on the grand jury!' – the Bianconi termed 'King of the Irish Roads' because of his coaching network. But Glengall insisted: 'Pray stop this ... coup ... Bian is a tradesman'.[98] Cosy clubs certainly but containing many men of the calibre of Dunalley and his allies. On the one hand they were all servants of an Empire whose vast span was indicated on the globe by the colour red – which to most subject nations at intervals betokened bloodshed. On the other hand, the best of them were local patriots who gave public service of varying degrees of dedication on multiple fronts.

As one arm of local government they continued in the grand jury to take care of roads and bridges, lunatic asylum and courthouse, and the employment of the executives who brought continuity to the work between assizes – the secretary and surveyors. In the boards of guardians they met with their tenants and jointly developed, firstly, the workhouses, then outdoor relief of the poor and other functions which were gradually added – the provision of dispensaries and hospitals, burial grounds and sewers, and the removal of nuisances and prevention of disease.

Town government in Nenagh, Templemore and Thurles, had its own, quite different, revolution in 1899. Agus sin scéal eile arís - a chapter in the next volume. Meantime town commissioners acquired in stages more extensive powers of public health and sanitary services.

Notes

1. Richard Lucas, *General Directory of the Kingdom of Ireland, 1788.*
2. King's Inns Admission Papers, by kind permission of the Benchers of the King's Inns. Garret died on 11 February 1826, aged 74 (Ormond Historical Society, *Kenyon St, Nenagh Gravestone Inscriptions,* 1982). Mary died at Nenagh in late November 1832 (*C.A.*, 28 Nov 1832).
3. He was baptised on 18 July 1794 – Nenagh R.C. parish register of baptisms.
4. (Langrishe's) Catholic Relief Act, 1792.
5. King's Inns Admission Papers. O'Brien Dillon was educated at Thomas O'Brien's school, Limerick city. The memorials addressed to the Right Honourable the Benchers of the Honourable Society of the King's Inns as sworn for Trinity term 1815, when he was just about a month over the minimum age for admission of sixteen years, highlighted his Limerick instruction in the Latin language and the following Latin books – Sallist, Virgil and Horace. He had also read part of the Greek Testament, Lucian and the first book of Homer. Edward Walsh, Upper Dominick St., Dublin, Attorney of the King's Bench and Exchequer and a solicitor of His Majesty's high court of Chancery, desired young Dillon's requisite apprenticeship.
6. Sheehan, *N. & its N.*, p. 85 – primary source not given.
7. *Limerick Evening Post and Clare Sentinel,* 4 Jan 1828. The paper on 1 Jan had reported a Catholic Association call for the meeting on Sunday 13 January to demand 'civil rights'.
8. ditto, also 4 Jan 1828.
9. ditto, 8 Jan 1828.
10. *T.F.P.*, 7 Jan 1829.
11. *D.E.P.*, 19 July 1828.
12. *D.E.P.*, 24 Dec 1828.
13. *W.M.*, 1 July 1826. Maunsell is identified by Daniel O'Connell as an attorney on Beresford's side and by the editor of his letters as the fourth son of John, Ballybrood, Co. Limerick, and Catherine Widenham – M. R. O'Connell ed, *Correspondence,* iii, Letter 1321, 28 June 1826.

14. Rev. John Sheehan, P.P., to O'Connell, iii, 3 Nov 1826, Letter 1349, *Correspondence*.
15. *T.F.P.*, 20 Aug 1828.
16. ditto, 23 Aug 1828.
17. *Limerick Evening Post and Clare Sentinel*, 1 July 1828.
18. *T.F.P.*, 23 Aug 1828.
19. ditto, 15 Oct 1828.
20. ditto, 11 Oct 1828.
21. ditto, 18 Apr 1829.
22. ditto, 4 Jan 1837. Hackett was rather inclined to lead with his chin. His *T.F.P.* on 29 Dec 1838 announced, apropos the 'celebrated letter' by Under-Secretary Drummond to the Tipperary magistrates: 'in order to gratify the calumniated jurors of this county who desire to have this splendid document in gilt frames to grace their mantelpieces, we have directed that some copies should be beautifully printed (but not in letters of gold) on superfine hot-pressed paper'.
23. Rev. John Gleeson, *History of Ely O'Carroll*, p. 189; Sheehan, *N. & its N.*, p. 23, quoting *The Nation*, 27 May 1843.
24. *D.E.P.*, 18 June 1839 ('from a Nenagh correspondent'); *N.G.*, 12 June 1839.
25. *N.G.*, 12 June 1839.
26. ditto, 1 June 1839. This first report was despite their reporter not being 'allowed to remain and make a note of the proceedings.' Hence, the inaugural meeting was termed a 'hole and corner conclave', despite which the paper for succeeding issues winkled out the full story of officers' elections. Within eighteen months, the Nenagh Union Guardians resolved to admit reporters (Minutes, N.B.G., 26 Nov 1840). The Attorney-General had 'given his opinion that the poor law guardians have not powers under the Poor Law Act to exclude strangers from meeting (*T.F.P.*, 2 Dec 1840).
27. *N.G.*, 7 Apr 1849.
28. Minutes, N.B.G., 22 Apr 1841.
29. *N.G.*, 30 Mar 1842.
30. ditto, 3 Apr 1852.
31. ditto, 1 Apr 1854.
32. ditto, 3 Feb 1855.
33. Minutes, N.B.G., 2 Sept 1858.
34. *N.G.*, 2 Apr 1853.
35. ditto, 28 Apr 1855.
36. Minutes, N.B.G., 22 Apr 1841. This capacity, as deduced in the text, could be categorised as: like father, like son. An 1815 poster offering £100 reward for information leading to the conviction of persons concerned in the issue of threatening notices has Garret Dillon as a signatory among fifty-five whose surnames included Dunalley, Holmes, Bayly, Finch, Going, Minnitt and Stoney (poster published by Watson & Mahony, props. of The *Limerick Chronicle*).
37. Minutes, N.B.G., 28 Apr, 5 May 1842.

38. ditto, 12 May 1842.
39. ditto, 18 May 1843.
40. ditto, 9 Feb 1843.
41. ditto, 25 July 1846.
42. ditto, 27 Dec 1849.
43. ditto, 30 Sept 1858, 27 Jan 1859.
44. ditto, 1 June 1843. While it is obvious that a body of politicians would be disposed to entrust such a task to one of their own, Dillon's reputation as a lawyer should also be affirmed. For instance, he acted as agent for the prosecution *in re* The King versus Dancer at the 1835 Spring Assizes – some weeks before the Whig government came into office – *The Pilot*, 1 Apr 1835.
45. ditto, 18 Apr 1846.
46. ditto, 25 Apr 1846.
47. ditto, 24 Oct 1850, 7 Oct 1858, 10 Feb 1859, 24 Oct 1861.
48. ss. 80, 81, 85 and 19, respectively, of the Irish Poor Relief Act, 1838, provided that every occupier paying rates and every person receiving rent from which rates were deducted was deemed a ratepayer; that every ratepayer would have a vote in the election of guardians; that no occupier would be entitled to vote unless he had paid all rates (excepting any due within the previous six months); that, among the qualifications for being a guardian, one was entitled to vote at an election for guardians.

     s. 22 of the Irish Poor Law Amendment Act, 1843, provided that among the disqualifications from being elected or acting as guardian were having forfeited £100 for having supplied 'any Materials, Goods or Provisions for the Use of any Workhouse' in one's own Union while holding office as one of its guardians. Such conflict of interest was prohibited by s. 93 of the parent 1838 Act which also specified the fine or forfeiture of £100 for a breach of the prohibition. This principle followed and elaborated on the headline s. 47 of the 1836 Grand Jury Act which declared that no magistrate, cess payer, any county officer or his employee could be interested in any contract; this followed another prohibition in its s. 32 on certain county officers serving on grand juries at presentments.

     Articles 16-18 of the Poor Law Commissioners' General Regulations of 8 June 1844 governed the execution of contracts and did not envisage among them contracts for services such as those of attorney. At or about the same time Michael Doheny acted as legal agent to Cashel Town Commissioners while he was a member of that body (Dr Thomas G. McGrath, 'Michael Doheny', lecture at Kickham Weekend, Mullinahone, Co. Tipperary, 6 Aug 1993).
49. Minutes, N.B.G., 5 Jan 1843.
50. ditto, 2 Feb 1843.
51. ditto, 5 Sept 1846.
52. ditto, 5 Dec 1846.
53. ditto, 12 Dec 1846.
54. *N.G.*, 18 Apr 1846.

55. ditto, 29 Apr 1843.
56. ditto, 3 Aug 1850.
57. ditto, 19 Aug 1851, 25 Mar 1859, 4 Apr 1860, 26 Mar 1862.
58. ditto, 15 Oct 1862.
59. *C.A.*, 23 Nov 1836.
60. *N.G.*, 13 Oct 1838.
61. ditto, 12 Dec 1838.
62. ditto, 29 Jan, 7 Mar 1840. The three other sub-committee members were Dr James Dempster, who was a T.C. and a fellow-Commissioner of Gason's for gaol and courthouse, James A. Foley and a Mr Falkiner. 'The Burr family was connected with the business life of Nenagh for half a century. Those who recollect Wm. Burr and his brothers, the extensive employment they gave and the munificent charities which they periodically bestowed, will bless their memory which is fragrant and perisheth not. As philanthropic a family as ever proved a blessing to any community.' (Sheehan, *N. & its N.*, p. 28).
63. ditto, 21 Jan 1846.
64. ditto, 29 May 1839.
65. ditto, 22 Apr 1840, repeated for effect 25 Apr 1840.
66. ditto, 18 Mar 1840, 25 Apr 1840.
67. ditto, 9 May 1840.
68. Devon Commission = Evidence taken before the Commissioners appointed to Inquire into the Occupation of Land in Ireland, PP, 1845, XXI, ii, Witness No. 562 pp. 608-14.
69. ditto, p. 614.
70. ditto, p. 608.
71. Sheehan, *N. & its N.*, p. 16. That residence-office was at the Market Cross or town centre end of that part of Pound Street later renamed Queen Street and was later incorporated into the National Bank premises.
72. The Burr brewery and maltings were formerly the Globe Inn, and later in succession the Munster and Leinster Bank, O'Neill's Nursing Home and (now) the Ormond Hotel. Brundley's Hotel at 14-15 Castle St was later and still O'Meara's Hotel, acquired through apparent O'Brien and Smith family connections. The Landed Estates Court prospectus, 1863, vol. 119, names a Brien Smith, son of a Barry Smith, for a 1780 lease of the Lough Field. Barry, William and Aquilla Smith, Denis and Matthew O'Brien and John Pyne surface in the same prospectus in relation to dealings in the O'Meara's Hotel site over the period 1738 to 1839. An American genealogical treatise identifies an 1804 mortgage between a John Pyne and an O'Brien Smith, Pyne's father-in-law. John Pyne was born in Nenagh in 1766 and had a brother Cornelius (b. c.1765, m. 1790, d. 1803). The name Cornelius appears in Sheehan, *N. & its N.*, p. 4, as the owner of The Star and Garter, following Barry Smith, on the O'Meara's Hotel site in 1790.

All this and further evidence, in that American treatise, of surnames brought forward as first names – a second O'Brien Smith, a Smith Pyne and an O'Brien Pyne – allow one to hypothesise as follows: O'Brien Dillon's first name may have been adopted from that of a possible grandfather and uncle, both named O'Brien Smith; the first was clearly John Pyne's father-in-law as father to Hanora Smith (Pyne's wife) and possibly father also of Mary Smith, O'Brien Dillon's mother. The American source is Frederick Wallace Pyne, *The John Pyne Family (1766-1813) in America*, pp. 22, 31-5.

The 97 acres which the Primary Valuation identified him as occupying were dispersed over Benedine, Shesherakeale and Nenagh North/ Annbrook.

73. Nenagh Union Rate Books 1846-52, Tipperary Co. Library, Thurles. The eleven acres were described in 1846 as Silver St and in 1850 as Pound St Fields – apparently the land lying between the two streets and which is now partly the area of the town's principal car park off John's Lane/Place.
74. Landed Estates Court Prospectus, vol. 119 (N.A.).
75. *C.A.*, 6 Sept 1828.
76. O'Brien Dillon, Jun., his eldest son is one of three lives fixing the duration of an 1837 lease for Lot 3 of the L.E.C. Prospectus cited above; the parish records of baptisms do not record this name.
77. Nenagh R.C. Parish Records. Garrett was baptised on 6 Aug 1831.
78. ditto, Theobald was baptised on 23 Dec 1838.
79. A thinner line of speculation than above can be drawn, upon noting in Arthur Vicars, *Index to the Prerogative Wills of Ireland, 1536-1810*, that a Garret Dillon, Dublin, gent, made a will in 1730 and that a Theobald Dillon, Dublin, merchant, made one in 1736.
80. *N.G.*, 10 Sept 1859, recording her marriage to John Gleeson of Lima, Peru; 'Mary Dillon, his eldest daughter' is one of three lives fixing the duration of an 1837 lease for Lot 3 of the L.E.C. Prospectus cited above; the parish records of baptisms do not record this name.
81. ditto, 30 May 1874 recording her death at Begard, Brittany, France; the parish records of baptisms do not record this name.
82. Nenagh R.C. Parish Records. Anna & Anastasia were baptised on 6 Dec 1840.
83. ditto, Dominick was baptised on 23 Feb 1845.
84. *N.G.*, 19 Mar 1859.
85. Sheehan, *N. & its N.*, p. 24; deed checked, courtesy of James O'Brien & Co., solicitors, Nenagh.
86. Minutes, N.B.G., 7 Nov 1861.
87. ditto, 13 Mar 1862.
88. ditto, 4 Sept 1862.
89. ditto, 29 Mar 1862.
90. ditto, 2 Apr 1863.
91. *N.G.*, 7 Jan 1863.
92. ditto, 7, 21 Oct 1863.
93. One hundred and forty years before the evocation of Social Employment

Schemes and Community Employment, Nenagh Relief Committee set about alleviating the problem of unemployment. The labourers were not their main worry as they would have work on the railway line between Nenagh and Birdhill which was opened in 1864. Instead employment was concentrated on the artizans. A fund was set up and it was decided to give employment to batches of 60 men daily for two days a week rather than full-time employment. Most of the money which was raised was given to the landowners as they would be creating most of the jobs for those men – *N.G.*, 7, 14 Feb 1863

94. *N.G.*, 4 Feb 1863.
95. ditto, 28 Jan 1863.
96. Certificate of Death, 10405.
97. The first Board of Guardians for Clonmel Poor Law Union were as follows. *Ex-officio* (significantly listed before the elected members in the Minutes of their first meeting on 1 May 1839 – County Library, Thurles): Stephen Moore, John Bagwell, James R. Smith, William H. Riall, Edmond Mulcahy, William Perry (absent from the first meeting); Lieut.-Col. Phipps (ditto). *Elected*: (District Electoral Division in brackets) Charles Bianconi (Clonmel); Patrick Fennelly (ditto); Thomas Cantwell (ditto); John Dunphy (ditto); Thomas O'Brien (ditto); John Lacy (ditto); William Mahony (ditto); William Smith (ditto); John Power (Kilsheelan); John Moloughney (Templeatiny); Patrick Wall (Lisronagh); Joseph Slattery (Newchapel); Thomas Hackett (Inishlounaght); Patrick Corcoran (ditto); Eccles Greene (Kilronan); Theobald Fitzpatrick (ditto); John Norris (ditto); Henry Pedder (St Mary's); Thomas Hughes Jun. (ditto); Michael O'Donnell (Killalone); Maurice Torpey (Rathgormack).

William Perry in his absence was unanimously elected Chairman on the proposition of Bianconi, seconded by Slattery. John Lacy was elected vice-chairman on the proposition of Greene and Power after a division (the votes were not specified) against Stephen Moore, proposed by Pedder and Mulcahy. Thomas Cantwell was elected deputy vice-chairman unanimously, proposed by Corcoran and Wall. The *Tipperary Constitution* of 3 May 1839, true to form, was rather sniffy about the one election: 'Mr John Lacy, shopkeeper, in preference to Stephen Moore, Esq., of Barn, and John Bagwell, Esq., of Marlfield – two of the largest landed proprietors in this county!!'

The rapport occurred in the following year when Bagwell, Moore and Mulcahy, all ex-officios, were unanimously elected in that order to the three officerships on propositions by a mix of elected and ex-officio members.

98. Donoughmore Papers, G 37/2.

ℰPILOGUE

'Separate Managers for the North and South Ridings'

1 The Genesis of the Council-Manager System

County management is now a sturdy Irish oak, with roots spread through the administrative soil for over five decades. The previous forty-three years, 1899-1942, had seen the democratically-elected successors of the grand juries at their monthly meetings and through finance and general purposes committees deal with both policy and what was clearly seen by corporate bodies generally as the day-to-day business of an executive. Such included, for instance, the recruitment and payment of all but professional staff of the local authorities, and the allocation of houses to applicants. A Department of Local Government and Public Health inspector's memoir of that era demonstrates a consciousness of the problem at central level.

> ... it became apparent that many decisions on minor matters called for the appointment of an executive head with power to deal with such matters without reference to the elected public representatives.
>
> Accordingly, at a conference of inspectors and auditors at Government Buildings at the time when Seamus Burke, B.L., was Minister, we advocated the transfer to County Secretaries and Town Clerks powers to deal with such, but the idea did not find favour at the time with the higher executives of the Department. The proposal then made was translated into law in 1942 (twenty years later) when County Managers were appointed but not exactly to our ideas.[1]

It was, however, grass roots disenchantment among business and professional people with inefficiency, particularly in regard to the collection of rates, and with corruption among some councils, which provided the strongest influence on government in replacing the existing system with a council-manager partnership.[2] The Offaly Roads Improvement Association claimed credit for the dissolution of Offaly County Council and its replacement by a commissioner in 1924.[3] Some twenty local government bodies were dissolved, 1923-6, and replaced

172

by commissioners.[4] Tipperary urban district council was the eighth authority and the second urban to be dissolved – on 22 October 1924.[5] The Minister for Local Government and Public Health, Seamus Burke, who appointed those commissioners to carry out all the council's functions, as a one-man tribunal in each case, was himself a Tipperary TD.[6]

Tipperary (South Riding) County Council was the first of another wave dissolved in 1934, for failing to co-operate in the collection of rates, allegedly because of a bias by their majorities against the new Fianna Fáil government.[7] South Tipperary, in another aspect, had already in 1923 provided a case for what transpired eventually as centralisation of the recruitment of senior grades and of pay bargaining. The proposer of one candidate for the position of its chief administrator, the County Secretary, listed as his attributes that 'during the Black-and-Tan regime the family did their part; there was not a man in the South of Ireland had a revolver put in his face so frequently'. The proposer of the only other candidate who gathered votes, from among a number of applicants, said simply that 'he suffered in the cause of Ireland'. There was no reported mention of job-related qualities or experience. The appointment was made on a vote of 14-13.[8]

At the previous meeting it was first revealed that the retired Secretary had enjoyed salaries, including as secretary also to various committees, which totalled £943. An inclusive salary of £600 was fixed for the incoming man on a vote of 11 as against 7 votes for a salary of £500. Not before Mr Morris, MCC, had made a case for a 'competitive examination', but of a rather special type: 'that each could tender for a lump sum and the lowest tender be accepted'. That proposal won 4 votes.[9]

The New Inn Ratepayers Association asked the Council to turn back the calendar to 1838: 'to hang up the appointment with a view to amalgamating North and South Ridings, and saving the rates'. The only reported comment was that of a Mr Morris: 'From an economic point of view he thought that the unit of South Tipperary was enough for one small county. He held if they centralised too much they would meet with difficulties'.[10]

County management began as a cutting from a sapling – city management, sown in Cork 1929, Dublin 1930, Limerick 1934 and Waterford 1939, with similar motivation and a similar impetus. The acorn came from America where city management was an offshoot of business management and saw its first appointee in 1908. The Irish foresters were J. J. Horgan, Solicitor and Coroner, and his Cork Progressive Association which succeeded in having a commissioner appointed by the Minister to replace Cork Corporation in 1924. The Greater Dublin Movement was a prime mover in the adoption of management in the capital.[11]

A council-manager partnership for the counties was announced by Finance Minister Ernest Blythe in 1931. But it failed to be planted in the political storms of 1931-2 when the Cumann na nGaedheal government's and Minister Richard Mulcahy's hands on the spade were replaced by Fianna Fáil's and Seán T. O'Kelly's. It took until 1939, before his Department of Local Government and Public Health, by then under Patrick J. Ruttledge, next a cabinet sub-committee, and finally the cabinet itself, after several bouts of shaping up to the task, put forward the County Management Bill, 1939.[12]

In Tipperary North Riding, Thurles UDC had joined the chorus of bodies seeking the extension of city management to the counties.[13] Collins points out that county and borough councils had themselves got power under the Local Government Act, 1925 (s. 73) to 'delegate to such person or persons as the Minister shall from time to time appoint for the purpose, all or any of its powers, duties and functions' – a power which was never exercised to delegate to a manager of some shape.[14]

TDs DIFFER

In focusing on Tipperary, the words of two deputies from the county pungently illustrate the contrasting views of the tender plant, during the debate on the Bill in Dáil Éireann in December 1939. Thus Dan Morrissey (Fine Gael, formerly Labour and ex Leas-Cheann Comhairle, TD 1922-57), from Nenagh in the North Riding:

> There is no demand for the Bill from any section as far as I know, but I believe the Government are bringing it in for the purpose of putting in managers to carry out a policy of ruthless economy …. As far as I am concerned, I can speak fairly freely of the county council that remains in one part of my county, and of the board of health and subsidiary bodies there, because I am not a member of any of them. The majority on these bodies are attached to the Minister's party. Leaving aside the usual little talk we hear about favouritism here and there for certain small positions, I can say that, so far as carrying out ordinary duties goes, they do it very well, and in a very creditable way …[15]

Jerry Ryan, from Liskeveen, Horse-and-Jockey, close to the north-south border (also Fine Gael – a 1933 amalgam in which Cumann na nGaedheal were the dominant founders, TD 1937-44):

> I live in a county where there are two county councils, North Tipperary and South Tipperary county councils. I remember we often had bets to know on which council was the greatest number of rogues – the fellows who would sell their votes .... During the past five or six years one of the Tipperary councils was wiped out. I, being one of the criminals that time, I suppose I was responsible for the wiping out of the council.[16]

'Colonel Jerry' (his Irish Free State army rank 'stuck to him') understated his achievement: two months after his Council was dissolved he took part in an armed raid on a rate collector's home in April 1934 and received a nine-month jail sentence. In the Dáil five years later, apparently with the same forthright mode of speech and clear mind as was characteristic of his nephew Tom Dunne, TD (1961-77), he went on to paint a picture of his South less flattering than that of Morrisey's benign North.

> Would it not be an awful thing to find a board of directors running a big house or a ship worth £100,000 and they had no man to control the staff? ... The directors did not bother about the business so long as the newspaper reported what they said. ... I am describing the councils as they are and as they have been in my time. Our functions were that we entered the council and whoever shouted the loudest got the ear of the Press.
>   Each and every one of us did a job for our relatives, or our best friends, or our protégés and that is all we did. ... I am sure that Deputies opposite from my county cannot deny that the cottiers, people receiving home assistance, and people in difficult circumstances have been better off under a commissioner than under the county council ... I appeal to Deputies to vote for this Bill ...[17]

They did. The final vote on the fifth stage was 23 for, 22 against. None of the seven Tipperary TDs from what was then a single constituency voted against. Andy Fogarty, Grange, Cashel, Frank Loughman, Clonmel and Martin Ryan, Knockfune, Newport, all Fianna Fáil, voted for. Their colleague Dan Breen, was not present. Fine Gaelers Morrissey and Ryan were not present for the foregone conclusion; their party colleague Richard Curran (FG), Carrick-on-Suir, though in opposition, voted for.

UNIQUE TIPPERARY

With the relatively light weight of powers and duties on local authorities of that era, Minister Ruttledge grouped twelve counties into six pairs, each pair under one manager, and also paired Dublin city and county. The Dublin City and County Manager and the Cork County Manager were each to get two assistant managers. The two Tipperarys were to get a shared assistant in addition to sharing a county manager. This was unlike the five other pairs of grouped counties, none of whom had an assistant manager.

Tipperary, as with the palatinate, the two grand juries and their successor county councils, was again unique.

The Dáil Debates yield contrasting thoughts on that aspect from Tipperary TDs.

Curran: The following counties are smaller than the South Riding and yet they are to have a county manager: Cavan, Louth, Meath, Monaghan, Roscommon and Wicklow. In the case of Louth, Meath, Monaghan and Wicklow the population is about equal to that of Tipperary North Riding and they are to have a manager. Even from the point of view of valuation I think there is every justification for asking that there should be a manager for both the North Riding and South Riding of Tipperary … I have not met anyone who is not in agreement with the principle of the Bill but I have met nobody who is in agreement with the idea of one manager and subordinate …[18]

Fogarty: We should prefer to have the whole county under one manager.[19]

Loughman: I tried to get the opinion of a number of people in the county, and I could not get anybody to take an interest in the matter at all. It seems to me that the majority of the people are satisfied with the Minister's arrangement, although I would like to see separate managers for the North and South Ridings.[20]

Minister Ruttledge said he could not accept an amendment by Deputy Curran which would install an individual manager in each riding. Professor John M. O'Sullivan, himself a former Minister who had put through the masterly Vocational Educational Act, 1930 and deputising here for Curran, asked in cold logic:

> What is gained by having one manager for each of these when you have to appoint another official under him to help to carry on the work?… who again suffers from dual personality.[21]

The Minister's rationale introduced one novel element to theories of organisation and management – sentiment:

This is a grouping that on sentiment and every other ground seems to be warranted. You have a joint mental hospital and a joint library service, and you have what is known as one county, so that if sentiment were involved, there would be no objection to amalgamating the two.[22]

II The Degrouping Saga

It was to be thirteen years before the North and South Ridings had an opportunity to alter the situation to accord with the Curran-Loughman line (both, interestingly in the light of the source of opposition to the 1838 division into ridings, from the deep South). It took a further fourteen years to arrive at agreement between both Councils and with the three Ministers involved. The bones of the story can be outlined in a chronology constituting Table 4.[23]

The opportunity arose upon the enactment of 1955 legislation by the second inter-Party government. It followed attempts in 1950 by the first such one and in 1953 by Fianna Fáil, back in power, to amend the County Management Act, 1940. In each case a bill reached the Dáil; in each case it lapsed upon a change of government. Each bill set out to redress dissatisfaction with several aspects of the system;[24] for the purpose of this study, it only needs to be said that Minister Paddy Smith's 1953 bill provided for de-grouping of the six pairs of counties. In other words, to give each of the twelve a separate county manager – if the Minister saw fit; there was no role for the council to opt one way or the other.[25]

The County and City Management (Amendment) Act, 1955 handed the power of initiative to the local rulers, as the 1835 Assizes Act did for grand jurors. The 1955 Act's s. 13 provided that both county councils would have to seek the cesser of grouping and hence separate county managers (which process was termed 'degrouping' in common reference). The final decision to terminate the grouping lay with the Minister for Local Government, with the consent of the Ministers for Health (because county councils ran the health services within their areas) and Social Welfare (because they also provided home assistance and allied services).

A quick conclusion from a scan of the chronology would be simply that the South were on balance for degrouping or two individual managers when the then County Manager was resident in Nenagh. The North, initially against, dithered through an uncertain period of 1963-4 and then became pro-independence when the new County Manager resided in Clonmel. The motivations for the respective votes were however more complex than that. One must examine the attitude

177

Table 4	THE CHRONOLOGY OF DEGROUPING
1 July 1955	City and County Management (Amendment)Act, 1955 came into operation. S. 13 allowed cesser of grouping of counties, i.e for a pair to discontinue sharing one County Manager.
3 Jan 1956	South deferred question, 13 votes to 12 ; resolution to degroup then declared lost.
6 Feb 1956	South for degrouping, i.e. for two individual Co.Managers, 16-8 after amendment to defer for 3 months was lost 13-10; decision followed by a strong lobby to rescind the decision.
27 Feb 1956	North against degrouping, i.e. for keeping a shared Manager, 12-4.
June 1960	Local elections; new Councils – 6 changes among North's 21 members; 10 changes among South's 26.
Mar 1963	John P. Flynn, Co. Manager for both counties since 1942, reached age limit, re-appointed in temporary capacity. He had always resided in Nenagh.
2 Oct 1963	Both councils sought Local Appointments Commission recommendation for one, shared Co. Manager following decisions to do so by TNR on 20 Aug and TSR on 2 Sept.
Apr 1964	Pádraig de Buitléir, Assistant Co.Manager for both counties since 1956 and previously Acting as such since 1948, appointed Co. Manager for the two grouped counties. He had always resided in Clonmel.
4 May 1964	South for degrouping, unanimously.
21 July 1964	North against degrouping, 13-6.
2 Nov 1964	Joint meeting of two councils. South in a separate, later meeting affirmed degrouping policy.
15 Dec 1964	North for degrouping, 13-0, one dissenting.
22 Mar 1966	Department of Local Government query whether councils still of same opinion 'in the light of the Government's proposal to transfer the administration of the health services. '
4 Apr 1966	South deferred question for six months, 12-5.
19 Apr 1966	North for degrouping, 8-7.
4 Mar 1967	South deferred question for a further 6 months, unanimously.
June 1967	Local elections, new councils – 7 changes North; 10 changes South.
6 Nov 1967	South for degrouping, unanimously: 'decision of 2 November 1964 confirmed'.
2 Feb 1968	Minister for Local Government, 'before making the necessary Order', gives newly-elected councils opportunity to consider.
20 Feb 1968	North for degrouping, 'adheres to decision of 15 December 1964', unanimously.
21 Jan 1969	Ministers' Order signed: degrouping to take effect from 1 April 1969.

of the party groupings and probe beyond statements on the public record for the private heart-searchings of the politicians and, perhaps crucially, of the managers.

• This part II examines the public on-the-record debate and decisions of the members assembled in Council, illuminated by the recollections of some key councillors. It concentrates on their views of the question from the perspective of organisation and structure.

• Part III introduces the personnel factor in two aspects:
   – the County Manager's opinion in his role as the council's chief executive;
   – the regard paid to the personal status of managers from their own viewpoints and those of the councils and of the Department of Local Government.

• Part IV views the stance of Ministers and their civil service on the proposed degrouping during the final phase of the saga, 1965-9.

IN THE NORTH

A look at the local swings on the question is rewarding. There was the inevitable banter. From J. B. (Barney) O'Driscoll (Fianna Fáil), Newtown, Nenagh: 'We should degroup Thurles out of the respectable part of the county'.

> *Jack Murphy* (Labour), Thurles: 'Thurles can well look after itself'.[26]

The North chairman in 1956, Dan Kennedy (Clann na Poblachta in 1956 and later Independent), who was the only councillor for degrouping in all four key votes of 1956, 1964 (twice) and 1966, went to the heart of the matter on the first occasion, when he proposed degrouping:

> The County Manager had a great deal of work to do between the two counties and he was hardly ever home in Nenagh and any person who wished to see him found it very hard to do so.[27]

Dan Kennedy (without the benefit of reference to the printed 1956 opinion when interviewed in 1982) echoed that, recalling the biggest factor as the workload the County Manager and Assistant County Manager were carrying. He remembered one or the other leaving a 12 midday to 5 p.m. County Council meeting in Nenagh to attend an Urban Council meeting in Carrick-on-Suir, 65 miles away, that night. County Manager J. P. Flynn's practice had been to spend Monday, Wednesday

179

and Friday in the larger South, and Tuesday, Thursday and a very hectic Saturday (half-holiday) morning in the North. That factor of one man in two halves was to be highlighted again and again over the years. Costs were seen not to be a factor; one estimate found the salaries of two full managers plus their travelling if confined to the respective counties to exceed the salary of a manager and an assistant plus travelling expenses in crossing the bounds, by only £40 per annum.[28]

FIANNA FÁIL

The North's Fianna Fáil group was mostly against degrouping although Jim Mounsey claimed in July 1964, when he was one of three among his party who voted for: '… every member would agree that thirty years ago this council had not a fraction of the work it was doing today.'[29] John Fanning, TD (1951-69), Mick Clohessy and Mrs Mary Bridget Ryan, TD (1944-61), voted on three occasions against the split and to retain the one, shared manager but Mrs Ryan 'now believed that it would be better for both North and South to have their own Manager'.[30] That opinion was given to the joint meeting of the two Councils, held in November 1964 at the invitation of the South, and followed within a month by the North's unanimous vote for degrouping.

Still focusing on Fianna Fáil, there remains a curiosity, which none of the survivors were able to satisfy, as to why, having divided their votes according to personal opinions in 1956 and July 1964, they became part of a unanimous vote in favour in December 1964 (after the change of County Manager had the consequence of his residing in Clonmel rather than in Nenagh as his predecessor had) and then did a complete turnabout in April 1966 (see Appendix Nine).

FINE GAEL

The Fine Gael record was quite different. Martin Cosgrave and Ned Kennedy were against degrouping in 1956 and July 1964 but converted in December 1964 along with Liam Whyte (Senator 1973-7) and Tom Dunne, TD (1961-77) who had both also been against degrouping in July 1964.

Liam Whyte in 1966, when the potential relief to the councils' workloads of the mooted health service regionalisation was tending to cloud the question, said:

> The Council gave the proposal a considerable amount of thought and they decided they would degroup the county for managerial purposes. There was nothing that came up to alter the opinion. They had made a decision and they should stand by it.[31]

Whyte has told me that for the July and December meetings in 1964 and again in 1966 there was a party consensus on the issue. He himself had been for degrouping all along and Tom Dunne had been neutral. Both went along with their colleagues against degrouping on the first occasion; on the second the party position was reversed. This does not indicate a regular Fine Gael procedure of agreeing a common line before meetings in that era; such had occurred only on rare occasions.

LABOUR

Just as crucial were the Labour attitudes, though also divided. Paddy Tierney, Senator in 1956 and TD from 1957 to 1969, was trenchantly against degrouping initially. He mellowed to the extent of abstaining, though recording his dissent, in December 1964, simply abstaining in 1966, and rowing in with the unanimous opinion in 1968.

Nov. 1964 – As it was there were far too many County Managers in the country – he never agreed with the Managerial Act anyway.[32]

Dec. 1964 – He hoped that he was not hitting too hard but he believed that it was the truth that they would finish up with two County Managers and two Assistant Managers for County Tipperary. If they thought that the Manager resided too far away, that Council and South Tipperary County Council could pass a resolution that he reside in Thurles and be accessible to both counties.[33]

Interpreting Tierney, one must recall that he was by nature Agin-the-Establishment, whoever and wherever. He had been, in the Flynn era prior to those quoted opinions, the veteran of a hundred public rounds vis-a-vis that manager. They were well-matched – assertive, combative, often abrasive; debate often livened and lightened with a mischievous wit and throwaway phrase; each informed and incisive – frequently on practical nuances which never reached print in local newspapers with a Councillor-Bites-Manager news sense; each, out of the arena, capable of considerate human relations (remembered by many for the big heart and the good turn) with a mix of genuine charm and purposeful *plamás*.

Jack Murphy (initially against the idea in 1956) and John Ryan (later TD, 1973-87, Leas-Cheann Comhairle of Dáil Éireann, 1983-7, Senator 1989-92, TD again 1992-) proposed and seconded degrouping in May 1964 when the Council went along with Tom Dunne's and Liam Whyte's proposal to adjourn, again in July 1964 when the Labour initiative lost 6-13, and in December 1964 when they won 13-0. John Ryan proposed the successful resolutions of 1966 and 1968, seconded respectively by Tom Dunne (FG) and Tom Shanahan (Labour).

J. Murphy, 1964 – there was no sense bringing a man from Nenagh to Carrick-on-Suir.[34]

J. Ryan, 1964 – if they had a manager of their own he would be present at the Urban Council meetings too.[35]

J. Ryan, 1968 – this would be a vast improvement; they were going to have a quicker service.[36]

T. Shanahan, 1968 – North Tipperary is big enough for its own Manager. Appointment would speed up the work and he hoped that they would get good results.[37]

IN THE SOUTH

South Tipperary councillors Ahessy, Boyle, Coffey, Duggan, P. Hogan, Thomas A. Hogan, Murphy and O'Donoghue were basically for degrouping from 1956 to 1967 although Ahessy, Boyle and the two Hogans voted for deferral of the question in April 1966 (see Appendix Nine). The eight represented both Fine Gael (5) and Fianna Fáil (3); T. A. Hogan (FF) proposed the defeated January 1956 motion for degrouping and seconded J. J. Morrissey's (FG) successful February 1956 resolution also for degrouping.

John Kennedy (FF), was initially against degrouping in 1956, one of the minority of eight who felt so strongly that they lodged a motion to rescind the two-to-one vote that February. The motion ran up against a three-month moratorium on rescissions and meantime became unnecessary to renew because North Tipperary's decision against degrouping meant that the statutory requirement that both Councils must agree could not be fulfilled.[38]

Objective consideration in 1956 appears to have been somewhat hindered by tangled party politics as revealed in the following exchanges when the question came up in March for the third successive month (along with legal opinion that they were not entitled to rescind within three months of the February decision).[39]

J. Kennedy (FF): At first there had been a free vote. We were told of Party Whips being brought into action up to last week when certain men who voted in favour of degrouping were asked to change and to fall into line with the Party Whips.

J. Morrisey (FG): Fine Gael left it to a free vote.

C. O'Donnell (Ind): was not influenced by managerial or party whips but voted on conscience.

G. Meskill (FF): had been for deferring but when it came to a showdown voted for degrouping because the Manager had told them they should put the county before the individual.

Kennedy altered opinion to the extent that he proposed the

November 1964 resolution for degrouping, seconded by John Boyle (FG) and adopted unanimously. As an Alderman of Clonmel (Borough) Corporation he had this angle in May 1964:

> If the county were divided it would mean that the Manager could look after the urban areas as well as the rural areas. This would give him a much more comprehensive picture of the running of the county.[40]

This radical thinking, as with John Ryan's in parallel in the North, arose from the division of managerial duties between County Manager and Assistant. John P. Flynn himself handled both County Councils' affairs and those of just one Urban District Council – Nenagh, at home. He delegated all the other Urbans to the Assistant County Manager, Pádraig de Buitléir – Carrick-on-Suir, Cashel and Tipperary in the South, Templemore and Thurles in the North as well as the much larger Clonmel Corporation.[41]

P. J. Kenny in 1964 echoed an 1838 consideration: 'The county was a long and narrow county and very difficult to deal with from a managerial point of view'.[42]

Paddy Hogan, TD (FG) (1961-72), known universally by his professional prefix, 'Surgeon', put both the sentimentality and difficulties of councillors and public in a nutshell in 1964: 'he did not really like to see the county divided, but for administrative purposes it was not realistic that the Manager should be in one riding for 3 days and 3 days in the other'.[43] He proposed both the May 1964 resolution, seconded by John Kennedy, and also proposed the 1967 resolution, seconded by Con Donovan. Both were accepted unanimously.

As with Jack Murphy in the North, a southern Labour leader's conversion to degrouping was a significant factor there. Sean Treacy, TD (1961-) was one of the eight against the idea in 1956, when he was another of the eight signatories to the aborted rescinding motion. Ironically, for a future Ceann Comhairle of Dáil Éireann (1973-7 and 1987-) whose role frequently involves rejecting on grounds of precedent stirring pleas for emergency debates, he was a protester in February 1956. Chairman Tom Duggan ruled out a debate in view of the lengthy one on the subject as recently as the previous month Treacy objected: 'the Council had been gagged all right'.[44]

By May 1963 Treacy believed 'that they might be better off if they had their own manager, as it was felt that South Tipperary Co. Council matters were not receiving the attention they deserved under the present system'.[45] It was he (seconded by T. K. O'Donoghue) who proposed the joint meeting of the two councils in November 1964 which helped to clear minds north and south. He chaired the South meetings in May 1964 and November 1967 which unanimously opted for separate managers.

MATURE REFLECTIONS

Deputy Treacy, interviewed in 1982, clearly remembered his motivation for both the initial stance and the change. He was loathe to see the county divided for managerial purposes; he rather wished to see its territorial integrity preserved. In 1956 he had expressed it thus: 'I can in no way approve of anything which involves the dismemberment of the Premier County'.[46] In 1982 he still somewhat regretted the degrouping and would consider a reversion to the former situation. He recalled that in the Sixties he recognised the growing consensus for degrouping and that there was no point in opposing it. A peaceful transition then became his main concern, a stance characteristic of the temperament of a future Ceann Comhairle.

Willie Ryan (Senator 1961-89), also one of the minority of 1956, went so far in 1982 as to believe that there should not be two councils; he would have favoured a single council for the whole county with its headquarters in Thurles. He recalled the workload on officials getting heavier and that he could see the need for two managers, given that there were two councils. His recollection was that J. P. Flynn over the years influenced the councils towards similar policies on a range of issues. While that is correct, incidentally illustrating the initiator role of a manager, Desmond Roche's Foreword instances independence also. The influence was certainly felt in both counties in organisation and methods; Flynn initiated a two-way exchange of bright ideas, not always implemented by the receiver with a gallantry or alacrity equal to the sender's. He was the epitome of efficiency and dedication – known to have called on occasion into Thurles or Nenagh hospitals, on his way home at night from Clonmel, to do a spot-check on the staff's response to the fire-alarms.

Willie Ryan's final summary was that the change had worked out well and that the amount of business became too great for other than two managers. Deputy Sean Treacy agreed that administratively the degrouping has worked well but still believed that there was no reason why the former system could not have done likewise.[47]

John Ryan believed in 1982 and still maintains today that the change brought a big improvement and that the former system was unwieldy. In addition he recalls a psychological feeling that the North was too far from what was regarded as the power base – Clonmel. Liam Whyte regards the change as a success and emphasises that large groupings create great difficulties, instancing the health boards – he was the Mid-Western Health Board Chairman 1979-82 and its Vice-Chairman for the preceding five years and the subsequent three years.

LONG-DISTANCE COUNCILLORS
Councillors Murphy, Ryan and Treacy all spanned close to thirty years from the 1956 debate to the end of the 1979-85 TSR Council's term. Willie Ryan was the only one to serve the full duration of the 1985-91 council; Treacy resigned in 1987 following his resumption of chairmanship of Dáil Éireann; Murphy was not re-elected in 1985. Tom Duggan and John Boyle were elected to the 1979-85 Council but died in office in 1981 and 1983 respectively. T. K. O'Donoghue was still in public life as a Tipperary urban councillor until his death in 1986. Con Donovan is now the South Riding's senior statesman, its only survivor (in the role of county councillor) of the 1964 debate and bidding fair for an unbroken spell from 1960 to 1998.

His counterpart in the North Riding is John Ryan. Only John Ryan and Liam Whyte of the 1964 debate were on the 1979-85 and 1985-91 Councils. Liam Whyte was a casualty in the 1991 swing to a Fianna Fáil majority on the Council. In North Tipperary, not a single councillor of the 1956 debate was on the 1979-85 Council or its 1985-91 or 1991-8 successors.

III The Managers
The only records which I can find of positive executive advice given Tipperary (N.R.) County Council are by J. P. Flynn in April 1963: 'I feel that there is plenty of work for two County Managers in Tipperary',[48] and by Tom Brophy as Acting Assistant County Manager in May 1964 to the Council in Committee: 'In my opinion the best interests of the county would be served by degrouping'.[49]

Jimmy Murphy's recollection was that the officials 'kept their cards close to their chests'. Dan Kennedy's was that there was no lobbying by management for the change, as distinct from the formal opinions given in public session. Willie Ryan believed that it was the weight of the work rather than any desire to upgrade an Assistant Manager which was the dominant consideration at any stage. Sean Treacy, however, believed that the personality factor did enter into the question at some point.

THE FLYNN FACTOR
Here again the dominant 'J. P.' enters the picture. His relations with

their Council were summed up in retrospect by two South Riding councillors, Jimmy Murphy and Willie Ryan respectively, thus: 'A stormy little man but a great character,' and 'A dictator but he could bend the rules for a good case'.

Des Hanafin (Senator 1969-1992), a youthful Chairman of the North Riding (1956-60), recalls an example.[50] Manager Flynn refused a plea by the Council in session on a case put forward by Hanafin for a subsidy to a private nursing home for a young girl terminally ill and for whom the alternative was a free bed in the Council's Hospital of the Assumption. The councillors maintained that that geriatric hospital was the wrong atmosphere for such a patient. The County Manager stoutly maintained his refusal even when the Council went into Committee. Shortly afterwards he discreetly conceded. Hanafin, three decades on, pointed to Flynn's boardroom wisdom in not presenting councillors in session with a seeming precedent for other cases and to his discreet charity in the essence of the outcome.

Whereas the Manager and Council were frequently embattled in the South, Hanafin portrays the position in the North as the once-a-month council tending to agree that the full-time manager knew best. Flynn, he recalls, returned this compliment by giving close attention to those clients' problems which councillors presented to him and on which it was the manager's prerogative to decide. Jim Mounsey's recollection of meetings is of J. P.'s 'treating councillors like schoolboys, both as regards his own and reserved functions'; in contrast both de Buitléir and Brophy acted as advisers and flexibly. Staff would agree that in one-to-one relationships Flynn dealt very courteously and on level terms with councillors – in fact set an ethos among his staff that the councillors were the bosses and to be treated accordingly.

All that, combined with the residence factor, might partly explain the contrasting 1956 votes – the South in favour of a manager for themselves, the North happy enough with sharing. Plus the factor, again Hanafin's insight and one which would be widely-shared, that Flynn liked the exercise of power and still had immense energy at 58 years of age. Indeed in the three years from ages 62 to 65 he became chairman of the County and City Managers Association. In that capacity he led with flair and determination one side of the negotiations which resulted in a conciliation and arbitration scheme (1963) for local authority officers – despite active reservations by a minority trade union. He still had enough vigour and interest at 65 to carry on in a temporary capacity for the twelve months it took to appoint his successor. That was followed by a spell as Governor of St Laurence's Hospital (the Richmond), Dublin, an indication also of the confidence reposed in him by the Department who asked him to take on that role.[51] A widower whose wife had died twenty years previously at 33 years of age, his family reared and in their own homes in Dublin and further afield, his work was at that stage his life. A mutual colleague told me at the time that Flynn confessed to a feeling of panic on the morning after he finally retired – following his habitual early morning Mass, breakfast and glance over the newspaper he 'did not know what to do with himself'.

Des Roche's view, as a former Department official, was that Flynn would have regarded degrouping as a personal diminution; he was in the premier division of managers together with the Dublin City and County Manager and the five other managers of grouped counties. Hanafin expresses agreement with Treacy that, whatever about their limited public statements, the views of Flynn – and, later, of both de Buitléir and Brophy – would have been sounded out. By that light Flynn would undoubtedly have let it be known in 1956, to the North's key figures at least, that he was quite keen to continue carrying the double burden.

DE BUITLÉIR IN THE WINGS

By that light also one newspaper report of J. P. Flynn's contribution to the North's 1956 debate is somewhat tantalising:

> I am speaking against my own personal issue when I say this but I … no, I will say nothing.
> [later]: at present de Buitléir had not got the same sense of authority as a Manager had. This made the work of both very hard …. In addition it was not fair to Mr de Buitléir. I have kept open since 1948 your chance of degrouping, but I will have to look for a second manager now. It is unfair to Mr de Buitléir to have kept him in a temporary capacity so long.[52]

I take it that his 'own personal issue' was his interest in continuing as County Manager for both ridings. But that a consequence of a decision not to degroup would be immediate attention to regularising the position of Assistant County Manager. The holder of that post for the joint counties, in a permanent capacity, had been Ruairí Ó Brolcháin from 1946. He had come from Mayo's County Secretary post in 1944 and became Meath County Manager on 1 April 1948.[53] At that point TSR's County Secretary, for almost two years, had been Pádraig de Buitléir , the only holder of the Butler surname to make any appearance in all the story of this second stage division of their palatinate.

He was appointed Acting Assistant County Manager, for both ridings, of course; by the time of the early 1956 debates he had held that status for almost eight years. I can only attribute that record tenure to Flynn's having two good reasons for it (always a happier state than having one good reason). Firstly, from an organisational point of view, he was, as he said, leaving the road open for the councils to degroup – with the 1950 and 1953 abortive legislation and the mooted 1955 bill all successively in mind (what would the councils do with a redundant Assistant County Manager if they degrouped). Secondly, he was also building up the experience of a colleague to a point where he was clearly ahead of the field of County Secretaries for a permanent managership; at that stage only Dublin and Cork had assistant managers and they were inclined to corral themselves, as did their staffs due to a practice of confined competitions in those proud fiefdoms. All sources agree that de Buitléir was held in very high regard by Flynn.

Likewise by the southern councillors. He was regarded as one of their own – born just over the border in Kilnamack, Co. Waterford, and a past pupil of Clonmel's Christian Brothers High School.[54] After fifteen years as a Great Southern Railway clerk, he had moved to his native Waterford's County Council as Rates Inspector, acquired associateship of the Chartered Institute of Secretaries in 1942. That obviously helped towards the position of Carlow County Accountant which he held for fourteen months before settling in South Tipperary, initially as its County Secretary as of May 1946. So that the majority who voted for degrouping in early 1956 may very well have had in mind, apart from structural considerations, freedom from Flynn and a high chance of a familiar figure replacing him.

Pádraig de Buitléir felt the need to attempt the protection of his own position. Early in 1955, he observed that the City and County Management (Amendment) Bill, 1954 (which became the 1955 Act) had special provisions to make permanent two named temporary Assistant Managers in Dublin. Having himself been temporary since 1 April 1948, he requested the Minister for Local Government, Patrick (Pa) O'Donnell, to provide for him similarly.

O'Donnell declined: 'but I am sure you will agree that the two cases are not comparable'. Eugene Ó Caoimh had, as Dublin County Secretary, 'a clear (if unintended) legal claim', as of 1948, to any additional office of assistant manager, by 1955 actually created. John P. Keane, though not having an analogous legal claim, had been Deputy City Manager for about eighteen years and was due to retire in a few months' time. 'The provision is of no real value to him and is intended to be simply a mark of honour'.[55]

There is no evidence that de Buitléir enlisted anybody's assistance in pursuing his case in 1955 – he would in any event still be County Secretary if he had not succeeded in the eventual competition for permanent Assistant County Manager. He did succeed ; the Local Appointments Commission (LAC) recommended him to the councils on 13 October 1956.

AVOIDING REDUNDANCY

For seven years the councillors north and south 'let the hare sit'. Obviously nobody felt strongly enough to push for a revision of management in the face of County Manager Flynn's taste for an undiluted job; I believe the Hanafin-Roche-Treacy interpretations, quoted above, to be accurate.

Come 1963, Flynn's reaching 65 years of age and compulsory retirement, and his acceptance of an acting (temporary) role until his successor could be appointed. Any personality or personnel consideration which may have been marginally present in 1956 was now a serious question. 'P de B' was probably favourite to fill this permanent County Manager vacancy. But, as the law stood, while the South would hope to gain de Buitléir they also stood the risk of losing him altogether. For, upon degrouping, the office of Assistant County Manager for the two ridings would cease to exist.[56] And favourite though he might be, there could not be a cast-iron certainty that de Buitléir would succeed in the competition for the South, as distinct from the North, or for either.

J. P. Flynn took the lead. He suggested to the South monthly meeting of 1 April 1963 'that the councils might wish to degroup but before doing so they should consider the position of the Assistant County Manager'.[57] At their next meeting on 6 May Flynn again led. After discussion, consideration of the question was adjourned to enable Flynn to ascertain from the Minister what de Buitléir's position would be. *The Nationalist* (Clonmel) headline of 11 May 1963 encapsulated the problem: 'If Ridings Divide, Assistant Co. Manager's Office Will Cease'. The newspaper's report quoted several contributions which showed concern for their highly appreciated assistant.

An internal TNR memorandum by Acting Secretary Tom Kirwan which updated the story as of 19 February 1968, five years later, recapitulated that his Council's decision of 21 May 1963 was that 'the question ... should be gone into thoroughly to ensure that if the Council passed a resolution to degroup it would not jeopardise his [de Buitléir's] position.'

Manager Flynn, by letter of 8 June seeking a discussion with the

Minister and the Secretary of the Department, was able to say:[58]

> It would appear to me that each Council would like to have their own County Manager. On my request, no resolution was passed to that effect as the degrouping of the county would cause serious embarrassment to Mr. P. de Buitléir, Assistant County Manager. I also feel that if both Councils passed a resolution, it would place the Minister in an embarrassing position.
>
> While the Councils are anxious to degroup, they do not wish to pass any resolution or take any step that would jeopardise Mr Butler who has given excellent service to the two counties.

The Department's Secretary Garvin was a master of propriety. His reply of 20 June to Flynn, apparently without having burdened the Minister with the problem, indicated that he had already told de Buitléir himself that conclusions were premature; both councils should first formally meet, decide and inform the Department 'whether or not they would be prepared to pass the necessary resolutions' (to degroup) 'before any discussion, however informal could properly take place … in regard to Mr Butler's position'. He turned the question to one that 'perhaps it should be put to the Councils … that the statutory request for the filling of the vacant office of County Manager' should be sent to the LAC. He pointed out that 'Mr Butler will be free to compete for the post'.

Flynn and the Councils were equally adroit. His draft letter to the Department was formally approved by the Councils, indicating that while the proposal to degroup 'has been favourably received by the members, they are reluctant to take a final decision in the matter as they do not wish to jeopardise in any way the position of Mr Butler'. However, 'having regard to the advice' given by Garvin and following liaison between the two councils, both asked the LAC to recommend a County Manager.

That body held the competition and recommended de Buitléir. Meantime an acknowledgement of Garvin's letter had subtly raised the bidding and concluded with vintage Flynn, in the vernacular of his roots, the arch Able Dealer (pronounced 'Daler'):

> The two County Councils hold him [de Buitléir] in very high esteem and would be reluctant to part with him in any managerial capacity.
>
> I would like to thank you for your consideration in this matter and I have always found that the interests of the Custom House

in Local Government Officers reaps for us in the counties a fruitful harvest of loyalty, integrity and work.

That could be translated, just possibly was intended to, and even may have been, as: (Local Appointments) Commissioner Garvin, see that we get the right man. But given the Sinn Féin-inspired ethos of meritocracy institutionalised in the LAC as of 1926 and, to the best of knowledge, maintained with integrity, it is likely to have been translatable and translated as: If we don't get our man as County Manager now and if subsequently the councils degroup and he doesn't succeed for the other manager's job, we'll expect ye to haul out s. 9(4) of the County Management Act, 1940 and create an office of assistant county manager for the South or for the South and North jointly (and nobody will match our man for *that* job as the incumbent of the present one).

PERSONAL SAFEGUARD
Overlapping with the Council's formal efforts on his behalf, de Buitléir had, in anticipation of Flynn's 65th birthday on 17 March 1963, already obtained by mid-February Counsel's opinion on four questions posed by his solicitor. The advice was that the two councils were entitled to pass degrouping resolutions, that such would involve the abolition of the office of Assistant County Manager, that de Buitléir's consent to the abolition was not necessary, and that his consequential rights depended on the statutory superannuation (pension) provisions.[59]

He was approaching 58 years of age, too young to retire and too settled to contemplate moving job, residence and family, very much a South Tippman. He requested the Minister by 'semi-official' letter of 11 April 1963 to the Secretary of the Department to take steps to safeguard his position before making any degrouping Order. The prudent Secretary replied on 30 April that it was premature to form any conclusions but that the matter had been 'noted specially and will receive consideration if the two Councils decide on degrouping'.[60] The formal Council decision to request the Minister to safeguard his position, already recounted, followed within a week, in turn followed by the June correspondence and the competition. As stated above, the favourite duly won and was appointed as of 1 April 1964.

BROPHY FOR MANAGER
Now it was the North's County Secretary, Tom Brophy, who became Acting Assistant County Manager until de Buitléir's vacancy could be filled. As of mid-1964 when the Councils came to consider degrouping

191

once more, though an experienced County Secretary with a national reputation (partly via Flynn's commendations for 'his' man throughout the grapevine),[61] he might not have clocked up enough hours as Manager to ensure that the North got *their* highly-appreciated one of their own – a native of Thurles within the Riding too.

While an entry grade clerk (with typing duties) in the North Riding's Board of Health and Public Assistance, he had acquired an ACCA qualification through an after-hours correspondence course. He brought the accountant's analytical mind to all types of problems and is recalled as heavily relied upon by Manager Flynn throughout his term as County Accountant and later County Secretary.

Perhaps somewhat austere in manner through the Flynn regime, he became a highly popular chief of staff, flexible and a good listener, usually succeeding also in a perceived aim to have a better grasp of the intricacies than others. Department officials sent him copies of draft bills on legislation, e.g. the eventual, complex 1956 Superannuation Act, on which he furnished incisive, case-oriented comments. He had an infinite respect for councillors and an open door to members of the public, for the plight of many of whom he had a flexible sympathy.

Brophy's assignments could in retrospect be seen as an overload. Nine years younger than de Buitléir, he was delegated all the urbans and performed the bulk of TNR's functions. The County Manager handled all of the larger TSR and Clonmel Corporation; he came to the north for Council meetings and to such as the finale of trade union negotiations. He relieved Brophy of Carrick-on-Suir U.D.C. duties after Brophy had suffered a set-back in his health.

THE MEMBERS' CONCERN

John Cahalan who was against degrouping in July 1964, when de Buitléir was some four months County Manager and Brophy his Acting Assistant, recalls being concerned about Brophy. It was he who was in mind in these illuminating contributions in July 1964:

Paddy Tierney, TD: Some man from some bad county or a man who was already a County Manager may apply for the position in North Tipp. If they did not appoint a Manager they had a good chance of a local man being appointed Assistant County Manager. The local man would be conversant with the affairs of the council, every member of the council and every employee of the council.

Michael F. Cronin: It would better to have the devil they knew rather than the one they did not know. The council should leave matters as they were.[62]

Those points, cautious and negative though they may have been, incidentally illustrate, via public representatives who could never be accused of gullibility, the popular perception of the Local Appointments Commission's impartiality. Likewise it is implied in the 1963 exchange between a new councillor in the South and his acceptance of Flynn's reply – and Sean Healy of Carrick-on-Suir was not noted for docility. Again, in the positive attitude expressed by Brophy's townsman Jack Murphy in 1964.

S. Healy: Will the man with the most political pull and push get in?

Manager: I will say this for the Appointments Commission – I know of no case where there was political pull in any appointment.[63]

J. Murphy: When he came to talk to the County Manager he wanted to talk to him, not to his assistant as he has not got the power of the County Manager: We must have a poor opinion of our own officials if we have to build a wall around them to give them a job. He did not care where a man came from. Let the best man jump the ditch whether he was from Cork, Donegal, Kerry or Roscommon or anywhere else.[64]

The councillors' protectionism cannot be regarded as machiavellian. Both elected councils were feeling their way, without an obvious need for urgency, towards decisions on two levels. The decision on structure would either leave administration as it had been, but under increasing strain, or change it with some promise of increased effectiveness but with irrevocable effect. A decision to change, either in 1956 or 1963-4, would leave the consequential and vital decision – who would manage their affairs – out of their hands.

But their intelligence grapevine overlapped with that of the national grid of county managers and Department of Local Government and Department of Health officials, both categories serving as members of interview boards selected by and acting for the Local Appointments Commission. That was itself composed of the Secretaries of the two departments, being career civil servants, and the elected Ceann Comhairle of Dáil Éireann The meritocracy implicit in the Commission's interview system was abated in this instance by what was legitimately within the politicians' control – the timing of the process. And that in turn was influenced by a desire to get not just the men acknowledged by their peers as best in the national field but best also in the sense of in-depth knowledge of all the local nuances. There was, too, a premium for long acquaintance on a personal basis between councillor policy-makers who were also reviewers of executive action and managers who were both draughtsmen and executives of Council policy.

193

IV   With the Departments

Following the November 1964 joint meeting of the two councils, the South affirmed its degrouping policy; the North reversed its previous decisions and in December finally voted for degrouping. The matter was now one for three Ministers and their Departments – Local Government, Social Welfare and Health. Local Government (LGD), as the prime one concerned, undertook the normal sequence of consideration and memoranda between February and May 1965.[65] Its key Establishment (the old name for Personnel) section had raised no objection. FGC [Conlon] of the General section recorded that it favoured degrouping. Figures of population, area, revenue and capital expenditure and the number of urbans in Cavan, Meath, Monaghan, Roscommon, TNR, TSR and Wexford had been analysed.

> These figures, the growth and expansion of the functions performed by local authorities, together with the increasing costs of services they are required to administer had indicated that degrouping is desirable and that management of the county as one unit might in future years become unwieldy.

Correspondence with Social Welfare and Health followed: would the Ministers [Kevin Boland, Social Welfare; Donogh O'Malley, Health] be prepared to consent? Within days Social Welfare replied: the Minister would be prepared. But in late July 1965 Health demurred:

> The Minister considers it desirable to defer until the Government has considered proposals in the draft White Paper recently sent to the Department of Local Government for its observations ... as the adoption of these proposals might leave the position such that a joint appointment of manager for local government functions would be preferable.

LGD POSITIVE

From LGD's Establishment section T. P. Rice sent a strong memo to Conlon. He did not agree with Health that the White Paper developments might influence their decisions to degroup. He instanced that: (a) there were in effect two managers already; (b) the savings in salary of an assistant were offset by travelling costs; (c) public representatives were irritated as the manager spent two to three days in the other half.

He concluded that everything pointed to degrouping and both local authorities wanted it. He claimed that it could not be seriously

194

contended that fifty per cent of a manager's time was taken up with health functions. There was a substantial expansion in housing, sanitary services etc and particularly town planning, additional to what local authorities had to do up to the previous October. Presumably the Department of Health would not object if health services stayed with local authorities; if taken away, why should they object.

HEALTH NEGATIVE

T. P. Rice's arguments were summarised in September 1965 to Health, but four weeks later Brendan Hensey, responded with a recapitulation of his Department's having a draft White Paper and 'the Minister meantime considers that a decision to approve degrouping should not be taken'.

Whether that was Hensey and other Department of Health officials talking, or Minister O'Malley himself, or the officials with O'Malley's agreement is unclear. Hensey (who became Secretary in 1973) was at the time the high flyer 'heading a Departmental team' planning divorce of the health services from local government and on a regional basis.[66] Whoever was responsible for the woolly thinking vis-a-vis the management of the two Tipperarys, it amounted to quite a contrast with the cogent Rice reasoning. If the wool can be partly excused on the grounds of total immersion in their own plans, then it becomes inexcusable from a point of view that it was none of their business except by way of a legal technicality. The nett effect was that it sparked off a loss of over two years in progress on management of a set of major services in which they had no involvement since the splitting of local government and health at government level in 1947, almost twenty years before.

In March 1966, SO'H [Hanlon] of LGD re-opened the question with both councils: 'Are you still of the same opinion in the light of the Government's proposal to transfer the administration of the health services?' Although LGD's question was inevitable, given Health's attitude, TNR's Councillor Jack Murphy (who was regarded as the member principally interested in and expert on the health service) received it with typical pungency.[67] Councillor Paddy Tierney focused on the implications for health administration.

J. Murphy described the Minister's letter as one that could be sent to school children. When this White Paper becomes red or black would the Council not retain the Assistant County Manager or would he be transferred to the Regional Board.

P. Tierney: the County Council should turn down this new proposal entirely, it would come to that, they would have regional county councils

195

and that seemed to be the Minister's idea, that these county councils were getting too burdensome and troublesome for his wishes. They could envisage the day when they would have a regional water scheme, a regional mental scheme.

In the event, the North affirmed its degrouping stance promptly in April, with the narrow margin of 8 votes to 7. Now came a valley period when twice in twelve months the South Riding deferred the question. The Council minutes and the reports by both the *Tipperary Star* and *Nationalist* are bereft of debate to illuminate the rationale. Local elections took place in June 1967. The LGD sent umpteen reminders during this period to both counties.

SELF-DETERMINATION
In November 1967 the South unanimously confirmed its decision of three years before to degroup. In the following month JAK [Keegan], LGD, wrote to Health – the Minister was firmly of the opinion that two managers would make for more efficient and less costly administration irrespective of developments in relation to the organisation of the health service. The Department was concerned at the number acting in higher grades over a long period with noticeable ill-effects. The permanent appointment of the South Tipperary County Secretary to another post on 1 January 1968 could very quickly lead to a serious breakdown in administration (Paddy Dowd was about to become Laois-Offaly County Manager).

On 10 Jan 1968 Hensey replied for Health that in the circumstances explained the Minister [by then Sean Flanagan] would be willing to consent. Nevertheless, the Minister for Local Government [by then Kevin Boland] considered that the new North Riding council should be given the opportunity of considering the question. The North promptly replied at its February 1968 meeting that it unanimously adhered to its decision of 15 December 1964 (curiously they by-passed any reference to the narrower April 1966 decision).

In a final flurry of internal memoranda ML [Lawless] to Mr [Gerry] Meagher pointed out that if a transfer of health functions reduced the work load substantially, the position could be reconsidered when de Buitléir retired and possibly the manager in the North Riding could be required to do both, but that this was unlikely as the North Riding was with Clare and Limerick in the Limerick region.

He noted that de Buitléir left the 'rather important' Thurles, Nenagh, Templemore, Tipperary and Cashel to the Acting Assistant Manager and that seven urban districts constituted the largest number in any county outside Kerry.

TT [Troy] adverted to the fact that, when degrouping had taken place, that did not prevent counties from being grouped again under s.12 of the 1955 Act. However, because of different planning regions, North and South should not be grouped.[68]

It had taken 342 days from the final clearance by the two councils to finalise the single sheet of paper constituting the signed Minister's Order; it had taken 321 days for the comparable steps in 1837-8 towards a proclamation which ran to a preamble, 81 clauses and an appendix. Dublin Castle then had to cope with a unique and complex situation; the Custom House in 1968 had a readymade prototype in the Kilkenny-Waterford degrouping Order only three years previously. The 1969 Order beat a type of deadline by two days; it was signed sixty-two days ahead of the date it came into operation, 1 April, which marked a most convenient start of a new financial year; the Act prescribed 'a day not earlier than sixty days'. The obvious pressure of other business within the Department had as a corollary human pressure and stress within the counties.

CONCLUSION

The fourteen years hiatus between the opportunity which was presented in 1955 for remedying the strange structure of 1942, and the implementation of that remedy can be analysed thus:

- some early months when the opinions differed as between the two sets of elected members, probably influenced by contrasting perceptions of the strong man, County Manager Flynn, resident in the north capital;
- seven years of members' silence during which Flynn and Assistant County Manager de Buitléir continued a régime divided, not as between the two counties, but broadly as between the counties under Flynn and the urbans under de Buitléir;
- twenty-one months of delicate deliberations, including personnel considerations, at the end of which both councils were for degrouping and separate managers;
- three years and some months of muddled to-and-froing, which included both the Department of Local Government's honest attempts to respect local self-determination but bedevilled by the virtually irrelevant health services question, and a South Riding reluctance to finally let go the subject;
- a year of inaction in LGD while managers and staffs in imposed inefficiency coped with an escalation in services to the public.

Overall, and as in 1838, a commonsense assessment of the increased workload and its effects decided the basic issue. The saga concluded when the modern form of government proclamation divided Tipperary for the second time: the Ministerial Order which was signed by three Ministers on 21 January 1969 came into operation on 1 April 1969 – baptism and confirmation dates of the second charter of independence. Statutory Instrument No. 8 of 1969, County Management (Tipperary North Riding and Tipperary South Riding) Order, 1969. The signatories were Kevin Boland as Minister for Local Government, making the order, and the Ministers for Health and Social Welfare consenting, Sean Flanagan and Joe Brennan, respectively.[69]

When the Ministers involved ordered the degrouping – and thus individual managers – Pádraig de Buitléir exercised his statutory option in the unsurprising favour of the homely South – technically by relinquishing the North.[70] Thomas Brophy became Acting County Manager for the North Riding until his selection by the LAC for the permanent position which he held from February 1970. Sadly neither of the central figures lived to enjoy retirement. Pádraig de Buitléir died in office on 25 August 1969, only five months after the degrouping and within eleven months of the age limit. Tom Brophy died suddenly on 29 May 1977, two years short of the age limit and with tentative plans for early retirement unfulfilled.

Notes

1. Sean MacCraith, *Early Irish Local Government 1921-27* (Clonmel, 1967), p. 12. The author was better known as John McGrath, Tipperary (North Riding) County Secretary, from shortly after 1942 until retirement in 1957, following which he practised as solicitor in Nenagh for some years.
2. Desmond Roche, *Local Government in Ireland* (Dublin, 1982), Chapter Nine, and Eunan O'Halpin, 'The Origins of City and County Managment' in Joseph Boland and others, *City and County Management 1929-90/A Retrospective* (Dublin, 1991) tell all.
3. Michael Byrne.
4. Roche, cited above, p. 53.
5. Joseph Boland and Eunan O'Halpin, Part VI, 'A Chronology ...' in Boland and others, cited above.
6. Seamus A. Burke (1893-1967), B. L., Rockforest, Roscrea, was elected MP for Mid-Tipperary constituency in the Sinn Féin interest in 1918. On the institution of Dáil Éireann in January 1919 he began a twenty-one year spell as TD. Following the formation of the Irish Free State, he joined Cumann na nGaedheal and later Fine Gael. He was Minister for Local Government and Public Health from 1923 to 1927. He was defeated in the 1938 general election, and again in 1943 when an independent. He wrote *Foundations of Peace* (Dublin, 1920). He is buried in Glenkeen

graveyard, near Borrisoleigh.

7. P. J. Meghen, TSR's commissioner, became the first Limerick County Manager as of 1942 (Roche, cited above, p. 105). TSR was dissolved on 20 February 1934; Kilkenny, Laois and Waterford on 2, 5 and 6 June. (Neil Collins, *Local Government Managers at Work* (Dublin,1987), p. 243, n 67).
8. *T.S.*, 18 Aug 1923.
9. *T.S.*, 21 July 1923.
10. Patrick C. Power, *History of South Tipperary* (Cork, 1989), p. 221.
11. Roche, cited above, pp. 100-4.
12. Roche, cited above, p. 105.
13. Collins, cited above, p. 30.
14. ditto, p. 242 n55.
15. *Dáil Debates*, vol. 78, cols 1246, 1250, 7 Dec 1939.
16. ditto   ditto   col. 1252, same date.
17. ditto   ditto   col. 1253-5, same date.
18. ditto   vol. 79   col. 1734, 1737, 24 Apr 1940.
19. ditto   ditto   col. 846, 14 Mar 1940.
20. ditto   ditto   same date.
21. ditto   vol. 79.   col. 845, same date.
22. ditto   ditto   col. 846, same date.
23. The decisions and voting are taken from the respective Council Minutes – in TNR's Minute Book and extracts on TSR's file MG/8. I am grateful to the respective County Managers, Messrs John McGinley and Seamus Hayes, for access, and to TNR's former County Secretary, Mr Tom Griffin, and TSR's former Administrative Officer, Mr Willie Moloney, for abstracts of voting lists utilised in Appendix Nine.
24. Roche, cited above, 107-9 which also deal with central-local interaction.
25. Minister Pa O'Donnell to Pádraig de Buitléir, Acting Assistant County Manager for Tipperary (both ridings), 9 March 1955. Moreover: 'unlike my predecessor I am providing in the [1955] Bill that Councils may continue to be grouped or to be degrouped, as they please.'
26. *N.G.*, 3 Mar 1956.
27. ditto, same date.
28. TNR file.
29. *N.G.*, 25 July 1964.
30. ditto, 14 Nov 1964.
31. ditto, 30 Apr 1966.
32. ditto, 14 Nov 1964.
33. ditto, 19 Dec 1964.
34. ditto, same date.
35. ditto, 25 July 1964.
36. ditto, 24 Feb 1968.
37. ditto, same date.
38. TSR file MG/8: Roger O'Hanrahan, S.C., 2 Mar 1956 to Francis Murphy, County Solicitor.

39. *The Nationalist*, 10 Mar 1956.
40. *N.G.*, 16 May 1964.
41. Personal recollection, checked with Mr Seamus Hayes.
42. *N.G.*, 14 Nov 1964.
43. ditto, 16 May 1964.
44. *The Nationalist*, 11 Feb 1956.
45. *The Nationalist*, 11 May 1963.
46. *The Nationalist*, 10 Mar 1956.
47. I am greatly indebted to those and the other public representatives, including former councillors, quoted above and below for their recollections and insights conveyed in a series of one-to-one conversations, mostly in mid-1982.
48. *N.G.*, 20 Apr 1963.
49. TNR Minutes, 19 May 1964.
50. In the course of an interview, 17 Aug 1988, and a follow-up shortly afterwards.
51. My own recollection, confirmed by his profile in Boland and others eds, cited above, p. 74. Flynn's early career was equally stimulating: born in Moyne, Thurles; a B. Comm. from U.C.C.; Cork, London and Argentina (five years) accounting and banking; Limerick County Accountant and Agricultural Credit Corporation Accountant; then twelve years as TNR County Secretary, 1930-42.

    In the early years of the latter post he introduced manilla folders to hold correspondence, memoranda and case studies, a technological revolution which won him for a short while the nickname 'File Flynn' from the slim staff who had retained information in pigeon holes and in their heads.
52. *Tipperary Star*, 3 Mar 1956.
53. Recollection of Mr Seamus Hayes, TSR County Manager, as of 1948 a Clerical Officer in that county; also in Boland and others eds, cited above.
54. TSR staff file.
55. I am most grateful to Dr Donal de Buitléir, the late County Manager's son, for copies of that exchange of correspondence.
56. s.13 (4) of the 1955 Act by deleting s. 9(3) of the 1940 Act which provided:

    There shall be an assistant county manager for the county of Tipperary, North Riding, and an assistant county manager for the county of Tipperary, South Riding, but one and the same person shall be the assistant county manager for each of those counties.
57. TSR Council Minutes.
58. This and the correspondence following: TSR file MG/8.
59. TSR file MG/8: Roger O'Hanrahan, S.C., 16 February 1963, in response to Francis Murphy, County Solicitor's queries of 30 October 1962. The key legal points were that (1) s. 13 of the City and County Management (Amendment) Act, 1955 provided that a Minister's Order for degrouping

would delete s. 9(3) of the 1940 Act, quoted at note 56 above, which provided for the two Ridings' assistant county manager (and to be the same person); (2) the general requirement for a permanent officer's consent to a local authority's abolition of his office (s. 10(5) of the Local Government Act, 1941, as added to by s. 12(1) of the Local Government Act, 1955) was over-ridden by the express provisions of the 1955 Management Act whereby the abolition was not at the hands of the local authority (it was both a statutory provision and stemming from a Minister's Order).

60. TSR file MG/8.

61. Since writing that I have come across Collins, cited above, p. 162: 'Some men are noted for promoting the image of their protégés. Several senior managers point with obvious pride at the numbers of "their men" who now hold managerial posts'. I had slipped into a parallel line of thought from a different perspective in preparing the first draft of the section, 'Graduates', in the Postscript.

62. *N.G.*, 25 July 1964.

63. ditto, 20 Apr 1963. Another view of the LAC surfaced in the Seanad debate on what became the 1955 (Amendment) Act – by Denis E. Burke, Clonmel (vol. 44, col. 1586, in 1955). This view, certainly not typical among public representatives in relation to the filling of senior posts by the LAC, might have had a subliminal source in the selection of county rate collectors by elected members by a vote. This followed a round of canvassing which called upon kinship, party political affiliation and past favours, with the occasional allegation of bribery and, once, a kidnapping of a wrongly-disposed South Tipp councillor. The whole scandal was ended in 1973 by the County Management (Amendment) Act, 1972. A diluted form still exists in the mix of politicians, management and Department of Education representative on Vocational Education Committee interview boards for the appointment of teachers. Senator Burke's view was:

> I would hate to think that there is no farmer in Kickham's county good enough to sit on a board with civil servants to pick a person to be a county manager ... mix the boards with different types of people, people with common sense and ability.

64. ditto, 25 July 1964.

65. Department of the Environment file G246/29/2, 'De-Grouping of Tipperary Nth and South Riding' inspected 8 Nov 1991 by much-appreciated permission of Mr Brendan O'Donoghue, Secretary.

66. Joseph Robins, *Custom House People* (Dublin, 1993), p. 158.

67. *N.G.*, 30 April 1966.

68. Messrs Lawless, Meagher and Troy became Secretaries of the Department on 1 October 1966, 7 June 1974 and 25 June 1985, respectively – Boland and others eds, cited above, Part VI, 'A Chronology of Local Government'.

69. The full set of degroupings is as follows:

County	Degrouping: Min's. Order per S.I. No.	Effective Date	Last Manager of Grouped Counties	First Managers of Degrouped Counties
Kilkenny Waterford	3 of 1965	1 Apr 1965	Simon Moynihan	Dion Donovan Charlie O'Connor
Tipp N.R. Tipp S.R.	8 of 1969	1 Apr 1969	Pádraig de Buitléir	Tom Brophy P. de Buitléir
Carlow Kildare	305 of 1974	1 Jan 1975	Edward M. Murray	Michael Boyce Gerald Ward
Sligo Leitrim	220 of 1976	1 Dec 1976	Thomas J. McManus	Paul Byrne P. J. Doyle
Longford Westmeath	296 of 1976	1 Jun 1977	Michael J. Boyce	Michael Killeen Dan Hurley
Laois Offaly	391 of 1981	1 Apr 1982	Patrick Dowd	Michael Deigan Seán P. MacCarthy

Sources: Department of the Environment; Boland and others, cited above.
70. Pádraig de Buitléir to the Secretary of the Department, 10 February 1969, TSR file CM/43. The option was prescribed in s. 13(3)(b) of the 1955 Act.

$\mathcal{P}OSTSCRIPT$

'Councillors Divided on Unity'

FURTHER ASSISTANCE

Tipperary South Riding developed sufficiently to acquire an assistant manager of its own in 1980. The South Riding has the lowest population of the twelve county councils enjoying the service of one or more assistant managers (Cork has three) – 75,000, with Clare at 91,000 and Wicklow at 97,000 the next lowest. Whether Paddy Tierney's forecast of two assistants in the two Tipperarys comes true probably depends partly on population and partly on the final shape of the local government reform of structures and functions. The North Riding at 58,000 ranks behind five other counties without assistant managers: Kildare, Louth, Kilkenny, Westmeath and Offaly (see Table 5). Still on the population factor, Offaly, Sligo and Roscommon would have more or less equal claims to North Tipperary's with the latter perhaps having a slight edge through the presence of three urban districts and the developing Lough Derg area.

RESIDUE

Two local government bodies covering both administrative counties remained after 1 April 1969, although one, the Tipperary Mental Health Board, succumbed exactly two years later to the embrace of the South-Eastern Health Board on its inauguration. Only one body now remains to cross the two Tipperarys' border – the County Tipperary Joint Libraries Committee which was formed as a result of resolutions on 17 November 1926 and 7 December 1926 by North and South County Councils respectively to adopt an 1855 Libraries Act and take over the Carnegie Trust libraries throughout both counties. That Act was repealed by the Local Government Act, 1994 whose s.32, 32(2) gives the modern constitutional basis for this joint committee, the only one in the State (see also Appendix Ten). Deputy Seán Treacy, consistent with his *grádh* for the single county concept, loved meeting his 'North Tipperary friends' in this forum and points to the great rapport among its members. He claims it to be a very effective committee. The chair and vice-chair rotate between the North and South.

At its meeting of 3 February 1969, the South Riding Council 'as the largest contributing body' requested the Minister for Local Government to appoint their man as manager for the Libraries Committee and Mental Health Board. However the Department raided their archives for the County Management (Joint Bodies) Orders of 1945 and 1960 respectively which specified that the North County Manager was to be both bodies' manager. That was logical for the library, having the centrally-placed Thurles as its headquarters; it ran counter to the logic of geography for the Mental Health Board, centred on St. Luke's Hospital, Clonmel, especially as the 1960 Order was promulgated five years after degrouping became possible. Perhaps the reason was no more profound than that N for North preceded S for South in the alphabet and so in all the statutory references to the pair. The question in relation to the Mental Health Board became academic with the inauguration of health boards on 1 April 1971.

Members of the two councils also meet in a weak descendant of that Mental Health Board – the Visiting Committee to St Luke's Psychiatric Hospital, Clonmel, although nominated to this by the South-Eastern and Mid-Western Health Boards (see Appendix Ten); in occasional consultation on housing in the Holycross area which consists of the finger or spur of the north which dips into the south, plus the surrounding area in both counties; on Clodiagh and Black River Joint Drainage District Committees; and in a full-scale joint session once every three years to nominate a member of the Senate of University College, Cork. It was on such an occasion in 1964 that the opportunity was taken to discuss degrouping. The Councils' present joint nominee is Most Rev. Dr Dermot Clifford, Archbishop of Cashel and Emly Diocese, who resides in Thurles. He succeeds his episcopal predecessor, Archbishop Thomas Morris, as nominee.

POLICE AND ELECTIONS

A brief examination is appropriate of two systems organised on a basis using the thirteenth to nineteenth century county. Police functions still have a geography close to the old. A Garda division under a Chief Superintendent consists of Tipperary plus the Oola-Doon-Galbally area of east Limerick, the Moneygall area of south Offaly and the Piltown-Urlingford-Johnstown area of west Kilkenny but minus North Tipperary's Redwood-Lorrha area (in Laois-Offaly Division) and the Rearcross-Newport-Ballina-Ballywilliam area (in Clare Division). There are six districts within the division, each under a Garda Superintendent, centred on Clonmel, Tipperary, Cahir, Thurles, Templemore and Nenagh.[1]

For parliamentary elections the geographical county continued after 1838 as a geographical unit, returning two members in common with the thirty-one other counties; then four single-seat divisions from 1885 to 1922 were succeeded from 1923 to 1947 by a single countywide seven-seat Dáil constituency. From the 1948 election onwards the two ridings became separate constituencies, with some reshaping (and larceny of part of Waterford on occasions) in 1961, 1969 and 1974, each dictated by the opinion of the ruling government as to electoral advantage.

Since 1980, following the Walsh Commission report, Tipperary North constituency has been given territorial integrity with three seats. Tipperary South constituency has acquired a small segment of County Waterford near Clonmel for its four seats consisting of the district electoral divisions of – Ballymacarbry, Graignagower, Gurteen, Kilmacomma, Kilronan and St Mary's in the former Clonmel No. 2 Rural District (i.e. that part of Clonmel poor law union which formed a rural district in County Waterford, as distinct from Clonmel No. 1 rural district in County Tipperary).[2] There have been two Constituency Commission Reports since then, on 29 July 1983 and 31 July 1990, but neither recommended any changes in the Tipperary constituencies.[3]

The Returning Officer for Dáil elections is the County Registrar whose office was created by the Court Officers Act, 1926. In taking over that former duty of the High Sheriff as election returning officer and other duties and powers of the Under-Sheriffs (both offices unaffected in 1838, as was specified in s.32 177 of the 1836 Grand Juries Act, but abolished by that 1926 Act) the role of County Registrar can be seen to be a tenuous link with medieval institutions (as also is that of coroner). And the North Tipperary ratepayers contribute, in this one common manner with their forbears, to the extent that the North Riding pays a sum towards the maintenance of Clonmel Courthouse because the County Registrar's office is there.[4]

DEVELOPMENT

The Vocational Education Committees of the two ridings, running second-level schools, have co-operated in leading a campaign of some years running for a third-level institution, to be located at Thurles and initially envisaged (1979) as a Regional Technical College. The case was approved by Government and a site purchased in 1985, but the RTC did not materialise due to public service expenditure cut backs in 1987. The plan was altered in concept, as of 1989, to the Tipperary Rural and Business Development Institute (TRBDI). An innovative case was developed in 1989 for a totally new concept in third level education, using the European Commission document 'The Future of Rural Society', as its inspiration.

Its management structure as designed would draw on the two VECs and the managements of voluntary secondary schools, Institute staff and students, the Department of Education, Aontas (National Association of Adult Education), the Science and Technology Office of the Department of Industry and Commerce, Teagasc (Agriculture and Food Development Authority), Shannon Development, rural interest groups, industry and trade unions.[5] Among its aims are to develop an effective model for rural development in Ireland and Europe, through partnership and active community involvement by such a third-level institution, and to develop an effective model for using technology in rural development.

The practicalities envisaged to cater for a target of 800 users each year (students, business people, adult and continuing education participants) include a distributed campus, with two core centres (Thurles and Clonmel), ten extended network centres and twenty-two outreach centres; a comprehensive range of people and technology support services to individuals, communities and businesses; an overseas development consultancy and training unit to carry out assignments in developing countries, and in areas such as Eastern Europe, specialising in the field of rural development.

Side by side with an escalating public relations campaign, imaginative, sustained and with widespread public involvement, the TRBDI name was used meantime for numerous pilot initiatives. They include a national pilot GAA coaching course; participation in the 'European Virtual Class Room EUROFORM Project' through delivering a certificate programme in health and safety at work; an advanced diploma in the organisation of community groups (1993-4). The members of the Action Committee are listed in Appendix Ten.

Amalgamation of the two VECs was one of a number of amalgamations, and notably the least sensible one because of the size of each Tipperary, mooted by the Minister for Education, Mrs Mary O'Rourke, TD, in late 1987; plans for new educational structures are not finalised at the time of writing, seven years and three Ministers later.

Shannon Free Airport Development Company have brought within their orbit the old Ely O'Carroll. That semi-state body has a basic remit of industrial development since 1959 for Clare, Limerick and North Tipperary (the mid-west region), with an extra dimension of tourism development for the expanded region since 1 January 1988. In this one curious respect the Ely O'Carroll territory transferred to King's

County (Offaly) in 1605 has been 'repatriated', and joined to a further area to its north-west, also in County Offaly and comprising Eglish and most of Garrycastle baronies, the whole area being the equivalent of most of Birr No.1 Rural District (1899-1925).[6]

In May 1991, the Minister for Agriculture and Food, Michael O'Kennedy, a North Tipperary TD, announced the national arrangements for implementing the European Commission initiative on rural development known as LEADER.[7] That is a happy acronym for *Liaison entre actions de dévelopement de l'économie rurale* – links between actions for the development of the rural economy. The full geographical Tipperary was selected as one of fifteen areas in the State for its impact. The first effort within the county had an unhappy termination; it was succeeded in mid-1993 by a group listed in Appendix Ten. At the time of writing they have applied for European Union designation to operate LEADER II from 1995. During their eighteen-month existence they sanctioned 200 projects and spent a budget of £1.906 million. The activities funded included technical support for rural development (e.g. surveys, assessments); vocational training and assistance for recruitment; rural tourism enterprises; small firms, craft enterprises, local services; development and marketing of local agricultural, forestry and fishery products; other activities which aspired to contribute to the development of the area.[8]

GRADUATES
V. T. H. Delany, drawn upon for the Prologue, listed a number of persons who had served in the palatinate court of Tipperary and who moved on to the national Bench. One applicant described the county's court 'a very lucky station to everyone else that has had it'. Delany concluded: 'It will be seen, therefore, that in many cases, appointment to office in Tipperary foreshadowed accession to higher places ...'.[9]

That comment in relation to the seventeenth and eighteenth centuries equally applies to the twentieth. A number of elected members who became Government Ministers, Teachtaí Dála and Senators are noted in Appendices Nine and Ten. Likewise, an impressive array of County Managers have graduated from the staffs of the county and urban district councils within Tipperary. They number twenty-six, including Flynn, the North County Secretary until 1942, de Buitléir, Assistant Manager for both ridings, and Brophy whose rise from Clerk-Typist through Accountant, Secretary and Assistant Manager, all within the North Riding, is unparalleled in Irish local government. Two chief executive officers of health boards add to the total.

Pat O'Halloran, TSR Staff Officer and then Chief Clerk of St Luke's

Mental Hospital, Clonmel, was seconded as Organisation and Methods officer for the two ridings in 1956-7, became Wexford's County Secretary, then the Kerry County Manager and died in office. Ruairí Ó Brolcháin, the two Tipperarys' 1946 Assistant County Manager, having been County Secretary in Mayo, went on to Meath as County Manager in 1948 and then to Dublin as Assistant County Manager assigned in effect as manager for Dublin County. Dion (Denis F.) Donovan, County Accountant, after a lengthy spell as Acting County Secretary during de Buitléir's acting assistant managership, became the Kilkenny County Manager following a term as Limerick's County Secretary.

Two former Accountants, Seamus Keating and Seamus Hayes, each of whom placed a step on the first rung of the ladder in 1948 as a Clerical Officer in the first post-war wave of recruitments, and a former Secretary of Tipperary (South Riding) Co. Council, Patrick Dowd, have been Managers in Galway County and City, South Tipperary and Cork County, respectively. Messrs Keating, Hayes and Dowd were in the meantime Managers in Kerry, Wicklow and Laois-Offaly, respectively. Two other former TSR County Secretaries, Michael N. Conlon and Joe (T. J.) McHugh, have been Cork County and Cork City Managers, respectively. Conlon became Chief Executive of Cork and Limerick Savings Bank and Chairman of Bord Gáis Éireann (The Irish Gas Board); McHugh, General Manager, Southern region, of Bord Gáis Éireann. Prior to his stint in TSR, McHugh was the pioneer of regionalism – as the first Director of a Regional Development Organisation, that for Limerick, Clare and TNR. It was set up in February 1968 by the local authorities themselves; seventeen months later the Minister enjoined the rest of the State to set up seven similar RDOs.[10]

Tommy (Thomas P.) Rice, a pioneer migrant in the modern era from the Department to become TNR County Secretary, retired as Cork City Manager, having been meantime County Manager in the South Riding and City Manager in Limerick. Two former engineers with TNR, Michael Deigan, for some time Roscommon County Manager, and Seán McCarthy for a spell Donegal County Manager, became managers for Laois and Offaly, the last pair of counties to be degrouped; a third engineer graduate of the North, Seán (Patrick J.) Murphy, was Limerick County Manager, succeeded by Deigan in his third such post. One of the first engineers to break the mould by entering top administration was Tom (T. F.) Collins, an Assistant County Engineer in TSR in the Fifties who became Kerry County Manager in 1974. He was succeeded by his assistant there, Paddy (D. P.) d'Arcy, yet another former TSR County Secretary.

Michael Killeen, Longford County Manager, was Town Clerk in Cashel and later in Nenagh. Another Cashel graduate, Jack Quinlivan, is Louth County Manager, having meantime followed a fairly typical itinerary via Athy, Castlebar, Carlow and Dundalk UDCs, Laois County Secretary and Wexford Assistant Manager. A full generation earlier, Michael Veale was Town Clerk at Carrick-on-Suir before three managerial posts, as Cavan and Laois-Offaly County Manager and Assistant for Dublin city and county, 1957-68. Another Carrick-on-Suir graduate, Tom (T. J.) McManus, was TSR's Acting County Secretary, 1945-6, and became the last Leitrim-Sligo County Manager before degrouping. Yet another Town Clerk, this time of Clonmel borough for eighteen years, James J. Berkery, went straight to his birthplace Limerick as its City Manager in 1939.

A fully-fledged County Manager, Thomas A. Hayes, Longford-Westmeath's first, chose to become the two Tipperarys' Assistant, 1944-5, before heading home to Cork for twenty years in a similar post. Donal Connolly, Waterford County Manager, was Staff Officer in North Tipperary and Assistant County Manager in South Tipperary before a spell as Roscommon County Manager. David Mackey, formerly County Secretary and then Assistant County Manager in the South Riding, was Cavan County Manager until his move into the private sector. Bob (R. N.) Hayes, not himself reared within either county, can be bracketed with Rice as the only migrants from Tipperary manager positions: Hayes became General Manager of the Dublin Port and Docks Board.[11]

The chief executives of health boards enjoy an increment of status and salary; the South-Eastern caters for five counties, including Tipperary South Riding. Its first two CEOs have a place in this roll of 'graduates'. Peter McQuillan came to TSR as County Secretary following successive terms as Kilkenny Borough Accountant and Wexford County Accountant. He became Deputy County Manager following de Buitléir's death until his appointment as the first Chief Executive Officer of the South-Eastern Health Board in October 1970 (the Department of Health gave the new chiefs a six-month run in to the statutory commencement of health boards). His successor, John Cooney, is a native of the South Riding, where he commenced as Clerical Officer, moved on promotion to Waterford's Ardkeen hospital and thence to the SEHB headquarters via three steps of the ladder there to the top.[12]

To this array of chief executives, can be added five others at the time of writing in the next immediate rank, assistant managers Ned Gleeson (Limerick), Michael Malone (Kerry), and Willie Moloney

(Donegal) – all ex-TNR, and the latter two also ex-TSR; and health board programme managers, Derry O'Dwyer (Midland) and Stiophán de Búrca (Mid-Western), both ex-TSR. Two other graduates of the south are retired programme managers – Christy Walsh (Southern), onetime TSR County Secretary, and Steve O'Donoghue, whose 1969-72 tenure as Chief Clerk of St. Luke's Mental Hospital, Clonmel was succeeded by upward mobility through three health boards culminating in the Western. His immediate predecessor in St. Luke's was Donal F. Murphy (1958-68) whose departure was to a chief executive post – as Secretary of the Hospitals Commission. On its abolition he joined the Institute of Public Administration's training function and retired from it as Health Program Manager.[13]

Special mention must be made of Paddy (Patrick J.) Meghen, best known as Limerick's first County Manager, writer and lecturer on public administration, and vice-President of Muintir na Tíre. The earliest engineer to become a local administrator, he was a Department's Engineering Inspector before becoming Commissioner to replace the dissolved Tipperary U.D.C., 1924-8. He moved to similar roles for no less than eight other authorities, culminating in eight years in TSR, in effect its combined council and manager immediately before newly-elected members and J. P. Flynn inaugurated the new concept of partnership in 1942. For his final two years there he was also designated County Commissioner. That was a shadow post, to become active if World War II spread to the State and normal government was interrupted. Commissioners would see to the supply of food and basic public health, continuity of welfare payments and the maintenance of order with the co-operation of the Garda Síochána.[14]

Meghen himself and seven others of the above listed have been among the twenty-five chairmen to date of the County and City Managers Association: Messrs Veale, Flynn, Conlon, Dowd, Keating, Rice and Deigan.[15]

ALWAYS THE SAME

Finally, echoes of two key points in the 1837 debate convince one that, despite the arrivals and departures of four or five generations meantime and despite radical changes in administrative structures, all is not changed utterly. *The Guardian* of 20 December 1980 reported:

> You are always the same – everything that comes up, you want it for Nenagh – if Rome got burned you would want the Pope to live in Nenagh, laughed Councillor Tom Shanahan at the VEC meeting in Templemore, when John Ryan, TD, was making a

case for some Nenagh organisations under the Youth and Sport Grant scheme.

Come 1993-4 and the institution of the Mid-West Regional Authority, one of eight in the State established by the Minister for the Environment, Michael Smith, a TD for North Tipperary. It is part of the reform of the local government system led by himself, his predecessor Pádraig Flynn, and Department Secretary (as of mid-1990) Brendan O'Donoghue (whose forbears include the Leahy surveyor-contractors of the 1830s' Clonmel and Cork).

Arising from the selection of Tom Kirby, a TNR County Council administrative officer, as the new authority's chief executive, *The Guardian* on 15 January 1994 boldly headlined 'Nenagh Headquarters for Regional Authority'. So it was – temporarily – and the chief executive himself, a native of neighbouring Kilruane, 'was hopeful that Nenagh would remain the headquarters… There is more to the mid-west than Limerick'.

There followed an exchange of printfire between *Limerick Leader* columnist Patricia Feehily (herself both a former TNR clerical officer and a *Guardian* reporter), pushing a 'natural capital' line on behalf of Limerick city and *The Guardian's* editor, Gerry Slevin. The politicians settled the matter in style at the first meeting. TNR's John Sheehy proposed County Limerick's Michael Healy from Newcastle West, far removed from the city, as chairman. They are both Fianna Fáil party members. He beat Limerick Corporation's John Quinn of the Progressive Democrat party, by 15 votes to 10.

Sheehy and Willie Kennedy, also TNR, proposed Nenagh as headquarters, supported of course by their countymen and by Clare councillors. The Mayor of Limerick, Senator Jan O'Sullivan, and County Limerick's James Houlihan, proposed Limerick city, the 'natural centre', as headquarters. The comparative costs of renting office space and the fact that Nenagh had the temporary headquarters – and in the Minister's constituency – entered the debate. Then Chairman Healy repaid the TNR compliment by expressing a long-held belief in 'having regions within regions', and backed Nenagh. Senator O'Sullivan withdrew Limerick 'in the interests of harmony' but got agreement that meetings 'should rotate between the three constituent counties'.[16]

THE THURLES ROAD

The *Tipperary Star* of 3 July 1982 reported, apropos what its maker claimed in 1837 as 'one of the finest in Europe', that David Molony,

211

TD, had raised in the Dáil the necessity to up-grade the Thurles-Nenagh road to national secondary road status:

> Mr Molony claimed that because of the geographical location of Thurles, placed on the periphery of the Mid-Western region, the poor quality of the Nenagh-Thurles road was seriously militating against the proper development and particularly industrial development of Thurles and its immediate surrounding areas.

As of the time of completing this text, in 1994, a section of that road, near The Ragg, is undergoing large-scale improvements. Removal of the bends near Borrisoleigh and Latteragh in a couple of more decades might yet make it one of the finest roads in North Tipperary.

FINAL DEGROUPINGS

The Local Government Act, 1991 provided for the penultimate management uncoupling as well as for an increase in the number of county councils from twenty-seven to twenty-nine. Working through a transition period as area managers for area committees which grew into separate administrative counties, there are now county managers for Fingal, Dun Laoghaire-Rathdown and South Dublin. The 'Reorganisation of Local Government for the County of Dublin' involved 'the abolition of the county' and hence the office of Dublin County Manager which the 1940 Act decreed would 'always be held by one and the same person' as was the office of Dublin City Manager.

There remains to mention one final pairing not envisaged in 1940 and 1955. The Local Government (Reorganisation) Act, 1985 gave Galway the higher status of county borough which was refused it in 1937 even when its dynamism promoted a private bill for the purpose (it did get plain borough status by legislation in that year). The Act was passed in the afterglow of Galway's quincentennial celebrations of Richard III's 1484 charter which made it a virtual city-state.[17] It went into effect as of New Year's Day 1986 and thus joined Cork, Dublin, Limerick and Waterford as county boroughs.

Each of the five has a manager distinct from its hinterland county manager(s). Seamus Keating, onetime South Riding's County Accountant, was, up to 1986, Galway's first City Manager, having already been Galway County Manager, the county having incorporated the borough for management purposes. Just as degrouping in the cases of paired counties followed the retirement or transfer of managers, Keating's retirement finally ended the Irish phenomenon of two divine offices in one person.

212

REUNIFICATION?

The quotation at the head of this Postscript is taken from the *Tipperary Star* of 17 July 1993. It headlined the report of a discussion on a motion by TSR's Councillor Tom Wood at a joint meeting of the two county councils at half-way Holycross on 12 July. The motion was to ask the Minister for the Environment to set up a review group to examine the possibility of reuniting the geographical county for administration. Senator Tony McKenna, TNR, got the meeting to agree instead on each council doing a review.

The TSR County Secretary's consequential memorandum set out ten 'matters to be addressed were such an amalgamation to take place'. They included the merging of policies and standards of services, the rationalisation of staffing and selection of a county headquarters.[18] Top of the list was a factor addressed in the Wood motion: 'that every effort be made to have County Tipperary placed within one region.' The pair of counties are in the Mid-West and South-Eastern regions for local government authorities and health boards; and are likewise serviced for both industrial development and tourism by different regional bodies, and by separate divisions of such as FÁS (the training and employment authority.)

STRENGTH OR WEAKNESS?

Former Taoiseach Liam Cosgrave's comment comes to mind on a proposal to restore health services to local authorities as against the then novel and controversial health boards, to the effect that it would be like unscrambling the egg. In fact, any in-depth feasibility study, as more recently called for by Councillor Wood, would inevitably address the disadvantage in regional terms of divorcing North Tipperary from its Clare and Limerick neighbours and of South Tipperary from its Waterford and Kilkenny ones. It would hardly be seriously argued that the two Tipperarys could constitute a region of the scale required by national and European policies. On a somewhat more theoretical level, and to whatever extent one thinks of Tipperary as a unit, it can be argued that its foot in two camps enhances its chances of optimum input into policy and entrapment of public funding.

Voluntary organisations differ as to use of the full county or the two ridings as federations of their clubs.

An extraordinary statement appears in the first, 1994, report of the new TSR County Enterprise Board, listed under 'Weaknesses of the County – External Perceptions and Image':

The existence of Tipperary North and South 'Ridings' has split the use of the well-known name across two local authorities.

Their existence has not inhibited the use of the name 'Tipperary' for such diverse, successful commercial enterprises as crystal in Carrick-on-Suir, civil engineering and construction in Clonmel, radio in both Clonmel and Tipperary, foodstuffs in Thurles, spring water in Borrisoleigh, glass in Templemore, wood and steel in Nenagh. It makes no difference to the common 'Welcome to Tipperary' signs at the borders of both ridings with other counties, or to the distinct 'TN' and 'TS' vehicle registration plates.

The implied assertion that the 'split' is a weakness is in the same category as an assertion by T. J. Maher, then MEP, in 1988 that the people 'were at a serious disadvantage by having their county divided under central government designated structures'.[19] Both are assertions without back-up reasoning.

SENTIMENT

A suspicion that sentiment, unleavened by serious study, lies partly behind the question is suggested by Minister Ruttledge's 1942 mention of the very word as quoted in the Epilogue, by Deputy Treacy's 'dismemberment of the Premier County' stance in 1956, and by a comment by Councillor Wood to the *Tipperary Star*, quoted on 7 May 1994:

> I am amused when I hear some politicians crying for a united Ireland and at the same time they cannot support a united Tipperary.

That former nationalist catch-cry has now been well supplanted by an appreciation of the doctrine of self-determination for all peoples, or, to put it another way, by the conversion of most nationalist politicians to the reality that people, not territory, matter. Which reminds one that self-determination was the impetus for Tipperary's division in 1838. Leaving such tangents aside, there are four practical factors which make a merger of the two county councils a non-runner.

REALITY

TSR have provided new headquarters at a cost of £3.736 million, completed as recently as December 1992. TNR are at the preliminary planning stage of a structure to replace prefabricated buildings which are now less than habitable. The cost of providing yet another new headquarters elsewhere would in itself daunt the bravest of public

214

representatives.

Next, the choice of its location – query Thurles, query Cashel; that would put in the halfpenny place the 1838 north riding assize town debate; the Kilkenny versus Waterford, and Tullamore versus Mullingar health board battles; and the Cashel versus Clonmel general hospital siting (currently referred by the Minister for Health to a committee, following stirring battles within the South-Eastern Board).

Thirdly, the powerful IMPACT (the administrative staff's union) would see only marginal advantage by way of a couple of extra layers of middle management posts, outweighed by the disturbance of homes and the imposition of new or lengthier travelling to work.

Finally, as can be readily interpreted from Table 5, a new council would justify a membership of perhaps thirty as against the twenty-six plus twenty-one at present. From both a politician's viewpoint and that of a public needing representation close to home, the inevitable reduction in representation would alone kill the idea. For instance, the change of the single four-seat electoral areas to three-seaters, of six five-seaters to four-seaters, of the six-seater Fethard to four, and the seven-seater Nenagh-Newport to five would still leave a council of thirty-six members. More drastic surgery would require a major carve-up of electoral areas, the very thought of it – or worse, the execution of it – not exactly evoking a unanimous round of applause.

It does not seem extravagant to have the numbers of 21 and 27 elected members in partnership with two chief executives and their staffs in charge of revenue expenditure, leaving aside fluctuating capital expenditure, of TSR's £22.239 million and TNR's £14.728 million or an approximate average of £278 per man, woman and child in the combined counties (1994 figures). It would be illusory to dream of large 'economies of scale' from a merging of staffs because of the nature of the inter-personal work and because of the slimming exercise of 1987-8, termed early retirement and voluntary redundancy.

There might be a saving to North Tipperary ratepayers in that their rate per £ valuation of business premises is £31.23 and their household service charges £133, as against the South Tipperary rate of £29.26 and service charges of £100. But, a saving for one body of ratepayers would mean an increase on the other.

Organisations, like nations and States, develop their individual cultures over a period of time, similar to others in many respects but still unique overall. It can be counter-productive to alter them drastically. Progress is more likely by way of fresh blood among both councillor policy decision takers and manager-executives at several levels, both guaranteed by time itself.

Table 5 Council	Popul.	Sq. miles	Valuation £	Cllrs.	Towns UD+TC	Asst. Mgrs
Cork	279,427	2,878	2,066,916	48	9+3	3
South Dublin	208,739	86	1,738,791	25	0+0	1
Dún L'aire-Rathdown	185,410	49	1,983,805	28	0+0	1
Fingal	152,766	174	1,306,526	24	0+1	1
Two Tipperarys Total	**132,747**	**1,647**	**935,068**	**47**	**7+0**	
Galway	129,462	2,350	758,793	30	1+2	1
Donegal	129,428	1,876	564,773	29	3+1	1
Kildare	122,516	654	801,579	25	2+2	
Kerry	121,719	1,815	584,954	27	3+0	1
Mayo	110,696	2,159	552,214	31	3+0	1
Limerick	109,816	1,064	915,670	28	0+0	1
Meath	105,370	905	849,092	29	3+0	1
Wexford	102,045	909	574,663	21	3+1*	1
Wicklow	97,265	782	716,611	24	3+1	1
Clare	90,826	1,262	748,781	32	2+2	1
Louth	90,724	318	309,312	26	2+0*	
Tipperary (SR)	74,918	872	470,665	26	4+0*	1
Kilkenny	73,613	796	242,857	26	1+1*	
Westmeath	61,182	692	512,117	23	1+1	
Offaly	59,835	771	354,178	21	2+1	
Tipperary (NR)	57,829	775	464,403	21	3+0	
Sligo	54,756	709	276,160	25	1+0*	
Roscommon	54,592	984	438,801	26	0+1	
Cavan	52,756	730	372,486	25	1+2	
Laois	52,325	664	374,513	25	0+2	
Waterford	51,296	713	374,470	23	1+2	
Monaghan	51,262	500	336,816	20	4+1	
Carlow	40,946	346	298,803	21	1+1	
Longford	31,496	403	204,125	21	1+1	
Leitrim	25,297	614	184,565	22	0+0	
Galway Co. Borough	50,853		451,422	15		1
Dublin Co. Borough	478,389		5,686,177	53		3
Cork Co. Borough	136,000		1,168,376	32		3
Limerick Co. Borough	52,040		432,956	18		1
Waterford Co. Borough	40,328		331,996	15		1

Note 1: The * indicates that one of the number under the heading UD (urban district councils) + TC (town commissioners) is in fact a borough council, i.e. Clonmel, Drogheda, Kilkenny, Sligo, Wexford.
Note 2: The figures for assistant managers include, in the case of the three Dublin counties, the rank of deputy manager; in the case of the county boroughs, they include the rank of assistant town clerk.
Source: *Administration Yearbook & Diary 1994*, pp. 72-92.

OPPORTUNITY

The further, essential spur for local authorities is legislation. It so happens that the legislation is already more than adequate and recently updated, only to be utilised, for cross-border co-operation between adjoining counties. Such includes the creation of bodies with executive powers if necessary, i.e. joint committees, with the consent or indeed under the direction of the Minister for the Environment.[20] They now also have a 'general competence' to promote the interests of the local community, avoiding only duplication of other bodies' statutory functions.[21]

In short, the route is open to elected members and/or managers to first study what precisely needs to be done, in any or all of a council's eight main programmes, in partnership with the neighbours and to their mutual benefit. Then to study the best avenues within the existing liberal law to achieve those common purposes. Such follow-up to Councillor Wood's initiative would be practical and potentially fruitful.

LOCAL GOVERNMENT REFORM

It is twenty-three years on from the White Paper, *Local Government Reorganisation*[22] and the *More Local Government* proposals in response,[23] already double the gestation period of county management. One notes that Minister Michael Smith in a relatively short tenure to date of the Department of the Environment piloted the Local Government Act, 1994 as well as the Local Government (Dublin) Act, 1993, together with three electoral acts, two planning Acts, a roads Act, a housing Act, the Environmental Protection Agency Act and the Road Traffic Act. The 1994 Act did repeal a number of outdated statutes and re-defined such matters as local authority membership, elections, estimates and rating, and personnel. More importantly, it provided power to make bye-laws, and it ensured the extension of a very large number of town boundaries in time for the 1994 elections.

Its contribution towards the long-running concern for sub-county structures is a provision for a Reorganisation Commission to submit proposals to the Minister in relation to town government. It would seem that only a very broad interpretation of the Commission's statutory remit would provide for town-and-hinterland district councils centred on towns as were the poor law unions.

The other outstanding issue adverted to in the Foreword, local financing, shows no sign of being addressed. There is a widespread, little-voiced belief that a property tax is inevitable, but at a huge risk of electoral retribution to whatever government would introduce it. No doubt, Irish eyes will be looking at the impact after a couple of years operation of the 1993 British Council Tax which replaced the Community Charge, otherwise known as Margaret Thatcher's poll tax. The new tax provides a single bill for each household, reflecting the value of the property on a broad-banded basis. There are discounts for single adults, students, and empty properties. There are rebates for certain income levels. It has been summarised as a combined property tax, personal tax and local income tax.[24]

This perennial question of local authorities needing their own finances, in addition to government block grants distributed equitably, will be tackled inevitably when a Taoiseach, Minister for Finance and Minister for the Environment have a meeting of minds to combine the vision and political courage of Seán Lemass's and Dr Jim Ryan's minority government which introduced turnover tax in 1963 to enhance essential services.

The signs of an early solution are not good. The annual chestnut about service charges being 'double taxation' reached its peak in early 1994 following increases by various local authorities, a couple of them teetering on the brink of dissolution if they had failed to complete their estimates. A mild extension of the very limited residential property tax in the national Budget was met by an outcry, led by media commentators who failed to declare their personal interest in the question. This was followed by a partial Government retreat. In April a political shambles occurred when Taoiseach Albert Reynolds thought out loud, at the annual Irish Management Institute conference, about funding local authorities by an amalgamation of property tax and service charges. Minister Smith told an interviewer that 'the government's position is that there will be no return to rates and neither is there a possibility of a general property tax being introduced'. A government source was quoted as saying, '*that's the end of it*'.[25] Which sounds like an echo of another political decision – that Tipperary was to be one county *for ever*.

If these paragraphs indicate a *seanchaí* turning hob politician, I can only plead the excuse of long-standing concern for real local government which would be close to 'the source of all legitimate power'.

I would also repeat the cliché that history can provide lessons. Alongside the many parallels evident between the 1830s and 1890s – creeping civilisation and strong reaction, doughty campaigners, strong leadership, cumulative political experience peppered with kinship, enduring alliances and short-term coalitions for specific interests, and honourable and entrepreneurial public officials – is another enduring aspect of human nature:

The comfortable mostly resist taxation for public services, especially if it does not appear to benefit themselves directly.

But political leadership at Westminister and Dublin Castle – the predecessors of our Brussels and Upper Merrion St – pushed ahead with progress and evoked a developmental response from town commissioners and, with some hesitation, boards of guardians. The Glengalls of today who parrot the sound-bite of the decade – reduced taxation and decimated public services – must be countered by the modern Mulgraves and Drummonds, Bloomfields and Dillons who want better roads, swifter health treatment and unpolluted waterways from governors locally accessible and accountable.

Notes

1. Information kindly supplied by Mr Paschal Feeney, Chief Superintendent's office, Thurles.
2. Schedule Electoral (Amendment Act, 1980 which is identical with the scheme of constituencies recommended in the Report of the Dáil Éireann Constituency Commission dated 21 April 1980 (Prl. 8878). The report's p. 32 gave the history of Tipperary boundaries since 1923; the then Minister for the Environment, Mr Ray Burke, TD, kindly gave me maps of the constituencies since 1961, per Mr John Keenan.
3. Ms Norma O'Shea, Department of the Environment, confirmed that the 1980 constituencies still hold.
4. Confirmed as still so with Mr Tom Kirwan, Co. Finance Officer, TNR.
5. *The Guardian* and *Tipperary Star* reports over the period, checked with Mr Luke Murtagh, Joint Secretary of TRBDI, and Chief Executive Officer of Tipperary (N.R.) VEC.
6. A comparison of maps of the Shannon Development area with ones of the Co. Offaly baronies and rural districts, kindly furnished respectively by Mr Joe Price, Shannon Development, and Mr Michael Byrne, Offaly Historical Society.
7. Press release from the Minister of Agriculture and Food, kindly supplied by Ms Jane Toomey, Tipperary LEADER.
8. *Tipperary Star*, 13 Aug 1994.
9. Delany, 'Palatinatinate Court', pp. 116-7.
10. Boland and others eds, *City and County Management, 1929-1990/ A Retrospective* (Dublin, 1991), pp. 154-5.
11. The present County Managers, Messrs John McGinley (North) and Seamus Hayes (South), added to my own knowledge of the managers. Gaps were filled in by the subsequent publication of Boland and others, cited above, Part IV 'Career Profiles' by Joseph Boland and James O'Donnell.
12. Information checked with Ms Jo Redmond, SEHB.
13. Personal knowledge; Eamonn Lonergan, *St Luke's Hospital Clonmel 1834-1984*.

14. Seán Lemass, TD, Minster for Supplies, broadcast 19 July 1940, quoted as Appendix 2 in Boland and others, cited above, pp. 186-8.
15. Boland and others, cited above, p. 184, updated by enquiry from Mr Michael Deigan.
16. *N.G.*, 4 Mar 1994.
17. N. Ó Gadhra, The *Galway Guide*, Bord Fáilte; Roche, cited throughout, p. 104.
18. Mr Tom Wood, MCC, Chairman of Cashel UDC, kindly supplied me with this memorandum.
19. *N.G.*, 5 Oct 1988.
20. Local Government Act, 1991, ss. 37 & 38.
21. ditto, s. 6.
22. *Local Government Reorganisation* (February, 1971), Prl. 1572, Stationery Office, Dublin.
23. *More Local Government, A Programme For Development* (July 1971), Institute of Public Administration Dublin, prepared by a study group set up by the Institute in response to the Minister's request for comments on the White Paper. The group was chaired by Dr Basil Chubb, Professor of Political Science, Trinity College, Dublin and included two members of the expert advisory group convened by Mr Pádraig Flynn, Minister for the Environment in 1990 and whose recommendations influenced the Local Government Act, 1991 – its Chairman, Dr T. J. Barrington, then Director of the Institute, and Mr Richard Haslam, then Limerick County Manager. It also included Messrs T. J. McHugh, mentioned above, D. Roche and D. A. Murphy, writers of the foreword and text of this book, then attached to the Institute and to the Limerick, Clare and North Tipperary Regional Development Organisation, respectively.
24. Christopher Giles and Michael Ridge, 'The Impact on Households of the 1993 Budget and the Council Tax' in *Fiscal Studies* (1993) vol. 14, no. 3, pp. 1-20; John Greenwood, 'Local Government in the 1990s: The Consultation Papers on Structure, Finance and Internal Management' in *Talking Politics*, vol. 4 (2) Winter 1991/2.
25. *The Sunday Tribune*, 24 April 1994.

Lewis's Topographical Dictionary, 1837, for County Tipperary and the towns of Clonmel, Nenagh and Thurles

This is a reprint of the extensive entry for the county and the three towns central to the story, in the 'Topographical Dictionary of Ireland' by Samuel A. Lewis,
* *minus only his two and one-half columns of potted history of the county and of the Butlers up to 1811. That section contains a few inaccuracies and is now seen to be rather selective (the notes to Chapter One refer to modern writings on aspects of the subject). A few essential corrections and amplifications are shown in square brackets thus: [ ]*
* *plus only sub-headings and paragraphing for ease of reading and reference.*
    Lewis includes mention of several persons and events that appear in the text of the book. His spelling of placenames has not been altered, even where it is different from the modern, settled spelling, except in one case to avoid confusion between two similar placenames.

AN OVERVIEW

TIPPERARY (County of), an inland county of the province of MUNSTER, bounded on the east by the King's and Queen's counties, and that of Kilkenny; on the south, by that of Waterford; on the west, by those of Cork, Limerick, and Clare, from which latter it is separated by the Shannon and Lough Derg; and on the north, by that of Galway and King's County. It extends from 52 12' to 53 9' N. Lat., and from 7 20' to 8 26' W. Lon.; comprising an area, according to the Ordnance survey, of 1,013,173 statute acres, of which 819,698 consist of cultivated land, 182,147 of bog, mountain, and unimproved waste, and 11,328 are covered with water.

The population, in 1821, was 346,896; and in 1831, 402,363.

The county is partly in the dioceses of Lismore, Emly, and Killaloe, but chiefly in that of Cashel. For purposes of civil jurisdiction it is divided into the baronies of Clanwilliam, Eliogarty, Iffa and Offa East, and Iffa and Offa West, Ikerrin, Kilnamanagh, Middlethird, Lower Ormond, Upper Ormond, Owney and Arra, and Slieveardagh. It contains the borough, assize and market-town of Clonmel; the city and borough of Cashel; the corporate, market, and post-town of Fethard, formerly a parliamentary borough; the market and post-towns of Nenagh, Thurles, Carrick-on-Suir, Tipperary, Roscrea, Clogheen,

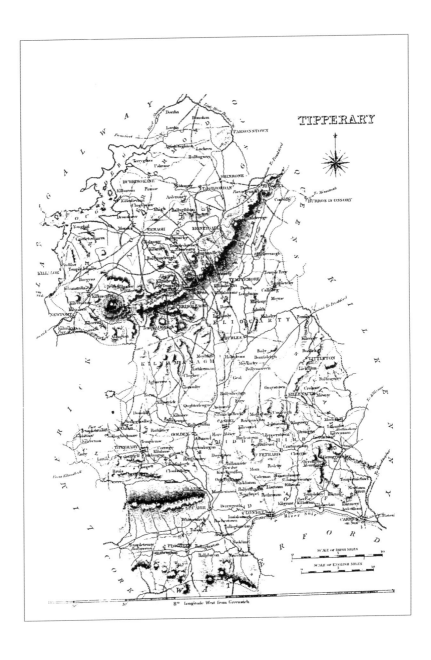

Fig. 7

Killenaule, Cahir, and Templemore; and the post-towns of Burris-o'-Leagh, Burris-o'-Kane, Cloghjordan, Newport, Golden, Littleton and New Birmingham: the largest villages are Bansha, (which has a penny post), Emly, Toomavara, Silvermines, Ballina, Ballingarry, and Mullinahone.

THE PUBLIC SERVICE
It sent eight members to the Irish parliament, two for the county, and two for each of the boroughs of Clonmel, Cashel, and Fethard; but since the Union its representatives in the Imperial parliament have been two for the county and one for each of the boroughs of Clonmel and Cashel. The county members are elected at Clonmel: the constituency, as registered up to Jan 1st, 1837, consisted of 837 £50,379 £20 and 1600 £10 freeholders; 62 £20 and 228 £10 leaseholders; and 16 £50 and 15 £20 rent charges; making a total of 3137 voters.

The county is included in the Leinster Circuit. The local government is vested in a lieutenant, 30 deputy-lieutenants and 153 other magistrates, with the usual county officers, including 4 coroners. There are 99 constabulary police stations, comprising altogether a force of 2 magistrates, 10 chief officers, 77 constables, 464 men and 21 horses. The county gaol is at Clonmel, and there are bridewells at Cahir, Clogheen, Tipperary, Cashel, New Birmingham, Thurles, Templemore, Roscrea, Nenagh, Burris-o'-Kane and Newport.

The lunatic asylum for the county is at Clonmel; where also is the county House of Industry, with a lunatic asylum attached to it, principally for cases of idiocy: the county infirmary is at Cashel: there are Fever hospitals at Clonmel, Tipperary, Cahir, Burris-o'-Kane, Clogheen, Cloghjordan, Cashel, Carrick-on-Suir, Nenagh, Roscrea, and Templemore; and dispensaries at Ballingarry, Bird Hill, Burris-o'-Leagh, Burris-o'-Kane, Ballyporeen, Clonmel, Drangan, Golden, Kilsheelan, Newcastle, Portroe, Poulmucka, Lorrha, Carrick-on-Suir, Cahir, Clogheen, Cappaghwhite, Cloghjordan, Dundrum, Fethard, Killenaule, Mullinahone, Nenagh, Newport, Ballynonty, Roscrea, Silvermines, Tipperary, Thurles, Templemore, Toomavarra, Littleton and Ballymacky, each maintained by equal Grand Jury presentments and private subscriptions.

The Grand Jury presentments for 1835 amounted to £56,795. 16. 0. of which £442. 6. 6. was for new roads and bridges, &c; £21,629. 2. 10. for repairs of roads and bridges; £20,065. 16. 1. for public buildings, charities, officers' salaries and incidents; £11,811. 7. 10. for the police; and £2847. 2. 9. for repayments of advances made by Government.

In the military arrangements the county is partly in the western, but chiefly in the south-western, district; and within its limits are nine barracks, or military stations: four for cavalry, at Cahir, Carrick-on-Suir, Clogheen, and Fethard; four for infantry, at Cashel, Nenagh, Roscrea, and Templemore; and one for cavalry, artillery and infantry at Clonmel; the whole capable of accommodating 139 officers and 2938 men.

THE GOLDEN VALE AND THE MOUNTAINS

The surface of the county is composed of several extensive and fertile tracts of champaign country, separated from each other by ranges of hills. The greatest tract of level country is that watered by the Suir, from its source near Roscrea to Ardfinnan, extending in length about 50 miles, and in breadth averaging 15. Although it presents a nearly level appearance, when viewed from the surrounding heights, owing to the general equality of its successive swells, it is found to be diversified with slightly depressed valleys and gentle elevations, which, combined with an exuberant fertility, present a pleasing though by no means a picturesque succession of scenery. The part of this plain between the Kilnamanagh and Galtee ranges, in the centre of which the town of Tipperary is situated, and which is bounded by a line drawn from Bansha and Thomastown near Golden on the east, and by another from Galbally through Pallasgreine to the Bilboa mountains on the west, has been designated the 'Golden Vale', on account of the surpassing richness of its soil.

The general elevation of its surface is about 400 feet above the level of the sea, though in some parts it does not exceed 250: from Cashel upwards it varies from 326 to 474 feet. On the east it is bounded at first by a large tract of bog, a branch of that of Allen, extending into the contiguous county of Kilkenny; farther south it is enclosed by the low range of the Slieveardagh hills, forming the Killenaule coal district, extending from the vicinity of Freshford, in the county of Kilkenny, a distance of eighteen miles south-westward, to a point five miles beyond Killenaule: the breadth of this range is about six miles; it is most elevated and abrupt towards the north-western side, where the height of the hills above the subjacent plain varies from 300 to 600 feet, while towards the south-east the surface gradually declines, and in that direction flow all the principal streams.

Farther south the boundary of the plain is terminated on this side by the elevated group of Slieve-na-man, to the south-east of Fethard, from which several ranges of hills extend into the county of Kilkenny. On the south the vale is immediately overlooked by the steep and towering heights of the Monevullagh and Knockmeledown mountains, which form the county boundary towards Waterford; and along the base of the latter, a branch of the plain extends westward from Cahir and Ardfinnan, by Clogheen and Ballyporeen, into the vale of the Blackwater, which forms the north-eastern part of the county of Cork.

On the north of this portion of the plain stands the noble range of the Galtees, which on this side rise for the most part with a gentle ascent, while on the north-west they are in many parts extremely precipitous. The length of this range is twenty miles to its termination at the river Funcheon near Mitchelstown, which river forms part of the boundary between Tipperary and Cork, and its breadth from five to seven.

The highest summit is Galtymore, which attains an elevation of about 2500 feet. The wild magnificence of this chain is, from its sudden elevation in the midst of a fertile plain, very striking; and its vast groupings present an assemblage of the most interesting features in boldness, freedom of outline, and variety of aspect. There are three curious circular lakes of small extent on these mountains, and the glens diverging from them present many natural beauties, particularly the western glen, in which is a fine cascade. North of these is a subordinate and lower parallel ridge, called Slieve-na-muck, near the base of which stands the town of Tipperary. From this vicinity a second branch of the great plain, through which a road runs from Clonmel to Limerick, extends to the western confines of the county, where it is met by the more elevated district in the vicinity of Pallasgreine, in the county of Limerick; and to the north of this vale rises the grand group of the Bilboa, Keeper, and Slieve-Phelim mountains, presenting a grand and varied outline. Among these, which occupy a wide district, is pre-eminently distinguished the Keeper mountain, between Newport and Silvermines, to the north-west of which lies another mountain group on the borders of the Shannon at Lough Derg, appearing to form part of a range extending by Killaloe to the vicinity of Six-mile-bridge, in the county of Clare, though here intersected by this grand watercourse.

The Bilboa mountains separate the baronies of Ormond from the other baronies; and from them the western boundary of the grand vale of Tipperary is continued by a narrow range of heights, called the Kilnamanagh hills, which stretches hence north-eastward above Thurles and Templemore, forming the Devil's Bit mountains; and from these, again, a lower series of hills extends by Roscrea to the more elevated Slievebloom mountains, separating the King's from the Queen's county, and which makes the length of the entire range not less than 40 miles. The Keeper mountains and their northern dependencies within the county of Tipperary form a wild tract of country, extending in length about 24 miles, and in breadth about 20, and comprehending an extent of about 480 square miles, throughout the whole of which there was, until lately, scarcely any road passable for wheel carriages; but two excellent lines have recently been constructed by Government.

From these mountains to the banks of the Shannon, and its expansion Lough Derg, extends the fertile plain of the Ormonds of similar character to the Golden Vale, like it highly cultivated, and adorned with many rich demesnes. The common elevation of this plain varies from 114 to 274 feet, gradually declining towards Lough Derg.

LAND AND FARMING

The soil of the great plains and vales consists of calcareous loams of various quality, but for the most part exuberantly fertile, and forming, in parts of the southern and south-western baronies of Clanwilliam, Middlethird, and Iffa and Offa, the most productive portion of the county; these baronies contributing more to the county cess than all the other seven, and comprising a greater number of highly cultivated farms. The rest of the low country is similar in character, forming extensive agricultural tracts; the hills are occupied by poorer soils on substrata of slate and sandstone, and are often very shallow.

Great progress, however, has been made in their improvement, by means of the facilities which the construction of new roads has afforded for the introduction of lime as a manure, which is procured in abundance in the low country.

The soil of the Slieveardagh hills is of a cold and wet nature, abounding in many places with yellow clay. Contiguous to the bog of Allen lies a great extent of flat marshy ground, producing little but sedges and aquatic grasses, used for thatching and litter. The diversified nature of its surface renders the county equally noted for its good sheepwalks, its rich corn-fields and its fertile grazing pastures.

In describing the husbandry of the county it may be classed into five districts, three agricultural, occupying the plains, and two of pasturage, comprising the mountain tracts. The principal of the former is the plain from Carrick to Tipperary, the superior quality of the soil of which, and its contiguity to Clonmel, the great mart for export, have caused it to be occupied by the more wealthy class of landholders, in farms averaging about 50 or 60 acres, though sometimes considerably more: here the lands under tillage exceed the quantity of pasture in the proportion of five to three. Of the other two agricultural districts, one occupies the upper part of the same plain, extending to Roscrea, Burris-o'-Leagh, Dundrum and Cappaghwhite, while the third forms the plain country extending from the northwestern mountains to the Shannon and Lough Derg.

The mountain districts are the coal tract of Slieveardagh and Killenaule, and the mountains of Upper Ormond and Kilnamanagh. By much the greater part of the hills of Slieveardagh are under tillage; the farms, which were of considerable size, averaging from 80 to 100 acres, have been in many instances so subdivided among the descendants of the original lessees, that they do not now average more than 10.

The mountain district of Upper Ormond, including the Keeper and Kilnamanagh mountains, though elevated, affords good pasturage to the summit; the bases of these mountains, particularly on the north, are fertile and under excellent cultivation, which is extending a considerable way up their sides. In the low lands the general course of crops is potatoes, wheat, and oats, sometimes for two years, after which the same course is resumed, after liming or manuring. On light and shallow soils barley sometimes succeeds the potatoes. Bere is usually taken off rich deep soils that have remained long under pasturage. In the mountain districts, wheat is cultivated only in a few peculiarly favourable valleys, except where the increased use of lime has extended its growth on the Slieveardagh hills. Sometimes the corn crops are repeated until the soil is entirely exhausted, and then it is left to regain its natural sward, and remains untilled for a few years. The common mode of planting the potatoes is in lazy beds, but in many parts they are now drilled.

The artificial grasses are red and white clover, rye-grass, and hay-seeds, which last are now almost invariably sown whenever land is laid down for grass. The grass lands are good and sound, and though not in general clothed with the luxuriant herbage that adorns the county of Limerick, the butter is of superior quality. The most productive lands are the abundant tracts of low meadow along the banks of the larger rivers descending from the mountains, and constantly enriched by their alluvial deposits. These lands are here designated *Inches*, signifying "islands".

A considerable portion of fertile land is devoted to the purposes of the dairy; and there are some extensive grazing farms, on which large herds of cattle are fattened. The butter, which is made in large quantities in the dairies, is mostly packed in firkins and sent to Clonmel, Waterford, or Limerick, for the English market, or by the canal to Dublin: the demand for it is annually increasing.

The principal manure is lime, which is extensively used on the rich lands of the vale, and in reclaiming and improving the colder soils of the high lands. A compost of turf mould mixed with the refuse of the farm-yard is also used, particularly for top-dressing. Limestone gravel is likewise in demand: that taken from the escars in the coal district between Killenaule and New Park, which form the fertile and picturesque hills chiefly composed of this material, was formerly in great repute as manure, and was always spread on the ground without being calcined. Agricultural implements and carriages of improved construction are every year coming more into use; a light car with a wicker body is common.

The fences are generally large mounds of earth from six to eight feet at the base, thrown up from the trench, frequently topped with white thorn or furze. In some districts stone walls are the general fence. A few resident gentlemen have set the example of an improved English system of fencing. Notwithstanding the undulatory character of the plain country, which renders the land less retentive of moisture than the contiguous county of Kilkenny, large tracts of the tillage land require draining. In many parts, a mode of drawing the water off pasture lands, called pipe-draining, has been introduced from Limerick: it consists of a narrow drain, covered with a thick surface sod, resting on an offset on each side.

In some parts of the Ormonds, and on the lands of the principal gentry, the most approved systems of green-cropping are practised: the raising of clover has become general among the farmers, by whom rape, flax, vetches, and hemp are occasionally sown, though not to any great extent. Flax is cultivated in small plots, on the headlands or in a corner of the field, for domestic use only. The fields are generally very small, even in the dairy districts seldom exceeding five or six acres, and in tillage land being from two to four. The number and width of the ditches in such a mode of arrangement must throw much land out of cultivation.

LIVESTOCK

Great improvements have taken place latterly in the breeds of every kind of cattle: the breed most esteemed for the dairy is the Irish cow crossed by the Holderness or Durham, the latter of which seems to thrive best on every soil but the limestone, where the cross between the Devon and Limerick answers better: the Kerry cow crossed by the Old Leicester is small, but fattens rapidly in the lowland pastures.

Sheep are seldom seen except with the gentry and large farmers: the defective system of fencing, the small holdings and subsequent minute subdivisions of the fields tend to exclude them from the management of the small farmer: in the mountain districts the small old hairy country breed is still to be found.

228

Pigs are very numerous, forming part of the stock from the highest to the lowest landholder: they grow rapidly, are easily fattened, and much care is bestowed on them: great numbers are shipped for England both alive and dead.

The breeding and improvement of horses is also much attended to, although the number is now less than what it formerly was, the farmers having brought into use a greater number of asses and mules to perform the drudgery. Some of the asses are of a large Spanish breed; they are almost everywhere used by the poorer classes.

TREES AND BOGS

There are very few woods, and these are mostly mere copses, consisting of underwood, or stunted oak, whitethorn and birch. The defect is in course of being remedied by the numerous plantations around the mansions of the gentry, in some of the glens and on the sides of hills; the most extensive wood of this description is that in the western Galtees, round the mountain lodge of the earl of Kingston. Several good nurseries for forest trees have been established, particularly in the neighbourhood of Clonmel, and great encouragement to plant is held out by many of the landed proprietors.

The greatest extent of bog is that formed originally by the obstructed waters of the Nore, which constitutes a tract of 36,025 statute acres, between Roscrea, Urlingford, and Killenaule, forming part of the bog of Allen: its general elevation is about 400 feet above the level of the sea. This vast tract, now wholly unprofitable except for fuel, is, according to a computation made by the surveyors in 1811, capable of being reclaimed at the moderate expense of 5s. per acre, and of being converted into land of the best quality; but with the exception of petty encroachments and improvements on the borders, no attempt has hitherto been made to carry into execution the plans then deemed practicable. The great object is the removal of obstructions in the bed of the Nore, which flows through these morasses, and must form their main drain.

There are several other detached bogs, all capable of being reclaimed, because they command a fall towards some one of the great rivers of the county. Yet, notwithstanding these extended tracts of turbary, the bog is so unequally distributed that the peasantry in many parts suffer much from the want of fuel; in the neighbourhood of Cahir, the women and children are chiefly employed in collecting everything of a combustible nature from the ditches and roads. In 1786, one of the smaller bogs of the county overflowed, and submerged some lands in its progress to the Suir at Ballygriffin.

MINERALS

The mineral productions are various and important. The plain country forms part of the great limestone field of Ireland. The Roscrea and Devil's Bit mountains, which are a continuation of the Slieve Bloom range, consist of sandstone in mass, whose covering everywhere assumes the form of conglomerate: the Keeper and Bilboa mountains, in which this range terminates, consist of a nucleus of clay-slate surrounded by sandstone, except on the north, near the village of Silvermines, where the clay-slate comes immediately in contact with the limestone of the flat district, extending nearly to Lough Derg: the surrounding sandstone in some parts forms a red coarse conglomerate, similar to that of Lyons and Donabate, near Dublin, and is quarried for mill-stones.

The Galtees, with the subordinate ridge of Slieve-na-muck, consist wholly of sandstone, the upper part of which forms strata from one to two feet thick, gradually curving in the form of the summit: the sandstone of Slieve-na-muck is arranged in horizontal strata, which yield excellent flags. The Knockmealdown and Monavullagh mountains, ranging along the southern boundary of the county, are likewise composed of clay-slate, with sandstone at the base and horizontal strata of the same formation on their summits: the Slieve-na-man group is of analogous structure, consisting of a nucleus of clay-slate surrounded and surmounted by sandstone, which is connected with the sandstone hills stretching by Nine-mile-house towards Carrick-on-Suir and Thomastown. The clay-slate to the east of Slieve-na-man, extending towards towards Kilmagany, yields good slates, particularly in the quarries of Inchinagloch, or the Ormond quarries.

MINING

The Killenaule coal district chiefly occupies a low range of heights extending to Coalbrook, on the north-east, a distance of about 5 miles. The strata constituting this formation are shale and sandstone, the principal bed of the latter forming the main body of the elevated part of the coal hills; the whole occupy a depression in the limestone strata, from the borders of which they dip to a common centre, those declining from the north-west having a descent about twice as rapid as those from the south-eastern margin. This bed of sandstone forms narrow troughs or basins lying north-east and south-west, in which are beds of fire-clay, forming the immediate floor of the coal and covered next it by two beds of shale and one of iron rock. In some instances this series appears to be repeated, two or more seams of coal lying one above the other in the same trough, which are generally from 40 to 43 yards from the surface to the upper bed of coal, with a breadth of from 500 to 700 yards. The fire-clay under the coal varies in thickness from four to nine feet, and is everywhere interspersed with vegetable impressions, apparently of grasses, which, when fresh, have a glossy surface. The roof also exhibits vegetable impressions of a similar kind, chiefly of ferns, reeds and grasses, but occasionally of shells. The coal of the whole district is of the kind called stone or blind coal, similar to that of Kilkenny and Queen's county. The value of the quantity annually raised, previously to 1825, amounted to about £12,000, but has since nearly doubled.

The increase is attributable in a great measure to the exertions of the Mining Company of Ireland, who took several of the mines on lease, among which were those of Glangoole, Ballygalavan, and Boulintlea, the last-named of which is said to be the most extensive coalfield in Ireland, and opened that of Mardyke in 1827. The principal colliery worked by an individual is that of Coalbrook, the property of Mr Langley, in which the beds of coal are not only more extended but nearer the surface and more regularly stratified than any others in the same neighbourhood: a singular feature in the strata of these collieries is their occasional interruption by what are technically called "hags"or "faults", which consist of substitutions of firm shale in lieu of coal, commonly from three to five yards broad, ranging across the troughs in a north-western and south-eastern direction.

The Coalbrook colliery has been worked for more than a century by the family of the present proprietor, and was the only mine of any importance kept open previously to the Mining Company's undertaking: the first steam-engine in this part of the country was erected in it. There are now extensive collieries in full operation at Ballinastick and earl's Hill, belonging to Mr Going. The troughs generally contain two or three seams of coal from one to two feet thick, covering a space varying from 50 to 600 acres. The undulating surface being favourable to the construction of adit levels, most of the seams were worked to the depth at which this mode was available before much use was made of steam power.

One fourth of the produce of the seam is pure coal and the remainder culm: the former is peculiarly adapted to every purpose where a strong regular heat is required; it possesses about 87 per cent, pure carbon, and, therefore, without any preliminary preparation, it is fit for the use of the maltster, and is carried to great distances for brewers, distillers, millers and smiths: the culm is in great demand for burning lime, and is likewise made up into balls with a mixture of clay, and used in the kitchen: the charge for the coal at the pit's mouth varies from 20s. to

40*s.* per ton, according to the quality; that of the culm from 16*s.* to 18*s.*

The collieries in which steam-engines are employed are worked on the most approved principles, the engine pits being sunk in the lowest part of the field whence the coal is raised; eight engines are now erected in the district, in which 34 pits are at work, giving employment to upwards of 1000 persons. In the Coalbrook pits several valuable seams of iron stone, yielding about 30 per cent of metal, have been found, which have not yet been turned to profitable account.

The Mining Company likewise possesses extensive slate quarries in the hilly tract adjoining the lower extremity of Lough Derg. Until a late period the produce of these quarries had to be conveyed by a land carriage of six miles to Killaloe, whence it was taken by boats along the Shannon or canal, although they lie within two miles of the Shannon navigation; but a new line of road thither, and the erection of a small quay in a bay in Lough Derg, allow it now to be conveyed at a greatly reduced scale of carriage to every part of the country with which the Shannon or the canals communicate. The produce of the mine has been about 7000 tons annually. The same company had the slate quarries at Derry, close to the shipping quay on the Shannon, but these are now held by John Salmon, of Derryville, near Killaloe, Esq.; and also those at Glenpatrick, east of Clonmel, of great magnitude and returning a good profit.

But the mineral works of earliest celebrity are the copper and lead mines near Silvermines. They were first worked by an English company who extracted a considerable proportion of silver from the ore; when their lease expired about a century ago, new veins were opened and the works extended in different directions by successive companies. Mr Hudson, the last lessee, sold his interest to the Mining Company, who, after sinking some expensive shafts, relinquished the attempt.

The works were opened in four places called the Old Works, Knockeen, and Kevestown, on Lord Dunally's estate, and Garryard, on that of Lord Norbury. The Old Works were carried on in a space between the clay-slate and limestone rock, which here approach each other, being several fathoms wide at the surface, but contracting until it closes at the depth of about 25 fathoms. This was filled with clay, sand, decomposed slate, and scattered blocks of limestone, lydian stone, and hornstone; the whole mass being penetrated and cemented by metallic deposits, consisting of iron ochre in various stages of induration, iron pyrites, white lead ore, galena, malachite (the value of which was unknown and it was therefore thrown away), copper pyrites, with calcareous spar and heavy spar. In Knockenroe is a powerful vein, consisting at the surface principally of quartz and iron pyrites, with some heavy spar galena, blende, and copper pyrites. In Knockeen are various others, comprising the same substances.

About five miles to the east of Newport is the old copper mine of Lackamore, the workings of which were very extensive, and an attempt was made to renew them at the beginning of the present century, but was abandoned on account of the insufficiency of the machinery to draw off the water. It was subsequently worked by the Mining Company and yielded ores worth from £20 to £30 per ton, but has again been abandoned as unprofitable.

Here are two veins running through clay-slate, and composed of brown spar, calcareous spar, clay and iron ochre, more or less indurated, a few inches in width; and a third vein of the same material, but of greater thickness, and comprising rich copper ore in bunches at Cappaghwhite, Ballysinode, and Gurtdrum, in this county: these were also held on lease by the Mining Company, who seem however, to have made no attempt to work the two first, but on the last they made an outlay, in 1826, of £300, apparently without any return. Ores of zinc and manganese are common in various places, but no efforts are now being made to work them.

MANUFACTURING

With the exception of an extensive cotton-manufactory at Clonmel, of recent establishment, the county may be considered to be wholly devoid of manufactures. The ancient staple manufacture of wool, of which Clonmel and Carrick-on-Suir formed the centre, was suppressed by the parliamentary regulations made shortly after the Revolution for the avowed purpose of confining the woollen manufacture to England and substituting that of linen in its place in Ireland; yet not withstanding this discouragement, stuffs and ratteens were made in large quantities until the close of the last century; and blankets and flannels, much prized for their warmth and durability, are still manufactured in various places.

Flax and linen had been manufactured on a small scale, chiefly for domestic consumption, for many years, and a few grants towards the erection of scutching mills were made by the Linen Board from 1817 to 1823. In 1822, the London Society for the relief of the western counties in Ireland, during the famine occasioned by the failure of the crops, besides supplying nearly £6000 to purchase food for the poor in this county, remitted £2500 for the employment of the peasantry in the linen manufacture; in addition to which grant, other sums were contributed by various charitable societies and by the Linen Board.

Societies were consequently formed in seventeen of the most important places by ladies of rank and respectability (among whom was the Countess of Glengall, who allotted 50 acres of land at Cahir for the growth of flax) to form and superintend establishments for carrying on the manufacture; but notwithstanding these exertions, the linen trade, after languishing a few years, may be said to be nearly extinct in the county. Flour is now the staple manufacture; there being 61 large mills for grinding it on the several rivers throughout the county; and this branch of industry is deemed to be of such importance that some of the wealthiest individuals in the country have embarked their property in it.

COMMERCE

The commerce of the county consists in the extensive exportation of its agricultural produce, the chief mart being Clonmel, from which the export trade is so great that the farmer is here always certain of a favourable market. The market of Thurles is the second in importance, and the others for agricultural produce are those of Carrick-on-Suir, Cahir, Tipperary, Cashel, Templemore, Roscrea, and Nenagh. Carrick-on-Suir, like Clonmel, exports by Waterford to the English markets, Nenagh sends to Limerick, by the Shannon navigation, and to Dublin by the Grand Canal; Roscrea, to Dublin by the Grand Canal; and Templemore, Thurles, Cashel, Tipperary, and Cahir generally send their products by land carriage to Clonmel or Waterford. The rich southern and eastern plains contribute, perhaps, one-half to the vast exports from Waterford of flour, oatmeal, barley, horned cattle, sheep, and pigs.

WATERWAYS

The principal rivers are the Shannon, the Suir, and the Nore. The Shannon, with its noble expansion, Lough Derg, forms the western boundary of the county from the mouth of the lesser Brosna to within a few miles of Limerick, a distance of about 40 statute miles, throughout the whole of which it is navigable and displays a grand succession of striking and beautiful scenery: it receives several streams from the Kilnamanagh hills, of which the most important is that from Nenagh. The Suir, in consequence of the great length of its course throughout the entire county from north to south, forms the grand outlet for the superfluous waters of by far the greater portion of it. The principal tributaries from the baronies to the east of its course are the Derryhogan, the Littleton, and the Anner; from the hills of Kilnamanagh, three considerable streams, which discharge their waters into it near Golden;

from the Galtee mountains, the Dunbeg, through the beautiful glen of Aherlow; and from the Cummeragh mountains in Waterford, the copious waters of the Nier. The Nore, from its source in the Slievebloom mountains, flows eastward for about ten miles through this county, in its way towards Burros-in-Ossory and Kilkenny; and though it has a fall of 71 feet in this distance, the various interruptions to its current have chiefly caused the formation of the vast tracts of bog extending along that part of the county.

With the exception of the Shannon and the Suir, the rivers present greater facilities for irrigation and millsites than for inland navigation. An extension of the Grand Canal by Mountmellick, Roscrea and Cashel, to Carrick-on-Suir, was at one period proposed. Another extension was designed to proceed along the western side of the Slievebloom and Keeper range: and in the report of the Board of Works, in 1831, it is recommended to form a still-water communication between Parsonstown and the river Shannon, by a canal, nearly parallel with the lesser Brosna.

RAIL AND ROAD

In 1825, the late Mr Nimmo by desire of the resident proprietors, made a survey and estimate for the construction of a railway, to connect the towns of Cahir, Clonmel, and Carrick-on-Suir, with an extension in one direction to Limerick and in the other to Waterford, and with a branch to the Killenaule coal district. It was proposed to extend this line from Cahir to Tipperary, with a branch to Thurles, but no steps have yet been taken to execute this plan.

A proposed line of railway from Dublin to Cork is intended to enter this county near Callen [i.e. Callan] and to proceed through Fethard, Cahir, and Clogheen to Ballyporeen, near which it is to enter the county of Cork. The roads of common construction are generally in good order, more especially the mail coach roads. Two lines of cross road deserve especial notice: they are called Anglesey's roads, from having been commenced in 1828 under the immediate order of the Marquess of Anglesey, then Lord Lieutenant: one, connecting the towns of Newport and Thurles, was completed in 1830, at an expense of £9857: the other, from Nenagh to Tipperary, has been more recently finished, at an expense of about £17,200. The great object of their construction was to open a communication into the mountains through which they extend, which had been for many years the asylum of outlaws and of robbers: they also afford the means of agricultural improvement to the whole district, by the introduction of lime from the surrounding quarries.

A new line has been opened from Mitchelstown to Tipperary; another from Lismore to Mitchelstown through the Knockmealdown

235

Plate 15

EXPEDITIOUS, COMFORTABLE AND
CHEAP TRAVELLING
DIRECT DAY CONVENIENCE
FROM MALLOW TO DUBLIN,
FOR ONE POUND.

The Public are respectfully informed, that a well appointed DAY CAR, leaves Mr Lawrence Murphy's House, Mallow, at half-past Six o'Clock every morning – passing through Doneraile, Kildorrery, Mitchelstown, Caher, Clonmel, Callon, and arrives at the Bush Tavern, Kilkenny, by 7 o'Clock p.m. – From whence the Day Coaches set off a quarter before Six next mroning, and arrives at 15 Duke-street, Dublin, by half past Four o'Clock. The Day Coaches leave Dublin at 9 o'Clock, and arrive at Kilkenny, by half-past 7 o'Clock; from whence the Day Car starts at 5 o'Clock in the morning and arrives at Mallow by half-past 5 o'clock, for the Sum of ONE POUND including all Fares. – Passengers for intermediate Stages and parcels carried equally cheap.

MALLOW AND WATERFORD CAR, starts at the same hour and arrives at Cumming's Hotel, Waterford, at 7 o'clock fare 11s. 6d.

Nenagh and Waterford Car, leaves William Gleeson's house, Nenagh, at 5 o'Clock, passing through Borrisoleigh, Thurles, Cashel, Fethard, Clonmel, Carrick, and arrives at Waterford by 7 o'Clock, leaves Waterford, at 5 o'Clock and returns to Nenagh by 7 o'Clock – Fare 11s. 6d.

A Car leaves Thurles at 2 o'Clock and arrives at Kilkenny by 7 o'Clock – Fare 4s. And from Thurles to Dublin, by this route 10s. 6d.

Cork and Dublin Car, starts from Mr Maulby's house, Patrick-street, corner of Princes-street, quarter before 6 o'Clock, through Fermoy, Mitchelstown, Caher, Clonmel, Callan, and Kilkenny, by 7 o'Clock, and Passengers and Parcels proceed next morning per Coaches as above. Leaves Kilkenny, at 5 o'clock in the morning, and arrives at Cork by 7 o'clock p.m. – Fare from Cork to Dublin £1 1s. 0d.

Cork and Waterford Car leaves this Office at five o'clock, and arrives at Waterford by 7 o'clock Fare, 12s. 6d.

Roscrea Car to Waterford, starts from McCauly's Hotel at 5 o'clock, (after the arrival of the Dublin Mail,) through Templemore, Thurles, Cashel, Fethard, Clonmel, Carrick, and arrives at Waterford by 7 o'clock. Fare, 10s. 6d.

Limerick, Tipperary, Thurles, Clonmel, Waterford, and Kilkenny Cars, which started heretofore from Glinn's Hotel with one horse, starts at present with two horses at 10 o'clock from same place at the following Fares:–

	s	d		s	d
Limerick to Tipperary	3	6	Waterford	10	6
Cashel	5	6	New Ross	12	6
Thurles	7	0	Enniscorthy	13	6
Caher	5	6	Wexford	16	6
Clonmel	7	0	Taghmon	15	6
Callan	10	6	Templemore	8	6
Kilkenny	12	6	Tramore	11	6
Carlow	15	6	Dungarvan	15	6
Carrick-on-Suir	8	6	Kilmacthomas	13	0

The above Establishment has been the result of twelve years' experience, and the Proprietor strongly recommends them as a most comfortable and safe mode of conveyance for Passengers and Parcels, the Horses being generally of the best description, the Cars mounted on Patent Axle-trees and Lancewood Shafts, and the men attendant as reward and unremitted attention could make them, in so extensive an Establishment, comprising a daily route of nearly 1600 miles.

The London Steam Packets generally sail from Waterford on Tuesdays; the Liverpool Packets on Thursday, as well as the Bristol on Saturdays, at 12 o'clock, and Passengers going by the Day Car the day before, will have passages secured to them.

The Proprietor will not be accountable for any Money, Plate, Jewellery, or Millinery sent by his Car, nor for any Parcel above the value of £2.

20lbs. luggage allowed to Passengers free of charge; for any above that, and under 50 miles, 1d. per lb.; 11/2 d. per lb. for any distance above that.

C. BIANCONI, PROPRIETOR

range; and a third is also in course of formation, being an extension of the Mitchelstown line, from Tipperary by Dundrum in the direction of Thurles, thence to be continued toward Durrow, and to form part of the grand mail line between Dublin and Cork, by which the distance between these cities will be shortened 33 miles.

Great facilities of intercourse throughout the country are afforded by the exertions of Mr Bianconi, an intelligent Italian settled at Clonmel, who first established a communication between Clonmel and Cahir by a jaunting car in 1815, and now has depots of cars and horses in every post-town in the county, and in all the counties of Munster except Clare, and of Connaught except Sligo, and in the counties of Carlow, Kilkenny, King's, Queen's, Longford, Westmeath, and Wexford in Leinster, in which 84 cars, 816 horses, and 469 men are constantly engaged; some of them carry the cross mails.

ANTIQUITIES

The most numerous remains of antiquity are the raths or earthworks of various kinds, scattered over the surface of the county. There are also many little mounds, called Clogh Breagh or "Stones of Sorrow", said to have been formed by passengers casting a stone each on a spot where any person had met with a violent death. There are yet standing within the limits of the county two ancient round towers, in good preservation, one on the rock of Cashel, and the other at Roscrea.

In a small bog near Cullen have been found an amazing number of valuable relics of a very remote period of antiquity: they include utensils of brass; ingots, plates, plain pieces, and numerous ornaments of gold; a quantity of arrow and spear heads; gold cups; tubes, rings, and chains; brass spears of very extraordinary form, and other articles of a similar kind.

The number of religious houses is stated to have been 40, and there are still remains of those of Ardfinnan, Athassel, the Dominican and Franciscan houses at Cashel, Clonmel, Corbally, Fethard, Holy Cross, Hore Abbey, Lorragh (where there are remains of three religious edifices), Monaincha, Roscrea, Thurles, and Kilcooly. There is also an old decayed ecclesiastical building at Mullinahone, and numerous decayed parish churches. But the ruins that claim pre-eminent notice are those on the rock of Cashel.

Remains of ancient castles are to be met with in every part. The most remarkable of the castles are those of Nenagh Round, Ardfinnan, Cahir, Lismalin, Grestown, Gralla near Killenaule, Mealiffe, Drumban in the parish of Mealiffe, two at Roscrea, and two at Thurles; besides which may be particularly noticed the old castellated mansion in the town of Carrick-on-Suir; Carrick Castle, formerly the seat of the earl of Carrick; and Killaghy Castle, that of F. Despard, Esq. Burnt Court is a very fine specimen of an ancient fortified mansion, and there are some remains of another at Thurles. The celebrated natural caves near Mitchelstown, lately discovered, are in the parish of Templetenny, in this county.

The title of earl of Tipperary is enjoyed by His Royal Highness Prince Adolphus Frederick, Duke of Cambridge.

CLONMEL

CLONMEL, a borough, market and assize town, and a parish, partly in the barony of UPPERTHIRD, county of WATERFORD, but chiefly in that of IFFA and OFFA EAST, county of TIPPERARY, and province of MUNSTER, 23 miles (W. by N.) from Waterford, and $82^{1}/2$ miles (S.W. by S.) from Dublin; containing 20,035 inhabitants, of which number, 17,838 are in the town.

It is situated on the banks of the river Suir, in a beautiful and fertile valley bounded by picturesque mountains, and on one of the two main roads from Dublin to Cork, and that from Waterford to Limerick. With the exception of that portion which is built on islands in the river, it is wholly on the northern or Tipperary side of the Suir, and is connected with the Waterford portion by three bridges of stone. The principal street is spacious, and extends from east to west, under different names, for more than a mile in a direction nearly parallel with the river; the total number of houses, in 1831, was 1532.

The town is lighted with gas from works erected, in 1824, by Messrs. Barton and Robinson, of London, who sold them, before they were completed, for about £8000 to the British Gas-Light Company of London, under whom they are now held on lease. The provisions of the act of the 9th of George IV [1828], for lighting and watching towns in Ireland, have been adopted here: the inhabitants are amply supplied with water by public pumps in the various streets. Several newspapers are published, and there are four news-rooms, one of which is a handsome building lately erected at the eastern end of the town, and called the County Club House. At the eastern entrance into the town are extensive barracks for artillery, cavalry, and infantry; behind them, on an elevated and healthy spot, is a small military hospital, capable of receiving 40 patients.

COMMERCE

In 1667, the plan of Sir Peter Pett for introducing the woollen manufacture into Ireland was carried into effect by the Duke of

Ormonde, then Lord-Lieutenant; and, in order to provide a sufficient number of workmen, 500 families of the Walloons were invited over from Canterbury to settle here. The manufacture continued to flourish for some time, but at length fell into decay, in consequence of the prohibitory statutes passed by the English parliament soon after the Revolution, and is at present nearly extinct. A factory for weaving cotton has been established by Mr. Malcomson, which at present affords employment to 150 girls; he has also an extensive cotton-factory at Portlaw, in the county of Waterford. A very extensive trade is carried on in grain and other agricultural produce of the district, principally with the Liverpool and Manchester markets; great quantities of bacon are also cured and sent to London and the channel ports. There are two very large ale and porter breweries in the town; and at Marlfield, about a mile distant, is a distillery for whiskey upon a very extensive scale. The Excise duties collected within this district, in 1835, amounted to £75,520. 16.

The only mineral production in the neighbourhood which forms an article of commerce is slate, of good quality, found at Glenpatrick and worked by the Irish Mining Company.

Though not a sea-port, the town, from its situation at the head of the Suir navigation, is the medium through which the corn and provision export trade is carried on between the southern and eastern portions of this large county and England. There are generally about 120 lighters, of from 20 to 50 tons burden, employed in the trade of this place; and several hundred carriers are engaged during winter on the roads communicating with Clonmel and the principal towns within 40 miles round: a considerable portion of the trade of Waterford also passes through the town. In the year ending April 30th, 1832, not less than 230,543 cwt. of flour, 28,678 barrels of wheat, 19,445 barrels of oats, 3878 barrels of barley, 21,559 cwt. of butter, 2769 cwt. of lard, and 63,751 flitches of bacon, besides smaller quantities not enumerated, were sent for exportation.

The navigation of the Suir was formerly very imperfect: in 1765, a parliamentary grant was obtained to form a towing-path, by which the passage of the boats has been greatly accelerated. The river is still in many places so shallow that, in dry seasons, the navigation is much impeded. An act has recently been obtained for its improvement; and it is proposed to form a railroad between Carrick, where a basin is intended to be formed, and Limerick, thereby opening a communication between the Suir and the Shannon. There is a salmon fishery in the river, the quays of which are spacious and commodious, extending from the central bridge along the north side.

The Bank of Ireland, the Provincial Bank, the Agricultural and Commercial Bank, and the National Bank of Ireland, have branch establishments here. The market days, under the charter of the 6th of Jas. I [5 July 1608], are Tuesday and Saturday; and fairs are held on May 5th and Nov. 5th, and also on the first Wednesday in every month (except May and November), for the sale of cattle, sheep, horses, and pigs, and on the preceding day for pigs only. The butter market is a spacious building, provided with suitable offices for the inspector and others; all butter, whether for home consumption or exportation must be weighed and duly entered: there are also convenient shambles and a large potatoe market.

The post is daily; the revenue of which, for 1835, was about £3000. The royal mail and day car establishment, under the direction of its proprietor, Mr. Bianconi (to whose enterprising exertions the south of Ireland is so much indebted for the establishment of public cars), is in this town. A chief constabulary police station has been established here.

LOCAL GOVERNMENT
The corporation is of great antiquity, and probably exists by prescription. Numerous charters have at various times been granted since the reign of Edw. I [eg. one of 8 April 1398 allowing 'the bailiffs and good men of Clonmel' to charge customs or tolls on a range of merchandise, both native and foreign]; that under which the borough is now governed was granted in the 6th of Jas. I (1608), and, under the title of "The Mayor, Bailiffs, Free Burgesses, and Commonalty of the Town or Borough of Clonmel," ordains that the corporation shall consist of a mayor, two bailiffs, twenty free burgesses (including the mayor and bailiffs), and a commonalty, with a recorder, chamberlain, town-clerk, and other officers. The freedom was formerly obtained by nomination of a burgess to the common council, a majority of whom decided on the admission; but at present the rights of birth, extending only to the eldest son, apprenticeship to a freeman within the borough, and marriage with a freeman's daughter, are recognised as titles to it. The borough returned two members to the Irish Parliament till the Union, since which time it has sent one to the Imperial Parliament. The elective franchise was vested in the freemen at large, amounting, in the year 1832, to 94 in number; but by the act of the 2nd [and 3rd] of Wm. IV, cap. 88, ['An Act to amend the Representation of the People of Ireland', 7 August 1832, 'whereby the right of voting in a county at large is extended to lease-holders and to copy-holders'] it has extended to the £10 householders: the number of voters registered at the close

of 1835 was 805; the mayor is the returning officer.

The electoral boundary, under the act of the 2nd and 3rd of Wm. IV, cap. 89, ['An Act to settle and describe the Limits of cities, towns and boroughs in Ireland, in so far as respects the Election of Members to serve in Parliament', 7 August 1832; the Act has a schedule describing thirty-three such areas] is confined to the town, including Long Island on the south and a space on the north side of the river for buildings contemplated in that quarter, and comprises an area of 361 statute acres, the limits of which are minutely described in the Appendix. The jurisdiction of the corporation extends over a large rural district comprising about 4800 statute acres, of which 3800 are in the county of Waterford, and 1000 in Tipperary: the mayor and recorder are justices of the peace.

JUSTICE

The Tholsel court, for determining pleas to any amount within the town and liberties, in which the cause of action must arise or the defendant reside, is held every Wednesday, before the mayor and bailiffs. The mayor's court, in which he presides, is held every Wednesday for the recovery of debts not exceeding 10s. late currency; and the mayor and bailiffs hold a court leet twice in the year. Petty sessions are held every alternate Friday. The elections for parliamentary representatives, and the assizes and quarter sessions for the county of Tipperary are held here, the last in April and October.

The old court-house, which was built after a design by Sir Christopher Wren, was some years since converted into shops; the new court-house is a light and handsome structure. The county gaol is a large stone building; but prior to the erection of the house of correction, which was completed in the year 1834, it was too small for the number of prisoners generally confined in it; it is now adapted to their classification, contains schools for both sexes and a tread-mill, which is applied to the raising of water for the supply of the prison.

THE PARISH

The parish extends beyond the Suir a considerable distance into the county of Waterford, and comprises 8907 statute acres, of which 5922 are applotted under the tithe act. The principal seats are Knocklofty, that of the earl of Donoughmore; Kilmanahan Castle, of Lieut.-Col. Nuttall Greene; Marlfield, of J. Bagwell, Esq.; Barn, of S. Moore, Esq.; Woodrooff, of W. Perry, Esq.; Rathronan, of Major-Gen. Sir H. Gough, K.C.B.; Kiltinane Castle, of R. Cooke, Esq.; Darling Hill, of the Hon. Baron Pennefather; and Newtown-Anner, of Lady Osborne: there are also many other handsome residences. The views from the demesnes of Knocklofty and Kilmanahan Castle abound with interest and variety, and are not surpassed by any in this part of the country. At Kiltinane Castle a very rapid stream issuing from a rock forms a remarkable natural curiosity.

The living is an entire rectory, in the diocese of Lismore, and in the gift of the Corporation: the tithes amount to £300. The glebe-house was built by aid of a gift of £100 and a loan of £650 from the late Board of First Fruits, in 1810; the glebe, dispersed in small parcels in the town and suburbs, comprises 2a. 1r. 2p. The R.C. parish is co-extensive with that of the Established Church, and is the benefice of the vicar-general of the united dioceses of Waterford and Lismore, and contains two chapels, one in Irishtown, and the other a large and neat modern building in Johnston-street; also a Franciscan friary in Warren-street, lately rebuilt, and a Presentation convent situated beyond the western bridge. There are places of worship for Presbyterians in connection with the Synod of Munster, the Society of Friends, Baptists, Unitarians, and Primitive and Wesleyan Methodists.

EDUCATION
The grammar school was founded in 1685, by R. and S. Moore, Esqrs., ancestors of the Mount-Cashel family, who endowed it with the lands of Lissenure and Clonbough, in the county of Tipperary, producing a rental of £369, for the gratuitous instruction of the sons of freemen in Latin. The old school-house having fallen into decay, a large and substantial building has been erected within the last few years at the western extremity of the town, on a site granted at a nominal rent by the late Col. Bagwell, and at an expense of nearly £5000, of which £4000 was advanced out of the consolidated fund, for the repayment of which £240 per annum is appropriated from the proceeds of the endowment: there are at present, including boarders, about 90 boys in the school.

A parochial school for boys is partly supported by a joint bequest from Dr. Ladyman and Mrs. Pomeroy, amounting to £7 per annum, late currency, and £2 per annum from the rector; and there are a parochial school for girls and an infants' school, both supported by voluntary contributions: a handsome and commodious building has been lately erected for these schools, containing three school-rooms, each capable of accommodating 100 scholars. Two schools for girls are superintended by two ladies, who teach the children gratuitously; a school for boys is supported by collections at the R.C. chapels, which are partly appropriated in paying the master's salary, and partly in providing clothing for the children; and there are Sunday schools in connection with the Established Church and the Presbyterian and Methodists' congregations. The number of children in attendance daily is, on an average, 580; and in the private pay schools are about 650 children.

WELFARE

The fever hospital and dispensary adjacent to it, both handsome and commodious buildings on the north side of the town, are liberally supported. The house of industry for the county of Tipperary, for the reception and support of 50 male and 50 female aged and infirm poor persons of good character, and for the restraint of male and female vagrants, is an extensive building in an airy situation at the foot of the western bridge, opened in 1811: it is supported by grand jury presentments, and is under the government of a corporation by act of parliament; it has a department for orphan children, who, when of proper age, are apprenticed to different trades; the receipts last year were £1543. 5., and the expenditure, £1335. 16.

A district lunatic asylum for the county of Tipperary was opened in 1835: the building is capable of accommodating 60 patients, and was erected at an expense, including the purchase of land, furniture, &c., of £16,588. A savings' bank has been established; and there are also a mendicity society and a clothing society, the latter established in 1833. A society has lately been formed for the maintenance and education of the orphan children of Protestant parents, and within the first year, 33 were so provided for. Several charitable bequests to a considerable amount have been left to the parish by different individuals.

Clonmel gives the titles of earl and Viscount to the family of Scott; the father of the present earl was the Rt. Hon. John Scott, the celebrated chief justice of the King's Bench in Ireland, who was created Baron earlsfort in 1784, and was advanced to the Viscounty of Clonmel in 1789, and to the earldom in 1793.

Appendix

From the Point at which the Western Enclosure Wall of the House of Industry meets the River Suir, along the said Western Wall to the Point at which the same meets Marl Street; thence along Saint Stephen's Lane to the Point at which the same meets the old Cahir Road; thence, Eastward, along the old Cahir Road to the Point at which the same is met by a Lane running Northward; thence, Northward along the said Lane to the Point at which the same is met by the first Bank on the Right; thence Eastward, along the said Bank to the Point at which the same is met by a Lane coming from the North and turning to the East;

243

thence, Eastward, along the last-mentioned Lane to the Point at which the same meets Heywood Street; thence along a Bank which runs Eastward from a House a little to the South of the Point last described to the Point at which the said Bank meets a small Bye Lane leading into the Cashel Road; thence along the said Bye Lane to the Cashel Road; thence Southward, along the said Cashel Road to the Point at which the same is met by the Southern Boundary Wall of the Park or Pleasure Grounds of Mr. David Malcolmson; thence along the said Boundary Wall to the Point where the said Wall meets Upper Johnson Street; thence, Eastward, along Backbone Lane to the Extremity thereof; thence to a Point in the new Road to Fethard, which Point is Sixty-four Yards to the North of the Spot at which the said Road is crossed by Bonlie Lane; thence, Southward, for Sixty-four Yards, to the said Spot where the Fethard Road is crossed by Bonlie Lane; thence, Eastward, along Bonlie Lane for about Six hundred and forty-four Yards, to a Point at which the same is met by a Bank on the Right opposite a small House; thence, Southward, along the said Bank, for the Distance of about Two hundred and nine Yards to the Point where it is met by another Bank running Eastward; thence, Eastward, along the last-mentioned Bank for about Fifty Yards to a Point where the same makes an Angle in turning to the South; thence, Southward, for about Fifty Yards along a Bank which leads to Bye Road to Powerstown until the said Bank reaches the said Bye Road; thence, Eastwards, along the said Bye Road for the Distance of Two hundred and seventeen Yards to the Spot where it is met by the first Bank on the Right; thence, in a straight Line to the most Northern Point of a Bank on the Southern Side of the Dublin Road, which Point is distant about Four hundred and sixty-four Yards from a Stone in Barrack which marks the South-eastern Corner of the Ordnance Land; thence, along the last-mentioned Bank to the Point at which the same meets the River Suir; thence along the Southernmost Channel of the River Suir as far as Moore's Island; thence along the Channel of the same to the North of Moore's Island to the Point first described.

NENAGH

NENAGH, a market and post-town, and a parish, partly in the barony of UPPER ORMOND, but chiefly in that of LOWER ORMOND, county of TIPPERARY, and province of MUNSTER, 19 miles (N.E.) from Limerick and 75 (S.W.) from Dublin, on the mail road between these cities; containing 9159 inhabitants, of which number, 8446 are in the town, which is the largest (except one), as to population, that does not return a member to parliament.

The town stands on a stream to which it gives name, that descends from the Keeper mountain to Lough Derg. It consists of four streets meeting in the centre. The market for corn and cattle, which is well attended, is held on Thursday: fairs are held under a grant by Hen. VIII to the Butler family, on April 24th, May 29th, July 4th, Sept. 4th, Oct. 10th, and Nov. 1st. The first fair held here was called *Eanaugh Airoon,* that is "a Fair in Ormond."

General sessions are held twice a year, and petty sessions weekly: there is a court-house for the meetings of the magistrates; also an old bridewell, consisting of 3 day-rooms, 9 cells and 2 yards. Application is about to be made to procure an act of parliament to make Nenagh an assize town. It is the residence of a stipendiary magistrate, and a chief constabulary police station. A seneschal's court for the manor was formerly held here. A fever hospital and dispensary are maintained in the usual manner: three physicians attend the former in monthly rotation, at a salary of £25 each. There is a small library of works of a religious and charitable tendency.

An infantry barrack has been built on an eminence at the east end of the town, on the principle of a field fortification, with accommodations for a field-officer, 12 commissioned officers, 208 non-commissioned officers and privates, and 4 horses, with hospital accommodation for 21 patients and a magazine.

A brewery is carried on in the town; and at Tyone, in its immediate vicinity, is a flour-mill, from which large quantities of flour are sent to Dromineer, the nearest steam-boat station on the Shannon, about five miles distant. There is also a small stuff manufactory. The town is supplied with water from wells, and is neither paved nor lighted. Near it, on the Dublin road, is a spring of excellent water, with a covering of masonry, on which are inscribed these words: "Erected by voluntary contribution, to commemorate the unparalleled benevolence of the English nation to the poor of Ireland at a season of extreme distress. A.D. 1822".

The fee of the land in and about the town, amounting to 500 acres, is vested in the Holmes family. The town is in a populous and well-cultivated district, in which are a considerable number of resident gentry. The seats in its immediate vicinity are Richmond, the residence of R. Wells [i.e. Wills] Gason, Esq.; Salisboro', of T. Poe, Esq.; Riverston, of John Bennett, Esq.; Smithfield, of Capt. Boucheir; Willington, of W. Smithwick, Esq.; and Brook Watson, of F. Watson, Esq.

The living is a rectory and vicarage, in the diocese of Killaloe, united by act of council, Feb. 16th, 1798, to the rectory and vicarage of Knigh, and in the patronage of the Bishop: the tithes amount to £350, and the gross tithes of the benefice are £636.3.1. The glebe-house was erected by a loan of £1200 from the late Board of First Fruits, in 1812; there are two glebes in the union, together containing 18*a*. 3*r.* The church, which is in the town, is a plain structure, built by a loan of £1300 from the same Board, in 1809; and the Ecclesiastical Commissioners have lately granted £101 for its repair. In the R.C. divisions the parish is the head of a union or district, comprising this parish and that of Lisbunny; it contains one chapel, situated in the town, where is also a meeting-house for Wesleyan Methodists, and another for Independents.

There are a parochial free school, a school under the trustees of Erasmus Smith's charity, and one under the Board of National Education, in which are about 290 boys and 150 girls. There are also six private schools, in which are about 170 boys and 80 girls.

THURLES

THURLES, a market and post-town, and a parish, in the barony of ELIOGARTY, county of TIPPERARY, and province of MUNSTER, 243/4 miles (N.) from Clonmel, and 75 (S.W.) from Dublin, on the road from Tipperary to Templemore; containing 10,031 inhabitants, of which number, 7084 are in the town.

The town is pleasantly situated on the banks of the river Suir, by which it is divided into two nearly equal parts, connected with each other by a low bridge; and consists of one spacious street, from each extremity of which smaller streets diverge in various directions. In 1831 it contained 1210 houses, most of which are neatly built and several are of handsome appearance: there are infantry barracks on a small scale. The environs in every direction are pleasant, and are enlivened by richly varied scenery: the surrounding country is extremely fertile, and the town is the commercial centre of a populous and highly cultivated district, and is rapidly increasing in wealth and importance.

A considerable trade is carried on in corn, which is sent by land carriage to Clonmel; it has also an excellent retail trade, and contains a large brewery and a tannery. The market days are Tuesday and Saturday; and fairs are held on the first Tuesday in every month, on Easter-Monday, and on the 21st of Aug. and Dec. The market-house is a neat building in the western part of the main street. A chief constabulary police force is stationed in the town; general sessions for the county are held twice in the year, and petty sessions every Saturday. The sessions-house is a neat modern building; and near it is a well-arranged bridewell, containing 22 cells, 4 day-rooms, and two airing-yards.

THE PARISH

The parish comprises 7290 statute acres, of which 5670 are arable, 810 pasture, and 810 bog and waste: the land in cultivation is of very good quality, producing abundant crops, and the system of agriculture is improved. An abundant supply of fuel is obtained from the bogs, and from the Slievardagh coal mines, which are about eight miles distant. Brittas Castle, the property of the Langley family, was commenced on a very extensive scale by the late Capt. Langley, but remains in an unfinished state. The Archbishop of Cashel has a handsome residence here, and there is also the residence of a stipendiary magistrate in the parish.

The living is a rectory, in the diocese of Cashel, partly impropriate in ____ Bagwell, Esq., and Mrs. Downes, and partly united, by act of council, in 1682, to the vicarages of Rahelty, Shyane, and Adnith, and in the patronage of the Archbishop. The tithes amount to £995, of which £135 is payable to the impropriators, and £860 to the vicar. The glebe-house, towards which the late Board of First Fruits contributed a gift of £100 and a loan of £1500, in 1820, is a good residence; the glebe comprises 68 statute acres, and the gross value of the benefice amounts to £1022. 3. 6 per annum. The church is a neat edifice at the east end of the town, towards the erection of which the late Board of First Fruits advanced a loan of £2000. The R.C. parish is co-extensive with that of the Established Church; it is the head of the diocese, and the mensal of the Archbishop. The chapel, which is the cathedral of the diocese, is a spacious and handsome structure, erected at an expense of £10,000, and one of the finest buildings of the kind in Ireland.

EDUCATION

Near it are the Ursuline and Presentation convents, the ladies of which employ themselves in the gratuitous instruction of poor female children; each has a private chapel. St. Patrick's College, established in 1836 for the liberal education of R.C. young gentlemen upon moderate terms, is a handsome building in an improved demense of 25 acres bounded on one side by the river Suir. About 700 children are taught in four public schools, of which the conventual schools are partly supported by a bequest of £2000 from the late Most Rev. Dr. James Butler, and those of the Christian Brethren by a similar bequest from the Most Rev. Dr. Bray, the interest of which he appropriated to the instruction and clothing of poor boys; and the parochial school is supported by

247

the incumbent. There are also 13 private schools, in which are nearly 700 children; and a dispensary.

It is said that till within the last 20 or 30 years there were the ruins of seven castles in this parish; there are still vestiges of two, and also of a large mansion, formerly the residence of the earl of Llandaff. The remains of the principal castle are situated close to the bridge, and consist at present of a lofty quadrangular keep, with various embattled walls and gables: the other, which is situated at the western extremity of the town, and is ascribed to the Knights Templars, appears to have been of very small extent; a little to the north of it was an ancient moat. In this part of the town are also the remains of the ancient monastery, consisting of a great part of a strong tower, with some mouldering walls.

The greater part of the parish is the property of Lady Elizabeth Matthew [i.e. Mathew], sister of the late earl of Llandaff. Thurles gives the inferior title of Viscount to the Marquess of Ormonde.

Extract from 'An Act for the Appointment of convenient Places for the holding of Assizes in *Ireland* [21st *August* 1835]':

5 & 6 Gulielmi IV, CAP XXVI (5 & 6 William IV c. 26)

'WHEREAS, by a Statute made in the Sixth Year of the Reign of King *Richard* the Second, it was ordained, that the Justices assigned to take Assizes and deliver the Gaols should hold their Sessions in the principal and chief Towns of every of the Counties where the Shire Courts of the same Counties should be holden: And whereas by a Statute made in the Eleventh Year of the same Reign, reciting so much of the said Statute of the Sixth Year as is herein-before recited, and stating that the said Statute was in part prejudicial and grievous to the People of divers Counties in *England*, it was provided that the Chancellor of *England* for the Time being should have Power thereof to make and provide Remedy, by Advice of the Justices, from Time to Time when Need should be, notwithstanding the said Statute: And whereas the Places at which the Assizes are now held in various Counties of *Ireland* are inconvenient to the Inhabitants thereof, and it would be conduce to the more cheap, speedy, and effectual Administration of Justice to appoint other Places instead thereof for the holding of Assizes; but Doubts may be entertained whether that Object can be fully effected by virtue of the Statutes herein-before referred to:' Be it therefore enacted by the King's most Excellent Majesty, by and with the Advice and Consent of the Lords Spiritual and Temporal, and Commons, in this present Parliament assembled, and by the Authority of the same, That so much of each of the said Statutes as relates or may be construed to relate to holding Assizes or Sessions in *Ireland* shall be and the same is hereby repealed.

II. And be it declared and enacted, That the Lord Lieutenant or other Chief Governor or Governors of *Ireland*, by and with the Advice of the Privy Council of *Ireland*, shall have Power from Time to Time to order and direct at what Place or Places in any County in *Ireland* the Assizes and Sessions under the Commissions of Gaol Delivery, and other Commissions for the Dispatch of Civil and Criminal Business, shall be holden, and to order and direct such Assizes and Sessions for the Dispatch of Criminal and Civil Business to be holden at more than One Place in the same County, and to order and direct the Assizes and Sessions under such Commissions for the Dispatch of Criminal or Civil Business to be holden at One or more Place or Places in such County;

and further to order and direct any Special Commissions of Oyer and Terminer and Gaol Delivery to be holden at any One or more Places in any such County.

III. Provided always, and be it enacted, That it shall not be lawful for the Lord Lieutenant or other Chief Governor or Governors of *Ireland*, and the Privy Council there, to make any Order for changing the Place for holding the Assizes in any County, or for dividing any County for the Purposes of this Act, unless a Memorial shall have been presented to him or them by a Majority of the Grand Jury of the Assizes of such County, praying that such Change or Division may be made.

IV. And be it enacted, That in case the Lord Lieutenant or other Chief Governor or Governors of *Ireland*, by and with the Advice of the Privy Council of *Ireland*, shall think fit to order and direct that the Assizes or any such Special Commissions shall be holden at more than One Place in any One County, it shall be lawful for the Lord Lieutenant or other Chief Governor or Governors, by and with the Advice aforesaid, to divide any such County for the Purposes of this Act, and to make Rules and Regulations touching the Venue in all Cases, Civil and Criminal, then pending or thereafter to be pending and to be tried within any Division of such County so to be made as aforesaid; and touching the Liability and Attendance of Jurors, whether Grand Jurors, Special Jurors, or Common Jurors, at the Assizes and Sessions as aforesaid, or at any Sessions under any Special Commissions, to be holden within any such Division; and touching the Use of any House of Correction or Prison as a Common Gaol, and the Government and Keeping thereof; and touching the Alterations of any Commissions, Writs, Precepts, or other Proceedings whatsoever for carrying into effect the Purposes of this Act; and touching any other Matters that may be requisite for carrying into effect the Purposes of this Act; and all such Rules and Regulations shall be of the like Force and Effect as if the same had been made by the Authority of Parliament, and shall be notified in the *Dublin Gazette*, or in such other Manner as the Lord Lieutenant or other Chief Governor or Governors of *Ireland*, by and with the Advice of the Privy Council of *Ireland*, shall think fit to direct.

NOTE: The Assizes Act, 1835, relating to Ireland, is virtually a transcript of the Assizes Act, 1833, which relates to England and Wales. The two have the same titles except for the countries' names; the 1833 one is described as 3 & 4 William IV, c. 71 and was passed on 21 August 1833. Each Act has only four sections. Section II in each is identical except for the countries' names and substitution in the Irish Act of 'Lord Lieutenant' etc for 'His Majesty' in the English Act.

Sections III in the English Act and IV in the Irish Act are likewise almost word for word the same. The final section IV in the English Act has special provisions relating to Lancaster.

Section III above of the Irish Act has no comparable section in the English Act. That is the section which prescribed as an indispensable condition a Grand Jury initiative or at least a request from them complementary to other requests for division. That requirement was inserted by the House of Lords at the last moment – on the bill's final reading [House of Lords Journal, 13 August 1835, p. 554]. No such requirement was included in s. 176 of the Grand Jury Act, 1836, given below. It will be noted that s. 176 (CLXXVI) enables both the appointment of a second assize town and, for that purpose, the division of a county into two ridings, whereas the corresponding 1835 provisions above are spread over sections II and IV and do not confine the number of assize venues or county divisions to two. Section 177 (CLXXVII) below, while bringing forward some of the 1835 s. IV clauses, is more comprehensive as to consequential provisions.

Section 110 of the Local Government (Ireland) Act, 1898, and Parts I & VI respectively of its Sixth Schedule repealed ss. 175-6 of the 1836 Act quoted in Appendix Three and the entire s. IV and relevant phrases of s. II & III of the 1835 Act above which enabled both the appointment of more than one assize town and the division of a county (see also the final paragraphs of Appendix Twelve).

251

Extract from 'An Act to consolidate and amend the Laws relating to the Presentment of Public Money by Grand Juries in *Ireland* [20th August 1836]':

6 & 7 Gulielmi IV, CAP CXVI (6 & 7 William IV, c. 116)

The words in italics within brackets in section CLXXVI (176) are those deleted by way of the Lords' amendments at the Committee stage in the House of Lords. They were replaced by the words in bold print which form part of the section as passed. The identification of deletions and additions was firstly done by reference to the Act and the House of Lords Journal, 3 August 1836, pp. 798-802. They were confirmed by reference to the successive prints of the bill – see Chapter One and its note.

CLXXVI. 'And whereas, from the great Extent of *(the County of Tipperary)* **certain Counties in Ireland**, and the inconvenient Situation of the *(Town)* **Towns** where the Assizes are now held in respect to *(the Northern Part)* **other Parts** of said *(County)* **Counties**, it *(is)* **may be** expedient that a Second Assize Town should be appointed at which Assizes shall be holden for *(the Northern)* Part of said *(County)* **Counties**, and for that Purpose that the said *(County)* **Counties** should be divided into Two Districts or Ridings;' be it therefore enacted, That it shall and may be lawful for the Lord Lieutenant or other Chief Governor or Governors of Ireland, by and with the Advice of the Privy Council, to order and direct that *(the)* **any** County *(of Tipperary)* **in Ireland** shall be divided into Two Ridings or Districts, *(to be called the Northern and Southern Ridings)* and to direct and appoint what Baronies or Half Baronies or other Portions of Land shall be contained in each of said Ridings, and to order and direct that Assizes and Sessions under the Commissioners of Assize and General Gaol Delivery, and other Commissions for the Dispatch of Civil and Criminal Business, or that any special Commission or Commissions of Oyer and Terminer and Gaol Delivery, should be holden in and for *(said)* **any** County *(of Tipperary)* **which now is or may hereafter be so divided** at such Town *(in the Northern Part of said County)* **within the same** as shall be deemed most expedient for the Purpose, in addition to and in like Manner as the same are now holden at the **usual Assize** Town *(of Clonmel)*; and from thenceforth the Assizes so to be holden in such Northern Part of said County shall be designated as the Assizes for the Northern Riding of the County of Tipperary, and the Assizes to be holden as heretofore at the Town of Clonmel shall be designated as the Assizes for the Southern Riding of said County.

CLXXVII. And be it further enacted, That it shall and may be lawful for the said Lord Lieutenant or other Chief Governor or Governors, with such Advice as aforesaid, to make Rules and Regulations touching the Venue in all Cases, Civil and Criminal, then depending or thereafter to be depending and to be tried within said Divisions or Ridings of *(said)* **any such** County, and touching the Alterations of any Commissions, Writs, Precepts, or other Proceedings thereby made necessary, and touching the Attendance and Liability of Jurors, whether Grand Jurors, Special Jurors, or Common Jurors, at such Assizes, or at any Sessions to be holden for such Ridings or Divisions, and to make such Orders, Rules and Regulations for the building or fitting up of any Gaol or Court House in such Town so to be appointed as the Assize Town of **any** such *(Northern)* Riding, and for ascertaining the Proportions to be borne by each Division or Riding of all Presentments or other Fiscal Charges affecting the County at large, and to make all such Rules, Orders, and Regulations touching all other Presentments as may be rendered necessary from Time to Time in consequence of the Division of said County, and all other Rules, Orders, and Regulations as may be necessary for carrying into full and complete Effect the Object of having Two Half-yearly Assizes holden in and for said County in manner aforesaid; and all such Rules, Orders, and Regulations shall be inserted in the *Dublin Gazette*, and notified in such other Manner as Orders of the Lord Lieutenant in Council are usually notified: Provided always, that such Division of said County for the Purposes aforesaid shall not be deemed, construed, or taken to damage, alter, limit, or abridge any Power, Authority, Jurisdiction, Right, Duty, or Privilege of any High Sheriff, Sub-Sheriff, or Justice of the Peace or other Magistrate of the said County, **or to affect the holding of an Election of a Member or Members to serve in Parliament for such County, which shall continue to be holden at the Town at which it is now by Law required to be holden until Parliament shall otherwise direct.**

Requisitionists of Thurles meeting, 1836, to consider 'the remote situation of the Town of Clonmel'

The following is an advertisement in the 'Clonmel Advertiser' on 17 December 1836. It is set out below as printed in the newspaper except by omitting the full stop after each name.

COUNTY OF TIPPERARY
ASSIZES

WE, the undersigned, request a Meeting of the Landed Proprietors and Inhabitants of this County at the COURT-HOUSE, in the Town of THURLES, at the Hour of One o'Clock on THURSDAY, the 22nd of December Instant, to consider the best mode of remedying the great public inconvenience and hindrance to the due administration of justice caused by the remote situation (in reference to the greater portion of the County) of the Town of Clonmel, in which the Assizes have been hitherto held:–

John Trant, D.L.
Wm. F. Mathew, D.L.
Geo. Ryan, D.L.
Valentine Maher, JP
Charles Clarke, JP
Robert Lidwell, JP
Wm. Armstrong, JP
John Russell, JP
James Lenigan, JP
John B. O'Brien, JP
John Maher, JP
Nicholas B. Grene, JP
Thos. Atkinson, Clk
John Pennefather Lamphier
Anthony Lamphier
Vernon Lamphier
Henry Langley
Jas. Knaggs
Robert Lawless
Luke Bray
Daniel Guider
Francis O'Brien
Charles O'Keefe
Marcus Carew Russell
James Chadwick

James Mockler
Thos. Kirwan
John Max
Wm. Ryan
Hugh Mulcahy
M.J. Quinlan, M.D.
Benjamin Russell
Wm. Langley
Thos. Bourke
John Mathew
John Lloyd
Adam Cooke
Thos. Browne
Mat. Quinlan
Robt. Knaggs, M.D.
Stephen Boyton
Edmd. Bourke
John Fanning
Patrick Cahill
Michael Boylson
John Saunderson
Wm. Saunderson
Stephen Saunderson
Peter Phelan
Thos. Bergin

Thomas Godfrey
Joseph Godfrey
Benjamin Whyte
Solomon Lalor Cambie
Michael Power
Patrick Kirwan
Patrick Fogarty
James Fogarty
Henry J. Creaghe
Richard Lalor Cambie
John Maher
Thos. McKenzie
Michael Harney
Robert Manning
Wm. Foley
Michael Mulvany
Timothy Cahill
Wm. Nagle
Michael Mara
Thos. Mara
Thos. Hennessy
Pierce McLoughlin
Patrick McLoughlin
Wm. McLoughlin
John Finn
Philip Fogarty
Daniel Fogarty
John Fogarty
James Russell
Edward Flanagan
John Manning
Geo. Grace
Denis Maher
Thomas Molony
Archibald Cooke
Patrick Ryan, M.D.
Geo. Bradshaw, M.D.
Michael Cormack
Wm. Mackey
Wm. Boyton
Patrick B. Ryan
Samuel Smyth
Wm. Large

John McCarthy
John Molony
Richd. Mullumby
Denis Maher
Patrick Scott
Nicholas Laffan
Wm. Beere
Thos. Miles
Arthur H. O'Connor
Thos. Butler
Wm. Bourke
Patrick Bourke
James Bourke
Martin Bourke
Daniel Maher
Joseph Long
Geo. Hall
John Dohan
Pat. Collier
Pat. Phelan
Denis Mullany
Wm. Hickey
David Cambie
John Boulger
Joshua Lester
Pat. Fanning
Richard Ryan
Wm. B. Fogarty
Usher Beere, Holles st.
Philip Fogarty, Mount-st
John Cahill
Nicholas Maher
Wm. Phelan
Francis Phelan
John Cooke
Richard Bourke
Wm. Bloss Armstrong
Wm. Bourke
John Grene, Sen.
John Grene, Jun.
Magrath Fogarty
Milo Bourke
Richard Beere

**Extract from a Proclamation of the Lord Lieutenant in Council
as printed in the *Nenagh Guardian,* issues of
8, 12 and 15 December 1838**

*The Proclamation had a lengthy preamble reciting the provisions of
the Grand Jury (Consolidation) Act, 1836, which enabled the division
of a county, the appointment of a second assize town within that county,
and the making of consequential 'orders, rules and regulations'.*

And whereas memorials have been presented unto the Lord Lieutenant
and Privy Council of Ireland, from several landed proprietors and
inhabitants of the northern baronies of the county of Tipperary, praying
that said county of Tipperary might be divided into two ridings or
districts, under and for the purposes of said recited act, and the said
memorials having been taken into consideration, it appears from the
great extent of the said county of Tipperary, and the inconvenient
situation of the town of Clonmel, at which the assizes for the said
county are now holden, in respect to the northern parts of said county,
that it would be expedient and highly beneficial to a great portion of
the inhabitants of the said county, that a second assize town should be
appointed, at which assizes for said county should be holden as well
as at the said town of Clonmel, and for that purpose that the said county
of Tipperary should be divided into two districts or ridings accordingly:
   Now We, Constantine Henry, Marquis of Normanby, Lord
Lieutenant General and General Governor of Ireland, by and with the
advice of Her Majesty's Privy Council in Ireland, do, in pursuance of
the powers vested in us for that purpose, and in order to carry into
effect the provisions of the herein-before in part recited act of
parliament, hereby order and direct, that henceforth the said county of
Tipperary shall be divided into, and the same is hereby accordingly
divided into two ridings or districts, the one to be called the south
riding, and the other the north riding of the county of Tipperary; and
that the south riding of the said county of Tipperary shall comprise
and contain the baronies and portion of a barony following, that is to
say, the barony of Iffa and Offa East, the barony of Iffa and Offa West,
the barony of Clanwilliam, the barony of Middlethird, the barony of
Slievardagh, and that part of the barony of Kilnemanagh, containing
the unions or parishes of Clogher, Clonoulty, Aughterleigue,
Ballintemple, Kilpatrick, and so much of the parish of Donohill as is
situate in the barony of Kilnemanagh:

And We, the said Lord Lieutenant General and General Governor of Ireland, by and with the advice aforesaid, further order and direct that the said town of Clonmel be the assize town for the said south riding of the county of Tipperary:

And We do, with the like advice, order and direct that the north riding of the said county of Tipperary shall comprise and contain the baronies and parts of a barony following, that is to say, the barony of Upper Ormond, the barony of Lower Ormond, the barony of Owney and Arra, the barony of Ikerrin, the barony of Eliogarty, and the barony of Kilnemanagh, save and except however so much of the said last-mentioned barony as is comprised in the unions or parishes, and part of a parish aforesaid, which, by this our proclamation, We have ordered and directed to be added to and form part of the south riding of the said county of Tipperary: and that the town of Nenagh be the assize town for the said north riding of the county of Tipperary:

NOTE 1: Neither the four civil parishes recommended for the North Riding by the Privy Council's Committee on 16 June 1837 nor the six civil parishes named by the Proclamation as allocated to the South Riding correspond to the total extent of Kilnamanagh Upper and Lower, respectively, as delineated in practice. Unaccountably, the Committee, or at least its Minutes, omitted all mention, for North or South, of sizeable Upperchurch and tiny Ballycahill (part of) – south of Glenkeen and north of Templebeg. Both omissions were included in the Upper half-barony and therefore in the North Riding by virtue of the Proclamation's not including them in the South.

Castletown, specified by the Committee, is actually the name of a small civil parish entirely in the barony of Coonagh, Co. Limerick, but described as partly in Kilnamanagh Upper in the Civil Survey of 1654. The Committee seems to have used the name Castletown to describe the area consisting of the larger, neighbouring civil parishes of Doon (part of) and Toem (part of) which were now placed in Kilnamanagh Upper and the North Riding in 1838. They comprise the portion transferred to the South Riding in 1899 with the advent of county councils to succeed grand juries as local government administration units (they remained in the North Riding for assizes purposes). They were then described as the electoral divisions of Cappagh, Curraheen and Glengar. The townlands comprising this territory, the only one subjected to a boundary change since 1838, are: Ardnagassane, Augvallydeag, Bahagha, Ballyhane East, Ballyhane West, Birchgrove, Blackstairs, Boolanunane, Brownbog, Cahernahallia, Cappagh, Clonmurragha, Commonealine, Cummerbeg, Cummer More,

Curraghmarky, Curraheen, Druminda, Foilaclug, Foildarg, Foilmahonmore, Foilycleary, Garracummer (also spelt as Garrycummer), Glengar, Gortaderry, Gortmahonoge, Inchinsquillib, Inchivara, Kilbeg, Kilmore, Knockanawar, Knockane, Knockduff, Knockshanbrittas, Leugh, Losset, Moanvaun (Cappagh), Moanvaun (Glengar), Moher East, Moher West, Oldcastle, Parkroe, Piperhill, Reafadda, Reagoulane, Shanacloon, Toem, Toreen.

The division of Kilnamanagh barony, by civil parishes, accordingly was (the modern spelling is used here): in Kilnamanagh Upper and the North Riding: Upperchurch, Ballycahill (part), Glenkeen (which included Borrisoleigh village), Moyaliffe, Templebeg, and the two which were later transferred to the South Riding in 1899: Doon (part) and Toem (part); in Kilnamanagh Lower and the South Riding: Aughacrew, Donohill (part), Kilmore, Ballintemple (which included Dundrum village), Clogher, Rathkennan, Clonoulty (part), Oughterleague and Kilpatrick.

The Proclamation does not specify three small parishes which finally found a resting place in Kilnamanagh Lower and the South Riding: Aghacrow and Kilmore, both south of some which they had listed, and Rathkennan, a debatable allocation on the border beside Holycross. It also overlooked indicating that only part of Oughterleague was in Kilnamanagh .

NOTE 2: The parts of the following civil parishes, other than their parts in one or other Kilnamanagh, are located as indicated in brackets: Ballycahill (Eliogarty, North Riding), Doon (Coonagh, Co. Limerick), Toem (Clanwilliam, South Riding), Clonoulty (do.), Donohill (do.), Oughterleague (do.).

References: Map Index to Townland Survey of the County of Tipperary, Townland Index Sheets No 4 & 6; Cashel and Emly Atlas (Thurles, 1970), ff 2a, 10, 1 1; John J. Clancy, MP, *A Handbook of Local Government in Ireland* (Dublin 1899), pp. 232-5, 436.

Ratepayers Appointed for Baronial Presentments in the Eleven Baronies, 1834

The following is an advertisement in the 'Tipperary Free Press' on 5 April 1834. It is set out below as printed in the newspaper except by omitting the full stop after each name and address..

COUNTY OF TIPPERARY.
Sessions under the Road Act.

Clonmel Spring Assizes, 1834.

We Present and appoint Special Sessions to be held under the Road Act, to take into consideration such PRESENTMENTS as are intended to be sought for at Summer Assizes, 1834; or accounted for at the Times and Places following, viz: –

Monday, May 5, at Clogheen, for the Barony of Iffa and Offa West.

Tuesday,	6, at Tipperary	Clanwilliam
Wednesday,	7, at Clonoulty	Kilnemanagh
Thursday,	8, at Cashel	Middlethird
Friday,	9, at Ballinonty	Slieveardagh
Saturday,	10, at Thurles	Eliogarty
Monday,	12, at Newport	Owney & Arra
Tuesday,	13, at Nenagh	Upper Ormond
Wednesday,	14, at Burris-o'kane	Lower Ormond
Thursday,	15, at Roscrea	Ikerrin
Saturday,	17, at Clonmel	Iffa & Offa East

Notices of Applications to be posted on Saturday, the 26th day of April, for the first Six Baronies, and on Saturday the 3rd day of May, for the Five last Baronies in the above list, between the hours of 9 and 12 o'Clock in the forenoon of said Days, at the usual Place of Posting such Notices.

All Presentments, Supervisorships, and Accounting Affidavits, to be lodged in the Secretary's Office in Clonmel, (and no where else,) on or before Thursday, the 24th day of April, which is the last day for receiving them.

All Persons intending to apply for Presentments, Surveyors, Estimators, Posters of Notices, Supervisors, and Deputy Supervisors, and all such Persons as are to Account for Presentments already granted, are to attend at their respective Baronies, on the days, and at the places above mentioned, precisely at 12 o'Clock in the morning of each Day, at which Hour the Court will proceed to Business.

No Supervisorship or Accounting Affidavit can be received at the Road Sessions.

For Self and Fellow Jurors

GEORGE O'CALLAGHAN, Foreman

We present and appoint the under-mentioned Persons, who appear to be the highest Rate Payers in the several Baronies, and are thereby entitled to sit in conjunction with the Magistrates, at the Special Road Sessions, to be held on the 5th day of May next, and succeeding days, under the Provisions of the 3rd and 4th William 4th, chap. 78, sec. 6.

IFFA AND OFFA WEST
1. John McCann	Ballyholan
2. Robert Prendergast	Marlhill
3. William R. Mulcahy	Burgessland
4. William Fennell	Rehill
5. Luke Hally	Lisnamucka
6. Denis Mulcahy	Shanbally
7. James Mulcahy	Ballysheehan
8. George Fennell	Caher Abbey
9. Patrick O'Brien	Garranlea
10. James Hally	Ballylegan

CLANWILLIAM
1. James Sadlier	Brookfield
2. Clement Sadlier	Shronehill
3. Nicholas Sadlier	Tipperary
4. Michael Green	Thomastown
5. Cornelius Manning	Tipperary
6. Peter Smithwick	Barnlough
7. Thomas Bolton	Ballylisteen
8. Walter Meade	Thomastown
9. Michael Dalton	Ballynaclough
10. Hugh Baker	Lismacue

KILNAMANAGH
1. John Greene	Cappaghmurra
2. John Murphy	Woodford

3. George Wayland	Ballywalter
4. Michael Dwyer	Coolacussane
5. William Murphy	Ballinamona
6. James Horan	Toragh
7. Daniel Murphy	Ballymore
8. Patrick Burne	Carrigeen
9. Thomas Crowe	Inchskillip
10. Francis Phelan	Shanballyduff

MIDDLETHIRD

1. John Millett	Lismortagh
2. Wray Palliser	Derrylusken
3. William Maher	Cloneen
4. Daniel Mansergh	Ballysheehan
5. James Millett	St. Johnstown
6. John Roe	Rockwell
7. Leonard Keating	Garranlea
8. Robert Cooke	Kiltinan
9. John Shea	Bannixtown
10. Avary Jordan	Race Course Lodge

SLIEVARDAGH

1. Brabazon Barker	Kilcooley-Abbey
2. James O'Halloran	Kilnegrannagh
3. Walter Maxey	Upper Noan
4. Michael Kirwan	Urard
5. John Power	Cleragh
6. John Shea	Ballywalter
7. Florence Carroll	Kilbragh
8. Robert Latouche	
9. John Sullivan	Cappagh
10. Robert Mason	Grange

ELIOGARTY

1. Theophilus Bennet	Templemore
2. Charles O'Keefe	Thurles
3. Henry Langley	Archestown
4. Luke Bray	Thurles
5. Philip Kirwan	Thurles
6. William Purcell	Drom
7. Thomas Kirwan	Thurles
8. Patrick Fennelly	Castletown

9. Richard Carden — Fishmoyne
10. Patrick Finn — Rathmoy

OWNEY AND ARRA
1. Finch White — Fort Henry
2. Michael Coffee — Killeen
3. Denis Gleeson — Shallee
4. Pierce Power — Monroe
5. Michael Deegan — Ballina
6. William Phillips — Mount Phillips
7. Richard O'Meara — Shallee
8. Robert Browne — Ballyhourigan
9. George Twiss — Roran
10. John Phillips — Bushfield

UPPER ORMOND
1. Thomas Going — Traverstown
2. Hastings Atkins — Monaquill
3. John Costelloe — Ballyvandran
4. Newton Short — Ballynamona
5. Robert Otway Cave — Castle Otway
6. Samuel Hill — Coolderry
7. William Cooper Crawford — Rapla
8. Matthew Kennedy — Ballyhane
9. David E. Young — Ballygibbon
10. Denis Crowe — Long John's Hill

LOWER ORMOND
1. Thomas Stoney — Portland
2. John Lalor — Gurteen
3. George Smith — Gurteen
4. Robert Robinson — Tenakella
5. Anthony Parker — Fortwilliam
6. Frederick French — Sopwell
7. Thomas G. Stoney — Arranhill
8. James Sheppard — Clifton
9. Marmaduke Thompson — Ballingarry
10. Nathaniel Falkiner — Ballingarry

IKERRIN
1. John Lloyd — Lloydsboro'
2. James Mason — Clonakenny

3. James Middleton   Dangan Lodge
4. Robert Lloyd   Longford
5. Wm H Hutchinson   Rockforest
6. Thomas Jackson   Inane
7. George Hewson   Clonakenny
8. Timothy Bridge   Ashbury
9. Thomas Crawford   Cranagh
10. Costney Egan   Cloncannon

IFFA AND OFFA EAST
1. William Greene   Powerstown
2. James Scully Jun.   Shanballyard
3. John Keating   Springmount
4. John Francis O'Ryan   Ballyenrkeen
5. Walter Asper   Ballyboe
6. Michael Hickey   Kilcash
7. Jeoffrey Prendergast   Ballymackey
8. Thomas Cleary   Lisadubber
9. Thomas O'Donnell   Seskin
10. Hugh McEnry   Lisronagh

For self and fellow Jurors

GEORGE O'CALLAGHAN, Foreman

Table 6   THE COST OF COUNTY GOVERNMENT 1834-44

	1834 £	1838 £	1839 £	1840 £	1841 £	1842 £	1844 £
1. New Roads, Bridges, pipes, gullets, walls, cutting down hills and filling up hollows	3,546	6,585	1,849	2,220	3,166	3,372	1,789
2. Repairs of roads, bridges, pipes, gullets &c.	699	15,572	20,196	19,872	24,831	23,307	21,905
3. Court or sessions houses, erection or repair	—	—	203	950	6,093	2,723	2,143
4. Gaols, bridewells, and district lunatic asylum, erection or repairs			1,627	4,000	4,698	1,265	1,315
5. County gaol, and all other bridewell and prison expenses	5,093	8,140	5,365	6,776	8,002	6,081	6,783
6. Salaries to officers in bridewells and keepers of sessions courts			250	237	303		
7. Constabulary, police, payments to witnesses, &c.	14,143	11,224	14,636	17,196	17,538	17,847	19,102
8. Salaries to all other county officers (not in No 6) and baronial collector's poundage	1,734	4,646	4,712	5,074	5,548	5,731	5,323
9. Public charities [hospitals and dispensaries]	5,642	7,958	7,382	6,409	7,423	6,783	5,546
10. Repayment to Government for support of district lunatic asylum	—	2,006	2,328	1,959	2,308	6,294	6,291
11. Miscellaneous, not included above	3,334	1,930	2,357	2,835	2,339	3,494	1,944
Deduct Re-presentments						1,372	3,390
TOTAL	**34,192**	**58,061**	**60,905**	**67,527**	**82,249**	**75,525**	**68,751**

The Cost of County Government, 1834-44

The rising cost of public services is not a modern phenomenon, as illustrated for the years 1834 to 1844 in the accompanying Table. The totals for the county expressed in *Thoms* 1846 as 'the amount of Grand Jury Cess for every tenth year from 1775 to 1835' are set out in the directory for each county without a breakdown into the components. The same directory is the source for the County Waterford figures (excluding the city), quoted here because of the tenor of the debate reported in Appendix Eleven.

	1775	1785	1795	1805	1815	1825	1835
	£	£	£	£	£	£	£
Tipperary	7,367	11,235	20,205	35,770	40,785	48,836	56,796
Waterford	2,033	2,627	4,139	13,770	10,635	18,459	23,807

Both counties had reviews of their finances in 1834. The *Tipperary Free Press* on 8 March 1834 had a letter from 'a Landholder, Kilsheelan re taxation of Iffa and Offa,' and reported a public accounts committee:

> The Grand Jury at the last assizes named seven as a committee to enquire into "the immense sum for this management" yearly £34,191.12.3: Sir Hugh Gough, J. Bagwell, T. E. Lalor, Thomas Ryan, S. Moore, I. Philips, R. Gason.

Waterford produced a *Report of the Committee appointed by the Grand Jury at the Summer Assizes of 1833 to equalize and facilitate the levying of the grand jury rates for the County of Waterford* (Waterford, 1834). As a consequence a committee was nominated by the grand jury at the Spring Assizes, 1834, as follows; all except two appear in Appendix Eleven as participants in one way or another.

Gaultier – George Meara and Shapland Carew Morris;
Middlethird – Alexander Sherlock and Edward Roberts;
Upperthird – Robert Uniacke and John Power O'Shee;
Decies w'out Drum – John Musgrave, Robert Power, Pierse Hely;
Decies w'in Drum – Sir Richard Musgrave, Bart. and William V. Stuart;
Coshmore and Coshbride – John Keily and William S. Currey;
Glenaheiry – Sir Richard Keane, Bart. and Nuttal Greene.

A presentment was also fiated for levying 10s. per ploughland towards defraying the necessary expenses, and an agreement has since been made for procuring authentic copies from the Registry-office, of all the parochial valuations relating to the County of Waterford.

In the case of Tipperary, it is difficult to pinpoint the increases as a result of the division effected in 1839. Those under items 3, 4 and 5 in 1840 and 1841 appear to reflect the commencement of Nenagh's courthouse and gaol, but that begs the question as to why the amounts fell when the gaol was fully staffed.

The 1834 figures as reported in the newspaper under somewhat different headings from the standard ones later adopted for parliamentary reports have been grouped to accord with the standard ones. 1834 had a final payment to the Peace Preservation Force which preceded Peel's constabulary; likewise the final instalments repaying a government loan for fighting the 1832 cholera epidemic, and a final payment for construction of the Anglesey roads.

Fiscal matters which engaged the attention of the north riding grand jury at the 1842 Spring Assizes before the completion of their new gaol and courthouse are quoted as follows from the first Presentments Book held at the County Library, Thurles: Henry Cole: Keeper of Nenagh Quarter Sessions courthouse, his half-year salary, £3.13s. 10d; Rice Lewis: fuel, £11. 5s. 6d; J. Fletcher: furniture, Nenagh courthouse, £2. 10s. 6d; Henry Cole: stationery for court at sessions, 7s. 6d; Board of Superintendence: salaries of officers in said gaol, £337. 8s.11d; Michael Harty: medicines for use of prisoners and turnkeys, £9. 12s. 0d; Thomas Prendergast: late master of the House of Correction, Clonmel, two-fifths of £50 a half-year superannuation, £20. 0s. 0d.

In addition Daniel Loeman was awarded £40 for taking charge of Nenagh's bridewell, and £5 for providing handcuffs. An amount of two-fifths of £127. 13s. 4d. was passed in respect of a half-year's rent of the ground under the county gaol at Clonmel payable to John Bagwell.

The following sample of matters dealt with at presentment sessions in five of the new north riding baronies is taken from the *Clonmel Advertiser*, 18 December 1838.

OWNEY & ARRA: all relate to repairs to roads except No. 25 – To open and make 77 perches of new line of road from Nenagh to Newport between Mulconroy's House at Crannagh and the mail coach road at

Scragg; UPPER ORMOND: All repairs except No 18 – To make 114 perches of new road from Cloughjordan to Silvermines between the pike road near the new road at Lisboney and William Walshe's gate on the road leading to Tyone; LOWER ORMOND: To build a bridge near the Ford at Lackeen on the road from Birr to Portumna; IKERRIN: No 12 – To build a small bridge on the road from Templemore to Borris-in-Ossory between the crossroads at Gurthderryboy and the chapel of Knock. No 15 – To make a new line of road from Roscrea to Rathdowney between William Carroll's house at the crossroads at the Sheehills and the old lime kiln on the same lands; ELIOGARTY: No 52 – To open and make 22 perches of new line of road from Clonmel to Thurles between the bounds of the baronies of Sliveardagh and Eliogarty and the Castle of Grallagh.

Looking slightly ahead and treating of grand jury expenditures countrywide, the cost of policing was transferred to central government in 1847; in 1851 dispensaries were taken over by the poor law unions; in 1877 gaols and bridewells were given into the care of the central government's General Prisons Board.

Sources of the figures in Table 6:
PP (Accounts) 1834 (174) xlviii. 717, quoted in *T.F.P.,* 8 Mar 1834.
PP (Accounts) 1837-8 (207) xlvi. 377.
PP (Accounts) 1839 (104) xlvii. 573.
PP (Accounts) 1840 (41) xlviii. 211.
PP (Accounts) 1841 (143) xxvii. 265.
PP (Accounts) 1842 (90) xxxviii. 321.
PP (Accounts) 1844 (194) xliii. 137.

Householder Requisitionists for a Nenagh Meeting to set up Town Commissioners, 1839

The two memorials to the Lord Lieutenant in each case requistioning a meeting were forwarded on 22 October 1838 and 15 December 1838.

• indicates names common to both October and December requisitions.
1 indicates names only in the October list.
2 indicates names only in the December list.

The letters TC and the numerals 39 and/or 42 indicate that the person was elected a Town Commissioner in 1839 and/or 1842.

• Abbott, T. T. (T.C. 42)
• Acres, James
2 Bayly, John
• Bayly, R. U., JP
• Bennett, John L.
• Bourchier, John
• Bourke, William (TC 39)
2 Brindley, A.
• Brundley, David (TC 39)
1 Burr, George
1 Burr, William
• Byron, Francis (TC.39)
• Cane, P. (TC 39 & 42)
• Cantrill, Joshua
• Cantrill, Wm. (TC 42)
1 Carroll, W. Parker, JP
• Consedine, Bryan (TC 42)
• Dempster, James, M.D. (TC 39)
• Dillon, O'Brien (TC 39 & 42)
Dobbs, John, Barrack Master
Dunalley, Lord
2 Dwyer, John McKeogh
1 Falkiner, Daniel
• Finucane, John, M.D.
2 Flannery, M.
1 Fletcher, Robert J.
• Frith, George
• Gleeson, Edward
1 Gleeson, William
• Glissan, Patrick, M.D.
• Going, Thomas
2 Hanly, Michael

• Hanly, Patrick
1 Harty, M. (TC 39)
2 Hill, Wm.
• Holmes, Peter, JP
• Kempston, John, Jun.
2 Kennedy, John (TC 39)
• Kennedy, Richard, M.D.
2 Kiernan, John
1 Kittson, J.
1 Langford, George, Solicitor
• Lee, Edward (TC 39)
• Lee, George
• Lewis, Rice (TC 39 & 42)
• Loeman, John
• Magrath, John
• Magrath, Patrick
• Maguire, Thomas
• Meagher, Francis, Solicitor
• Meara, Patrick (TC 39 & 42)   •
• Nolan, Anthony (TC 39 & 42)   1
• O'Brien, John, Solicitor (TC 39)
1 O'Connor, Ambrose, P.P.
• O'Leary, Ignatius
• O'Shea, Thaddeus (TC 39)
1 Parker, Edward
• Poe, James H., Rector
• Poe, Samuel
• Quin, O'Neil, M.D. (TC 39)
2 Spain, Rody (TC 39 & 42)
1 Switzer, Christopher
• Tracey, Daniel (TC 39)

Votes on Degrouping for County Management

The crucial votes on the question of degrouping the two counties for management purposes were as follows.
Abbreviations: FF – Fianna Fáil; FG – Fine Gael; Lab – Labour; C na P – Clann na Poblachta; Ind – Independent; SF – Sinn Féin.

Tipperary (N.R.) County Council
27 February 1956
For Degrouping: John Cahalan (FF), Coolagorna, Borrisokane; Daniel Kennedy (C na P), Foilduff, Rearcross, Chairman; Patrick Ryan (FF), Gortnagoona, Templederry and James O'Meara (FF), Valley Place, Roscrea – **4**.

Against: Martin Collins (FG.), Knockanacartan, Puckane; Senator Patrick Tierney (Lab), Coolbawn; Mary Bridget Ryan, TD (FF), Knockfune, Newport; Jeremiah B. O'Driscoll (FF), Newtown; Martin Brislane (FG), Coologe, Toomevara; Martin Cosgrave (FG), Longford, Templemore; Edmond Kennedy (FG), Longorchard, Templetuohy; John Fanning, TD (FF), Borris, Two-Mile-Borris; Desmond Hanafin (FF), Parnell Street, Thurles; John Murphy (Lab), 10 Iona Avenue, Thurles; Edward Flanagan (FG), Graigue, Thurles and Michael Clohessy (FF), Cleakile, Ballycahill, Thurles – **12** .

Absent: Michael Cronin (C na P), Lorrha; John Gleeson (C na P), Benedine, Nenagh; Patrick Ayres (Lab), 41 Summerhill, Nenagh; Thomas F. Meagher (FF), Patrick Street, Templemore and Edward Byrne (FF), Ballysorrell, Clonmore, Templemore – **5**.

D. Hanafin is the later Senator (1969-92).

21 July 1964
For Degrouping: D. Kennedy (Ind); John Ryan (Lab), 26 St Patrick's Tce., Nenagh; James Mounsey (FF), Clashnevin, Nenagh; E. Byrne (FF); J. Murphy (Lab); T. F. Meagher (FF), Chairman – **6**.
Against: P. Tierney, TD (Lab); J. Cahalan (FF); Liam Whyte (FG), Ballyhough, Aglish, nr. Borrisokane; M. B. Ryan (FF); M. Brislane (FG); Aindreas MacDomhnaill (SF), Gralladh, Aonach Urmhumhan; J. O'Meara (FF); E. Kennedy (FG); Martin Cosgrave (FG); J. Fanning, TD (FF); Thomas Dunne, TD (FG), Friar Street, Thurles; M. Clohessy (FF) and M. Cronin (Ind) – **13**.
Absent: P. Ryan (FF); D. Hanafin (FF) – **2**.

J. Ryan is the later TD (1973-87 and 1992-), Leas-Cheann Comhairle (1982-7), and Senator (1989-92); L. Whyte is the later Senator (1973-7).

15 December 1964
For Degrouping: T. F. Meagher (FF), Chairman; L. Whyte (FG); M. B. Ryan (FF); D. Kennedy (Ind); J. Ryan (Lab); J. Mounsey (FF); P. Ryan (FF), J. O'Meara (FF); E. Kennedy (FG); J. Murphy (Lab); T. Dunne, TD (FG); M. Clohessy (FF); M. Cosgrave (FG) – **13**.
Against: **Nil**.
Dissenting: P. Tierney, TD (Lab) – **1**.
Absent: J. Cahalan (FF); M. Cronin (Ind); M. Brislane (FG); A. MacDomhnaill (SF); E. Byrne (FF); J. Fanning, TD (FF); D. Hanafin (FF) – **7**.

19 April 1966
For Degrouping: L. Whyte (FG); D. Kennedy (Ind); J. Ryan (Lab); A. MacDomhnaill (SF); E. Kennedy (FG); M. Cosgrave (FG); J. Murphy (Lab); T. Dunne, TD (FG) – **8**.
Against: M. B. Ryan (FF); J. O'Meara (FF); E. Byrne (FF); J. Fanning, TD (FF); D. Hanafin (FF); M. Clohessy (FF); T. F. Meagher (FF), Chairman – **7**.
Abstained: P. Tierney, TD (Lab) – **1**.
Absent: J. Cahalan (FF); M. Cronin (Ind); M. Brislane (FG); J. Mounsey (FF); P. Ryan (FF) – **5**.

20 February 1968
Passed unanimously: L. Whyte (FG), Chairman; P. Tierney, TD (Lab); James Darcy (FG), Clashateaun, Ardcroney; J. Ryan (Lab); M. Brislane (FG); Daniel Moylan (FG), Rathnaleen, Nenagh; P. Ryan (FF); Joseph Bergin (FF), Cudville, Nenagh; Edward Meagher (FF), Patrick Street, Templemore; Michael Smith (FF), Behagloss, Roscrea; Thomas Shanahan (Lab), 19 Cnoc Mhuire, Roscrea; M. Cosgrave (FG); E. Kennedy (FG); T. Dunne, TD (FG); J. Fanning, TD (FF); J. Murphy (Lab); J. Doyle (FF), Holycross, Thurles – **17**.
Absent: J. Cahalan (FF); D. Kennedy (Ind); J. Mounsey (FF); Thomas Moloney (FG.) Holycross, Thurles – **4**.

M. Smith is the later TD (1969-73, 1977-82, 1987-), Senator (1982-7), Minister for Energy (Jan-June 1989), Minister for the Environment (1992-) and Minister of State at the Departments of Agriculture (1980-1), Energy (with special responsibility for Forestry,1987-9) and

Industry and Commerce (with special responsibility for Science and Technology, 1989-91).

It can be noted that John Cahalan and Jimmy O'Meara were for degrouping in 1956 but against it in July 1964 and 1966. Tommy Meagher and Ned Byrne were for it in July 1964 but switched in the Fianna Fáil block vote against in 1966.

The thirteen Councillors unanimously in favour in December 1964 included Mounsey, Clohessy, Mrs Ryan, O'Meara and Meagher referred to above or in the text. The only other Fianna Fáiler present was Paddy Ryan who was consistent with his 1956 vote for; he was absent in July 1964 and April 1966. Cahalan and Mounsey were also absent in 1966 when the remaining seven of their party switched to a solid vote for degrouping.

Tipperary (S.R.) County Council
6 February 1956

For Degrouping: John Ahessy (FF), Fethard; John Boyle (FG), Ardfinnan; Patrick Brett (FG), Killenaule; Michael Buckley (FF), Cappawhite; Denis E. Burke (FG), Clonmel; Richard Coffey (FG), Emly; Patrick Crowe, TD (FG), Dundrum; Thomas Duggan (FF), Gortnahoe; Michael Fitzgerald (FG), Golden; Patrick Hogan (FG), Cashel; Thomas Hogan (FF), Tipperary; Gerard Meskill (FF), Ardfinnan; John Morrissey (FG), Clonmel; James Murphy (FG) Grangemockler; Colm O'Donnell (Ind), Cahir; Timothy K. O'Donoghue (FG), Tipperary – **16.**

Against: Daniel Feehan (FF), Cashel; James Hennessy (FF), Cahir; John Kennedy (FF), Clonmel; Patrick J. Kenny (FF), Carrick-on-Suir; William O'Dwyer (FF), Boherlahan; Denis O'Sullivan (Lab), Ballingarry; William Ryan (FF), Kilfeacle; Sean Treacy (Lab), Clonmel – **8.**

Absent: John Kearney (FF), Clogheen; Michael Lacy (FF), Clonmel – **2.**

S. Treacy is the later TD (1961-), Member of the European Parliament (1981-4) and Ceann Comhairle (1973-7) and (1987-).

4 May 1964

Unanimously for Degrouping: S. Treacy, TD (Lab), Chairman; J. Ahessy (FF); J. Boyle (FG); M. Buckley (FF); Edward Clancy (FG), Drangan; R. Coffey (FG); P. Crowe (FG); Don Davern, TD (FF), Cashel; Con Donovan (FF), Ballyporeen; T. Duggan (FF); M. Fitzgerald (FG); P. Hogan, TD (FG); T. A. Hogan (FF); J. Kennedy (FF); Roger McGrath (FF), Burncourt; J. Murphy (FG); Christopher O'Brien (Lab),

Cahir; Patrick O'Brien (Lab), Cashel; T. K. O'Donoghue (FG); John O'Meara (FF), Cahir; Senator W. Ryan,(FF); P. J. Kenny (FF) – **22** .
Absent: D. E. Burke (FG); Sean Healy (Lab), Carrick-on-Suir; Michael Norris (FF), Clonmel; Pierce Power (FG), Kilsheelan – **4**.

6 November 1967

Unanimously for Degrouping: S. Treacy, TD (Lab), Chairman; J. Ahessy (FF); Ned Brennan (Lab), Killenaule; J. Boyle (FG); Sean Byrne (FF), Cahir; Willie Byrne (Lab), Clonmel; Peter Carew (FF), Cashel; Paddy Caplice (FF), Cahir; E. Clancy (FG); R. Coffey (FG); C. Donovan (FF); T. Duggan (FF); Michael Ferris (Lab), Bansha; Jim Hanly (FF), Cappawhite; S. Healy (Lab); P. Hogan, TD. (FG); T. A. Hogan (FF); J. Murphy (FG); M. Norris (FF); P. O'Brien (Lab); T. K. O'Donoghue (FG); John P. Ryan (FG), Cappawhite; Sean Sampson (FG), Cahir; W. Ryan (FF) – **24**.
Absent: D. E. Burke (FG); Eddie O'B. Hogan (FF), Clonmel – **2**.

S. Byrne is the later TD (1982-7) and Senator (1987-). M. Ferris is the later Senator(1981-9 and TD (1989-).

Members of Countywide Bodies

As of 1830 County Tipperary was assigned as part of the catchment area of the new Maryboro (now Portlaoise) District Lunatic Asylum. The Tipperary Grand Jury immediately sought one at Clonmel for counties Tipperary and Waterford. The Lord Lieutenant and Privy Council over the period 1831-2 decided, firstly, that Waterford would be given its own asylum, then that the Maryboro accommodation was insufficient to cater for Tipperary which would also be given separate status as a district and an asylum provided at Clonmel. One was built there in 1833-4.

The first Governors and Directors of Clonmel District Lunatic Asylum, 1834

Their first meeting took place on 15 November 1834. Note the proportion of twelve southerners to three northerners.

The earl of Glengall [Cahir Castle, Cahir]; Viscount Hawarden [Dundrum, Cashel]; Viscount Lismore [Shanbally Castle, Clogheen]; Baron Dunalley [Kilboy, Nenagh]; Baron Bloomfield [Loughton House, Moneygall]; Sir Hugh Gough [Rathronan House, Clonmel]; John Bagwell [Marlfield, Clonmel]; Stephen G. Moore [Barn House, Clonmel]; William Perry [Woodroffe, Clonmel]; Samuel Barton [Rochestown, Cahir]; David Malcolmson [Clonmel]; George Ryan [Inch House, Thurles]; Rev. J. P. Rhoades; M. D. Moore [possibly a misprint for Maurice Crosbie Moore [Mooresfort, Lattin]; J. H. Massy-Dawson [Ballinacourty, Tipperary].

The last Board of Governors of Clonmel District Lunatic Asylum, 1898

The Board of Governors was abolished as of 1 April 1899 upon the advent of county councils. Its twenty-two members included fifteen from the South Riding (first in the list below) and seven from the North. It can be noted that the list includes five Deputy Lieutenants of the county and only one Poor Law Guardian, and that all except three are Justices of the Peace or magistrates (the D.L.s were all magistrates).

Richard Bagwell, D.L., Marlfield, Clonmel; Alderman Edward Cantwell, JP, Clonmel; Edmund Cummins, JP, Brookhill, Fethard; Richard B. Feehan, JP, Carrick-on-Suir; Rev. C. J. Flavin, P.P., Clonmel; Jerome J. Guiry, JP, Peppardstown, Fethard; Captain M. V. S. Morton, D.L., Little Island, Clonmel; Captain John R. Mulcahy, JP, Ballyglass,

Tipperary; Patrick O'Donnell, JP, P.L.G., Clonmore, Cahir; R. P. L. Pennefather, JP, Marlow, Cashel; William Rochfort, JP, Cahir Abbey, Cahir; Colonel W. A. Riall, D.L., Heywood, Clonmel; John R. Scott, Bagwell-street, Clonmel; Darby Scully, JP, D.L., Silverfort, Fethard; Hugh Scott, JP, Kilbeg, Cappawhite; R. G. Carden, JP, Fishmoyne, Borrisoleigh; C. Neville Clarke, JP, Graiguenoe Park, Thurles; John Connolly, JP, The Mills, Templemore; Fitzroy Knox, D.L., Brittas Castle, Thurles; Anthony Parker, JP, Castlelough, Portroe; Colonel Fitzgibbon Trant, D.L., Dovea, Thurles; James Walsh, Killenaule.

The first Joint Committee of Management of Clonmel District Lunatic Asylum, 1899

Upon the institution of county councils, elected upon a partially democratic basis, by the Local Government (Ireland) Act, 1898, lunatic asylums were to be managed by the county councils and the former boards of governors abolished. As the Clonmel asylum catered for patients from the two Tipperarys a joint committee was set up under s. 9(7) of the Act.

The attendance at the first meeting on 12 June 1899 comprised eleven from the South Riding and four from the North. All the laymen were members of the county councils except the two O'Donnells who were rural district councillors and poor law guardians. Only Messrs Cummins, P. O'Donnell and Walsh were brought forward from the 1898 Board of Governors.

Very Rev. Dean McDonnell, P.P., VG., SS. Peter and Paul's, Clonmel, Chairman; Edmund Cummins [Brookhill, Fethard]; James Walsh [Main St, Killenaule]; Dr J. F. O'Ryan [Tipperary]; W. P. Mullalley, Wm Dwyer [Elmville, Clonmel]; P. O'Donnell, JP, D.C. [Clonmore, Fethard]; Con O'Donnell, D.C. [Seskin, Kilsheelan, Clonmel]; John Heffernan [Mocklerstown, Clerihan, Clonmel/Cuckoohill House, Cahir]; E. Murphy, Mayor of Clonmel; John Cullinan [Dobbyn's Hotel, Tipperary/Bansha, Tipperary]; Thomas Duggan [Two-Mile-Borris, Thurles]; Timothy Ryan [Ileigh, Borrisoleigh, Thurles]; Thomas Collier [Tempetouhy, Thurles]; Patrick Maher [Templetouhy, Thurles].

Edmund Cummins was Chairman of Tipperary (S.R.) County Council and Wm Dwyer its Vice-Chairman.; John Cullinan was MP for Tipperary South constituency, 1900-18.

The Joint Committee of Management of Clonmel District Mental Hospital, 1942

The institution's title had been changed by the Local Government Act,

274

1925, having been informally changed by the Joint Committee of Management in June 1921 following a unanimous decision of an Irish Asylums conference in May 1921 to ask Committees throughout the country to do so.

The reconstituted twenty-two man Joint Committee of Management of the Clonmel District Mental Hospital, whose first meeting took place on 9 September 1942, succeeded a Committee consisting of nine Tipperary North members and Commissioner P. J. Meghen who was appointed in March 1934 after the dissolution of Tipperary (S.R.) County Council. He replaced that Council's thirteen nominees. The 1942 members, all county councillors, were:

Tipperary (S.R.) County Council: Richard Curran, TD, Cregg, Carrick-on-Suir; Denis O'Sullivan, The Commons, Thurles; John O'Reilly, Pegsboro, Tipperary; Joseph Cahill, Bank Place, Tipperary; Richard Coffey, Ballynacree, Emly; Daniel Kennedy, Ballagh, Gooldscross; Thomas Ryan, Cappawhite; Jeremiah O'Dwyer, Moheragh, Annacarty; Alderman R. Stapleton, Árd na Gréine, Clonmel; John Cronin, 3 Mitchel St, Clonmel; Alderman Denis E. Burke, Norman Lea, Clonmel; William F. O'Donnell, Glenreigh, Clonmore S., Cahir; Patrick Mulcahy, The Square, Cahir.

Tipperary (N.R.) County Council: James Maher, Friar St, Thurles; J. P. Stakelum, Ballinahow, Thurles; Thomas Maher, Kilcoake, Strogue, Templemore; Martin Ryan, TD, Knockfune, Newport; Patrick Tierney, Ballyscanlon, Coolbawn, Borrisokane; Thomas Meagher, Patrick St, Templemore; Denis O'Neill, Mitchel St, Nenagh; Senator Seán Hayes, Cabra Rd, Thurles; James A. Boland, Kenyon St, Nenagh.

Tipperary Mental Health Board, 1971

The title of the governing body of the institution had been changed by the Mental Treatment (Names of Joint Bodies) Order, 1946 to the Clonmel Mental Hospital Board and again by the Mental Health Board Order, 1960 to the Tipperary Mental Health Board.

The members listed are of the final board at the time of dissolution in 1971 upon the transfer of health functions from county councils to the new regional health boards. The representation had switched to fourteen from the South Riding and eight from the North. Only Messrs Coffey and Tierney were still members since 1942.

Tipperary (S.R.) County Council: Seán Treacy, 'Rossa', Heywood Rd, Clonmel; Michael Norris, Shanbally, Lisronagh, Clonmel; Seán Cooney, Suir Island, Clonmel; Con Donovan, Ballyporeen; Seán

Sampson, Church St, Cahir; Josephine Quinlan, Glengar, Cappawhite; Timothy K. O'Donoghue, Garryskillane, Tipperary; Richard Coffey, Ballynacree, Emly; Edward Clancy, Glengoole, Thurles; Thomas Duggan, Knockboy, Gortnahoe, Thurles; John Ahessy, Tinakelly, Fethard; Peter Carew, The Green, Cashel; Thomas Kevin, Nodstown, Cashel; Patrick Fahey, Parkroe, Cappawhite.

Tipperary (N.R.) County Council: Patrick Tierney, Ballyscanlon, Coolbawn, Nenagh; Martin Brislane, Coologue, Toomevara, Nenagh; Edmond Kennedy, Longorchard, Templetuohy, Thurles; Thomas Molony, Holycross, Thurles; John Ryan, 26 St. Patrick's Terrace, Nenagh; John Murphy, 10 Iona Avenue, Thurles; Daniel Kennedy, Rearcross, Newport; John Fanning, Borris, Two-Mile-Borris, Thurles.

St. Luke's Hospital Visiting Committee, 1972
The title St. Luke's was attached to the hospital in the early 1950s.
South-Eastern Health Board nominees: Joseph Cummins, MCC, Ferrybank, Waterford; Roland Gallagher, B.D.S, Parnell St, Waterford; Bridget McCarthy, S.R.N., St. Joseph's Hospital, Clonmel.
Mid-Western Health Board nominees: Tom Molony, MCC, Holycross, Thurles; Michael Smith, MCC, Lismackin, Roscrea; Liam Whyte, MCC, Aglish, Borrisokane.

St. Luke's Hospital Visiting Committee, 1993
South-Eastern Health Board: Pat Power, B.C., 67 Doyle St, Waterford; Tom Ambrose, MCC, 'Dun Mhuire', Melview, Clonmel; Deirdre Bolger, MCC, Gorey, Co. Wexford; Dr Finian Gallagher, Gowran, Co. Kilkenny; Dr Neville De Souza, Co. Clinic, Clonmel.
Mid-Western Health Board: Jim Casey, MCC, Knockanacree, Cloughjordan; Jane (Binkie) Hanafin, MCC, Parnell St, Thurles; Dr John Hennigan, Richmond, Templemore; Michael Lowry, TD, MCC, The Green, Holycross, Thurles; Dr Mary O'Mahoney, Acting Director of Community Care, St. Camillus' Hospital, Limerick.
Source for St. Luke's: Eamonn Lonergan, 'St. Luke's Hospital, Clonmel, 1834-1984': pp. 22-4 quoting National Archive papers for its origins, pp. 56-7 and 75 for its changes of title, and pp. 24, 38, 186-7 for memberships to 1971. Mr Lonergan has also supplied the more recent lists. The addresses of the 1834 and 1899 memberships have been reconstructed from 'Thoms' and other directories.

Co. Tipperary Joint Library Committee
Like its bookshelves, the committee filled up gradually. Six were appointed initially from each county council, all MCCs, by Tipperary

(North Riding) at its meeting on 13 January 1927, and by Tipperary (South Riding) at its meeting on 8 March 1927.

Tipperary (S.R.) County Council: P. L. Ryan, Russelstown House, Tipperary; Wm J. Mulcahy, Ardfinnan Castle, Cahir; James Timoney, Cappawhite; Patrick Morris, Crohane, Killenaule; Captain C. M. Moore, Mooresfort, Tipperary; Richard Curran, Cregg, Carrick-on-Suir.

Tipperary (N.R.) County Council: Wm Butler, Friar St, Thurles; Jeremiah Ryan, Friar St, Thurles; Martin Cunningham, Timeighter, Roscrea; John J. Hassett, Killoskehane, Barnane, Templemore; Joseph Morrissey, Moynetemple, Templemore; James Bourke, Clonakenny, Roscrea.

P. L. Ryan was Chairman of Tipperary (S.R.) County Council. The Committee held its first meeting on 18 March 1927, chaired by J. J. Hassett, and agreed on P. L. Ryan in his absence as the Committee's Chairman. The first meeting co-opted five North Tipperary persons: Paul Dempsey, Secretary, Committee of Technical Instruction, County Courthouse, Nenagh; Jeremiah Ryan, Secretary, Co. Committee of Agriculture, County Courthouse, Nenagh; Seán O'Byrne, Roscrea; Rev. W. Fitzgerald, C.C., The Presbytery, Thurles; Dr William Callanan, The Mall, Thurles.

Its second and third meetings were chaired by Fr Fitzgerald and Dr Callanan. At its fourth meeting, on 7 December 1927, the Committee co-opted five South Tipperary persons: W. E. Ryan, 49 St. Michael St, Tipperary; C. V. Barrington, Maryville, Cashel; T. F. O'Brien, Glenarm, Clonmel; Rev. Dr Seymour, Cappawhite; Rev. N. Ryan, Dundrum.

By 18 July 1928 Clonmel Corporation and the Urban District Councils had nominated their representatives: Francis Phillips, Chairman, U.D.C., Cashel; P. Butler, Brookdale, Clonmel; Seán T. O'Neill, Town Clerk, Nenagh; Thomas F. Meagher, Town Clerk, Templemore; Thomas Corcoran, St. Michael St, succeeded immediately by M. Kirby, Town Clerk, Tipperary; J. M. Kennedy, Town Clerk, Thurles.

The 1993-4 Committee, listed by nominating bodies (each was a councillor except Mr Billy Healy):

Tipperary (S.R.) County Council: Denis Bourke, St. Anne's, Castle Park, Carrick-on-Suir; Michael Anglim, Ballylaffin, Ardfinnan, Clonmel; Michael Maguire, Lattin, Tipperary (succeeding Willie Ryan, Kilfeacle, Tipperary, an ex-Councillor who died in 1992-3); Jimmy Hogan, 7 Dunbane, Carrick-on-Suir; Jack Crowe, Convent Cross, Dundrum; Billy Healy, County Council Offices, The Square, Cahir.

Tipperary (N.R.) County Council: Denis Ryan, Parkmore, Roscrea; Tom Ryan, Rathnaleen, Nenagh; Mattie Ryan (Coole), Coolecarra, Kilcommon, Thurles; John Sheehy, Garryneel, Ballina, Killaloe, Co. Clare; Seán Mulrooney, Millpark, Roscrea; Dan Smith, Timeighter, Roscrea.

Thurles U.D.C.: Seán Costello, St. Anne's, Bohernamona Rd, Thurles, succeeding Kevin O'Dwyer, 2 Davitt Terrace, Dublin Rd, Thurles (1992-3).

Templemore U.D.C.: Mary Meagher, Patrick St, Templemore, succeeding Tony Shelley, 13 Park Avenue, Templemore (1992-3).

Nenagh U.D.C.: Sally Gardiner, 11 St. Patrick's Terrace, Nenagh.

Cashel U.D.C.: Martin Browne, Dualla Rd, Cashel.

Carrick-on-Suir U.D.C.: Noel Torpey, Coolnamuck Rd, Carrick-on-Suir.

Tipperary U.D.C.: Ned Walsh, 126 St. Michael's Avenue, Tipperary.

Clonmel Corporation: John Kennedy, 72 Árd-na-Gréine, Clonmel.

Under its new charter given by the Local Government Act, 1994, which brought forward a provision of the Local Government Act, 1991, the two county councils appointed seven each, rather than six as heretofore, to be members. Their nominees are the same as the outgoing six, plus TNR's Martin Kennedy, Gortaggart, Thurles, and TSR's Tom Wood, 12 Old Rd, Cashel. The U.D.C. and Corporation nominees as members of this revived body for its first year, 1994-5 (each is an urban/borough councillor) are as follows. Because of s. 39(3) of the 1991 Act, they and Mr Healy are non-voting members, as they are not themselves members of either county council; the county council is the appointing, as distinct from nominating, body.

Thurles U.D.C.: Mary Fogarty, Maple View, Abbey Rd, Thurles.

Templemore U.D.C.: Tony Shelley, 13 Park View West, Templemore.

Nenagh U.D.C.: Máire Hoctor, 33 Pearse St, Nenagh.

Cashel U.D.C.: William McInerney, Camas Rd, Cashel.

Carrick-on-Suir U.D.C.: Patsy Murphy, Abbey Square, Carrick-Beg, Carrick-on-Suir.

Tippperary U.D.C.: Jim O'Shea, 5 Martin Breen Court, Tipperary.

Clonmel Corporation: Niall Dennehy, 23 Inislounaght, Marlfield Rd, Clonmel.

Source for County Library: Mr Martin Maher, County Librarian.

The County Councils
The members of both county councils as of the time of publication are also set out for the historical record. They were elected in 1991; the normal five-year period of office is superseded by s. 20(2) of the Local

Government Act 1994; which extends the 1991-6 term and specifies the next election date as 1998.
Party affiliations: FF – Fianna Fáil; FG – Fine Gael; Lab – Labour; NP – Non Party; Ind – Independent.

Members of Tipperary (North Riding) County Council

Borrisokane Area: Jim Casey (FF), Knockanacree, Cloughjordan; Michael Hough (FF), Coorevan, Borrisokane; Tony McKenna (FF), Ballyhaden, Borrisokane; Gerard Darcy (FG), Clashteeaun, Ardcroney.

Templemore Area: John Egan (FF), Inch House, Bouladuff, Thurles; Noel Coonan (FG), Gortnagoona, Roscrea; Seán Mulrooney (FF), Millpark, Roscrea; Denis Ryan (FG), Parkmore, Roscrea; Dan Smith (FF), Timeighter, Roscrea.

Thurles Area: Jane (Binkie) Hanafin (FF), Parnell St; Martin Kennedy (Lab), Castlemeadows, Gortataggart; Michael Lowry (FG), The Green, Holycross; Harry Ryan (FF), Galboola, Littleton; Mae Quinn (FG), Rossestown, Thurles.

Nenagh Area: Tom Harrington (FF), Upper Knockalton, Nenagh; Willie Kennedy (FG), Glastrigan, Borrisoleigh; Joseph O'Connor (NP), Tyone, Nenagh; John Ryan (Lab), 26 St. Patrick's Terrace, Nenagh; Mattie Ryan (Coole) (FF), Coolecarra, Kilcommon; Tom Ryan (FG), Rathnaleen, Nenagh; John Sheedy (FF), Garryneel, Ballina, Killaloe.

Chairmen Tipperary (N.R.) County Council 1991-5:
1991-2 – Senator Tony McKenna.
1992-3 – John Sheehy.
1993-4 – Seán Mulrooney.
1994-5 – Jim Casey.

Members of Tipperary (N.R.) County Council on the inaugural Mid-West Regional Authority, 1994: Harry Ryan, Willie Kennedy, John Sheehy, Mattie Ryan (Coole), Seán Mulrooney, Noel Coonan.

Staff at Mid-West Regional Authority seconded from the Council: Tom Kirby, Chief Executive; Marion Hickey, Clerical Officer.

Members of Tipperary (South Riding) County Council

Cahir Area: Therese Ahern (FG), TD, Ballindoney, Grange, Clonmel (Cathaoirleach 1994-5); Senator Seán Byrne (FF), Tubrid, Ballylooby, Cahir; Michael Anglim (FF), Ballylaffin, Ardfinnan; Seán Sampson (FG), The Mall, Cahir; Con Donovan (FF), Ballyporeen, Cahir.

Cashel Area: Jack Crowe (FG), Convent Green, Dundrum; Seán McCarthy (FF), John St, Cashel; Tim Hammersley (FF), Clonoulty, Cashel; Tom Wood (FG), 12 Old Rd, Cashel; Tom Hayes (FG), Cahervillahow, Golden, Cashel.

Bridie Hammersley was co-opted following her husband Tim's death in November 1994.

Clonmel Area: Seamus Healy (Ind), Scrouthea, Old Bridge, Clonmel; Pat Norris (FF) (co-opted on Noel Davern's becoming Minister of Education in mid-Nov 1991), Rathronan, Clonmel; Ted Boyle (Ind), 140 Elm Park, Clonmel; Tom Ambrose (FF), 'Dun Mhuire', 7 Melview, Clonmel; Seán Lyons (Lab), 20 Powerstown Rd, Clonmel.

Fethard Area: Susan Meagher (FF), Shangarry, Ballingarry, Thurles (Cathoirleach, 1993-4); Ned Brennan (Lab), Pike St, Killenaule; John Holohan (FG), Ballinard, Fethard; Denis Landy (Lab), Greystone St, Carrick-on-Suir; Denis Bourke (FF), 1 Castle St, Carrick-on-Suir; Jimmy Hogan (FG), 7 Dunbane, Carrick-on-Suir.

Tipperary Area: Michael Ferris (Lab), TD, Rosanna, Tipperary; Brendan Griffin (FG), 'Cnoc Pic', St. Michael St, Tipperary; Michael Maguire (FF), Lattin, Tipperary; Michael Fitzgerald (FG), Rathclogheen House, Rathclogheen, Golden; Christy Kinahan (NP), 19 Cashel Rd, Tipperary.

Tipperary (S.R.) Co. Council Chairmen 1991-5:
Jul-Dec 1991 – Noel Davern, TD.
Dec-June 1991-2 – Tom Ambrose.
1992-3 – Michael Fitzgerald.
1993-4 – Susan Meagher.
1994-5 – Theresa Ahern.

Mr Davern resigned from the Council on becoming Minister for Education (1991-2). He was an MEP (Member of the European Parliament) for Munster, 1979-84.

Members of Tipperary (S.R.) County Council on the inaugural South-East Regional Authority, 1994: Jack Crowe, Michael Fitzgerald, John Holahan, Seán Byrne, Con Donovan, Michael Maguire.

Staff of South-East Regional Authority seconded from the Council: Tom Byrne, Parnell St, Clonmel, Chief Executive.

Tipperary LEADER Group

Board of Directors: Michael J. Lynch, Chairman; Seamus Hayes, Tipperary (S.R.) County Council; Tom Kirby, Mid-West Regional Authority; James Finn, Thurles Development Association; Michael Ryan, Co. Tipperary Community Groups; Noel Horgan, Co. Tipperary co-operatives; Joan O'Dwyer, Muintir na Tíre; Denis Ryan, Co. Tipperary unemployed groups; Frank O'Donnell, representing the Minister of State at the Dept. of Agriculture; Jim Gilligan, County Tipperary Chambers of Commerce.

Staff: John G. Devane, Manager; Jane Toomey, Administrative Officer;

Tom Fitzgerald, Administration Supervisor; Isabel Cambie, Field Officer; ~~Field~~Edward Fox, Accountant; Ann Lynch, Assistant Administrative Officer.

Coiste Gniomhaíochta don Fhoras Forbartha Tuaith agus Gnó Thiobraid Árann – Action Committee, Tipperary Rural and Business Development Institute

Most Rev. Dermot Clifford, Archbishop of Cashel and Emly, Thurles – Patrún; Lucas Ó Muircheartaigh, P.O.F., Coisde Gairm Oideachais, Chondae Thiobraid Arainn Thuaidh, Bóthar na h-Eaglaise, Aonach Urmhumnan; John Slattery, C.E.O., Co. Tipperary (S.R.) V.E.C.

Members of the Oireachtas: Theresa Ahern, TD; Senator Seán Byrne; Noel Davern, TD, Tannersrath, Clonmel; Michael Ferris, TD; Michael Lowry, TD; Senator Seán McCarthy; Senator Michael O'Kennedy, Gortlandroe, Nenagh; John Ryan TD; Michael Smith, TD, Minister for the Environment, Lismackin, Roscrea; Seán Treacy, TD, Ceann Comhairle, 'Rossa', Haywood Rd, Clonmel.

Tipperary North Riding County Councillors: Jim Casey, Noel Coonan, Gerard Darcy, John Egan, Jane (Binkie) Hanafin, Tony McKenna, Mae Quinn, Tom Ryan.

Tipperary South Riding County Councillors: Jack Crowe, Michael Fitzgerald, Brendan Griffin, Tom Hayes, Denis Landy, Susan Meagher.

Seán Mac Fhionnlaoich, Bainisteoir An Chondae Thiobraid Arann Thuaidh; Seamus Hayes, South Tipperary County Manager, Emmet St, Clonmel; Tomás Ó Domhnaill, TNR Development Manager, Shannon Free Airport Development Co, Silver St, Nenagh; Brian Callanan, Planning Manager, SFADCo, Town Centre, Shannon, Co. Clare; Michael Maher, C.A.O., Teagasc, Castlemeadows, Thurles; Maura Scully, UDC, Cathedral St, Thurles; Marius Cassidy, N.R.B., 75 John St, Kilkenny; Gerry Ryan, FÁS, Raheen, Limerick; Antóin Ó Briain, UDC, 'Caragh', Brittas Rd, Thurles.

Pat Donnelly, A.C.C., 7 Liberty Square, Thurles; John O'Donoghue, Gortmore Upper, Carrigatoher, Nenagh; Larry Looby, Liscrea, Bouladuff; Thurles. Des Hanafin, Littleton, Thurles; William Byrne, 31 Baron Park, Clonmel; Mary Eakins, Freghduff, Cashel; Olive Cornelia, Seskin, Kilsheelan, Clonmel; Sr. Berchmans, Principal, Ursuline Convent Secondary School, Thurles; Tim O'Brien, Tim O'Brien & Associates, Park House, Arthurs Quay, Limerick, PRO.

Members of Tipperary (N.R.) County Enterprise Board

Members of Tipperary (N.R.) County Council: Mattie Ryan (Coole),

Ger Darcy, Michael Hough, Jane (Binkie) Hanafin.
Executive Agencies: Gerard Ryan, FÁS, Raheen Industrial Estate, Limerick; Michael Maher, Chief Agricultural Officer, Teagasc, Castlemeadows, Thurles; John McGinley, Tipperary (N.R.) County Manager, Courthouse, Nenagh; Tomás Ó Domhnaill, Regional Development Manager Tipperary (N.R.), Shannon Development, Silver St, Nenagh.
Social Partners: Ger Lewis, Chairman, 16 Knights Crescent, Nenagh, (ICTU); Frank Reddin, Operations Manager, Rhone-Poulence Rorer, Pharmaceuticals Ltd., Lisboney Industrial Estate (IBEC/CIF); Jimmy Murphy, Chief Executive, Nenagh Co-op Creamery Ltd (FARMING).
General: Angela Quinn, Federation President, North Tipperary ICA, 1 Sarsfield St, Thurles; Kathleen Costello, Ciamaltha Rd, Nenagh, T. F. Costello & Sons; Hilary Henry, Lakeshore Mustard, Ballinderry, Coolbawn, Nenagh.
Staff: Peggy Roche, Acting County Enterprise Officer; Noel Cleary, Acting Assistant County Enterprise Officer; Hellen Spillane, Clerical Officer.

Members of Tipperary (S.R.) County Enterprise Board

Members of Tipperary (S.R.) County Council: Susan Meagher, Shangarry, Ballingarry, Thurles; Denis Landy, Greystone St, Carrick-on-Suir; Patrick Norris, Rathronan, Clonmel; Thomas Hayes, Cahervillahow, Golden.
Executive Agencies: Tom McAuliffe, Regional Manager, Forbairt, Industrial Estate, Cork Rd, Waterford; Liam O'Dea, Manager, Employment Services, FÁS, Cork Rd, Waterford; Patrick Nolan, Tourism Officer, South East Regional Tourism Organisation, Rose Inn St, Kilkenny; Edmond O'Connor, (Chairman), Assistant County Manager, Tipperary (S.R.) County Council, County Hall, Clonmel.
Social Partners: Willie Joe Dwyer, Elwill, Ballytarsna, Cashel (IFA); Rory Kirwan, Managing Director, Medite of Europe Ltd., P.O. Box 32, Clonmel (IBEC); Seán Kelly, c/o ATGWU Offices, 20 Parnell St, Clonmel (ICTU).
General: Michael Lynch, National President, Muintir na Tíre, Rosanna Rd, Tipperary; Mrs Maureen McNamara, Secretary, Clonmel Chamber of Commerce, 38 Shamrock Hill, Clonmel; Ms Ellen O'Donnell, Youth Training Enterprise, Mulcahy House, Clonmel.
Staff: Kieran O'Brien, Acting County Enterprise Officer; Thomas Hayes, Acting Assistant County Enterprise Officer; Anne O'Donnell, Clerical Officer.

Dungarvan Versus Waterford as County Capital

'All politics is local' – Tip O'Neill

Counties Waterford and Cork experienced local agitation and consequent central arbitration on issues partly like the Tipperary ones. Whereas the Tipperary politics had focused on both division of the county and a second assize town, Waterford had at issue only the removal of assizes from one venue to another. The Cork campaign was similar in objective to Tipperary's but took place six decades later in different legislative circumstances and with a contrasting outcome; it is described in Appendix Twelve.

The Waterford debate evoked far more participation by the general public than did either of the others. It was in the public eye, with short intervals, in four successive years – 1834, 1835, 1836 and 1837. The feelings aroused were expressed in stronger terms. The local newspapers played a more active role – two of the three in increasingly heated, partisan terms. It involved a trial of strength which was not between equals. It had also the spicy element that the enabling act of parliament was introduced by the MP for the borough which was bidding to be the new assize venue. Finally, after an interval of six decades, the saga had an epilogue in which the earlier losers became the eventual victors.

1 Shaping Up

At about the same time as the soldier-diplomat Lord Bloomfield was mobilising support for redress of north Tipperary's grievance, some Waterford parliamentarians were taking steps which had received little enough public notice as yet. The *Waterford Mail* on 6 August 1834 was 'informed by respectable authority that'

> Henry Villiers-Stuart, Esq., Lord Lieutenant of the County, Sir Richard Keane, Bart., MP, and John M. Galwey, Esq., MP, have been deputed to present memorials from the towns of Dungarvan, Lismore and Tallow to the Marquis of Wellesley, Lord Lieutenant of Ireland, praying that he may be pleased to direct his Secretary to apply for an Act of Parliament, to have the town of Dungarvan made the assize town for the County, and that a Record and Criminal Court be built there, also a County Jail; or that his Excellency may have it in his power at any time on a proper representation, to change the Assize town in any County in Ireland;

the memorialists also propose to have the County Jail and Court House at Waterford sold. The memorials are very respectably and numerously signed, and the gentlemen are very sanguine that their expectations will be realised.

The *Tipperary Free Press* report added the gloss that Dungarvan was the centre of the county.

The three named by the *Mail* were men of wealth and were experienced political operators in a county which had seen nigh a decade of hectic and heady politics. Donal McCartney and L. J. Proudfoot have explored the nuances of its parliamentary election battles.[1] Villiers-Stuart had been MP for the county, 1826-9, after a famous election had climaxed a two-year campaign which had local undertones as well as the obvious Catholic Emancipation issue. Galwey had been his campaign treasurer.[2]

Almost eight months later what became an act of parliament enabling such changes as were proposed by the trio and associates, was introduced into the House of Commons on 26 March 1835 as the Assizes Removal (Ireland) Bill; the MP was Michael O'Loghlen, the member for Dungarvan. During the second reading of the Bill in the Commons on 27 May 1835, by which time he was Solicitor-General for Ireland, and obviously conscious of being open to accusations of a conflict of interest, O'Loghlen recalled the 1834 memorials or petitions which were 'long before he was connected with Dungarvan'.

> He had done nothing more, therefore, than act upon a resolution, being at the same time convinced of the necessity of such a Bill when he saw that in Tipperary witnesses were obliged often to travel sixty Irish miles and in Cork seventy or eighty or about 100 English miles. When Honourable Members talked of the expense they seemed to forget the poor suitors and that it was meant that everything should be done by a county to diminish their expenses as much as possible.[3]

A RISING STAR

O'Loghlen, born in Ennis, County Clare, had been a favourite junior barrister of Daniel O'Connell, King's Counsel and MP for Clare. He first contested a seat for Parliament in Dublin City in 1832 but failed.[4] In October 1834 he was appointed Solicitor-General for Ireland in Lord Melbourne's first Whig-Liberal government, though not an MP. He was unopposed for Dungarvan borough in the general election of January 1835. He was re-appointed Solicitor-General on 29 April 1835 on the formation of Lord Melbourne's second government, following the short-lived intervening Tory-Conservative government under Peel.[5]

As a consequence, like all new Ministers, he had to fight a by-election in May for Dungarvan and won by 360 votes to 88 for J. M. Galwey, an 1832-5 MP for the county. Although Galwey ran as a Repeal of the Union candidate, that campaign's leader, Daniel O'Connell, had supplied O'Loghlen with a letter of recommendation to the electors.[6] O'Loghlen was not an open supporter of Repeal and ran under the Liberal banner. He was aided by the ending of an O'Connell-Galwey alliance.[7] A further indication of the Clareman's capacity as a politician of the inner circle was his promotion in August of the same year to the post of Attorney-General for Ireland.

In November 1836 he was further promoted, this time to the judges' bench as Baron of the Court of Exchequer. He became Master of the Rolls in January 1837 and as such has been encountered in Chapter Two as a member of the Privy Council adjudicating on the Tipperary division.[8]

As a barrister he had been a favourite of the judges due to the simplicity and clarity of his argument, according to the *Dictionary of National Biography*. He had the distinction of being the first Catholic either as Solicitor-General or Attorney-General or as a judge in Ireland since the reign of James II. In that latter role also he was highly regarded:

> The late Sir Michael O'Loghlen it is scarcely too much to say, was one of the best judges that Ireland ever possessed. Able, acute, clear-headed, and thoroughly just, he towered above his fellows…. On the Bench he maintained and, if possible, increased the reputation he had won at the bar. All parties and all creeds honoured and respected the upright judge, and the urbane and accomplished gentleman. There was a general feeling of gratification, at the bar, and among the public, when, in 1837, he was raised to the dignity of Master of the Rolls. In this capacity, he showed the great grasp of his mind, for, though his bar-practice had chiefly been at *common law*, his decisions in *equity* were irrefragable.[9]

> There never was a judge who gave more entire satisfaction to both suitors and the profession; perhaps never one sitting alone and deciding so many cases of whose decisions there were fewer reversals.[10]

> He was so industrious, and so anxious to save the suitors of his

court from unnecessary costs, that he frequently undertook work which might properly have been referred to the Master. He was very courteous, carried patience almost to a fault, and was especially kind and considerate to young men appearing before him.[11]

The concern he expressed in the Commons for suitors at court thus appears to have been genuine. His introduction of the 1835 Assizes Removal Bill applied practical politics to this sympathy.

THE ASSIZES REMOVAL BILL, 1835

The Waterford-Dungarvan question came to the forefront of intimately local politics in July 1835, five weeks after the key second reading of the bill. On 4 July a letter from 'Civis' at Dungarvan to the editor of the *Waterford Chronicle* struck a note quite different to the anti-removal one being sounded in the editorial columns of that city-published paper.

> ... the improvement of this town, and the advancement of its interest ... for Mr Bagge has, in a most strenuous manner, commenced the work ... I have no doubt of its success, for it could not by possibility fall into better hands for its accomplishment as he is the most persevering individual I ever knew in anything he takes up, regardless of trouble or expense. It is to him, and to his exertions we may mainly attribute the making this the Assizes town, if the bill succeed ...

Henry Bagge, a Dungarvan attorney, was the one thus lauded. The bill did succeed in the Commons within days; opposition to it had been expressed on the second reading but not pressed to a vote. The opponents included the two Waterford City MPs, Thomas Wyse, who had been the strategist behind the milestone emancipationist Waterford election victory in 1826, and Henry Winston Barron, and the MP for Waterford County, Sir Richard Musgrave, Tourin, Cappoquin. (Barron and Musgrave had been 1826 colleagues of Wyse, Villiers-Stuart and Galwey).[12] One reason expressed for opposition was similar to one adduced in Tipperary's case as related in Chapters One and Four – inevitably increased taxation, which of course 'the country could not bear'. Another reason was the power of decision which was being given to the Privy Council of Ireland – 'individuals whom the nation would not trust'. But O'Loghlen and the Privy Council were defended just as eloquently. Clonmel's liberal *Tipperary Free Press* on 15 July 1835 reviewed the measure in broad, national terms.

We sincerely congratulate the country on the passing of this important measure. To the activity of the Honourable Member for Dungarvan, aided by some of the best Irish Representatives, is attributable this triumph over a paltry clique of self-interested individuals, who perceiving at length the injustices and silliness of opposing a measure of such utility, did not, when it went into Committee, raise their voices against it. Besides the incalculable benefits that may be expected to accrue from this Bill, it will tend materially to give an impetus to industry in several towns in Ireland. Public buildings, such as Gaols, Court-Houses, &c. shall be raised at once under its provisions, and this, added to the influx of visitors during the Assizes in those towns, where Court-houses &c., shall be built, must tend to alter their condition considerably for the better.

ONE COUNTY, TWO INTERESTS

The very local politics firmed up as, on the left, a Dungarvan/western county lobby for 'removal' versus, on the right, a Waterford city/eastern county group defending the status quo. There was a certain David versus Goliath flavour about the duel. The respective complements of Dungarvan borough's single MP and Waterford city's two MPs were in line with the respective populations of 6,527 and 28,821.[13] Other reflections of comparative statures can be seen in the following quotations from *Thoms Directory*.

DUNGARVAN, a maritime town and parliamentary borough … The public buildings are, the Parish Church, 4 Roman Catholic Chapels, 1 Convent, a Fever Hospital, Sessions' House, Union Workhouse, Market House, and an ancient Castle, used as a barrack. The inhabitants are chiefly supported by the resort of summer visitors, and by the fisheries, the principal of which are the hake and herring fishery. The trade is limited, as vessels of not more than 150 tons can discharge at the quay.[14]

WATERFORD, a county of a city and parliamentary borough … The public buildings are, the Cathedral, 2 Parochial Churches, the Roman Catholic Cathedral, 5 Roman Catholic Chapels, a Presentation Convent, Presbyterian, Baptist, Independent, Methodist, and Friends' Meeting-houses, the Protestant Episcopal Palace, the Roman Catholic College of St. John, the endowed school, the Blue Coat schools for boys and girls, the City and County Court Houses and Prisons, the Penitentiary, House of Correction, Leper Hospital, Glynn's Poor House, Lunatic Asylum,

Fever Hospital, Lying-in Hospital, Union Work-house, County Hall, Custom House, Military Barracks, and Reginald's Tower. The principal manufactures are glass and beer. There are 3 breweries, 4 foundries, and a ship yard with a patent slip; together with several flour mills in the neighbourhood .... The superintendence of the port is vested in 24 Commissioners appointed by the Corporation and Chamber of Commerce. Vessels of 800 tons can discharge at the quay, which is a mile in length. The navigation is continued in the Suir, by barges, 34 miles to Clonmel, and in the Barrow by sailing vessels to New Ross, and thence by barges up that river to Athy, and up the Nore to Inistiogue.[15]

One might note here that Waterford would retain its separate city assizes, whatever the outcome of its battle to retain county capital status; as will become clear, it was in no mood to share power.

THRUSTING DUNGARVAN

The endeavours of O'Loghlen and Bagge apart, there was a certain thrust, a development culture, about Dungarvan in the era. A Clonmel-Dungarvan run had been added to the Bianconi coaching network in 1831.[16] Visits by Daniel O'Connell and Lord Lieutenant Mulgrave to the city were matched by their visits to Dungarvan.[17] The *Waterford Mail's* correspondent from there in 1834 was 'happy to inform you that our Town is improving daily. The County Surveyor has opened an office here and several new buildings are in course of erection'.[18] An 1835 public meeting considered 'the propriety of opening a branch of the National Bank of Ireland'.[19] Although that took place at an interval of just a year after a similar meeting in Waterford, both Dungarvan and the city opened branches during 1835. Dungarvan also got a branch of the Provincial that year, but Waterford already had two banks for almost a decade and acquired a fourth in 1836.[20]

All this followed an extensive reconstruction of the town by its lord of the manor, the Duke of Devonshire, and his agents. A central square, new streets, and a bridge to replace a ferry were all provided between 1807 and 1816. These were followed by a Roman Catholic church, a bridewell and a courthouse.[21]

II Round One, 1835

However, the Goliath of this contest struck an early blow. There were 148 signatories, including three MPs and thirteen JPs, to a requisition for a county meeting of freeholders and ratepayers which was held on

Saturday 18 July. The *Waterford Mirror* in its issue of the previous day gave the only indication over the entire duration of the controversy of a stance one way or another by publishing an anonymous letter. The letter set a tone adopted for much of the subsequent polemics reported and generated by the other media. It had three main points against a change. On 'the question, whether is it more grievous that the occidentals should come to the east, or the orientals go to the west', the writer listed the attractions of Waterford for westerners, as against 'no other business in Dungarvan' for easterners. Then, too, justice would be difficult to administer in Dungarvan because of the factions 'armed with bludgeons, pitchforks, and scythes, hanging on the brow of the mountain'. In addition a change of venue would

> prove that there ought to be a Court-house in every village, and every townland. Our County will then present a novel scene, unlike whatever before existed, when Temples of Justice are as numerous as Churches and Chapels. Moreover, by-and-bye our country gentlemen, oppressed by corpulence and inertia, will find it grievous to leave their pleasant domestic retreat, in order to mingle in the turmoil and hustle of the county business; and as the Judge is, *ex-officio*, an itinerant, it will be necessary for him, if he has business with them, to wait upon them on their sofas and loungers.

The *Waterford Chronicle* of 21 July 1835 reported on the meeting itself:

> Sir Richard Keane remarked that in the case of King's County the assizes had been removed from Philipstown to Tullamore. Counsellor Walsh [Kilduff] – There was a particular Act.[22]… The Solicitor-General first brought in a bill which had as the sole purpose the removal of the County Waterford Assizes. But as he encountered smart opposition with that bill, he brought in a new bill of general application.[23]

A resolution was prompted by two magistrate-landowners in the eastern lobe of the county close to the city, Thomas Carew, Ballinamona, and James Esmonde, Pembrokestown. It was passed – to forward a petition to the House of Lords against removing the assizes from Waterford to Dungarvan, characterising the bill thus:

> … While it professes to be general in its objects, we have strong

reason to believe that it is intended to have a local application in this County.[24]

During the month further, similar accusations were made against O'Loghlen. This controversy was carried in the two Waterford papers. O'Loghlen's acceptance speech two months previously, in May, on being re-elected became contentious with hindsight. The *Waterford Mail* on 6 May had reported that 'the Honourable and Learned Gentleman also expressed his intention of bringing in another bill for the purpose of removing the County Assizes to Dungarvan' (the implied 'other' being a bill proposing the reclamation of land in Dungarvan, at the seaside by the Cumergard river). O'Loghlen strongly denied having made this statement, by way of a letter to Major Simon Newport, JP, which was published in the *Waterford Chronicle* on 30 July 1835.

The neighbourly *Tipperary Free Press* has no qualms two months previously, in its issue of 2 June, about perceiving an overlap in the interests of O'Loghlen the legislator and O'Loghlen the political patron: 'This is the first and great proof he has given of the efficiency and attachment to the interests of his constituents'.

III The Policy Changes, 1836

On 13 August 1835 the House of Lords passed the Assizes Removal Bill. A week previously Lord Wicklow had presented a petition against the Bill stated to have been on behalf of the Waterford County Grand Jury.[25] Because of the necessity, built into s.3 of the Act as passed, to have a majority of the Grand Jury formally present a memorial to the Lord Lieutenant 'praying' a change of assizes venue, the Dungarvan-Waterford question was thus set to rest for the moment.

There was no discussion of the subject at the 1836 Spring Assizes. But at the Summer Assizes, on 9 July of that year, the newly-selected grand jury, which included eleven men not among the 1835 objectors to the Assizes (Removal) Bill, discussed the topic afresh, as reported in detail by the *Waterford Chronicle*.[26]

Sir Richard Keane moved that a memorial be forwarded to the Lord Lieutenant for the removal of the assizes from Waterford to Dungarvan. His main argument was 'the inconvenience to which the western portion of the County was put, in having to come down to Waterford periodically'. That becomes a most interesting choice of words when set side by side with the key phrase of the 1836 Grand Juries Act, highlighted at the start of Chapter Two, which flowed from the Lefroy amendment. That amendment was introduced that very week in the House of Commons and focused on the northern part of neighbouring

Tipperary and the perceived inconvenient situation of Clonmel.

A curious point here is that Keane had not been among the twenty-three who constituted the grand jury when it first assembled on Friday 8 July. When they reassembled the following morning Keane was present among twenty-two, apparently a deputy for Sir Richard Musgrave who had been present on the Friday but was not now mentioned in the report of the proceedings of Saturday 9 July. Musgrave had been among the opponents of the Assizes Removal Bill in the House of Commons.

Mr William Christmas, JP, 'spoke very ably against the bill, pointing out the enormous charge that the alteration would entail upon the county, for not only a new gaol and courthouse but a new barrack and other public buildings would be requisite'. Messrs Esmonde, Uniacke and O'Meara sided with Christmas, quoting an estimate of cost as £40,000 'but undoubtedly likely to amount to much more': the Glengallian scepticism of the following year *in re* Tipperary.[27]

This anti-removal group lost a quadruple manoeuvre no less adroit than any within the capacity of politicians 160 years on: proposing to postpone consideration for six months; proposing to send an alternative memorial to the Lord Lieutenant seeking the appointment of commissioners to enquire whether the present gaol and courthouse were fit; proposing to first take 'the sense of the cess-payers at a public meeting'; and a formal amendment, from Uniacke, which attracted only three supporters, to repair and enlarge the existing county gaol in Waterford city.

Keane's motion for removal was carried by 14 votes to 8 after a discussion which lasted three hours (see list of voters at the start of the Notes to this Appendix). So confident were they of approval by the Privy Council that they thereupon appointed a jail committee to select ground in Dungarvan for jail and courthouse buildings.[28]

THE GRAND JURY'S DISTRIBUTION

The *Waterford Chronicle* of 19 July 1836 reported that six of the eight grand jurors who opposed the removal represented four out of the seven baronies of Waterford and the remaining two were interested in the three western baronies for whose exclusive benefit the change was sought, while the fourteen in favour of the memorial represented three western baronies only. Among the fourteen, P. G. Barron of Tramore could hardly be identified as a westerner despite landholding at Seafield in the barony of Decies without Drum, but the point in general remained valid.

One must note that the inconvenience felt by the westerners was not so great as to prevent them travelling in force to the city. This was in contrast to the absence of Tipperary northerners from the Clonmel assizes. The distances involved were, however, much less within the tidier shape and size of county Waterford.[29] The duration of the assizes was considerably less – three to four days as against Tipperary's nine to twelve; the discrepancy is accounted for by a lesser population, a lesser crime rate and the draw-off of city business to the city's own assizes.

That particular jury list underlines another general point – that grand jurors were the wealthiest of the wealthy. Stuart, Keane, Smyth, Keily, Chearnley, Bushe, Wall, Meara, Greene and Uniacke owned ten of the twenty-five Big Houses of highest value in the county c.1850. Five others, Christmas, Fitzgerald, Barron, Hely and Ronayne, joined them in a listing of 112 landowners having lands valued at £500 or more, likewise identified in the Primary Valuation c.1850.[30]

Reverting to the *Chronicle's* geographical analysis, one must ask – why the imbalance? The table looks at the respective populations of the opposing sets of baronies vis-a-vis their 'representation' in successive assizes over the period of the debate and the following year, 1838. Glenahiry is isolated in the table because of the small population, a later statement as to its being 'indifferent' in the debate, and the later, neutral stance of its resident Nuttal Greene. Barron is re-allocated to the east, and the *Chronicle's* stretching their case by adverting to (property) interests in the west of two easterners is ignored. The non-voting Foreman is excluded in all cases.

Barony	Popul 1831	Sub-totals	Su 35	Sp 36	Su 36	Sp 37	Su 37	Sp 38	Su 38
Coshmore & Coshbride	29,662								
Decies w'in Drum	23,823								
Decies w'out Drum	37,739	91,224	14	14	16	17	15	16	13
Gaultier	10,209								
Middlethird	14,034								
Upperthird	27,596	51,839	7	7	5	4	5	6	5
Glenahiry	5,170	5,170	2	1	1			1	1
Total	**148,233**	**148,233**	**23**	**22**	**22**	**21**	**20**	**23**	**19**

Summer 1837: Greene did not vote and Gumbleton arrived late (from Lismore in the west).

292

For the 1836 Summer assizes under immediate scrutiny, the three western baronies had one grand juror per 7,000 people, while the three eastern baronies had one per an approximate 6,500. Collapse of the *Chronicle's* case defending the interests of its own patch. But only through the modern perception of representation of people; the 1830s focused on the political interests of large landowners.

Which brings one to the method of their selection, by a one-man tribunal – the High Sheriff. The incumbents of that office for the years in question were as follows; comment is hardly necessary.

1835 Pierse G. Barron, Eastlands/Tramore Lodge, Tramore in the eastern Middlethird barony but with land interests at Seafield in the western Decies without Drum barony.

1836 Robert Power, Clashmore House in the north-western segment of the western barony Decies within Drum.

1837 Gervaise Bushe, Glencairn Abbey, Lismore in the heart of the far western barony Coshmore and Coshbride.

1838 John Purcell Fitzgerald, Little Island, Waterford [and Portland Place, London] on the doorstep of the city in the far eastern barony of Gaultier.

INTENSE POLITICKING

The memorial was sent to the Lord Lieutenant. The *Waterford Chronicle* reported, also in its issue of 19 July 1836, that those who had voted against the memorial had forwarded a separate petition to Dublin Castle which voiced their opposition to the bill for the following reasons, in addition to the one just quoted which adverted to a geographical imbalance in the grand jury:

• the eastern extremity was as far distant from Dungarvan as the western extremity was from Waterford;

• Dungarvan could not give sufficient accommodation for the increased numbers expected to attend the assizes;

• it would be a waste to abandon present institutions;

• it was mutually advantageous to the city and county for th e respective assizes to be held at the same time and place;

• the alleged saving in transmitting prisoners could be effected by making Dungarvan and Lismore bridewells available as county gaols for local purposes;

• there had already been enormous expense in improving the present County Gaol and therefore further expenditure would be impractical at present;

• Gaultier, Middle Third and Upper Third baronies were opposed to the removal and Glenahiry barony was indifferent.

On 23 July 1836 a notice appeared in the *Waterford Chronicle* calling for another meeting of freeholders and cess-payers on the removal question. It was signed by Thomas Wyse, [Ballynacourty House, Dungarvan]; and Henry Winston Barron, [Belmont House, Waterford], the two MPs for Waterford City, Patrick Power, MP for the county (with Sir R. Musgrave); William Christmas, JP (the defeated candidate in 1835 for the city); twenty magistrates or JPs who included seven deputy lieutenants of the county and fifty-five others. They included six who had been among the losers in the grand jury vote only days previously (see second list at the start of the Notes).

There was a large meeting in Waterford at the beginning of August which was against a removal to Dungarvan. For the next two months a spate of meetings took place throughout the county. Dungarvan argued for the removal, of course; Kilmacthomas in the middle east, Tallow in the far west, and Waterford again (which held several) argued against. The *Chronicle* nailed the city's colours to its mast by the tone of its reporting, on 5 November 1836, that it had just seen a 'long list of signatures from the distant parishes of Ballyduff and Stradbally, against the barefaced and scandalous job of removing the Assizes'. In fact, those parishes, taken as a pair, could be argued as virtually equidistant from Waterford and Dungarvan.

In the intervening period the Grand Jury Bill passed through the House of Lords and received royal assent on 21 August 1836. This, however, was irrelevant to the Waterford question as the county had already established a majority of the Grand Jury in favour of the move and thus activated the 1835 Assizes Act, unlike the Tipperary agitators who depended on the 1836 provisions.

IV At The Privy Council, 1836

The conflicting memorials came before the Lord Lieutenant and Privy Council on 18 August and 30 September. Additional to the pair from the opposing wings of the grand jury was one obviously emanating from the series of public meetings, signed by no less than 2,164 landowners and land holders and 'praying that his Excellency will withhold his sanction from the removal of the Assizes'.[31] The Council referred the whole question to a Committee of itself.

A Committee of the Privy Council convened on 27 October 1836 to consider the memorial.[32] The case for a removal was heard first. The members of the Privy Council present were the Lord Chancellor, the Archbishop of Cashel, the Master of the Rolls, the Chief Justice of the Common Pleas, the Right Hon. Judge Perrin, the Right Hon. Dr.

Radcliffe and the Attorney-General – who was the Dungarvan MP, Michael O'Loghlen, and who did not suffer from any appearance of a conflict of interest on this occasion either (nor was there any comment to that effect in the newspaper). The Counsel who appeared for the memorialists were Messrs Moore, K.C.; T. B. C. Smith, K.C.; and Brewster, K.C.; and for the counter memorialists Sergeant Green and Messrs Hatchell, K.C., and Holmes.

Mr Moore put forward the arguments for the removal:
• the imperfections in the Waterford Gaol which hindered the Act of Parliament with respect to classification of prisoners being carried out. He felt that the erection of a new gaol was necessary and that it would be no more expensive to construct a gaol in Dungarvan than it would be to raise one in Waterford;
• the cost for a 'poor ten pound lease-holder', for example, to travel up to 50 miles in order to claim his elective franchise before the judge of assizes by way of appeal against the decision of a registering barrister sitting at Dungarvan or Lismore;
• there would be no lack of accommodation for grand jurors, counsel and litigants, etc. that the assizes would draw to the town;
• the more central position of Dungarvan in relation to Waterford county as a whole;
• the change was desired by the majority of the Grand Jurors and a large percentage of the cess-payers.

Mr Moore added weight to his arguments by calling as expert witnesses: Mr Keane, an architect, obviously John B. Keane who was destined to leave his mark on Nenagh; Major Woodward and Major James Palmer, Inspectors-General of Prisons; Robert Longan, JP, from near Dungarvan and who had been O'Loghlen's seconder in the May 1835 by-election.[33]

The following Thursday, 3 November 1836, the case against the removal was heard. The members of the Privy Council Committee present were the same as the previous week, but with the exception of O'Loghlen, Perrin and Radcliffe and the addition of Mr Solicitor-General John Richards.[34]

THE PRICE OF CHANGE

The opposition felt that the present gaol in Waterford city was adequate for the purpose of carrying out the classification of prisoners without the building of a new one. They suggested instead further improvements to the existing gaol by way of a plan drawn up by Thomas Ryan, the governor,[35] supported by Terence O'Reilly, builder and architect. O'Reilly deposed that cracks in the walls were long-standing and not likely to create any danger; the walls had lately been raised. They cited cess-payers' opposition to the move, due to the cost. This was demonstrated by the public meetings, particularly at Tallow where the rate-payers called for 'no tax'.

Henry Winston Barron, MP for Waterford City, claimed that 'so heavily has the county been taxed that the money for the most useful roads had been raised by long instalments; in fact the county was, if I may so say, mortgaged'. Upon cross-examination he was handed a placard and asked to read it. He admitted that part of it was his own composition; it was headed: 'Robbery of Poor Farmers'. It went on to claim that the change of the assizes was to be made to bring it nearer to some gentlemen's doors, and that the expense would be very great on the tax-payers. It concluded with the words 'No Dungarvan Assizes', 'Justice for Ireland'. The newspaper added the word: '(Laughter)'.[36]

Barron also argued that Dungarvan would be unable to provide suitable and sufficient accommodation for an influx of gentlemen attending the assizes if it were moved. And that 'it had been said that eleven post towns had roads running through Dungarvan, but there are only three'. Twenty-nine of the thirty magistrates for removal were resident in the Dungarvan-oriented west of the county, whereas nineteen of the twenty-six opponents were resident in the county as a whole. James Esmonde stated that 'some of those who had signed the memorial for the removal had now changed their minds'. Alexander Sherlock, with east county addresses at Butlerstown Castle, Waterford, and Darrigal, near Kilmeaden, but stated to hold 1,300 acres near Dungarvan, also came forward to quote cess-payers' objections.

DECISION NOT TO DECIDE
The Privy Council Committee's minutes record its decision:

> The Lord Chancellor announced to the Counsel for the Parties That the Committee are all of opinion That it would be premature now to come to any decision in the Matter, Nor until the Grand Jury of the said County of Waterford shall have had an opportunity of deliberating upon the change proposed, upon consideration of Plans and Estimates of the Expense of altering and improving the present Gaol so as to make the same fit and convenient, As also if necessary upon Plan and Estimate of the Expense of erecting a New Gaol and Court House for same County – The Committee thereupon adjourned *Sine die*.[37]

The *Waterford Chronicle* on 8 November 1836 felt that the 'question [had been] set aside forever' – a vulnerable word is that one: 'forever'. They congratulated the county as a whole and especially Mr Esmonde whom they felt had roused the rate-payers to action and had been the 'life and soul of the organisation.'

> We may now say that a determination prevailed, to a great extent, among the farmers, under all circumstances not to pay this tax; and who, amongst those who say that taxation and representation should go together, could blame them? Assuredly none: for never, not even in the struggle between Great Britain and her American colonies was the flagitious principle of "taxation without representation" acted upon, more openly and avowedly, than in the recent attempt to mult the cess-payers of this county without their participation.

The *Chronicle*, consciously or otherwise, was echoing the sentiments of English radicals like Joseph Hume; of O'Connell in 1833 that 'grand juries should, in his opinion, be elected by the cess-payers'; of William Smith O'Brien's hope, expressed in April of that year and quoted in Chapter One for 'something of the principle of representation'. It was to be over sixty years before the principle was adopted for a reformed county government.

V The Battle Resumes, 1837

In the following year, 1837, further attempts at removal were made. The first occurred at the Spring Assizes, with the *Waterford Chronicle* breathing down the necks of the grand jurors. They referred to complaints against the High Sheriff for his selection:

> Sixteen of the twenty-three who compose it are from the western part of the county and few of the others are from the neighbourhood of the city. The property east or south of Dungarvan, though very great, is scarcely represented.[38]

The *Chronicle* spotlit a couple of gentlemen of property, easterners and past grand jurors, who had been 'set aside'. At a public meeting of the city's inhabitants on 9 March, a parish priest, Rev. John Sheehan,[39] developed the theme with a detailed listing in denigratory terms of twelve from the baronies of Coshmore and Coshbride and Decies within Drum. He proceeded with a list of men of the east whose property (much emphasised) was not represented. Punctuations of 'cheers' and 'hear, hears' may have encouraged him to evoke the 'laughter' reported upon his summary of 'the parties interested in this project':

They employed a speculating architect to come down from Dublin [obviously John B. Keane], to draw out plans and make estimates – a rebellion attorney from Dungarvan [Henry Bagge], and a baronet of chameleon character from the west [Sir Richard Keane] ... . Is it from this man [Keane, following the PP's further unfavourable examination of his political c.v.] that the citizens of Waterford should bear the insult that their city ... this *urbs intacta* ... should be sacrificed to the fishing hamlet of Dungarvan.[40]

Meantime, on Monday 6 March, the grand jury cross-examined Major Woodward, one of the two Inspectors-General of Prisons. He had found 93 prisoners in 57 cells; he declared that the separation or classification of debtors, and of others, tried and untried, was inadequate though required by law. He concluded, 'I do not think that anything but building a new gaol for the County Waterford would do'.

Whereupon, Sir Richard Keane and John Keily moved 'that measures be taken for the speedy erection of a new gaol for the county Waterford'. That was passed on a vote of 16 to 5, the same numbers as defeated an amendment by William Christmas and George Meara 'that government should send down a certain number of qualified and impartial persons to inspect the gaol'. Those were fresh words on one of the four manoeuvres floated less formally at the previous assize, Summer 1836. The Foreman did not vote and Nuttal Greene 'declined voting as the representative of the barony of Glanahiry'[41] which petitioners had categorised in the previous year as 'indifferent'.

THE DUBLIN ROUND TWO, MAY 1837

Round Two of the Privy Council Committee deliberations took place on Friday 12 May 1837. There were this time only three Privy Councillors present – Lord Chancellor Plunkett, Justice Perrin, and Master O'Loghlen.[42] Although Henry Villiers-Stuart had been added to the Privy Council by Lord Lieutenant Mulgrave in December 1836,[43] he was an interested absentee. So were John Richards and Richard Blake, also new appointees, who would deliberate in a month's time on Tipperary's case. Even O'Loghlen 'left the room early in the day', causing the remaining two to indicate at the close of evidence that they 'should consult' him 'before they made their decision'.[44] They had before them two memorials. One was from the Foreman and sixteen soul-mates of the Spring Assizes. The other was from the dissident five sticking to the line of seeking 'thoroughly competent' examiners of the existing gaol and courthouse.[45]

The thrust of the evidence was similar to that of the previous hearing, with some new witnesses. John Semple, Jun., identified as an architect of city prisons, concluded that 'it was not possible to make the gaol of Waterford a good one according to the present law … a workhouse, an infirmary, or a mendicity might be made of it'. Mathew Bodkin had been two months a debtor among seven in the gaol; four of them shared a room thirteen feet by eleven.

Major James Palmer reiterated the faults of Waterford gaol, 'the worst county gaol in Ireland'. John B. Keane estimated £25,000 for a gaol and courthouse in Dungarvan to accommodate 150 males and 25 females. A Richard Owen, however, produced a plan 'by which he considered that all the imperfections of the two buildings in Waterford would be remedied, and by this means the necessity of erecting a new gaol and court-house in Dungarvan would be obviated'.[46]

Despite the weight of evidence against Waterford, 'the Committee signed a Report setting forth that they do not deem it expedient at present to Recommend to the council to make any Order for the removal of the said assizes from Waterford to Dungarvan or for the erection of a new Gaol or Courthouse either at Waterford or Dungarvan'.[47]

THE GRAND JURY'S ROUND THREE, 1837

But when the Grand Jury assembled for the 1837 Summer Assizes that brave baronet Sir Richard Keane proposed further pressure.

> In consequence of no official answer having been received to the late memorial of the Grand Jury, the question was in abeyance, and he wished now to awaken the attention of Government to the subject, and to show them that the sentiments of the Grand Jury were still the same. Gentlemen were aware that the law permitted the Grand Jury to build the jail where they liked, but in common courtesy they wished the Assizes to accompany the jail … He would now move the forwarding of a memorial that the Assizes should accompany the jail to Dungarvan. Government had required them to build a new jail – the present jail was considered by every one to be incompetent, and if all the improvements suggested were made, it would still be imperfect.

Messrs Morris, Uniacke, Meara and Barron challenged the existence of such a government view on the matter of the jail. Keane in response asserted such a view by the Inspectors-General of Prisons and that he 'was a functionary of the government'. The proven pro-removal Foreman, William Villiers-Stuart, MP, observed protocol in not voting on a J. W. Barron-Meara amendment in favour of postponement of a Keane-Keily motion to reactivate the memorial for a transfer. The amendment was defeated by 12 votes to 8 and the original motion so carried (see the third list at the start of the notes). Among the twelve pro-Dungarvan voters was Pierse George Barron, a first cousin of the anti-removal Henry Winston Barron,[48] MP for the city[49] whose younger brother John Winston Barron was among the anti-removal minority eight.

There were three postscripts to the vote. Richard Gumbleton arrived late, no doubt out of breath, and sought to have his name recorded as voting with the twelve. This was refused, but he was allowed to sign the memorial. Next, Mr Bagge, obviously the *Waterford Chronicle* 1835 Dungarvan correspondent's 'most persevering individual', identified here as solicitor to the 1836 Summer grand jury majority, produced a plan or drawings for a new gaol and attempted to have it considered. Uniacke objected that 'for all they knew it could be the farm offices to be built at Strancally' (which was Keily's estate). The foreman ruled that the plan could not be considered as there was no name attached and as Bagge was acting unofficially.

Finally, Meara risked his case against removal by challenging Keane to 'at once bring forward the question of the new gaol'. Keane had already adverted to the King's County case when the assizes move to Tullamore had been preceded, perhaps precipitated, by the grand jury's building a gaol there. But Keane, more gentleman than politician at that point, declined: 'They proceeded as they did in courtesy to the Privy Council, reserving the case of the new gaol'.

RECIDIVIST DUNGARVAN, LATE 1837

The removal campaign was still simmering some months later, in the very month in which the Tipperary case was brought to a conclusion by the Privy Council's committee. Thomas Ryan, the governor of the County Gaol, was accused of misappropriation of funds. Petitions were circulated. Both the Waterford newspapers reported the move but neither felt that Ryan was guilty (nor was he, and he was still governor a decade later) or indeed that it would give cause for the removal of the Assizes to Dungarvan. The ubiquitous Mr Bagge appears to have been behind the attempt, but it was to no avail.[50] The *Waterford Mail* of 9 December 1837 was as crystal clear in its feelings as its city-centred competitor, the *Chronicle* had been a year earlier:

> We fancied that the chimerical ideas which had seized the thoughtless heads of a few individuals, of removing the Assizes

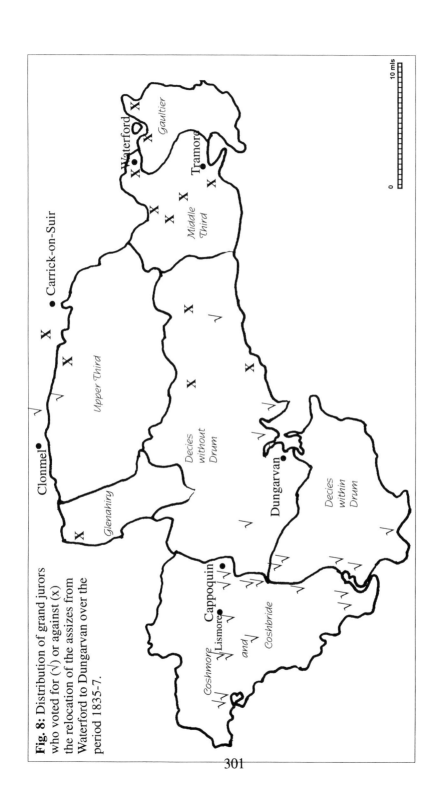

Fig. 8: Distribution of grand jurors who voted for (√) or against (x) the relocation of the assizes from Waterford to Dungarvan over the period 1835-7.

301

from a great commercial and populous city, to an obscure, insignificant village, would, in the lapse of a little time, have given place to good sense and sound reason – more particularly when they saw the fate of their exertions before the Privy Council.

You will have your town filled up with adventurers seeking employment, working under rate, sowing disturbance, and plundering your properties.

We call upon you to hold parochial meetings, make your opinions known by petitions to the Privy Council, and if the measure be carried, you will have the heart-felt gratification of reflecting that you have done your duty.

Three weeks later, on 2 January 1838, the *Waterford Chronicle* railed that:

The unprincipled projectors of this mad scheme are yet at work, cajoling, misrepresenting, deceiving and mulcting the innocent country people ... the document which is industriously hawked about.

It pinpointed the persistent Sir Richard Keane, former MP, as now pushing the relocation which would cost money, though he 'told the last Spring Assizes that the county was too poor to refund the Cholera grant of 1832-3'.

VI The Governor Rules, 1837-8

But Keane was Foreman of the grand jury at the 1838 Spring Assizes when 'nothing of public importance occurred',[51] although the grand jury included eight who had voted for removal at the 1836 Summer Assizes, as well as five who had been against it on that occasion. And reports of the Governor of the County Gaol, and of a Committee appointed to inspect it, revealed that improvements already made had included the raising of the boundary wall, and provision of a gate lodge and work rooms; they recommended additional building to cost £1,000.[52]

Again, at the 1838 Summer Assizes, when the grand jury included five of the 1836 campaigners and two of those then against, the Foreman, Henry Villiers-Stuart, and 'nearly all the grand jurors inspected the County Gaol and expressed high approbation'.[53]

The Fifteenth Report of the Inspectors-General for Prisons for the year 1836 had recorded the removal of the governor and other officers as a result of an enquiry into a gaol break by the Connery brothers and associates.[54] That report also recorded the 'great loss' to Clonmel of Thomas Ryan's transfer to Waterford as governor. The reports for 1837, 1838 and 1839 clarify the reasons for the grand jurors' approbation, arising from the rare case of the right man in the right place at the right time.

> *1837* ... What was considered impracticable in this old and imperfect Gaol has been affected by Zeal and Intelligence of the Governor and his Assistants supported by the Board of Superintendence and Local Inspector ... . Mr Ryan the Governor.... In a very short time he has created a great change in this Gaol, every Prisoner is employed at Trades or some profitable work ... an excellent school is conducted by the Turnkeys, a good System of Silence is established, so that no criminal communicates with others. Each prisoner is clothed in Prison Dress and each at present sleeps in a single cell. ...
>
> *1838* ... The Board of Superintendence at Waterford having been anxious to introduce the system of workshops (in compliance with the terms of the Act) conferred the office of Governor on Mr Ryan in 1836 and I can now report that in the face of many difficulties he has (under the liberal support of the Board and Local Inspector) brought the interior description and reformatory character of Waterford to a degree of perfection which fully answers the intentions of the legislature, and is unequalled in any other county. The progress of trades has been supported by the appointment to the office of training of persons conversant with trades and taking advantage of tradesmen who are committed, and who aid in the instruction of beginners.
>
> *1839* ... from being decidedly one of the worst managed and constructed County Gaols in Ireland, it has, in the short space of less than three years, become one of the first as to discipline, good order and industry and the confused and ill-arranged accommodation so altered ... . I need scarcely say that the merit of these interval arrangements is due to Mr Ryan, the new Governor.[55]

On that sustained note the Dungarvan campaign seems to have ended, in effect by the implementation of the Uniacke 1836 proposal, discounted at the time, to improve the existing gaol – thereby focusing on avoidance of the cost of a new one. One of the main purposes of the campaigners, namely providing a more central location for an assizes, was thereby sidelined. It will be noted that the west Waterford campaigners did not follow the example of the north Tipps in seeking a division of the county. Waterford's county's population (excluding the separate 'county of the city's' 28,821), at 148,233 in 1831 was just 37% of its neighbour's; its 721 square mileage was just 43% of Tipperary's 'great extent'. Whether the crime rate was influenced by the breeze that blew along the Suir, might be a fruitful exercise in exploration for a local historian.[56]

It remains only to recall that Michael O'Loghlen, ex-MP for Dungarvan, sat in on the 1836 and 1837 Privy Council Committee meetings *in re* Dungarvan versus Waterford. We do not know whether he acted behind closed doors as advocate or impartial judge. A pointer to the latter might be the hostile *Dublin Evening Mail*'s perception of his initial days on the bench.

> Baron O'Loghlen has been sitting alone (we will not say 'in his glory') for the last two days in the Court of Exchequer, disposing of the motions and meting out justice to 'rebellious ruffians' with as even a hand as heart could wish; and adjudicating points, and deciding questions precisely as Barons Pennefather, Foster, or the Chief Baron would have done if they were the presiding Judges. We can tell our contemporaries that it is one thing, as an advocate, to advance arguments against a point or a practice, of which the same individual, as a Judge, takes a very different view.[57]

The *Clonmel Herald* on 3 December 1836 turned the knife by expressing the point thus: 'It is one thing to be a Whig advocate and another to be associated with sound laws and honest judges.'

VII Sixty Years On

Dungarvan's David had been well beaten in the 1830s. However, the grandsons of David entered a new arena in 1899 when Waterford County Council replaced the grand jury for its local government functions. O'Brien Dillon's 'people: the source of all legitimate power' had replaced the High Sheriff as selector of county governors. Hume, O'Connell and Smith O'Brien had not lived to see implemented the principle of representation which they had advocated. The leader of the lobby for the proud *urbs intacta* was a grandson of Thomas Wyse (1791-1862), the 1830s MP and meantime Sir Thomas, K.C.B., 'distinguished as a statesman, scholar and orator', Lord of the Treasury, joint Secretary of the Board of Control, and Her Britannic Majesty's Envoy Extraordinary at the Court of Athens. Villiers-Stuart, pro-Dungarvan in 1899, was a grand-nephew of the committed westerner

MP of the 1830s.[58]

The Council's inaugural meeting was held on 22 April 1899 in the grand jury room of Waterford courthouse. Thomas Power, UDC, PLG, Dungarvan, was elected Chairman after a series of votes, and subsequently got a celebratory welcome home in the light of blazing tar barrels. Capt. H. C. Villiers-Stuart was unanimously elected as vice-chairman, probably honoured as the grandson of the emancipationist 1826 election victor who was later Lieutenant of the county and became Baron Stuart of Decies. The Waterford debate, proved to be an echo of the discussions of 1835-7, including the argument of distance from the western section of the county. James Hayes moved that the adjourned meeting be held in Dungarvan. He pointed out that some members had to travel to Waterford from Youghal, the Halfway House, Clonmel and the mountains, and Dungarvan was the most central place. Edmond O'Shea seconded the motion. Matthew Drohan moved that meetings be held in the County Courthouse, Waterford. Captain L. W. P. Wyse moved that as a compromise alternate meetings should be held in each town. This motion was defeated by 20 votes to 9 (see the fourth list at the start of the notes).

> Mr Keily asked was it possible that the committee meetings were to be held in Dungarvan also. Mr Curran – certainly; all meetings (laughter). Mr Hayes: we are going to make Dungarvan the county town (laughter).

A Committee was appointed to consult with the County Surveyor as to what was necessary to be done to Dungarvan Courthouse 'in view of the meeting being always held there': Messrs Stuart, Hayes, Flahavan, Nugent, Queally, Coghlen and Drohan.[59]

Any derision in the laughter recorded at the thought of the 'fishing hamlet' being a county town must have been swallowed hard. And Sir Richard Keane must have turned, just once, contentedly, in his burial place. The statuesque Sir Michael O'Loghlen, lifelike in the foyer of Ennis courthouse, would have adjusted the folds of his judicial robes and inclined his head in what almost approached an approving nod.

On 6 May, 1899, at the next meeting, the Council met at an unidentified location in Dungarvan.[60] They decided to have minor repairs carried out to Dungarvan Courthouse for meetings and temporary offices. Not without another vote. The bold Captain Wyse, undeterred by his defeat on alternating venues, called for a poll on the venue for all future meetings. This time he mustered nine votes for Waterford against Dungarvan's conclusive nineteen. One councillor

Plate 16: This life-size marble representation of Michael O'Loghlen, Master of the Rolls and Privy Councillor, is located in the foyer of the courthouse in his native town, Ennis, Co. Clare.

deserted the captain's company of a week before. Dungarvan lost two of the previous week's voters against alternating, through absence on this occasion.

GO TO DUNGARVAN

The administrative offices continued, in Waterford for a while, but on 1 March 1900 the Council decided on an 11 to 7 vote that the offices of the County Secretary and County Surveyor be changed to the Courthouse, Dungarvan, within two months from that date. The proposer and seconder of that motion were Patrick F. Walsh, Tallow, and James Hayes, Dungarvan. They were both appointed to a committee to enquire into the suitability of offices in Dungarvan Courthouse. The other Committee members were Dungarvan's Thomas Power, who was the Council's chairman, John Flavin, Thomas Murphy and William Kearney, according to the Council minutes, with O'Shea added by the *Waterford Mail* report of 5 March 1900. Neither minutes nor newspaper records who voted for and against, but the information can perhaps be gauged by reference to the April vote and to the attendance for the milestone occasion: which forms the fifth list at the start of the notes.[61]

Mr P. F. Walsh thought it was only right that the office of the Council should be where the Council meets. Besides there was expense in the officials coming there at each meeting. From what had transpired there their Secretary should be their servant, not their master.

He had gone through this courthouse and he thought they had as good offices here as in any place in Ireland. He was glad they had repudiated the courthouse of Waterford, as it was a harbinger of evil. He liked the people of Dungarvan, and he hoped there would be bonfires lighted when their respected County Surveyor and County Secretary got their offices fixed up here.

Hayes – Geographically Dungarvan was the centre of the county.

Capt. Wyse suggested that the matter be referred to a committee.

Mr O'Shea – at present they were paying at the rate of £32 a year expenses of the officials to come to Dungarvan; that would mean interest on £700. They also had ample accommodation in these buildings for double the number of their staff.[62]

Following many committee meetings the County Secretary transferred in September 1903 from Waterford to new offices erected beside the Courthouse in Dungarvan.[63] Thus the long-standing junction of local government and justice was sundered in the county, unlike the case of either riding in Tipperary. Waterford, of course, continued to hold the city assizes and retained its gaol and courthouse.

In 1886 Dungarvan's bridewell was closed. The city continued to provide accommodation for the assizes until a new order replaced assizes in 1923. Under a native government a fair divide of former assizes business occurs with five weeks of Circuit Court sittings in the city and three at Dungarvan which deals with all aspects except criminal trials. The County Registrar's office continues in the city,[64] as does the (full county) Tipperary one in Clonmel and the County Meath one in Trim, even though Meath County Council offices moved to Navan.[65]

Notes

The voters on the crucial occasions, together with one select list of requisitionists of a meeting, are placed here for easy cross-reference.

Early July 1836 Summer assizes – for and against removal of the assizes from Waterford to Dungarvan. The addresses, in square brackets, have been assembled from *Thoms*, 1846, pp. 530-1, information contained in the two articles named in note 30 and in another article by Henry F. Morris in the same invaluable publication, 'The "Principal Inhabitants" of County Waterford 1746'.

For removal: Capt. William Villiers-Stuart, MP (Waterford County), [Dromana House, Cappoquin]; Sir Richard Keane, (former MP for Waterford County), [Cappoquin House, Cappoquin]; Richard Smyth, [Ballinatra/Ballynatray House, Youghal]; John Keily, [Strancally Castle, Tallow]; Thomas Joseph Fitzgerald, [Ballynaparka House/Ballinaparke, Cappoquin]; Pierse George Barron, [East Lands, Tramore; John Musgrave, [Tourin, Cappoquin]; Richard Chearnley, [Salterbridge House, Cappoquin]; Pierse Hely, [Rockfield House, Cappoquin]; Gervaise Bushe, [Glencairn Abbey, Lismore]; George Beresford Poer [Belleville, Cappoquin]; Richard Power Ronayne, [D'Loughtane House, Youghal]; Thomas Walsh, [Woodstock, Cappoquin]; Robert Longan, [Ballinacourty/Ballynacourty, Dungarvan] – **14.**

Against removal: James William Wall, [Coolnamuck, nr Carrick-on-Suir]; William Christmas, (MP for Waterford City, 1832-5), [Whitfield, Tramore/Waterford]; George Meara, [Maypark, Waterford]; Nuttal Greene, [Kilmanahan Castle, Clonmel]; Wray Palliser, [Comeragh Lodge, Kilmacthomas]; Robert Uniacke, [Woodhouse, Stradbally/Kilmacthomas]; James Power, [Rossess/Ballydine]; James Esmonde [Pembrokestown House, Waterford] – **8.**

Later July 1836 requisitionists of a meeting of freeholders and cess-payers (obviously an anti-removal lobby). Addresses have been assembled as for above list of voters; in addition, *'The General Alphabetical Index to the Townlands and Towns, Parishes and Baronies of Ireland'* (Dublin 1861, re-printed in Baltimore, Maryland, 1984 and 1986); *Philips' Handy*

308

Administrative Atlas, and Ordnance Sheet 22. The following lists only the MPs and JPs among a total of some eighty signatories.

Thomas Wyse, [Ballynacourty House, Dungarvan]; Henry Winston Barron, [Belmont House, Waterford]; Patrick Power, MP; William Christmas, D.L.; Nuttal Greene, D.L., John Congreve, D.L., [Mount Congreve, Waterford]; Nik Power, D.L., [Faithlegg, nr Passage/Waterford]; James Power, D.L.; John P. O'Shee, D.L.; Sir Joshua Paul, [Ballyglan, Waterford], Shapland Carew Morris, D.L., [Harbour View, Waterford]; Rev. J. T. Medlycott, [Rockett's Castle, Portlaw]; Simon Newport, [John's Hill, Waterford]; John Winston Barron, [Killsteague, Kilmacthomas]; James Esmonde, George Meara, Lorenzo Power, James William Wall, Roger Hayes, Maurice Ronayne, John Coghlan, Thomas Carew; John Power (who became MP for the county, replacing Musgrave in 1837), [Gurteen House, Clonmel; he was a step-son to Richard Lalor Sheil, the Tipperary MP].

1837 Summer assizes – 'ayes' (for an amendment to postpone a motion to reactivate the memorial for removal of the assizes from Waterford to Dungarvan) and 'noes' (against postponement and hence for removal)

AYES: Richard Duckett [Tramore], J. W. Barron, Shapland Carew Morris, George Meara, James William Wall, Robert Uniacke, Wray Palliser, John Congreve – **8**.

NOES: Robert Longan, Thomas Walsh, Richard Power Ronayne, J. M. Galwey (a former MP for Waterford County) [Glen Lodge, Clonmel], George Bennett Jackson, Thomas Joseph Fitzgerald, Pierse Hely, John Musgrave, John Keily, Pierse George Barron, Richard Smyth, Sir Richard Keane – **12**.

ABSENT: Nuttal Greene and Richard Gumbleton, [Castleview/Castlerickard, Lismore]

22 Apr 1899 – inaugural County Council vote for and against alternating meetings between Waterford and Dungarvan (those against were for holding all meetings in Dungarvan)

For alternating: Thomas Flahavan, Glen House, Portlaw, (Portlaw); Captain William Charles Coughlan, JP, Dromina, Passage East (Ballinakill); Patrick William Keily, 34 Catherine St., Waterford (Kilbarry); Matthias Walsh, Rathgormack, Carrick-on-Suir, (Rathgormack); Martin J. Murphy, JP, Atlantic Tce. (Tramore); Captain Lucien William Bonaparte Wyse, JP, Manor of St John's, Waterford (grand jury nominee); Edward Flahavan, Kilnagrange, Kilmacthomas (Kilmacthomas); Thomas Sullivan, Kilmeaden; Matthew Drohan, JP, Ballynevin, Carrick-on-Suir, (Carrick-on-Suir No. 2) – **9**

Against alternating: Mark Smyth, Flowerhill, Lismore, (Ballyduff); William Fitzgerald, Cappoquin (Cappoquin); James Vincent O'Brien, JP, Aglish House, Cappoquin (Clashmore); Captain H.C. Villiers-Stuart, JP, Dromana, Cappoquin (Dromana); James Lawlor, Kilmacthomas (Kilmacthomas); Edmond Nugent, Ballymacarbery, Clonmel (Kilronan); Patrick O'Gorman, Main St., Lismore, (Lismore); Charles John Curran, JP, Ballinamuck House, Dungarvan (Modeligo); John Flavin, Clashmore, Youghal

(Ardmore electoral division); James Hayes, JP, Dungarvan (Ringville); Patrick F. Walsh, Barrack St., Tallow, (Tallow); Richard J. Ussher, JP, Cappagh House, Cappagh, (grand jury nominee); Michael Mulcahy, Castlequarter, Ballymacarberry, Clonmel (Clonmel No. 2, Co. Waterford); Thomas Power JP, O'Connell St, Dungarvan (Dungarvan Urban); John McCarthy, Dungarvan (Dungarvan Rural); James O'Brien, JP, Lismore (Lismore Rural); James Kennedy, Newtown, Ferrypoint, Youghal (Youghal); Edmond O'Shea, JP, Mary St, Dungarvan, (co-opted); John Morrissey, Cappagh (co-opted); James Quelly, Barracrea, Ballinamult, Clonmel. – **20**

1 Mar 1900 – the attendance when the Council voted 11-7 to transfer the offices to the Courthouse, Dungarvan.
Thomas Power, Chairman, W. C. Coghlan, Charles J. Curran, Edward Flahavan, John Flavin, James Hayes, William Kearney, John McCarthy, John Morrissey, Martin J. Murphy, Thomas Murphy, Edmond Nugent, James O'Brien, Edmond O'Shea, James Queally, Mark Smyth, Thomas Sullivan, R. J. Ussher, Mathias Walsh, Patrick F. Walsh, L. W. Wyse.

1. Donal McCartney, 'Electoral Politics in Waterford in the early 19th Century', *Decies*, No. XX, May 1982; L. J. Proudfoot, 'Landlords and Politics: Youghal and Dungarvan in the 1830s', *Decies*, No. XXXIV, Spring 1987.
2. Galwey is one of a galaxy of 1826 characters in a particularly lively chapter, 'The Whole Nation in One Cry', in Fergus O'Ferall, *Catholic Emancipation* (Dublin, 1985).
3. *W.M.,* 3 June 1835.
4. In the Dublin 1832 vote for two seats, won with 1292 and 1250 votes, O'Loghlen ran fourth with 937 votes – Walker, Parliamentary Elections Results, p. 211.
5. *D.N.B.*
6. *W.M.,* 6 May 1835.
7. McCartney, cited above, p. 49.
8. *DNB; The London Gazette's* official announcement of 31 January as quoted in the *Waterford Chronicle*, 4 February 1837, gives O'Loghlen's formal title and conveys the imperial flavour of 1830s government.
   Whitehall, Jan 28 – The King has been pleased to direct letters patent to be passed under the Great Seal of the United Kingdom of Great Britain and Ireland, constituting and appointing the Right Hon. Michael O'Loghlen, Keeper or Master of the Rolls and Records of the Court of Chancery, in that part of the said United Kingdom called Ireland, in the room of Sir William McMahon, Bart., deceased.
9. Note by R. Shelton Mackenzie, D.C.L. at p. 116, vol. ii of *Sketches of the Irish Bar* by Rt. Hon. Richard Lalor Sheil, MP (New York).
10. [Irish Equity Reports, V 130].
11. *DNB*
12. McCartney, cited above, p. 42.

13. 1831 Census..
14. *Thoms*,1846, pp. 623.
15. ditto, pp. 648-9.
16. Burke, *History of Clonmel*, p. 194.
17. *C.A.*, 23 Aug 1834; *T.F.P.*, 6 Aug 1836.
18. ditto, 23 Aug 1834.
19. *T.F.P.*, 19 Aug 1835.
20. G. L. Barrow, *The Emergence of the Irish Banking System, 1820-45* (Dublin, 1975), Appendix Three, pp. 215-16.
21. William Fraher, 'The Reconstruction of Dungarvan 1807-c.1830: A Political Ploy' in *Decies*, No. XXV, Jan. 1984, pp. 2-21, including seven maps and drawings from contemporary papers and a conjectural drawing by the author on the cover; Patrick C. Power, *History of Waterford City and County* (Cork, 1990), pp. 125, 133. Power dates the bridewell as completed in 1827.
22. 1 & 2 William IV, c. 60 An Act for holding the assizes for the King's Co. in *Ireland*, Twice in every Year, at Tullamoore, instead of Philipstown (4 July 1832). The Act is bound in the 1832 volume of statutes with other 'Local and Personal Acts, declared public, and to be judicially noticed', as distinct from the 'Public General Acts'. It specified (in old-style spelling and typography), without reciting a rationale, that from 1 July 1835 'the ſaid Town of Tullamoore aforeſaid shall be deemed and taken to be the Shire Town of the ſaid County'.

    Michael Byrne, *A Walk Through Tullamore* (Tullamore, 1980), pp. 26-32, recounts attempts in the pre-Union Irish parliament in 1784 and 1786 to effect the transfer from Philipstown (now Daingean). These were defeated through the influence of that town's dominant family, the Ponsonbys. Successive grand juries between 1820 and 1826 forced a change by, firstly, deciding against using the existing county gaol at Philipstown and then deciding to build a new county gaol at Tullamore.

    Byrne highlights the central role of Lord Tullamore in promoting the change, a role acknowledged by a huge attendance at his laying of the foundation stone. The Lord, one of the Bury family who provided the earls of Charleville, proposed the second reading of the bill on 23 May 1832. He was supported by Messrs Shaw (Dublin University), Spring Rice (Limerick), Edward Ruthven (Kildare) and Lord Oxmanstown (Birr). Lord Ponsonby was defeated on an amendment involving the time-honoured ploy of a postponement of the bill for six months. – *Hansard*, vol. 12, cols 1414-5. The House of Lords received petitions in favour of the bill from the King's County magistrates and inhabitants of Tullamore, naturally, but also Frankford, Clara and Parsonstown (Birr) – *Lords' jn.*, vol. 64, pp. 296, 301.

    John B. Keane was the architect of Tullamore courthouse next door to the gaol following the transfer of assizes.
23. I have failed to find in *Hansard* or the Waterford newspapers any indication of an O'Loghlen bill prior to the Assizes Removal (Ireland)

Bill. Mr Stephen Ellison, Deputy Clerk of the Record, House of Lords, has kindly double checked and found no reference to any such bill in the indexes.

24. *W.C.*, 21 July 1835.
25. One presumes here that *The Pilot* report of 10 August 1835 telescoped two matters: firstly, a verbal interjection by Lord Wicklow quoting the resolution of the 'county meeting'; secondly, a petition (recorded in the *Lords' jn.*, vol. 67, p. 444, for the same date, 6 August) from the grand jury of 'the County of the City of Waterford' praying exemption from the provisions of the bill. On the other hand, a petition by 'inhabitants' against the bill had already been received by the Lords on 21 July (vol. 67, p. 313) and there may well have been another one from the county's grand jury not recorded in the Journal or the newspapers.
26. *W.C.*, 12 July 1836.
27. ditto, same date.
28. *Evening Packet,* 12 July 1836.
29. *W.M.*, 2, 5 Mar, 13 July 1836. The city court had two days' and one day's business respectively, at those 1836 Spring and Summer Assizes.
30. The full listings of landowners, both sourced in the Richard Griffith Primary Valuation of 1848-51, are respectively Table 1, p. 558 of Jack Burtchaell, 'A Typology of Settlement and Society in County Waterford c. 1850' and Table 1, pp. 522-4 and Figure 20.2, p. 534 of Lindsay Proudfoot, 'The Estate Systems in mid-nineteenth-century Waterford'; both articles are in Nolan and Power eds, *Waterford History & Society* (Dublin, 1992).
31. Privy Council Minutes, PCO MB 7.
32. *W.C.*, 3 Nov 1836.
33. *W.M*, 6 May 1835.
34. PC Minutes, PCO MB 7.
35. Ryan was a native of Clonmel whose appointment as governor was noted by the *T.C.*, on 12 July 1836.
36. *C.A.*, Wed 9 Nov 1836.
37. PC Minutes, PCO MB 7.
38. *W.C.*, 7 Mar 1837.
39. Sheehan was 'one of the strongest activists in the area and was perhaps Daniel O'Connell's most faithful link with Waterford over the next quarter of a century' [from 1825] – McCartney cited above, p. 42.
40. *W.C.*, 11 Mar 1837.
41. ditto, 7 Mar 1837.
42. PC Minutes, PCO MB 8.
43. *C.H.*, 31 Dec 1836.
44. *C.A.*, 17 May 1837 quoting *Saunders Newsletter.*
45. PC Minutes as above.
46. *C.A.*, 17 May 1837 quoting *Saunders Newsletter.*
47. PC Minutes, PCO MB 8. The conclusions of Inspectors-General Woodward and Palmer in their evidence to the Grand Jury and the Privy

Council Committee, respectively, reflected their annual reports. Their comments in their reports had moved from being 'satisfied with the general good order' and a 'zealous and intelligent' governor in 1832, though also then pointing out lack of employment and school instruction. By 1834 a great increase in committals had the number of prisoners equal double the number of cells. The Inspectors were now insisting on employment and schooling 'in order to keep the inmates from the evils of total idleness'. A year later there was a certain vehemence in the report about three or four prisoners sleeping in one cell and the lack of a schoolmaster, steam kitchen, bye-laws and an RC chaplain. In their 1836 report, printed in March 1837, they went so far as to commend the grand jury's resolution for a new gaol as 'judicious', despite the plan for alterations. – Appendixes to the Tenth to Fourteenth Reports of the Inspectors-General of the State of Prisons in Ireland.

48. *Journal of the Waterford and South East of Ireland Archeological Society*, vol. 18, pp. 150-1.
49. *W.M.*, 15 July 1837.
50. ditto.
51. *W.C.*, 30 Nov and 5 Dec 1837.
52. ditto, 3 Mar 1838.
53. ditto, 17 July 1838.
54. M. B. Kiely and W. Nolan, 'Politics, Land and Rural Conflict in County Waterford, c.1830-1845', p. 481 (in Nolan and Power eds, *Waterford: History and Society* (Dublin 1992).
55. Sixteenth to Eighteenth Reports of Inspectors-General of the State of Prisons in Ireland. The Inspectors continued to press in successive reports for a new gaol and/or uniting the city and county gaols.
56. M. B. Kiely's and W. Nolan's essay, 'Politics, Land and Rural Conflict in County Waterford, c.1830-1845' (in Nolan and Power eds, *Waterford: History and Society* (Dublin, 1992) is a searching examination of a larger question. One of its conclusions is that 'in terms of lawlessness and rural anarchy, Waterford does not even approach Tipperary'. There seems to be scope for further exploration on the lines of Hurst's for Tipperary, quoted in Chapter Two, and by examining any regional difference within County Waterford and distinctions in types of crime. For instance, a quite random spot-check (for differing dates between 1834 and 1837) gives the following totals of the respective calendars of crime, in each case for one assizes: Tipperary – 218, 192; Waterford county and city combined – 40, 69, 41 – *T.F.P.*, 12 Mar, 30 July 1834; *Waterford Mirror*, 18 July 1835, 9 July 1836, 4 Mar 1837.
57. Quoted by *C.A.*, 30 Nov 1836.
58. P. Higgins, 'The Wyses ...', *Journal of the Waterford & South-East of Ireland Archeological Society*, vol. v, 1899.
59. *W.M.*, 25 Apr 1899.
60. The information following has kindly been supplied by Mr Brian J. McNally, County Secretary, from the Council minutes.

61. Council Minutes, courtesy of Mr Brian J. McNally, Co. Secretary.
62. *W.M.*, 5 Mar 1900.
63. Council Minutes.
64. Information courtesy of Mr Niall Rooney, Co. Registrar.
65. Meath County Council at its first meeting in April 1899 decided to hold its further meetings at Navan. The move from the assize town was debated on similar lines to Waterford's – Navan's centrality versus Trim's peripheral position. A compromise sharing of meetings between those two venues was rejected. The vote was 14 to either 13 (the newspaper's figure) or 12 (the count of reported names) – *Meath Herald*, 29 April, 22 July 1899. The Council minutes have not been checked. Their offices moved to Navan.

Cliona Lewis and Donal A. Murphy

Partitioning Cork and Limerick

The county of Cork, like Tipperary after its division, had two 'county' surveyors for its east and west ridings since the inception of those offices in 1834. That shadowy division into ridings was initially the outcome of an 1823 Act (4 of Geo. IV, c. 93) 'for the purpose of holding general sessions of the peace and no other'. There remained just one assizes for the county, one grand jury and one county gaol.

Over six decades on, an opportunity arose to expand that limited role for the ridings with the introduction on 21 February 1898 of a Local Government (Ireland) Bill. It proposed to replace the long-targeted gentry as county rulers by elected county councils. The Chief Secretary for Ireland, Gerald Balfour, had included a clause which provided for a formal and full-scale division of Cork into two ridings, each of which would thus have a county council. Within three weeks the *Eagle and County Cork Advertiser*, published at Skibbereen, reported:

> On Wednesday last, a public meeting was held in the Town Hall, Skibbereen, for the purpose of discussing the Local Government Bill and pushing forward the claims of Skibbereen as the town in which the county council of the West Riding should assemble.

Mr T. Sheehy, Chairman, Town Commissioners, presided and the attendance included local political representatives, clergy and gentry.

EPISCOPAL LEAD

Those first two surveyors in the Cork ridings had been the Leahy brothers from Mullinahone at the fringe of the Golden Vale in county Tipperary. Another Tipperaryman, from Templederry near Nenagh, now played a major and probably decisive role in the 1898 debate on enhancing the status of the ridings. He was Denis Kelly, Bishop of the Roman Catholic diocese of Ross, then independent of the diocese of Cork with which it was later and controversially merged. A letter from him was read at the Skibbereen meeting.

'The question is of vast and enduring importance. The end to be aimed at in making the divisions is that the burden of local taxation may be spread equally over the two new counties. The chief factors in modifying the pressure of local taxation are area, population and valuation. The greater the area, the greater will be, speaking generally, the mileage of roads, the numbers of bridges and gullets and the expenses of making and repairing them. In a hilly country, like West Cork, roads and bridges are liable to damage from heavy rains and floods.

The greater the population, the more numerous will be the destitute poor, the sick poor, the insane poor; and the heavier the expenses of public relief. This is more particularly so when the means of the entire population are narrow and rather incline towards poverty. The lower the valuation, the higher must be the poundage rate to meet these public expenses. The West Riding of Cork is, with the single exception of Co. Kerry, the barrenest and poorest fiscal area in Munster.'

TWO RIDINGS CONTRASTED

'In order then that the burden of taxation should be fairly distributed over the two new counties, they should as far as possible be equal in valuation, population and area. Let us now examine these conditions in the two existing Ridings of Cork. The valuation of the East Riding is £770,000 and of the West Riding, £304,000. The valuation of the East Riding is consequently twice and a half as great as that of the West Riding, i.e., a rate of 1/- in the £ in the East Riding will produce as much money as a rate of 2/6 in the £ in the West Riding. While there is this enormous difference in the valuation of the two Ridings, there is only a slight difference in areas and populations. The West Riding only falls short by one-fifth of the East Riding in these regards.

The official and other working expenses of the various County Councils will be almost equal and hence it is obvious that if the present West Riding of Cork were elevated to the dignity of an administrative county, the unhappy residents should pay dearly for their honours. Hence the West Riding of Cork should be so enlarged that its valuation would rise from £300,000 to over £500,000; and while this is effected, the addition to the area and population should be as small as it is possible to have it. I believe it is with this in view that Mr Balfour in his Bill, while accepting the two Ridings of Tipperary as the two future counties, proposes to redivide Cork.'

The Bishop was attributing to Chief Secretary Balfour a line of thought contradicted by Balfour's own statement, quoted by Maurice Healy, MP, and given below. There was not any official intention to divide the county on a line any different from that dividing the existing limited-purpose ridings. Kelly indeed misread the clause in the Bill as is clear from its quotation by W. Abraham, MP, below: alteration of bounds or re-division was designed for existing judicial counties only, i.e. some cities, thirty-one geographical counties, and the two ridings of Tipperary. Alteration was not necessarily envisaged in the working of the Bill for the Cork ridings. The remainder of the Bishop's letter was therefore unwittingly just academic; it is reproduced as follows for local interest.

EQUALISING THE RIDINGS
'Now, County Cork cannot be divided by a line drawn form north to south. There is not, and cannot be, direct communication between Duhallow, in the north west, and Carbery in the south west. Nature has effectually forbidden such a course by casting up huge mountain barriers. Besides, if such a division were made, all the mountains, waste and the lowly valued lands would be in West Cork and all the rich fertile lands in East Cork. Duhallow at present belongs to the East Riding and should continue so to belong.

The new division will follow Poor Law Unions. The Millstreet Union is partly in Duhallow and partly in West Muskerry. The whole Union should go to the east county. It is not the class of country that would aid in bringing about equality between the new counties. Indeed, perhaps more of Muskerry, too, might be added to the East Cork; it is connected with it by road and rail while it is physically separated from South West Cork. The additions to the West Riding must be made by advancing to the east along the seacoast. The natural eastern boundary is Cork Harbour. West Cork administrative county should extend from Kenmare Bay to Cork Harbour and to the bounds of the municipal borough of Cork and as far to the north as will secure that the burden of local taxation will press with exactly equal weight on East Cork and West Cork.

It is at present unnecessary to work out the problem in greater detail; nor indeed have I the required knowledge to do so. Being but a recent resident amongst you, I have not yet seen a copy of the County Cork presentment book. In this letter I wish merely to draw attention to the principles which, in my opinion, must indisputably guide an equitable division and then practical men, with sufficient local knowledge, will work the matter out.

I have gathered from the local press that there is a rivalry in this matter among the towns of West Cork. Where important interests are concerned and where those interests are identical, there is no room for rivalry, except in promoting the common cause. Whatever division is made all these towns must, of necessity, be in the same financial county, and therefore the paramount consideration for them all, and for the rural districts as well, is that the burden of taxation laid upon them shall not be more than they can bear. If they act otherwise, they will, in my view, be playing the "Beggar's Opera" in the sober and grim of financial life.

Denis Kelly, Bishop of Ross'

Kelly's catholic intellect became prominent in the sphere of Technical Instruction (later and now termed Vocational Education and assigned for administration to the new county councils by the same 1898 Act). This breadth and depth of thought, combined with the promptings of his basic vocation, are evident in the following quotations from his follow-up letter also published in the *Eagle* on 12 March 1898.

'The new County Councils will have the right of declaring any further roads they deem fit main roads, and thus transferring half the expenses from the district to the county. I hope that this provision shall be largely availed of. The law of the Gospel and the law of humanity equally ordain that the strong should aid in carrying the burdens of the weak … .

In conclusion, I would venture to appeal to the rate-payers of West Cork to examine this matter carefully, as it will affect themselves, their children and their childrens' children. They and their fathers before them have been paying county rates for the last 264 years and very few among them seem to have taken any trouble to inquire how their money was expended. If there be intelligence, public spirits and a zeal to promote the common-good of our new west county, the proposed system of Local Government will prove a blessing – financial, social and political: but if the electors tolerate petty jealousies, self-interest, and a base seeking to serve friends at the expense of the public, the new system will prove a curse.'

There was one further meeting to promote division. Fermoy was the venue according to the *Cork Constitution* of 20 May 1898:

> The Town Commissioners had met under the chairmanship of Mr E. Byrne, JP. A resolution was proposed by Mr Coughlan and seconded by Mr Tapley (solicitor): "We the Town Commissioners of Fermoy request that the government retain in the local government bill the clause dividing Cork county for the purpose of the Act into East and West Ridings. The interests of the two ridings being entirely dissimilar. If the county be not divided, the main object of the Act – Local Government – will be defeated and great injustice to the East Riding will result. We take the opportunity of calling attention to the fact that the

resolutions passed at the various presentment sessions in favour of not dividing the county have emanated from and been passed in the interest solely of the existing officials of the Grand Jury of the County of Cork.

However on the same day as this report appeared the crucial Committee stage of the Bill was reached in the House of Commons.

THE COMMONS DEBATE

Bishop Kelly's intervention may have had a more significant influence on Cork opinion in that he identified the questions of cost and equalisation at an early stage in the debate and these factors feature in the contributions of Cork MPs in the Commons. At the Committee stage in May 1898, just over two months after the Kelly correspondence, Maurice Healy (Cork) proposed an amendment by way of deletion of the phrase, 'in the case of Cork to divide the same into two ridings'.

Healy: The West Riding of Cork is so remote from the east riding and it might desire to have a sort of home rule, and to set up a county council of its own. Well naturally, under these circumstances, all the expressions of opinion would come from the west because it is the west riding which has most interest.

Every body in the West Riding is of this opinion. My honorable friend says the opinion is machined. If that is so I am not aware of how it has been machined. When the figures were first investigated, it was suggested that the west riding would be hampered by any division at all, but if any division took place it ought to be upon the basis of equal rating. When the Chief Secretary announced publicly that if there was a division it would be upon the lines of the ridings, and not upon equal ratings, public opinion in the West Riding declared against the division. ... The county has, at an enormous expense, erected a building for the use of the county council of the whole county, and if the county is now divided all that expense will have to be incurred again.

Captain A. Donelan (Cork East): I do not think that a single public body in the east riding has passed or adopted any resolution upon this matter. All the resolutions have come from the west riding ... I think there is a good deal to be said for the provision in this clause with reference to the period of six months being allowed to elapse, in order that information may be gathered as to the desire of the people upon this point ... There is a very considerable difference of opinion upon this point in the different ridings.

William Abraham (Cork North East): What I should very much like to hear is who are the public bodies who have put forward those representations. So far as I have ascertained we have received representations from three poor law unions out of the seventeen, one from one board of town commissioners, one from the harbour commissioners and from other boards who called themselves Presentment Associations and in my belief, there is only one opinion among them, and that is that the county should be divided in two.

Gerald Balfour (Leeds Central): This particular question has excited a great deal of interest.

Abraham: But the Right Honourable Gentleman has taken care to say in this bill within six months after the passing of this Act, may alter for the purposes of the election of such council the boundaries of any existing judicial county, and in the case of Cork, divide the same into two ridings ... I declare that those expressions of opinion are machined and do not represent the true opinion of the county.

James Christopher Flynn (North Cork): The best way is that members representing the county of Cork should come together and then communicate their views upon the subject to the Right Honourable Gentleman.

Abraham: The East Riding has £700 thousand on the valuation; the west riding is £300; ... But as the west riding is practically unanimous upon this subject, though I feel we should prefer a division of the county, I do not myself propose to stand in the way of this amendment.

Charles K. Tanner (Cork County Mid): Opinions of both nationalist and Conservative, and others belonging to the county, is that there should be only one county of Cork, that there should be only one centre, and only one method of dealing with matters material to the county.

The amendment was put and agreed to.

THE OUTCOME
The clause giving power to divide Cork into fully-fledged ridings, each to have a county council, was thus deleted by Healy's amendment from what became section 68 of the Act. That section's enabling power to define boundaries was exercised by the Local Government Board – the predecessor of the native Department of Local Government (now Environment). By an Order of 1 November 1898, 'the boundaries of the administrative County of Cork' were fixed as 'the existing judicial county of Cork.'

By a similar Order Waterford's boundaries were fixed as 'the existing judicial county of Waterford (except the portion of the town of Carrick-on-Suir and of the borough of Clonmel situated therein, and the district electoral division of Kilculliheen).' Kilculliheen transferred to county Kilkenny.

The portions of that town and borough at the toe and heel of county Tipperary went into its South Riding which also acquired three electoral divisions from the North Riding. The latter's boundaries as an administrative county were described as 'the existing judicial county of the North Riding of the County of Tipperary (except the district electoral divisions of Cappagh, Curraheen and Glengar).' [*Dublin Gazette*, 1 November 1898, p. 1461] For other aspects of Tipperary's status see the final paragraph of the section headed 'Proclamation' in Chapter Four. The 1898 Act repealed both the 1835 Assizes Act and 1836 Grand Jury Act provisions which had enabled the division of a county.

NOTE 1: The provenance of the single-purpose division of County Cork and its rationale and delineation of the two ridings – was summarised thus in s. 23 of the Civil Bills and Quarter Sessions (Consolidation) Act, 1851 (14 & 15 Vic, c. 57):

XXIII, 'And whereas an Act was passed in the Fourth Year of His late Majesty King *George* the Fourth [1823], intituled *An Act to divide the County of Cork for the Purpose of holding additional General Sessions therein*, whereby after reciting that the County of *Cork* is very extensive and populous, and that it is requisite, for the due Administration of Justice within the said County, and the Preservation of the Peace therein, that General Sessions of the Peace should be holden frequently therein, it was enacted, that from and after the First Day of *September* One thousand eight hundred and twenty-three, for the Purpose of holding the General Sessions of the Peace in the said County of *Cork*, and for and in respect of all Matters relating to such General Sessions, but not for any other Purpose or in another respect, the said County of *Cork* should be and the same was thereby declared to be divided into Two Ridings, to be called the East Riding and the West Riding of the County of *Cork*; and that the East Riding of the said County of *Cork* should comprise and contain the Baronies and the Liberties following, that is to say, the Barony of *Duhallow*, the Barony or united Baronies of *Orrery* and *Kilmore*, the Barony or united Baronies of *Condons* and *Clongibbons*, the Barony of *Fermoy*, the Barony of *Kinnatalloon*, the Barony of *Imokilly*, the Barony of *Kerry-Currihy*, the Barony of *Kinnalea*, the Barony of *Barrymore*, the Barony of *Barretts*, the Barony of *East Muskerry* (except only the Parishes of *Aheena* and *Ahabullog* within the said Barony), the Liberties of the City of *Cork*, the Liberties of *Youghal*, and the Liberties of *Kinsale*; and the West Riding of the said County of *Cork* should comprise and contain the Baronies and Parts and Divisions of the Baronies following, that is to say, the Barony of *Beer* or *Bear*, the Barony of *Bantry*, the Barony of *West Muskerry*, the Parishes of *Aheena* and *Ahabullog* in the Barony of *East Muskerry*, the Barony of *Kinalmeaky*, the Barony of *Courcies,* the Barony of the united Baronies of *Ibanne* and *Barryroe* otherwise called *Barryroe* and *Ibanne*, and the Baronies of *East Carberry* and *West Carberry*, consisting of the Eastern and Western Divisions of *East Carberry* and the Eastern and Western Divisions of *West Carbery* … .

NOTE 2: Six counties, in addition to Tipperary, had two county surveyors. 'Ridings' or 'divisions' were specified in the County Surveyors, &c. Act, 1861 as counties for that purpose. They were classified for salary purposes, together with the undivided counties, as follows:

Class 1 (£600 per annum): East Cork, West Cork and South Tipperary; Down, Antrim, Kerry, Clare, Wexford, Londonderry, Meath.

Class 2 (£500): North Tipperary, North Donegal, East Galway, West Galway, North Tyrone and South Tyrone; Roscommon, Waterford, Armagh, Kilkenny, Wicklow, Cavan, Fermanagh, Queen's County, Sligo, Kildare.

Class 3 (£400): East Limerick, West Limerick, South Donegal, North Mayo and South Mayo; Monaghan, Westmeath, King's County, Leitrim, Louth, Carlow, Longford.

LIMERICK

Over fifty years after West Cork's drive for partition a surprising motion for division of the not so vast County Limerick was put forward at the normal fortnightly County Council meeting at Croom on Saturday 14 Feb 1953.

That the Minister for Local Government be requested to introduce legislation to divide the administrative area known as Limerick County Council division into two administrative areas to be known as East and West Limerick.

The motion was in the joint names of D. P. Quish [Ballyfroota, Knocklong], J. W. Canty, W. O'Connor [Main St, Abbeyfeale], J. Hayes [Cooga, Doon], J. J. McNamara [Toureen, Croom], P. H. Donegan [Cloghaderreen, Pallasgreen].

The *Limerick Leader* of the following week quoted the exchanges: Quish: all suggestions for schemes come from the west, we (in) the highly-valued lands of the Golden Vein in East Limerick must pay for them,

Donegan: did not see why the ratepayers of East Limerick should have to carry the West on their backs.

P. J. Lillis [Lissaleen]: I thought this was a joke.

D. J. Madden, TD [The Square, Rathkeale]: ... two separate staffs – surely you cannot be serious in that.

Cornelius Keane [Shears Street, Kilmallock] opposed the motion and said that he understood a similar effort to divide the county was made with Mr McEntee, Minister for Local Government [18 August 1941 to 17 April 1948], and had failed.

The Council's minutes throughout that period of Seán McEntee's tenure of office do not contain any record of such a previous attempt. The 1953 minutes, however, record that in addition to Lillis, Madden and Keane, Senator Hartney, Messrs. Maguire, G. Hayes, and the Chairman, spoke against the motion and pointed to the fact that the splitting of the County into two administrative areas would lead to a duplication of the existing officials as well as to the necessity for the provision in the eastern portion of the County of a new County Home and County Hospital, the capital cost of which would be colossal.

The Chairman, J. J. Collins, TD [Abbeyfeale], gave details of valuations of the rural districts in the county which he contended showed that parts of the western areas were as highly valued as any in the eastern. The question of reverting to the system of district charges for the financing of water supplies and sewerage schemes and public lighting was also discussed.

The diplomatic County Manager, Patrick J. Meghen, stated that the discussion provoked by the motion moved by Mr Quish had been very informative. He was of the opinion that the creation of two administrative areas in the county could be uneconomical and would be to the disadvantage of the two areas so created; the rates would go up in both. In so far as the motion arose from consideration of proposals to build cottages on voluntary sites offered by landowners for the accommodation of relatives, he reiterated the fact that the County Council was legally authorised to do so. The object in bringing offers of sites before the members for consideration was to allow an opportunity to have the system reviewed at any time that the Council considered that the commitments in relation thereto were becoming too heavy.

Mr. Quish, apparently the leader of the proposers, eventually agreed on being appealed to by several members that consideration of the motion be adjourned *sine die*.

Sources for Limerick:Limerick County Council Minutes, 14 Feb 1953; Limerick Leader', 21 Feb 1953.

Bibliography

Primary Sources

Unpublished Documents

Bloomfield, Benjamin, letter to his brother-in-law, privately held.
Book of Survey and Distribution for Co Tipperary - Offaly Hist. Soc.
Council Office Papers – N.A.
Day, Judge, Diary of - R.I.A.
de Buitléir, Pádraig, correspondence, privately held.
Department of the Environment file G246/29/2.
Donoughmore Papers – T.C.D.
Dunalley Papers – N.L.I.
Dunalley, Desmond, sixth Baron, *History of the Prittie Family in Ireland* (privately-held typescript).
Holmes Deeds – Limerick Regional Archives.
Howard Bury Papers – Longford-Westmeath Co. Library.
King's Inns Admission Papers – King's Inns.
Landed Estates Courts Records – N.A.
Limerick County Council Minutes – Co. Buildings, Limerick.
Nenagh Board of Guardian Minutes – Co. Library, Thurles.
Nenagh Poor Law Union Rate Books – ditto.
Nenagh R.C. Register of baptisms – indexed transcript, TN Family History Foundation.
Parker Papers – NLI.
Privy Council Letter Book – N.A.
Privy Council Minutes – N.A.
Ryan Papers – privately held.
Tithe Applotment Composition Books, c.1823-5 – N.A.
TNR County Council Minutes – Courthouse, Nenagh.
TSR County Council Minutes - Co. Buildings, Clonmel.
TSR files MG/8, CM/43 – ditto.

Official Publications

Assizes Act, King's Co.,1832.
Assizes Act (E. & W.), 1833.
Assizes Act, 1835.
Census of Population, 1831.
Civil Bills & Quarter Sessions Act, 1851.
County Management Act, 1940.
County Surveyors Act, 1861.
City and County Management (Amendment) Act, 1955.
Dáil Éireann Constituency Commission, Report of, Prl. 8878, 1980.
Dáil Éireann Debates

324

Electoral (Amendent) Act,1980.
Grand Jury Act, 1833.
Grand Jury Act, 1836.
Hansard, 1835-7, 1899.
House of Lords Journal, ditto.
Lighting of Towns Act, 1828.
Local Government (Ireland) Act, 1898.
Local Government Reorganisation, Prl. 1572, 1971.
Local Government (Reorganisation), Act, 1985.
Local Government, Act, 1991.
Local Government, Act, 1994.
Parliamentary Papers:
  Inspectors-General of Prisons of Ireland, Appendices to the Seventh to Twenty-Second Reports, 1829-44.
  Commissioners Report of Mr Griffith, Engineer, On Roads in the Southern District of Ireland, 1831.
  Correspondence … between Her Majesty's Government and the Magistrates of the County of Tipperary, relative to the disturbed state of that County, 1838.
  Reports of the Commission of Inquiry into the Law and Practice of the Occupation of Land in Ireland, 1845.
Poor Relief Act, 1838.
Poor Law Amendment Act, 1847.
Poor Law Commissioners' General Regulations, 8 June 1844.
Presentments, Co. Tipperary, An Abstract of, 1842.
Prisons Act, 1826.

Newspapers

Clare Journal
Clonmel Advertiser
Clonmel Herald
Cork Constitution
Dublin Evening Mail
Dublin Evening Post
Dublin Gazette
Dungannon Observer
Eagle & Co. Cork Advertiser
Evening Packet
Limerick Evening Herald
Limerick Chronicle
Limerick Evening Post and Clare Sentinel
Limerick Times
Meath Herald
Nation, The
Nationalist, The
Nenagh Guardian

Pilot, The
Sunday Tribune, The
Tipperary Star
Tipperary Constitution
Tipperary Free Press
Waterford Chronicle
Waterford Mail
Waterford Mirror

Other Printed Sources

Curtis, Edmund ed, *Calendar of Ormond Deeds*, vols i-v.

Deputy Keeper of the Public Records, *Appendix to the Fifth Report of (1873)*.

Griffith, Richard, General Valuation of Rateable Property in Ireland, 1848-51.

Laffan, T., *Tipperary Families: Being the hearth money records for 1665-6-7* (Dublin, 1911).

Lucas, Richard, *A General Directory of the Kingdom of Ireland* (Dublin, 1788).

Ormond Historical Society, *Ballinaclough, Nenagh and Borrisnafarney Gravestone Inscriptions* (Nenagh, 1982).

Pender Seamus, ed, *A Census of Ireland c.1659*

Pettigrew and Oulton, Directories, 1835-8.

Philips' Handy Administrative Atlas of Ireland (London, n.d.).

Pigot's Directory, 1824.

Seanad Debates

Shearman's Directory, 1839.

Simington, R.C., *The Civil Survey 1654-56 for Tipperary,* vols I & II (Dublin 1931).

Sweetman, H. S., ed, *Calendar of Documents Relating To Ireland* (Dublin, 1875).

Thom's Official Directory 1844, 1845, 1846 and 1847.

Watsons Treble Almanack 1825-30, 1832-4, 1836-9.

Secondary Sources

AA Touring Guide to Ireland (London, 1976).

Barrow, G. L., *The Emergence of the Irish Banking System, 1840-45* (Dublin, 1975).

Beames, Michael, *Peasants and Power; the Whiteboy Movements and their Control in Pre-Famine Ireland* (Sussex, 1983).

Beckett, J. C., *The Making of Modern Ireland* (London, 1966).

Bentley, Michael, *Politics without Democracy, 1815-1914* (London, 1984).

Bianconi, M. O'C and Watson, S. J., *Bianconi: King of the Irish Roads* (Dublin, 1962).

Bloomfield, Georgiana, Baroness, *Memoir of Lord Bloomfield* (London, 1844).

Bloomfield, Georgiana, Baroness, *Reminiscences of Court and Diplomatic Life* (London, 1883).

Boland, Joseph and others, *City and County Management 1929-1990/A Retrospective* (Dublin, 1991).

Boyce, George D, *Nineteenth-Century Ireland: The Search for Stability* (Dublin, 1990).

Breathnach, Seamus, *The Irish Police* (Dublin, 1974).

Burke, Sir Bernard, *Dictionary of Peerage and Baronetage (1878)*.

Burke, Sir Bernard, *A Genealogical and Heraldic History of the Landed Gentry of Ireland* (1904).

Burke's Irish Family Records (London, 1976).

Burke, Very Rev. William P. Canon, *History of Clonmel* (Waterford, 1907, Kilkenny, 1983).

Burtchaell, Jack, 'A Typology of Settlement and Society in County Waterford c.1850' in Nolan and Power eds, *Waterford History & Society* (Dublin, 1992).

Byrne, Michael, *A Walk Through Tullamore* (Tullamore, 1980).

Byrne, Michael, 'Who Killed Lord Norbury?', *Ireland's Own*, Summer Annual 1988.

Cahir Tourist Guide (Junior Chamber, Cahir).

Canny, Nicholas P., *The Elizabethan Conquest of Ireland: a Pattern Established 1565-76*.

Carte, *An History of the Life of James, Duke of Ormond* (1736).

Clancy, John J., MP, *A Handbook of Local Government in Ireland* (Dublin, 1899).

Collins, Neil, *Local Government Managers at Work* (Dublin 1987).

Corbett, William, 'The Anglesey Road', *Tipperary Association Yearbook 1981- 2* (Dublin).

Costello, Con, *Botany Bay: The Story of the Convicts transported from Ireland to Australia, 1791-1853* (Cork, 1987).

Craig, Maurice, *Dublin 1660-1860* (Dublin, 1969).

Crossman, Virginia, *Local Government in Nineteenth century Ireland* (Belfast, 1994).

Cullen, L. M., 'The Social and Economic Evolution of Kilkenny in the Seventeenth and Eighteenth Centuries' in William Nolan and Kevin Whelan eds, *Kilkenny History and Society* (Dublin, 1990).

Cunningham, George, *The Anglo-Norman Advance into the South-West Midlands of Ireland, 1185-1221* (Roscrea, 1987).

Davies, Gordon L. Herries and Mollan, Charles R., *Richard Griffith, 1784-1878*.

Delany, Michael, 'The Tithe Question in the Silvermines Area', in *The*

Guardian (Nenagh), 31 Dec 1938.

Delany, V. T. H., 'The Palatinate Court of the Liberty of Tipperary' in *American Journal of Legal History*, 5, 1961.

Delany, V. T. H. and Lysaght, Charles, *The Administration of Justice in Ireland* (Dublin, 1975).

Department of the Environment file G246/29/2.

Dictionary of National Biography.

Doran Liam, 'Gems of Local Verse' no. 31 in *The Guardian.*

Dunboyne, Lord, *Butler Family History* (Kilkenny,1972)

Empey, C. A., 'The Butler Lordship' in *Journal of the Butler Society no. 3*, (1970-1).

Empey, C. A., 'The Settlement of Limerick' in James Lydon ed, *England and Ireland in the Latter Middle Ages.* (Dublin, 1981).

Empey, C. A., 'The Norman Period, 1185-1500' in William Nolan and Thomas G. McGrath eds, *Tipperary History and Society* (Dublin, 1985).

Empey, C. A., 'Kilkenny in the Anglo-Norman Period' in William Nolan and Kevin Whelan eds, *Kilkenny History and Society* (Dublin, 1990).

Empey, C. A., 'Anglo-Norman County Waterford, 1200-1300' in William Nolan and Thomas P. Power eds, *Waterford History and Society* (Dublin, 1992).

Encyclopedia Britannica.

Falkiner, C. Litton, *Illustrations of Irish History*, (Dublin, 1904).

Foster, R. F., *Modern Ireland, 1600-1972* (London, 1989).

Fraher, William, 'The Reconstruction of Dungarvan 1807-c.1830: A Political Ploy' in *Decies*, No. XXXV, Jan 1984.

Giles, Christopher and Ridge, Michael, 'The Impact On Households Of The 1993 Budget and The Council Tax' in *Fiscal Studies*, vol. 14, no. 3 (1993).

Gleeson, Dermot F. and Harold G. Leask, *The Castle and Manor of Nenagh* (Nenagh, 1971).

Gleeson, Dermot F., *The Last Lords of Ormond* (London, 1938).

Gleeson, Rev. John, *History of Ely O'Carroll* (Dublin, 1915).

Greenwood, John, 'Local Government in the 1990s: ...' in *Talking Politics*, vol. 4 (2), Winter 1991-2.

Grimes, Richard H. and Horgan, Patrick T., *Introduction to Law in the Republic of Ireland.*

Hand, G. J., *English Law in Ireland 1290-1324* (Cambridge, 1967).

Hickey, D. J. and Doherty, J. E., *A Dictionary of Irish History since 1800* (Dublin, 1980).

Higgins, P.,'The Wyses ...', *Journal of the Waterford & South-East of Ireland Archeological Society*, vol. v, 1899.

Hurst, James W., 'Disturbed Tipperary: 1831-1860' in *Éire -Ireland*, Autumn 1974.

Institute of Public Administration, *More Local Government, A Programme For Development* (Dublin, July 1971).

Jackson, R. M., *The Machinery of Justice in England*, 1940.

Kiely, M. B. & Nolan W., 'Politics, Land and Rural Conflict in County Waterford, c.1830-45' in Nolan and Power eds, *Waterford History and Society* (Dublin, 1992).
Kirwan, John, 'Thomas Butler, 10th Earl of Ormond ...' in *Jn. Butler Soc.* vol 3, no. 4.

Lewis, Samuel A., *Topographical Dictionary of Ireland* (1837).
Local Government Board, *Return of Owners of Land in Ireland, 1876* (Dublin, 1876 & Baltimore, 1988).
Lonergan, Eamonn, *St Luke's Hospital Clonmel 1834-1984* (Clonmel, 1985).

MacCárthaigh, Micheál, *A Tipperary Parish: A History of Knockavilla-Donaskeigh* (Cork, 1986).
McCartney, Donal, 'Electoral Politics in Waterford in the early 19th Century' in *Decies*, No. 20, May 1982.
McClintock, Aileen, 'The Earls of Ormond and Tipperary's Role in the Governing of Ireland (1603-41) in *Tipperary Historical Journal*, 1988.
MacCraith, Seán, *Early Irish Local Government 1921-27* (Clonmel, 1967).
Marnane, Denis, *Land and Violence* (Tipperary, 1982).
Marshall, John J., *History of Dungannon* (1929).
Maunsell, Robert, *Recollections of Ireland*, 'by a Late Professional Gentleman' (Dublin, 1865).
Meghen, P. J., 'The Administrative Work of the Grand Jury' in *ADMINISTRATION*, Autumn 1958.
Meskell, Peter, *History of Boherlahan-Dualla* (Cork, 1987).
Murphy, Donal A. and Nancy, 'The Toomevara Shamrock in Louisiana', Part 1 in *The Guardian*, 3 April 1993.
Murphy, Donal A., 'Emancipation and the Tipperary Marches, 1828', Parts 6-9, *The Guardian*, 12 May, 2, 16, 23 June 1990.
Murphy, Donal A., 'The Redwood Railway Reformer' ('From Script and Stone' series), *The Guardian*, 12, 19 April 1986.
Murphy, Nancy, *Walkabout Nenagh* (Nenagh, 1994).

Nenagh District Heritage Centre, 'The Gaol Story' display in the Gatehouse.

O'Connell, Maurice R., *The Correspondence of Daniel O'Connell.*
O'Ferrall, Fergus, *Catholic Emancipation* (Dublin, 1985).
Ó Gadhra, N., The *Galway Guide*, Bord Fáilte. (Dublin, 1982)
Ó Raifeartaigh, T., 'The State's Administration of Education' in ADMINISTRATION, vol. 2, no. 4.

Ó Riain, Seamus, *Dunkerrin: A Parish in Ely O'Carroll* (Dunkerrin, 1988).
Oram, Hugh, *The Newspaper Book* (Dublin, 1983).
Ó Tuathaigh, Gearóid, *Ireland before the Famine 1798-1848* (Dublin, 1972).
Otway-Ruthven, A. J., *A History of Medieval Ireland* (London, 1940).

Peel, Sir Robert, *Memoirs* (London, 1856).
Power, Patrick C., *History of South Tipperary* (Cork, 1989).
Power, Thomas P., *Land, Politics and Society in Eighteenth-Century Tipperary* (Oxford, 1993).
Proudfoot, L. J., 'Landlords and Politics: Youghal and Dungarvan in the 1830s', Decies, No. XXXIV, Spring 1987.
Proudfoot, L. J., 'The Estate Systems in mid-nineteenth century Waterford' in Nolan and Power eds, *Waterford History & Society* (Dublin, 1992).
Pyne, Frederick Wallace, *The John Pyne Family (1766-1813) in America.*

Quarton, Marjorie, *The Renegade* (London, 1991).

Robertson, June O'Carroll, *A Long Way from Tipperary* (Upton-Upon-Severn, 1994).
Robins, Joseph, *Custom House People* (Dublin, 1993).
Roche, Desmond, *Local Government in Ireland* (Dublin, 1982).
Rolleston, C. H., *Potrait of an Irishman* (London, 1939).
Ryan, Mary T., 'The First Lord Bloomfield', *Newport News* , 1990.
Ryan, Mary T., 'John Arthur Douglas Bloomfield, 1802-1879', *Newport News,* 1992.

Shee, Eliizabeth and Watson, S.J., *Clonmel* (Clonmel, 1992).
Sheehan, E. H., *Nenagh and its Neighbourhood* (Bray, 1949, Nenagh 1976).
Sheil, Richard Lalor, *Sketches of the Irish Bar* (New York, 1858).
Sheil, Richard Lalor, *Speeches* (Dublin, 1872).
Smyth, T. S., *The Civic History of the Town of Cavan.*
Sillard, P. A., ed, *The Poems of Richard D'Alton Williams* (Dublin, 1894).

Thomson, David, *England in the Nineteenth Century* (London, 1971).
Tipperary Historical Society Journal (Thurles, 1988, continuing annually).
Trench, Charles Chenevix, *The Great Dan* (London, 1986)

Vicars, Arthur, *Index to Prerogative Wills of Ireland, 1536-1810.*

Walker, Brian M., *Parliamentary Election Results in Ireland 1801-1922.*
Webb, Sidney and Beatrice, *English Local Government.*

Index

This index does not reference persons in the Appendices.
Page references of a biographical nature are in bold.

Murray, Edward M. 202

National Bank 61, 119
national education 12
National Loan Fund Life Assurance Society 119
Nenagh 14, 21, 41, 52, 60, 61, 67, 72, 86, 95, 122, 149, 151, 179, 204, App 1, App 8
  analysis of civil & crown cases 86
  banks 118, 119
  canal proposal 106, 158
  case for assizes 30, 69, 83, 87, 89, 91
  Catholic civil rights 148
  chapel 122
  county gaol 95, 104, 121, 122, 124, 125 126, 132, 160
    Board of Superintendence 126
    public clock 132
  courthouse 95, 104, 122, 132
  distress 1863 164
  division lobby 42, 61, 64, 86
  famine relief 157
  first execution 128
  flagging of footways 131, 132
  Headquarters for Regional Authority 211
  memorial 42, 83
  military barracks 88, 122
  Poor Law Union 152
  population of 69
  Pound Street courthouse 122, 128
  public transport 115
  quarter sessions 71, 105, 121
  Savings Bank 106
  streets 128
  town government 129, 166
  workhouse 105, 106, 156
Nenagh Board of Guardians 152
  chair 86, 152
Nenagh Gas Company 159
Nenagh Guardian 73, 116, 131, 158, 211
Nenagh Minstrelsy, The 73
Nenagh Relief Committee 171
Nenagh Town Commissioners
  chair 131, 152
  election 130, 157, 158
  fundraising 131
  gas contract 159
  members 130
  no. of Catholics 139

rates 132
Nenagh UDC. 183
Newport 32, 59, 69, 88, 153
Nicholls, George 13
Nolan, – 158
Nolan, Anthony 144, 145
Norbury, 1st earl of 142
Norbury, 2nd earl of 89, 97, 105, 123, 124
  murder of 123
  promise of gaol site 122
Norbury, 3rd earl of 124, 161
  donation of gaol site 124
  scandal 124
Norfolk 36
Normanby, Marquess
  81, 104, 105, 107. See Mulgrave, 2nd earl
Normans 1, 6
Norris, John 171
Nugent, Thomas 148, 150

O'Brien, Daniel 146
O'Brien, Francis 68
O'Brien, James 144, 145
O'Brien, John Bray 58, 68, 85
O'Brien, John, Jun. 152
O'Brien, John, Sen. 124, 144, 152, 155
O'Brien, Stafford 161
O'Brien, Thomas 146, 171
O'Brien, William Smith 38
Ó Brolcháin, Ruairí 187, 208
O'Callaghan, Anne Maria Louise 79
O'Callaghan, Cornelius. See Lismore, Viscount
Ó Caoimh, Eugene 188
O'Carroll, Sir Charles 21
O'Connell, Daniel
  11, 17, 43, 52, 64, 81, 105, 107, 120, 133, 150, 151, 152, 159, 166
O'Connor, Charlie 202
O'Connor, Fergus 105
O'Connor, Rev. Ambrose 129, 144, 148
O'Donnell, Michael 171
O'Donnell, Patrick 188, 199
O'Donoghue, Brendan 211
O'Donoghue, Steve 210
O'Donoghue, T. K. 182, 183, 185
O'Driscoll, J. B. 179
O'Dwyer, Derry 210
O'Farrell, James 146
Offaly 4, 31, 203, 207

Toomevara 59, 60, 88, 121, 150
Torpey, Maurice 171
Tory party 69
town government 13, 138
Townsend, Horace Uniacke 118, 140
Tracy, Daniel 144
Tralee 50
Trant, John 67, **80**
Trant, Maria
    first wife of Dunalley, 2nd baron 75
Treacy, Seán 183, 185, 203, 214
Trench, William Steuart 66, 119
Troy, Thomas 197, 201
TSR County Enterprise Board 213
Tucker, – 158
Tullamore 122, 124
Tydd, Henry 146
Tyrone 30, 40, 41, 47, 48, 50

Wicklow 138, 203
William IV 9, 91
William, Richard Dalton 59
Williams, Michael 145
Willington, James 125, 126, 154
Winchelsea, earl of 97
Wood, Tom 213, 214, 217
working hours for children 12
Woulfe, John 144

Yorkshire 1
Youghalarra 4

Union of Great Britain and Ireland (1801)
    11
United Kingdom 9
United States of America 85

Veale, Michael 209, 210
Victoria, Queen 91
Villiers-Stuart, Henry 150, 151,
Vocational Education Committees 205, 206
Vocational Educational Act, 1930 176

Wall, Patrick 171
Wall, Rev. D. H. 145
Waller, Samuel 78
Walsh, Christy 210
Walsh, Jonathan 126
Ward, Gerald 202
Waterford 5, 6, 30, 37, 40, 42, 43, 50,
86, 122, 173, 205, 212, App 11
Waterford, Lord 97
Wayland, Francis 105
Wellesley, Richard Colley 35, 60, 66
Wellington, Duke of 12, 35, 66, 75
Wexford 50
Whately, Archbishop, Dublin C of I 13
White, Francis 125
Whitten, William 145
Whyte, Liam 180, 181, 184